MW00843518

Vlad Mihalcea

High-Performance
Java Persistence

Cluj-Napoca

2016

Copyright © 2016 Vlad Mihalcea

All rights reserved. No part of this publication may be reproduced, stored, or transmitted in any form or by any means – electronic, mechanical, photocopying, recording, or otherwise – without the prior consent of the publisher.

Many of the names used by manufacturers and sellers to distinguish their products are trademarked. Wherever such designations appear in this book, and we were aware of a trademark claim, the names have been printed in all caps or initial caps.

While every precaution has been taken in the preparation of this book, the publisher and author assume no responsibility for errors and omissions, or for any damage resulting from the use of the information contained herein. The book solely reflects the author's views. This book was not financially supported by any relational database system vendors mentioned in this work, and no database vendor has verified the content.

Publisher:

Vlad Mihalcea

mihalcea.vlad@gmail.com

Jupiter 9/27

900492 Cluj-Napoca

Romania

Cover design:

Dan Mihalcea

danmihalcea@gmail.com

Cover photo:

Carlos ZGZ[1] - CC0 1.0[2]

ISBN: 978-973-0-22823-6

---

[1] https://www.flickr.com/photos/carloszgz/19980799311/
[2] https://creativecommons.org/publicdomain/zero/1.0/

To my wife and kids

Contents

II JPA and Hibernate **121**

Preface

In an enterprise system, a properly designed database access layer can have a great impact on the overall application performance. According to Appdynamics[3]

More than half of application performance bottlenecks originate in the database

Data is spread across various structures (table rows, index nodes), and database records can be read and written by multiple concurrent users. From a concurrency point of view, this is a very challenging task, and, to get the most out of a persistence layer, the data access logic must resonate with the underlying database system.

	Hibernate specific features	
	JPA	
Type-safe dynamic queries (jOOQ)	Object-relational structural patterns	
JDBC		
DB specific SQL enhancement	DB specific concurrency control	
SQL Standard	Transactions / ACID	

Figure I.1: Data access skill stack

A typical RDBMS (Relational Database Management System) data access layer requires mastering various technologies, and the overall enterprise solution is only as strong as the team's weakest skills. Before advancing to higher abstraction layers such as ORM (Object-Relational Mapping) frameworks, it is better to conquer the lower layers first.

---

[3]http://www.appdynamics.com/solutions/database-monitoring/

The database server and the connectivity layer

The database manual is not only meant for database administrators. Interacting with a database, without knowing how it works, is like driving a racing car without taking any driving lesson. Getting familiar with the SQL standard and the database-specific features can make the difference between a high-performance application and one that barely crawls.

The fear of database portability can lead to avoiding highly effective features just because they are not interchangeable across various database systems. In reality, it is more common to end up with a sluggish database layer than having to port an already running system to a new database solution.

All data access frameworks rely on JDBC (Java Database Connectivity) API for communicating with a database server. JDBC offers many performance optimization techniques, aiming to reduce transaction response time and accommodate more traffic.

The first part of the book is therefore dedicated to JDBC and database essentials, and it covers topics such as database connection management, statement batching, result set fetching, and database transactions.

The application data access layer

There are data access patterns that have proven their effectiveness in many enterprise application scenarios. Martin Fowler's Patterns of Enterprise Application Architecture[4] is a must read for every enterprise application developer. Beside the object-relational mapping pattern, most ORM frameworks also employ techniques such as *Unit of Work*, *Identity Map*, *Lazy Loading*, *Embedded Value*, *Entity Inheritance* or *Optimistic and Pessimistic Locking*.

The ORM framework

ORM tools can boost application development speed, but the learning curve is undoubtedly steep. The only way to address the inherent complexity of bridging relational data with the application domain model is to fully understand the ORM framework in use.

Sometimes even the reference documentation might not be enough, and getting familiar with the source code is inevitable when facing performance related problems. JPA (Java Persistence API) excels in writing data because all DML (Data Manipulation Language) statements are automatically updated whenever the persistence model changes, therefore speeding up the iterative development process.

The second part of this book describes various Hibernate-specific optimization techniques like identifier generators, effective entity fetching, and state transitions, application-level transactions, and entity caching.

---

[4]http://www.amazon.com/Patterns-Enterprise-Application-Architecture-Martin/dp/0321127420

The native query builder framework

JPA and Hibernate were never meant to substitute SQL[5], and native queries are unavoidable in any non-trivial enterprise application. While JPA makes it possible to abstract DML statements and common entity retrieval queries, when it comes to reading and processing data, nothing can beat native SQL.

JPQL (Java Persistence Querying Language) abstracts the common SQL syntax that is supported by most relation databases. Because of this, JPQL cannot take advantage of Window Functions, Common Table Expressions, Derived tables or PIVOT.

As opposed to JPA, jOOQ (Java Object Oriented Query)[6] offers a type-safe API, which embraces any database-specific querying feature offered by the underlying database system. Just like Criteria API protects against SQL injection attacks when generating entity queries dynamically, jOOQ offers the same safety guarantee when building native SQL statements.

For this reason, the third part of the book is about advanced querying techniques with jOOQ.

About database performance benchmarks

Throughout this book, there are benchmarks aimed to demonstrate the relative gain of a certain performance optimization. The benchmarks results are always dependent on the underlying hardware, operating system and database server configuration, database size and concurrency patterns. For this reason, the absolute values are not as important as the relative optimization gain. In reality, the most relevant benchmark results are the ones against the actual production system.

To prevent the reader from comparing one database against another and drawing a wrong conclusion based on some use case specific benchmarks, the database names are obfuscated as DB_A, DB_B, DB_C, and DB_D.

All the source code, for every example that was used in this book, is available on GitHub[a].

---

[a]https://github.com/vladmihalcea/high-performance-java-persistence

---

[5]https://plus.google.com/+GavinKing/posts/LGJU1NorAvY
[6]http://www.jooq.org/

I JDBC and Database Essentials

1. Performance and Scaling

An enterprise application needs to store and retrieve data as fast as possible. In application performance management, the two most important metrics are response time and throughput.

The lower the response time, the more responsive an application becomes. Response time is, therefore, the measure of performance. Scaling is about maintaining low response times while increasing system load, so throughput is the measure of scalability.

1.1 Response time and throughput

Because this book is focused on high-performance data access, the boundaries of the system under test are located at the transaction manager level. The transaction response time is measured as the time it takes to complete a transaction, and so it encompasses the following time segments:

- the database connection acquisition time
- the time it takes to send all database statements over the wire
- the execution time for all incoming statements
- the time it takes for sending the result sets back to the database client
- the time the transaction is idle due to application-level computations prior to releasing the database connection.

$$T = t_{acq} + t_{req} + t_{exec} + t_{res} + t_{idle}$$

Throughput is defined as the rate of completing incoming load. In a database context, throughput can be calculated as the number of transactions executed within a given time interval.

$$X = \frac{transaction\ count}{time}$$

From this definition, we can conclude that by lowering the time it takes to execute a transaction, the system can accommodate more requests.

Testing against a single database connection, the measured throughput becomes the baseline for further concurrency-based improvements.

$$X(N) = X(1) \times C(N)$$

Ideally, if the system were scaling linearly, adding more database connections would yield a proportional throughput increase. Due to *contention* on database resources and the cost of maintaining *coherency* across multiple concurrent database sessions, the relative throughput gain follows a curve instead of a straight line.

USL (*Universal Scalability Law*)[1] can approximate the maximum relative throughput (system capacity) in relation to the number of load generators (database connections).

$$C(N) = \frac{N}{1 + \alpha(N-1) + \beta N(N-1)}$$

- C - the relative throughput gain for the given concurrency level
- α - the contention coefficient (the serializable portion of the data processing routine)
- β - the coherency coefficient (the cost of maintaining consistency across all concurrent database sessions).

When the coherency coefficient is zero, USL overlaps with Amdahl's Law[2]. The contention has the effect of leveling up scalability. On the other hand, coherency is responsible for the inflection point in the scalability curve, and its effect becomes more significant as the number of concurrent sessions increases.

The following graph depicts the relative throughput gain when the USL coefficients (α, β) are set to the following values (0.1, 0.0001). The x-axis represents the number of concurrent sessions (N), and the y-axis shows the relative capacity gain (C).

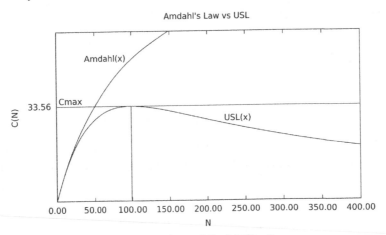

Figure 1.1: Universal Scalability Law

The number of load generators (database connections), for which the system hits its maximum capacity, depends on the USL coefficients solely.

[1]http://www.perfdynamics.com/Manifesto/USLscalability.html
[2]http://en.wikipedia.org/wiki/Amdahl%27s_law

$$Nmax = \sqrt{\frac{(1 - \alpha)}{\beta}}$$

The resulting capacity gain is relative to the minimum throughput, so the absolute system capacity is obtained as follows:

$$Xmax = X(1) \times C(Nmax)$$

1.2 Database connections boundaries

Every connection requires a TCP socket from the client (application) to the server (database).

The total number of connections offered by a database server depends on the underlying hardware resources, and finding how many connections a server can handle is possible through measurements and proven scalability models.

SQL Server 2016[a] and MySQL 5.7[b] use thread-based connection handling.

PostgreSQL 9.5[c] uses one operating system process for each individual connection.

On Windows systems, Oracle uses threads, while on Linux, it uses process-based connections. Oracle 12c[d] comes with a thread-based connection model for Linux systems too.

---

[a]https://msdn.microsoft.com/en-us/library/ms190219.aspx
[b]https://dev.mysql.com/doc/refman/5.7/en/connection-threads.html
[c]http://www.postgresql.org/docs/9.5/static/connect-estab.html
[d]http://docs.oracle.com/database/121/CNCPT/process.htm

A look into database system internals reveals the tight dependency on CPU, Memory, and Disk resources. Because I/O operations are costly, the database uses a buffer pool to map into memory the underlying data and index pages. Changes are first applied in memory and flushed to disk in batches to achieve better write performance.

Even if all indexes are entirely cached in memory, disk access might still occur if the requested data blocks are not cached into the memory buffer pool. Not just queries may generate I/O traffic, but the transaction and the redo logs require flushing in-memory data structures periodically so that durability is not compromised.

To provide data integrity, any relational database system must use exclusive locks to protect data blocks (rows and indexes) from being updated concurrently. This is true even if the database system uses MVCC (Multi-Version Concurrency Control) because otherwise atomicity would be compromised. This topic is going to be discussed in greater detail in the Transactions chapter.

This means that high-throughput database applications experience contention on CPU, Memory, Disk, and Locks. When all the database server resources are in use, adding more workload only increases contention, therefore lowering throughput.

Resources might get saturated due to improper system configuration, so the first step to improving a system throughput is to tune it according to the current data access patterns.

 Lowering response time not only makes the application more responsive, but it can also increase throughput.

However, response time alone is not sufficient in a highly concurrent environment. To maintain a fixed upper bound response time, the system capacity must increase relative to the incoming request throughput. Adding more resources can improve scalability up to a certain point, beyond which the capacity gain starts dropping.

At the Velocity conference[a], both Google Search and Microsoft Bing teams have concluded that higher response times can escalate and even impact the business metrics.

Capacity planning is a feedback-driven mechanism, and it requires constant application monitoring, and so, any optimization must be reinforced by application performance metrics.

[a]http://radar.oreilly.com/2009/06/bing-and-google-agree-slow-pag.html

---

1.3 Scaling up and scaling out

Scaling is the effect of increasing capacity by adding more resources. Scaling vertically (scaling up) means adding resources to a single machine. Increasing the number of available machines is called horizontal scaling (scaling out).

Traditionally, adding more hardware resources to a database server has been the preferred way of increasing database capacity. Relational databases have emerged in the late seventies, and, for two and a half decades, the database vendors took advantage of the hardware advancements following the trends in Moore's Law.

Distributed systems are much more complex to manage than centralized ones, and that is why horizontal scaling is more challenging than scaling vertically. On the other hand, for the same price of a dedicated high-performance server, one could buy multiple commodity machines whose sum of available resources (CPU, Memory, Disk Storage) is greater than of the single dedicated server. When deciding which scaling method is better suited for a given enterprise system, one must take into account both the price (hardware and licenses) and the inherent developing and operational costs.

Being built on top of many open source projects (e.g. PHP, MySQL), Facebook[3] uses a horizontal scaling architecture to accommodate its massive amounts of traffic.

StackOverflow[4] is the best example of a vertical scaling architecture. In one of his blog posts[5], Jeff Atwood explained that the price of Windows and SQL Server licenses was one of the reasons for not choosing a horizontal scaling approach.

No matter how powerful it might be, one dedicated server is still a single point of failure, and throughput drops to zero if the system is no longer available. For this reason, database replication is not optional in many enterprise systems.

1.3.1 Master-Slave replication

For enterprise systems where the read/write ratio is high, a Master-Slave replication scheme is suitable for increasing availability.

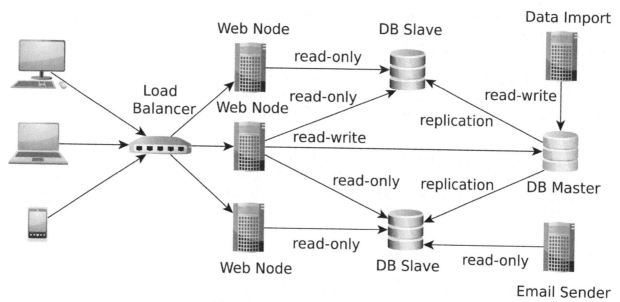

Figure 1.2: Master-Slave replication

The Master is the system of record and the only node accepting writes. All changes recorded by the Master node are replayed onto Slaves as well. A binary replication uses the Master node WAL (Write Ahead Log) while a statement-based replication replays on the Slave machines the exact statements executed on Master.

Asynchronous replication is very common, especially when there are more Slave nodes to update.

---

[3]https://www.facebook.com/note.php?note_id=409881258919

[4]http://stackexchange.com/performance

[5]http://blog.codinghorror.com/scaling-up-vs-scaling-out-hidden-costs/

The Slave nodes are eventual consistent as they might lag behind the Master. In case the Master node crashes, a cluster-wide voting process must elect the new Master (usually the node with the most recent update record) from the list of all available Slaves.

The asynchronous replication topology is also referred as *warm standby* because the election process does not happen instantaneously.

Most database systems allow one synchronous Slave node, at the price of increasing transaction response time (the Master has to block waiting for the synchronous Slave node to acknowledge the update). In case of Master node failure, the automatic failover mechanism can promote the synchronous Slave node to become the new Master.

Having one synchronous Slave allows the system to ensure data consistency in case of Master node failures since the synchronous Slave is an exact copy of the Master. The synchronous Master-Slave replication is also called a *hot standby* topology because the synchronous Slave is readily available for replacing the Master node.

When only asynchronous Slave nodes are available, the newly elected Slave node might lag behind the failed Master, in which case consistency and durability are traded for lower latencies and higher throughput.

Aside from eliminating the single point of failure, database replication can also increase transaction throughput without affecting response time. In a Master-Slave topology, the Slave nodes can accept read-only transactions, therefore routing read traffic away from the Master node.

The Slave nodes increase the available read-only connections and reduce Master node resource contention, which, in turn, can also lower read-write transaction response time. If the Master node can no longer keep up with the ever-increasing read-write traffic, a Multi-Master replication might be a better alternative.

1.3.2 Multi-Master replication

In a Multi-Master replication scheme, all nodes are equal and can accept both read-only and read-write transactions. Splitting the load among multiple nodes can only increase transaction throughput and reduce response time as well.

However, because distributed systems are all about trade-offs, ensuring data consistency is challenging in a Multi-Master replication scheme because there is no longer a single source of truth. The same data can be modified concurrently on separate nodes, so there is a possibility of conflicting updates. The replication scheme can either avoid conflicts or it can detect them and apply an automatic conflict resolution algorithm.

To avoid conflicts, the two-phase commit protocol can be used to enlist all participating nodes in one distributed transaction. This design allows all nodes to be in sync at all time, at the cost of increasing transaction response time (by slowing down write operations).

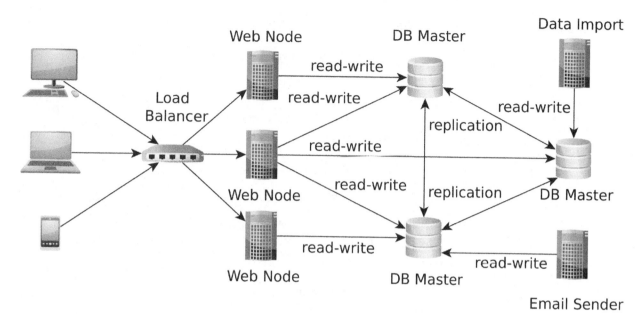

Figure 1.3: Multi-Master replication

If nodes are separated by a WAN (Wide Area Network), synchronization latencies may increase dramatically. If one node is no longer reachable, the synchronization will fail, and the transaction will roll back on all Masters.

Although avoiding conflicts is better from a data consistency perspective, synchronous replication might incur high transaction response times. On the other hand, at the price of having to resolve update conflicts, asynchronous replication can provide better throughput,

The asynchronous Multi-Master replication requires a conflict detection and an automatic conflict resolution algorithm. When a conflict is detected, the automatic resolution tries to merge the two conflicting branches, and, in case it fails, manual intervention is required.

1.3.3 Sharding

When data size grows beyond the overall capacity of a replicated multi-node environment, splitting data becomes unavoidable. Sharding means distributing data across multiple nodes, so each instance contains only a subset of the overall data.

Traditionally, relational databases have offered *horizontal partitioning* to distribute data across multiple tables within the same database server. As opposed to *horizontal partitioning*, sharding requires a distributed system topology so that data is spread across multiple machines.

Each shard must be self-contained because a user transaction can only use data from within a single shard. Joining across shards is usually prohibited because the cost of distributed locking and the networking overhead would lead to long transaction response times.

By reducing data size per node, indexes also require less space, and they can better fit into main memory. With less data to query, the transaction response time can also get shorter too.

The typical sharding topology includes, at least, two separate data centers.

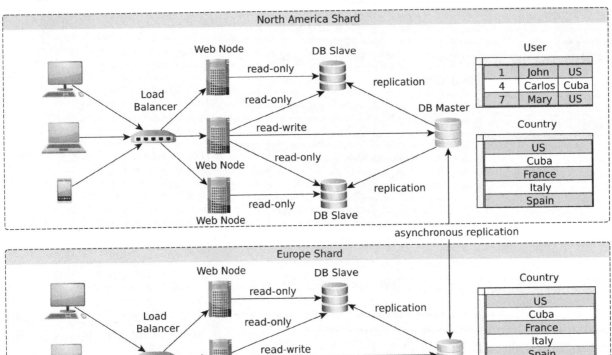

Figure 1.4: Sharding

Each data center can serve a dedicated geographical region, so the load is balanced across geographical areas. Not all tables need to be partitioned across shards, smaller size ones being duplicated on each partition. To keep the shards in sync, an asynchronous replication mechanism can be employed.

In the previous diagram, the country table is mirrored from one data center to the other, and partitioning happens on the user table only. To eliminate the need for inter-shard data processing, each user along with all user-related data are contained in one data center only.

In the quest for increasing system capacity, sharding is usually a last resort strategy, employed after exhausting all other available options, such as:

- optimizing the data layer to deliver lower transaction response times
- scaling each replicated node to a cost-effective configuration
- adding more replicated nodes until synchronization latencies start dropping below an acceptable threshold.

MySQL cluster auto-sharding

MySQL Cluster[a] offers automatic sharding, so data is evenly distributed (using a primary key hashing function) over multiple commodity hardware machines. Every node accepts both read and write transactions and, just like Multi-Master replication, conflicts are automatically discovered and resolved.

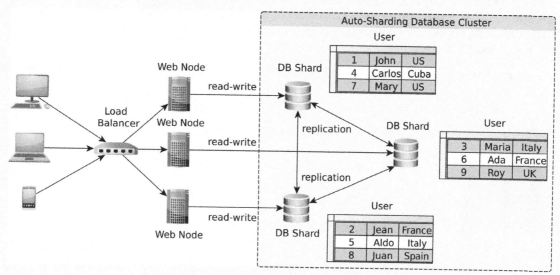

Figure 1.5: Auto-sharding

The auto-sharding topology is similar to the Multi-Master replication architecture as it can increase throughput by distributing incoming load to multiple machines. While in a Multi-Master replicated environment every node stores the whole database, the auto-sharding cluster distributes data so that each shard is only a subset of the whole database.

Because the cluster takes care of distributing data, the application does not have to provide a data shard routing layer, and SQL joins are possible even across different shards. MySQL Cluster 7.3 uses the NDB storage engine, and so it lacks some features provided by InnoDB[b] like multiple transaction isolation levels or MVCC (Multi-Version Concurrency Control).

---

[a]https://www.mysql.com/products/cluster/scalability.html
[b]http://dev.mysql.com/doc/mysql-cluster-excerpt/5.6/en/mysql-cluster-ndb-innodb-engines.html

Little's Law

In any given system, the ultimate relationship between response time and throughput is given by Little's Law[a] and, high values of incoming throughput can cause an exponential growth in response time due to resource saturation.

Nevertheless, when taking a single database connection, by lowering the average transaction response time, more transactions can be accommodated in a given time unit. For this reason, the following chapters explain in greater detail what is needed to be done in order to reduce transaction response time as much as possible.

[a]https://people.cs.umass.edu/~emery/classes/cmpsci691st/readings/OS/Littles-Law-50-Years-Later.pdf

2. JDBC Connection Management

The JDBC (Java Database Connectivity) API provides a common interface for communicating with a database server. All the networking logic and the database-specific communication protocol are hidden away behind the vendor-independent JDBC API. For this reason, all the JDBC interfaces must be implemented according to the database vendor-specific requirements. The `java.sql.Driver` is the main entry point for interacting with the JDBC API, defining the implementation version details and providing access to a database connection.

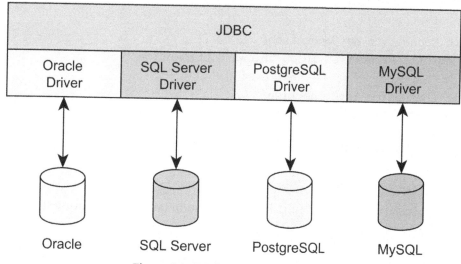

Figure 2.1: JDBC plugin architecture

JDBC defines four driver types:

- Type 1: It is only a bridge to an actual ODBC driver implementation.
- Type 2: It uses a database-specific native client implementation (e.g. *Oracle Call Interface*).
- Type 3: It delegates calls to an application server offering database connectivity support.
- Type 4: The JDBC driver implements the database communication protocol solely in Java.

Being easier to setup and debug, the Type 4 driver is usually the preferred alternative.

To communicate with a database server, a Java program must first obtain a `java.sql.Connection`. Although the `java.sql.Driver` is the actual database connection provider, it is more convenient to use the `java.sql.DriverManager` since it can also resolve the JDBC driver associated with the current database connection URL.

> Previously, the application required to load the driver prior to establishing a connection but, since JDBC 4.0, the *Service Provider Interfaces* mechanism can automatically discover all the available drivers in the current application classpath.

2.1 DriverManager

The `DriverManager` defines the following methods:

```
public static Connection getConnection(
        String url, Properties info) throws SQLException;

public static Connection getConnection(
        String url, String user, String password) throws SQLException;

public static Connection getConnection(
        String url) throws SQLException;
```

Every time the `getConnection()` method is called, the `DriverManager` requests a new *physical* connection from the underlying `Driver`.

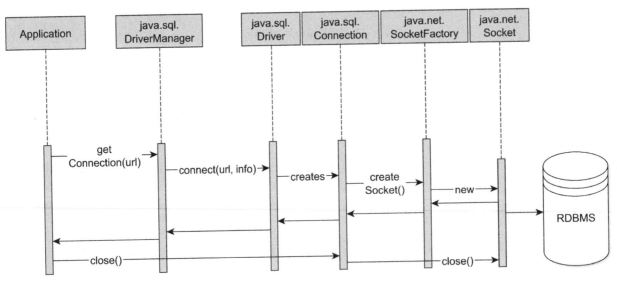

Figure 2.2: DriverManager connection

The first version of JDBC was launched in 1997, and it only supported the `DriverManager` utility for fetching database connections. Back then, Java was offering support for desktop applications which were often employing a two-tier architecture:

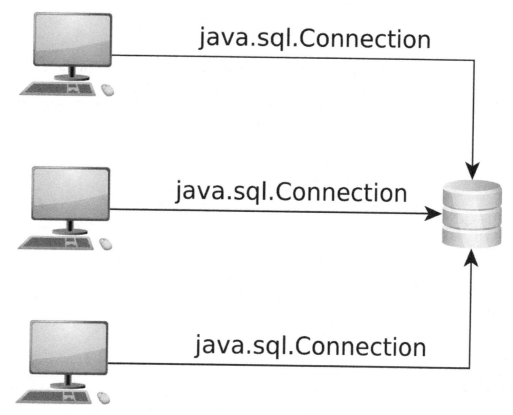

Figure 2.3: Two-tier architecture

In a two-tier architecture, the application is run by a single user, and each instance uses a dedicated database connection. The more users, the more database connections are required, and based on the underlying resources (hardware, operating system or licensing restrictions), each database server can offer a limited number of connections.

Oracle mainframe legacy

Oracle had gained its popularity in the era of mainframe computers when each client got a dedicated database connection.

Oracle assigns a distinct *schema* for each individual *user*, as opposed to other database systems where a schema is shared by multiple user accounts.

In PL/SQL, the *Packaged public variables* scope is bound to a *session*, instead of to the currently running transaction. The application developer must be extra cautious to unbind these variables properly since connections are often reused and old values might leak into newer transactions.

2.2 DataSource

In 1999, J2EE was launched along with JDBC 2.0 and an initial draft of JTA (Java Transaction API)[1], marking the beginning of Enterprisc Java. Enterprise applications use a three-tier architecture, where the middle tier acts as a bridge between user requests and various data sources (e.g. relational databases, messaging queues).

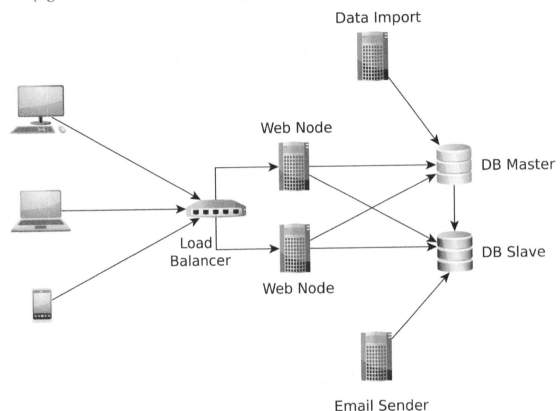

Figure 2.4: Three-tier architecture

Having an intermediate layer between the client and the database server has numerous advantages.

In a typical enterprise application, the user request throughput is greater than the available database connection capacity. As long as the connection acquisition time is tolerable (from the end-user perspective), the user request can wait for a database connection to become available. The middle layer acts as a database connection buffer that can mitigate user request traffic spikes by increasing request response time, without depleting database connections or discarding incoming traffic.

Because the intermediate layer manages database connections, the application server can also monitor connection usage and provide statistics to the operations team.

For this reason, instead of serving physical database connections, the application server

---

[1]https://jcp.org/en/jsr/detail?id=907

provides only logical connections (proxies or handles), so it can intercept and register how the client API interacts with the connection object.

A three-tier architecture can accommodate multiple data sources or messaging queue implementations. To span a single transaction over multiple sources of data, a distributed transaction manager becomes mandatory. In a JTA environment, the transaction manager must be aware of all logical connections the client has acquired as it has to commit or roll them back according to the global transaction outcome. By providing logical connections, the application server can decorate the database connection handles with JTA transaction semantics.

If the `DriverManager` is a physical connection factory, the `javax.sql.DataSource` interface is a logical connection provider:

```
Connection getConnection() throws SQLException;
Connection getConnection(String username, String password) throws SQLException;
```

The simplest `javax.sql.DataSource` implementation could delegate connection acquisition requests to the underlying `DriverManager`, and the connection request workflow would look like this:

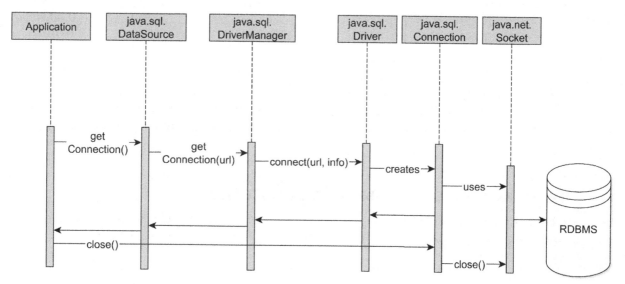

Figure 2.5: DataSource without connection pooling

1. The application data layer asks the `DataSource` for a database connection.
2. The `DataSource` uses the underlying driver to open a physical connection.
3. A physical connection is created, and a TCP socket is opened.
4. The `DataSource` under test does not wrap the physical connection, and it simply lends it to the application layer.
5. The application executes statements using the acquired database connection.
6. When the connection is no longer needed, the application closes the physical connection along with the underlying TCP socket.

Opening and closing database connections is a very expensive operation, so reusing them has the following advantages:

- It avoids both the database and the driver overhead for establishing a TCP connection.
- It prevents destroying the temporary memory buffers associated with each database connection.
- It reduces client-side JVM object garbage.

To visualize the cumulated overhead of establishing and closing database connections, the following test compares the total time it takes to open and close 1000 database connections of four different RDBMS against HikariCP[2] (one of the fastest stand-alone connection pooling solutions in the Java ecosystem).

Table 2.1: Database connection establishing overhead vs. connection pooling

Metric	Time (ms) DB_A	Time (ms) DB_B	Time (ms) DB_C	Time (ms) DB_D	Time (ms) HikariCP
min	11.174	5.441	24.468	0.860	0.001230
max	129.400	26.110	74.634	74.313	1.014051
mean	13.829	6.477	28.910	1.590	0.003458
p99	20.432	9.944	54.952	3.022	0.010263

When using a connection pooling solution, the connection acquisition time is between two and four orders of magnitude smaller. By reducing the connection acquisition interval, the overall transaction response time gets shorter too. All in all, in an enterprise application, reusing connections is a much better choice than always establishing them on a transaction basis.

Oracle XE connection handling limitation

While the Enterprise Edition does not entail any limitations, the Oracle 11g Express Edition throws the following exception when running very short transactions without using a connection pooling solution:

ORA-12516, TNS:listener could not find available handler with matching protocol stack

A connection pooling solution can prevent these intermittent connection establishment failures and reduce the connection acquisition time as well.

---

[2]http://brettwooldridge.github.io/HikariCP/

2.2.1 Why is pooling so much faster?

To understand why the connection pooling solution performs so much better, it is important to figure out the connection pooling mechanism:

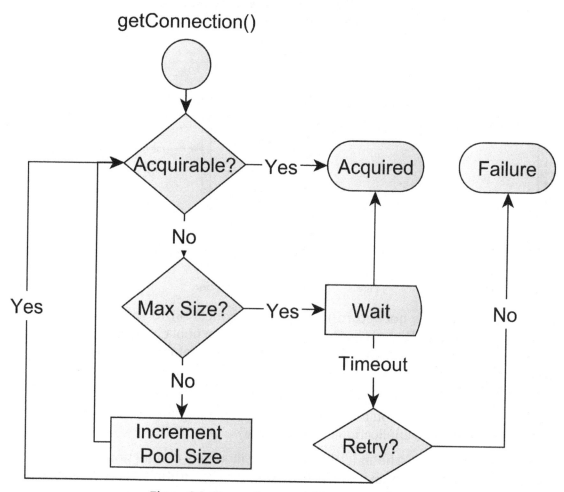

Figure 2.6: Connection acquisition request flow

1. When a connection is being requested, the pool looks for unallocated connections.
2. If the pool finds a free one, it will be handled to the client.
3. If there is no free connection, the pool will try to grow to its maximum allowed size.
4. If the pool already reached its maximum size, it will retry several times before giving up with a connection acquisition failure exception.
5. When the client closes the logical connection, the connection is released and returns to the pool without closing the underlying physical connection.

Most connection pooling solutions expose a `DataSource` implementation that either wraps an actual database-specific `DataSource` or the underlying `DriverManager` utility.

The logical connection lifecycle looks like this:

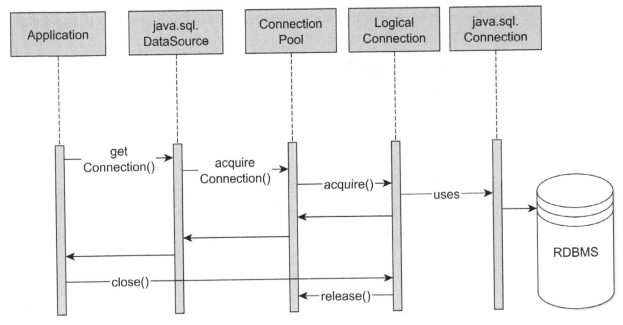

Figure 2.7: **DataSource connection**

The connection pool does not return the physical connection to the client, but instead it offers a proxy or a handle. When a connection is in use, the pool changes its state to *allocated* to prevent two concurrent threads from using the same database connection. The proxy intercepts the connection close method call, and it notifies the pool to change the connection state to *unallocated*.

Apart from reducing connection acquisition time, the pooling mechanism can also limit the number of connections an application can use at once.

The connection pool acts as a bounded buffer for the incoming connection requests. If there is a traffic spike, the connection pool will level it, instead of saturating all the available database resources.

All these benefits come at a price since configuring the right pool size is not a trivial thing to do. Provisioning the connection pool requires understanding the application-specific database access patterns and also connection usage monitoring.

Whenever the number of incoming requests surpasses the available request handlers, there are basically two options to avoid system overloading:

- discarding the overflowing traffic (affecting availability)
- queuing requests and wait for busy resources to become available (increasing response time).

Discarding the surplus traffic is usually a last resort measure, so most connection pooling solutions first attempt to enqueue overflowing incoming requests.

By putting an upper bound on the connection request wait time, the queue is prevented from growing indefinitely and saturating application server resources.

For a given incoming request rate, the relation between the queue size and the average enqueuing time is given by one of the most fundamental laws of queuing theory.

2.3 Queuing theory capacity planning

Little's Law[3] is a general-purpose equation applicable to any queueing system being in a stable state (the arrival rate is not greater than the departure rate).

According to Little's Law, the average time for a request to be serviced depends only on the long-term request arrival rate and the average number of requests in the system.

$$L = \lambda \times W$$

- L - average number of requests in the system (including both the requests being serviced and the ones waiting in the queue)
- λ - long-term average arrival rate
- W - average time a request spends in a system.

Assuming that an application-level transaction uses the same database connection throughout its whole lifecycle, and the average transaction response time is 100 milliseconds:

$$W = 100 \, ms = 0.1 \, s$$

If the average connection acquisition rate is 50 requests per second:

$$\lambda = 50 \, \frac{connection \, requests}{s}$$

Then the average number of connection requests in the system will be:

$$L = \lambda \times W = 50 \times 0.1 = 5 \, connection \, requests$$

A pool size of 5 can accommodate the average incoming traffic without having to enqueue any connection request. If the pool size is 3, then, on average, 2 requests will be enqueued and waiting for a connection to become available.

Little's Law operates with long-term averages, and that might not be suitable when taking into consideration intermittent traffic bursts. In a real-life scenario, the connection pool must adapt to short-term traffic spikes, and so it is important to consider the actual connection pool throughput.

---

[3]http://en.wikipedia.org/wiki/Little%27s_law

In queueing theory, throughput is represented by the departure rate (μ), and, for a connection pool, it represents the number of connections offered in a given unit of time:

$$\mu = \frac{Ls}{Ws} = \frac{pool\,size}{connection\,lease\,time}$$

The following exercise demonstrates how queuing theory can help provisioning a connection pool to support various incoming traffic spikes.

Reusing the previous example configuration, the connection pool defines the following variables:

- There are at most 5 in-service requests (Ls), meaning that the pool can offer at most 5 connections.
- The average service time (Ws) or the connection lease time is 100 milliseconds.

As expected, the connection pool can deliver up to 50 connections per second.

$$\mu = \frac{Ls}{Ws} = 50\,\frac{connection\,requests}{s}$$

When the arrival rate equals departure rate, the system is saturated with all connections being in use.

$$\lambda = \mu = \frac{Ls}{Ws}$$

If the arrival rate outgrows the connection pool throughput, the overflowing requests must wait for connections to become available.

A one-second traffic burst of 150 requests is handled as follows:

- The first 50 requests can be served in the first second.
- The following 100 requests are first enqueued and processed in the following two seconds.

$$\mu = \frac{Ls}{Ws} = \frac{5}{0.1} = \frac{Lq}{Wq} = \frac{10}{0.2}$$

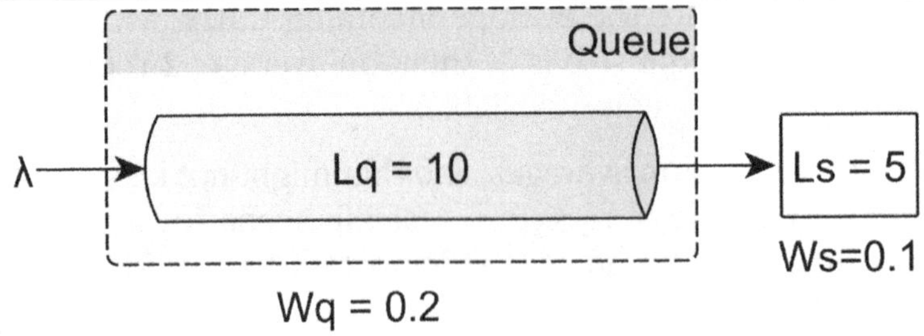

Figure 2.8: Little's Law queue

For a constant throughput, the number of enqueued connection requests (Lq) is proportional to the connection acquisition time (Wq).

The total number of requests in any given spike is calculated as follows:

$$Lspike = \lambda spike \times Wspike$$

The total time required to process the spike is given by the following formula:

$$W = \frac{Lspike}{\mu} = \frac{\lambda spike \times Wspike}{\lambda}$$

The number of enqueued connection requests and the time it takes to process them is expressed by the following equations:

$$Lq = Lspike - Ls$$

$$Wq = W - 1$$

Assuming there is a traffic spike of 250 requests per second, lasting for 3 seconds.

$$\lambda spike = 250 \frac{requests}{s}$$

$$Wspike = 3\,s$$

The 750 requests spike takes 15 seconds to be fully processed.

$$Lspike = 250 \frac{requests}{s} \times 3\,s = 750\,requests$$

$$W = \frac{750\,requests}{50 \frac{requests}{s}} = 15\,s$$

The queue size grows to 700 entries, and it requires 14 seconds for all connection requests to be serviced.

$$Lq = Lspike - Ls = 700\,requests$$

$$Wq = W - 1 = 14\,s$$

2.4 Practical database connection provisioning

Even if queuing theory provides insight into the connection pool behavior, the dynamics of enterprise systems are much more difficult to express with general-purpose equations, and metrics become fundamental for resource provisioning. By continuously monitoring the connection usage patterns, it is much easier to react and adjust the pool size when the initial configuration does not hold anymore.

Unfortunately, many connection pooling solutions only offer limited support for monitoring and failover strategies, and that was the main reason for building FlexyPool[4]. Supporting the most common connection pooling frameworks, this open source project offers the following connection usage metrics:

Table 2.2: FlexyPool metrics

Name	Description
concurrent connection requests	How many connections are being requested at once
concurrent connections	How many connections are being used at once
maximum pool size	If the target `DataSource` uses adaptive pool sizing, this metric will show how the pool size varies with time
connection acquisition time	The time it takes to acquire a connection from the target `DataSource`
overall connection acquisition time	The total connection acquisition interval (including retries)
retry attempts	The connection acquisition retry attempts
overflow pool size	How much the pool size can grow over the maximum size until timing out the connection acquisition request
connection lease time	The duration between the moment a connection is acquired and the time it gets released

While metrics are important for visualizing connection usage trends, in case of an unforeseen traffic spike, the connection acquisition time could reach the `DataSource` timeout threshold.

The failover mechanism applies various strategies to prevent timed-out connection requests from being discarded. While a batch processor can retry a failing request (although it increases transaction response time), in a web application, the user is much more sensitive to unavailability or long-running transactions.

---

[4]https://github.com/vladmihalcea/flexy-pool

FlexyPool comes with the following default failover strategies:

Table 2.3: FlexyPool failover strategies

Name	Description
Increment pool size on timeout	The connection pool has a *minimum size* and, on demand, it can grow up to its *maximum size*. This strategy increments the target connection pool maximum size on connection acquisition timeout. The *overflow* is a buffer of extra connections allowing the pool to grow beyond its initial *maximum size* until it reaches the *overflow size* threshold
Retrying attempts	This strategy is useful for those connection pools lacking a connection acquiring retry mechanism, and it simply reattempts to fetch a connection for a given number of tries

2.4.1 A real-life connection pool monitoring example

The following example demonstrates how FlexyPool failover strategies can determine the right connection pool size. The application under test is a batch processor using Bitronix transaction manager[5] as the database connection pooling provider.

The batch processor is given a certain data load, and the pool size automatically grows upon detecting a connection acquisition timeout occurrence. The average and the maximum pool size are determined experimentally, without the need of any prior mathematical calculations.

Prior to running the load testing experiment, it is better to know the current application connection pool settings. According to the Bitronix connection pool documentation[6] the default acquisitionTimeout (the maximum time a connection request waits before throwing a timeout exception) is 30 seconds.

A connection acquisition timeout threshold of one second is sufficient for the current experiment, allowing the application to react more quickly to a traffic spike and apply a compensating failover strategy.

The initial maxPoolSize is set to one connection, and, upon receiving a connection acquisition timeout, it grows until the maxOverflow threshold is reached.

The retryAttempts value is intentionally set to a reasonably large value because, for a batch processor, dropping a connection request is a much bigger problem than some occasional transaction response time spikes.

---

[5]https://github.com/bitronix/btm
[6]https://github.com/bitronix/btm/wiki/JDBC-pools-configuration

The experiment starts with the following initial connection pool settings:

Table 2.4: Initial connection pool settings

Name	Value	Description
minPoolSize	0	The pool starts with an initial size of 0
maxPoolSize	1	The pool starts with a maximum size of 1
acquisitionTimeout	1	A connection request waits for 1s before giving up with a timeout exception
maxOverflow	4	The pool can grow up to 5 connections (initial `maxPoolSize` + `maxOverflow`)
retryAttempts	30	If the final maxPoolSize is reached, and there is no connection available, a request will retry 30 times before giving up.

2.4.1.1 Concurrent connection request count metric

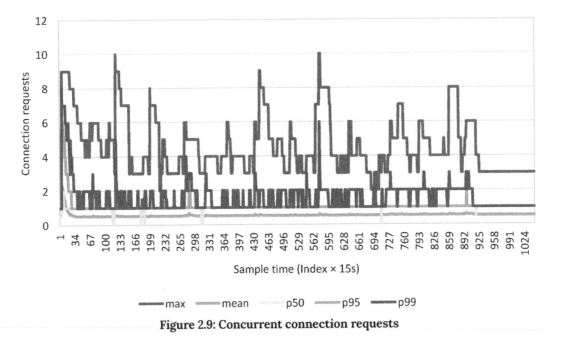

Figure 2.9: Concurrent connection requests

The more incoming concurrent connection requests, the higher the response time (for obtaining a pooled connection) gets. This graph shows the incoming request distribution, making it ideal for spotting traffic spikes.

The average value levels up all outliers, so it cannot reflect the application response to a given traffic spike.

When the recorded values fluctuate dramatically, the average and the maximum value alone offer only a limited view over the actual range of data, and that is why percentiles are preferred in application performance monitoring.

By offering the maximum value, relevant to only a percentage of the whole population, percentiles make outliers visible while capturing the immediate effect of a given traffic change.

2.4.1.2 Concurrent connection count metric

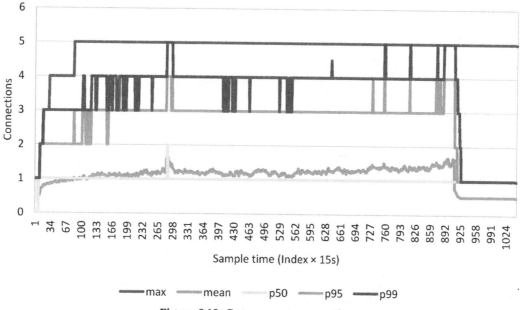

Figure 2.10: Concurrent connections

The average concurrent connection metric follows a gradual slope up to 1.5 connections. Unfortunately, this value is of little use for configuring the right pool size. On the other hand, the 99th percentile is much more informative, showing that 3 to 5 connections are sufficient. The maximum connections graph reconfirms that the pool size should be limited to 5 connections (in case the connection acquisition time is acceptable).

If the connection pool supports it, it is very important to set the idle connection timeout threshold. This way, the pool can release unused connections so the database can provide them to other clients as well.

2.4.1.3 Maximum pool size metric

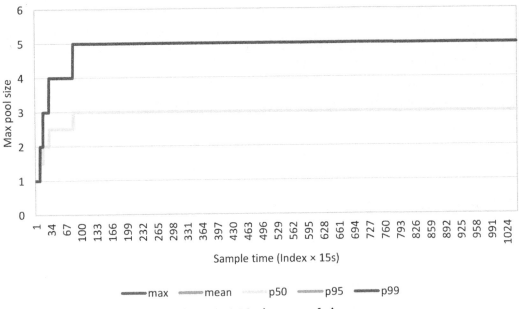

Figure 2.11: Maximum pool size

According to the 99th percentile, the pool gets saturated soon after the job process starts.

2.4.1.4 Connection acquisition time metric

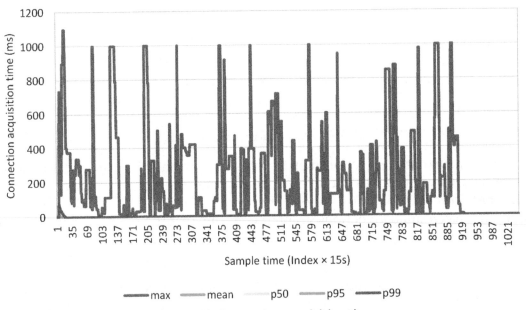

Figure 2.12: Connection acquisition time

The traffic spikes are captured by the maximum graph only. The timeout threshold is hit multiple times as the pool either grows its size or it retries the connection acquisition request.

2.4.1.5 Retry attempts metric

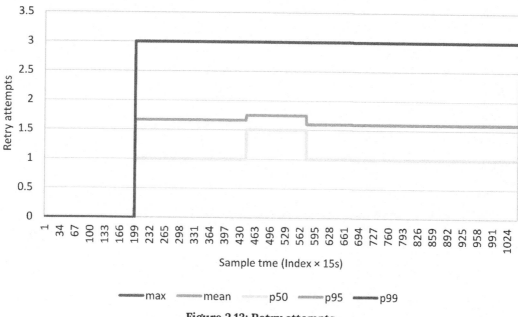

Figure 2.13: Retry attempts

When limiting the connection pool to 5 connections, there are only 3 retry attempts.

2.4.1.6 Overall connection acquisition time metric

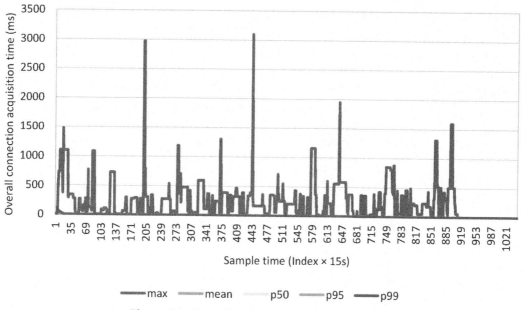

Figure 2.14: Overall connection acquisition time

While the retry attempts graph only shows how the retry count increases with time, the actual effect of reattempting is visible in the overall connection acquisition time.

2.4.1.7 Connection lease time metric

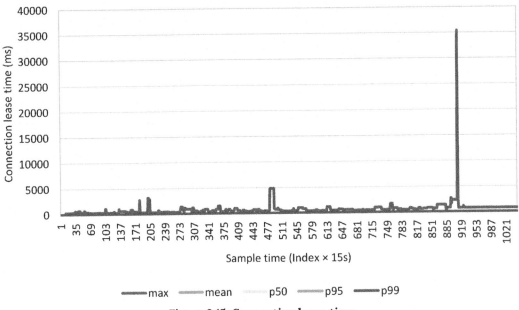

Figure 2.15: Connection lease time

The 99th percentile indicates a rather stable connection lease time throughout the whole job execution. On the other hand, the maximum graph shows a long-running transaction lasting over 35 seconds.

Holding connections for long periods of time can increase the connection acquisition time, and fewer resources are available to other incoming clients.

Most often, connections are leased for the whole duration of a database transaction. Long-running transactions might hold database locks, which, in turn, might lead to increasing the serial portion of the current execution context, therefore hindering parallelism.

Long-running transactions can be addressed by properly indexing slow queries or by splitting the application-level transaction over multiple database transactions like it is the case in many ETL (Extract, Transform, and Load) systems.

3. Batch Updates

JDBC 2.0 introduced *batch updates* so that multiple DML statements can be grouped into a single database request. Sending multiple statements in a single request reduces the number of database roundtrips, therefore decreasing transaction response time. Even if the reference specification uses the term *updates*, any *insert*, *update* or *delete* statement can be batched, and JDBC supports batching for `java.sql.Statement`, `java.sql.PreparedStatement` and `java.sql.CallableStatement` too.

Not only each database driver is distinct, but even different versions of the same driver might require implementation-specific configurations.

3.1 Batching Statements

For executing static SQL statements, JDBC defines the `Statement` interface, which comes with a batching API as well. Other than for test sake, using a `Statement` for CRUD (Create, Read, Update, Delete), as in the example below, should be avoided for it's prone to SQL injection attacks.

```
statement.addBatch(
    "INSERT INTO post (title, version, id) " +
    "VALUES ('Post no. 1', 0, default)");

statement.addBatch(
    "INSERT INTO post_comment (post_id, review, version, id) " +
    "VALUES (1, 'Post comment 1.1', 0, default)");

int[] updateCounts = statement.executeBatch();
```

The numbers of database rows affected by each statement is included in the return value of the `executeBatch()` method.

> ### Oracle
>
> For `Statement` and `CallableStatement`, the Oracle JDBC Driver[a] does not actually support batching For anything but `PreparedStatement`, the driver ignores batching, and each statement is executed separately.
>
> ---
> [a]http://docs.oracle.com/cd/E11882_01/java.112/e16548/oraperf.htm#JJDBC28752

The following graph depicts how different JDBC drivers behave when varying batch size, the test measuring the time it takes to insert 1000 *post* rows with 4 *comments* each:

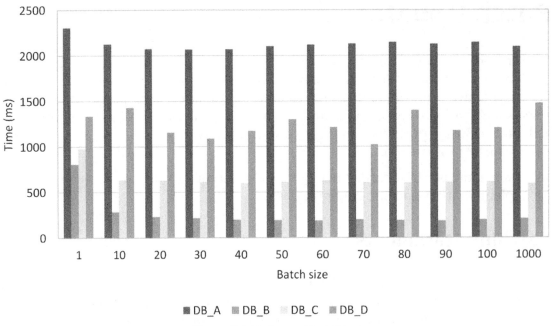

Figure 3.1: Statement batching

Reordering inserts, so that all *posts* are inserted before the *comment* rows, gives the following results:

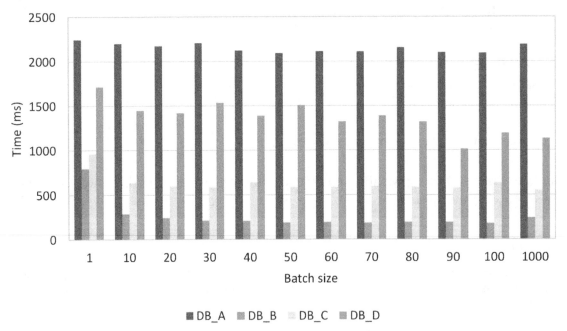

Figure 3.2: Reordered statement batching

Reordering statements does not seem to improve performance noticeably, although some drivers (e.g. MySQL) might take advantage of this optimization.

MySQL

Although it implements the JDBC specification, by default, the MySQL JDBC driver does not send the batched statements in a single request.

For this purpose, the JDBC driver defines the `rewriteBatchedStatements`[a] connection property, so that statements get rewritten into a single `String` buffer. In order to fetch the auto-generated row keys, the batch must contain insert statements only.

For `PreparedStatement`, this property rewrites the batched insert statements into a multi-value insert. Unfortunately, the driver is not able to use server-side prepared statements when enabling rewriting.

Without setting this property, the MySQL driver simply executes each DML statement separately, therefore defeating the purpose of batching.

---

[a]http://dev.mysql.com/doc/connector-j/en/connector-j-reference-configuration-properties.html

The following graph demonstrates how statement rewriting performs against the default behavior of the MySQL JDBC driver:

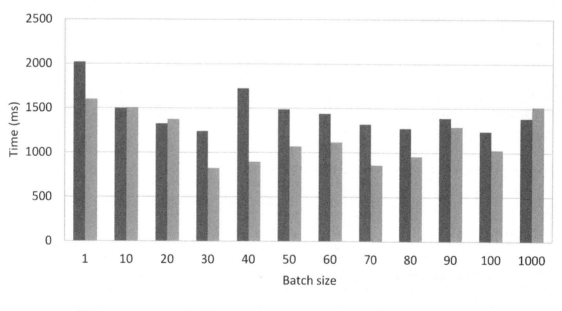

Figure 3.3: MySQL Statement batching

Rewriting non-parameterized statements seems to make a difference, as long as the batch size is not too large. In practice, it is common to use a relatively small batch size, to reduce both the client-side memory footprint and to avoid congesting the server from suddenly processing a huge batch load.

3.2 Batching PreparedStatements

For parameterized statements (a very common enterprise application requirement), the JDBC Statement is a poor fit because the only option for varying the executing SQL statement is through String manipulation. Using a String template or concatenating String tokens is risky as it makes the data access logic vulnerable to SQL injection attacks.

To address this shortcoming, JDBC offers the PreparedStatement interface for binding parameters in a safe manner. The driver must validate the provided parameter at runtime, therefore discarding unexpected input values.

Because a PreparedStatement is associated with a single DML statement, the batch update can group multiple parameter values belonging to the same prepared statement.

```
PreparedStatement postStatement = connection.prepareStatement(
    "INSERT INTO post (title, version, id) " +
    "VALUES (?, ?, ?)");

postStatement.setString(1, String.format("Post no. %1$d", 1));
postStatement.setInt(2, 0);
postStatement.setLong(3, 1);
postStatement.addBatch();

postStatement.setString(1, String.format("Post no. %1$d", 2));
postStatement.setInt(2, 0);
postStatement.setLong(3, 2);
postStatement.addBatch();

int[] updateCounts = postStatement.executeBatch();
```

SQL injection

For an enterprise application, security is a very important technical requirement. The SQL Injection attack exploits data access layers that do not use bind parameters. When the SQL statement is the result of String concatenation, an attacker could inject a malicious SQL routine that is sent to the database along the current executing statement.

SQL injection is usually done by ending the current statement with the ; character and continuing it with a rogue SQL command, like modifying the database structure (deleting a table or modifying authorization rights) or even extracting sensitive information.

All DML statements can benefit from batching as the following tests demonstrate. Just like for the JDBC Statement test case, the same amount of data (1000 *post* and 4000 *comments*) is inserted, updated, and deleted while varying the batch size.

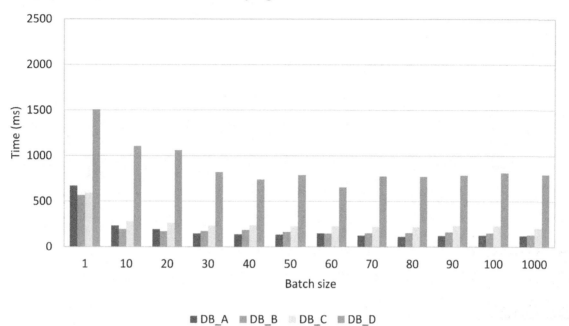

Figure 3.4: Insert PreparedStatement batch size

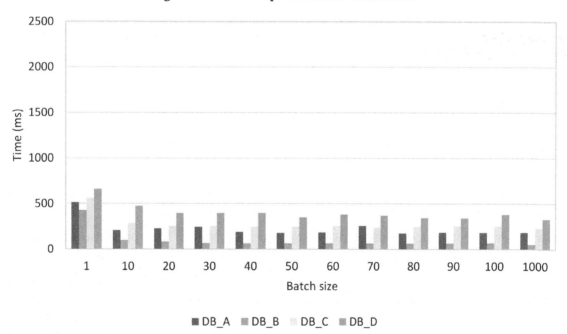

Figure 3.5: Update PreparedStatement batch size

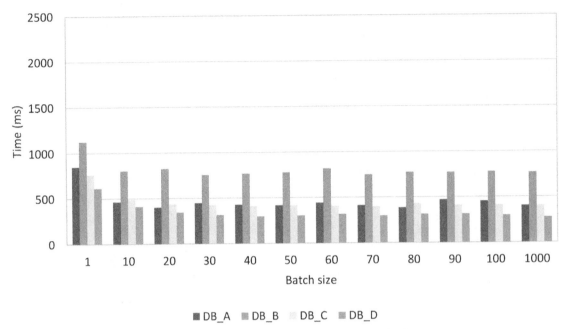

Figure 3.6: Delete PreparedStatement batch size

All database systems show a significant performance improvement when batching prepared statements. Some database systems are very fast when inserting or updating rows, while others perform very well when deleting data.

Compared to the previous Statement batch insert results, it is clear that, for the same data load, the PreparedStatement use case performs just better. In fact, Statement(s) should not be used for batching CRUD operations, being more suitable for bulk processing:

```
DELETE from post
WHERE spam = true AND created_on < current_timestamp - INTERVAL '30' day;
```

3.2.1 Choosing the right batch size

Finding the right batch size is not a trivial thing to do as there is no mathematical equation to solve the appropriate batch size for any enterprise application.

Like any other performance optimization technique, measuring the application performance gain in response to a certain batch size value remains the most reliable tuning option.

The astute reader has already figured out that even a low batch size can reduce the transaction response time, and the performance gain does not grow linearly with batch size. Although a larger batch value can save more database roundtrips, the overall performance gain does not necessarily increase linearly. In fact, a very large batch size can hurt application performance if the transaction takes too long to be executed.

As a rule of thumb, you should always measure the performance improvement for various batch sizes. In practice, a relatively low value (between 10 and 30) is usually a good choice.

3.2.2 Bulk processing

Apart from batching, SQL offers bulk operations to modify all rows that satisfy a given filtering criteria. *Bulk update* or *delete* statements can also benefit from indexing, just like select statements.

To update all records from the previous example, one would have to execute the following statements:

```
UPDATE post SET version = version + 1;
UPDATE post_comment SET version = version + 1;
```

Table 3.1: Bulk update time

DB_A time (ms)	DB_B time (ms)	DB_C time (ms)	DB_D time (ms)
26	13	58	9

The bulk alternative is one order of magnitude faster than batch updates. However, batch updates can benefit from application-level optimistic locking mechanisms, which are suitable for preventing *lost updates* when data is loaded in a read-only database transaction and written back in a successive transaction.

Like with updates, bulk deleting is also much faster than deleting in batches.

```
DELETE FROM post_comment WHERE version > 0;
DELETE FROM post WHERE version > 0;
```

Table 3.2: Bulk delete time

DB_A time (ms)	DB_B time (ms)	DB_C time (ms)	DB_D time (ms)
3	12	1	2

Long-running transaction caveats

Processing too much data in a single transaction can degrade application performance, especially in a highly concurrent environment. Whether if using 2PL (Two-Phase Locking) or MVCC (Multiversion Concurrency Control), writers always block other conflicting writers.

Long running transactions can affect both batch updates and bulk operations if the current transaction modifies a very large number of records. For this reason, it is more practical to break a large batch processing task into smaller manageable ones that can release locks in a timely fashion.

3.3 Retrieving auto-generated keys

It is common practice to delegate the row identifier generation to the database system. This way, the developer does not have to provide a monotonically incrementing primary key since the database takes care of this upon inserting a new record.

As convenient as this practice may be, it is important to know that auto-generated database identifiers might conflict with the batch insert process.

Like many other database features, setting the auto incremented identifier strategy is database-specific so the choice goes between an *identity* column or a database *sequence* generator.

Oracle

Prior to Oracle 12c, an auto incremented generator had to be implemented on top of a database sequence.

```
CREATE SEQUENCE post_seq;

CREATE TABLE post (
    id NUMBER(19,0) NOT NULL,
    title VARCHAR2(255 CHAR),
    version NUMBER(10,0) NOT NULL,
    PRIMARY KEY (id));

CREATE OR REPLACE TRIGGER post_identity
BEFORE INSERT ON post
FOR EACH ROW
BEGIN
    SELECT post_seq.NEXTVAL
    INTO   :NEW.id
    FROM   dual;
end;
```

Oracle 12c adds support for identity columns as well, so the previous example can be simplified as follows.

```
CREATE TABLE post (
    id NUMBER(19,0) NOT NULL GENERATED ALWAYS AS IDENTITY,
    title VARCHAR2(255 CHAR),
    version NUMBER(10,0) NOT NULL,
    PRIMARY KEY (id));
```

SQL Server

Traditionally, SQL Server offered identity column generators, but, since SQL Server 2012, it now supports database sequences as well.

```
CREATE TABLE post (
    id BIGINT IDENTITY NOT NULL,
    title VARCHAR(255),
    version INT NOT NULL,
    PRIMARY KEY (id));
```

PostgreSQL

PostgreSQL 9.5 does not support identity columns natively, although it offers the SERIAL column type which can emulate an identity column.

```
CREATE TABLE post (
    id SERIAL NOT NULL,
    title VARCHAR(255),
    version INT4 NOT NULL,
    PRIMARY KEY (id));
```

The SERIAL (4 bytes) and BIGSERIAL (8 bytes) types are just a syntactic sugar expression as, behind the scenes, PostgreSQL relies on a database sequence anyway.

The previous definition is therefore equivalent to:

```
CREATE SEQUENCE post_id_seq;

CREATE TABLE post (
    id INTEGER DEFAULT NEXTVAL('post_id_seq') NOT NULL,
    title VARCHAR(255),
    version INT4 NOT NULL,
    PRIMARY KEY (id));
);
```

> **MySQL**
>
> MySQL 5.7 only supports identity columns through the AUTO_INCREMENT attribute.
>
> ```
> CREATE TABLE post (
>     id BIGINT NOT NULL AUTO_INCREMENT,
>     title VARCHAR(255),
>     version INTEGER NOT NULL,
>     PRIMARY KEY (id));
> ```

Many database developers like this approach since the client does not have to care about supplying a database identifier upon inserting a new row.

```
INSERT INTO post (title, version) VALUES (?, ?);
```

To retrieve the newly created row identifier, the JDBC PreparedStatement must be instructed to return the auto-generated keys.

```
PreparedStatement postStatement = connection.prepareStatement(
    "INSERT INTO post (title, version) VALUES (?, ?)",
    Statement.RETURN_GENERATED_KEYS
);
```

One alternative is to hint the driver about the column index holding the auto-generated key column.

```
PreparedStatement postStatement = connection.prepareStatement(
    "INSERT INTO post (title, version) VALUES (?, ?)",
    new int[] {1}
);
```

The column name can also be used to instruct the driver about the auto-generated key column.

```
PreparedStatement postStatement = connection.prepareStatement(
    "INSERT INTO post (title, version) VALUES (?, ?)",
    new String[] {"id"}
);
```

It is better to know all these three alternatives because they are not interchangeable on all database systems.

> ### Oracle auto-generated key retrieval gotcha
>
> When using `Statement.RETURN_GENERATED_KEYS`, Oracle returns a `ROWID` instead of the actually generated column value. A workaround is to supply the column index or the column name, and so the auto-generated value can be extracted after executing the statement.

According to the JDBC 4.2 specification, every driver must implement the `supportsGetGeneratedKeys()` method and specify whether it supports auto-generated key retrieval. Unfortunately, this only applies to single statement updates as the specification does not make it mandatory for drivers to support generated key retrieval for batch statements. That being said, not all database systems support fetching auto-generated keys from a batch of statements.

Table 3.3: Driver support for retrieving generated keys

Returns generated keys after calling	Oracle JDBC driver (11.2.0.4)	Oracle JDBC driver (12.1.0.1)	SQL Server JDBC driver (4.2)	PostgreSQL JDBC driver (9.4-1201-jdbc41)	MySQL JDBC driver (5.1.36)
executeUpdate()	Yes	Yes	Yes	Yes	Yes
executeBatch()	No	Yes	No	Yes	Yes

If the Oracle JDBC driver 11.2.0.4 cannot retrieve auto-generated batch keys, the 12.1.0.1 version works just fine. When trying to get the auto-generated batch keys, the SQL Server JDBC driver throws this exception: *The statement must be executed before any results can be obtained.*

3.3.1 Sequences to the rescue

As opposed to identity columns, database sequences offer the advantage of decoupling the identifier generation from the actual row insert. To make use of batch inserts, the identifier must be fetched prior to setting the insert statement parameter values.

```
private long getNextSequenceValue(Connection connection)
    throws SQLException {
    try(Statement statement = connection.createStatement()) {
        try(ResultSet resultSet = statement.executeQuery(
            callSequenceSyntax())) {
            resultSet.next();
            return resultSet.getLong(1);
        }
    }
}
```

For calling a sequence, every database offers a specific syntax:

Oracle

```
SELECT post_seq.NEXTVAL FROM dual;
```

SQL Server

```
SELECT NEXT VALUE FOR post_seq;
```

PostgreSQL

```
SELECT NEXTVAL('post_seq');
```

Because the primary key is generated up-front, there is no need to call the `getGeneratedKeys()` method, and so batch inserts are not driver dependent anymore.

```
try(PreparedStatement postStatement = connection.prepareStatement(
    "INSERT INTO post (id, title, version) VALUES (?, ?, ?)")) {
    for (int i = 0; i < postCount; i++) {
        if(i > 0 && i % batchSize == 0) {
            postStatement.executeBatch();
        }
        postStatement.setLong(1, getNextSequenceValue(connection));
        postStatement.setString(2, String.format("Post no. %1$d", i));
        postStatement.setInt(3, 0);
        postStatement.addBatch();
    }
    postStatement.executeBatch();
}
```

Many database engines use sequence number generation optimizations to lower the sequence call execution as much as possible. If the number of inserted records is relatively low, then the sequence call overhead (extra database roundtrips) will be insignificant. However, for batch processors inserting large amounts of data, the extra sequence calls can add up.

Optimizing sequence calls

The data access layer does not need to go to the database to fetch a unique identifier if the sequence incrementation step is greater than 1. For a step of N, the sequence numbers are 1, N + 1, 2N + 1, 3N + 1, etc. The data access logic can assign identifiers in-between the database sequence calls (e.g. 2, 3, 4, ..., N -1, N), and so it can mitigate the extra network roundtrips penalty.

This strategy is going to be discussed in greater detail in the Hibernate types and identifiers chapter.

4. Statement Caching

Being a declarative language, SQL describes the *what* and not the *how*. The actual database structures and the algorithms used for fetching and preparing the desired result set are hidden away from the database client, which only has to focus on properly defining the SQL statement. This way, to deliver the most efficient data access plan, the database can attempt various execution strategies.

4.1 Statement lifecycle

The main database modules responsible for processing a SQL statement are the *Parser*, the *Optimizer*, and the *Executor*.

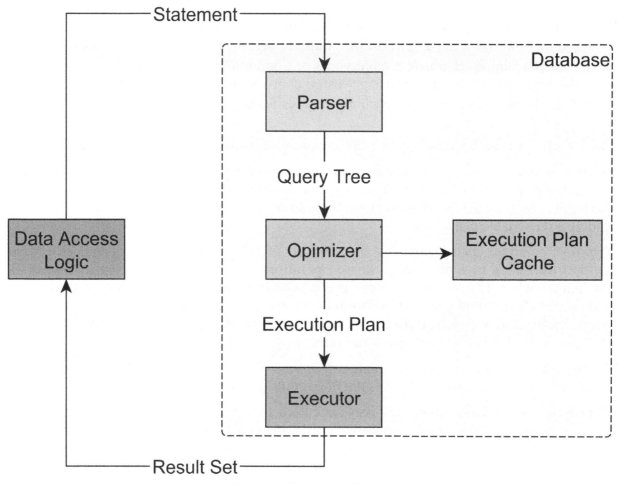

Figure 4.1: Statement lifecycle

4.1.1 Parser

The Parser checks the SQL statement and ensures its validity. The statements are verified both syntactically (the statement keywords must be properly spelled and following the SQL language guidelines) and semantically (the referenced tables and column do exist in the database).

During parsing, the SQL statement is transformed into a database-internal representation, called the *syntax tree* (also known as *parse tree* or *query tree*). If the SQL statement is a high-level representation (being more meaningful from a human perspective), the syntax tree is the logical representation of the database objects required for fulfilling the current statement.

4.1.2 Optimizer

For a given syntax tree, the database must decide the most efficient data fetching algorithm. Data is retrieved by following an *access path*, and the Optimizer needs to evaluate multiple data traversing options like:

- The access method for each referencing table (table scan or index scan).
- For index scans, it must decide which index is better suited for fetching this result set.
- For each joining relation (e.g. table, views or Common Table Expression), it must choose the best-performing join type (e.g. Nested Loops Joins, Hash Joins, Sort Merge Joins).
- The joining order becomes very important, especially for Nested Loops Joins.

The list of access path, chosen by the Optimizer, is assembled into an execution plan.

Because of a large number of possible action plan combinations, finding a good execution plan is not a trivial task. The more time is spent on finding the best possible execution plan, the higher the transaction response time gets, so the Optimizer has a fixed time budget for finding a reasonable plan.

The most common decision-making algorithm is CBO (Cost-Based Optimizer). Each access method translates to a physical database operation, and its associated cost in resources can be estimated. The database stores various statistics like table sizes and data cardinality (how much the column values differ from one row to the other) to evaluate the cost of a given database operation. The cost is calculated based on the number of CPU cycles and I/O operations required for executing a given plan.

When finding an optimal execution plan, the Optimizer might evaluate multiple options, and, based on their overall cost, it chooses the one requiring the least amount of time to execute.

By now, it is clear that finding a proper execution plan is resource intensive, and, for this purpose, some database vendors offer execution plan caching (to eliminate the time spent on finding the optimal plan). While caching can speed up statement execution, it also incurs some additional challenges (making sure the plan is still optimal across multiple executions).

Each execution plan has a given memory footprint, and most database systems use a fixed-size cache (discarding the least used plans to make room for newer ones). DDL (Data Definition Language) statements might corrupt execution plans, making them obsolete, so the database must use a separate process for validating the existing execution plans relevancy.

However, the most challenging aspect of caching is to ensure that only a good execution plan goes in the cache, since a bad plan, getting reused over and over, can really hurt application performance.

4.1.2.1 Execution plan visualization

Database tuning would not be possible without knowing the actual execution plan employed by the database for any given SQL statement. Because the output may exceed the length of a page, some execution plan columns were removed for brevity sake.

Oracle

Oracle uses the EXPLAIN PLAN FOR syntax, and the output goes into the dbms_xplan package:

```
SQL> EXPLAIN PLAN FOR SELECT COUNT(*) FROM post;
SQL> SELECT plan_table_output FROM table(dbms_xplan.display());


---------------------------------------------------------------
| Id  | Operation             | Name        | Rows  | Cost (%CPU)|
---------------------------------------------------------------
|   0 | SELECT STATEMENT      |             |     1 |     5   (0)|
|   1 |  SORT AGGREGATE       |             |     1 |            |
|   2 |   INDEX FAST FULL SCAN| SYS_C007093 |  5000 |     5   (0)|
---------------------------------------------------------------
```

PostgreSQL

PostgreSQL reserves the EXPLAIN keyword for displaying execution plans:

```
EXPLAIN SELECT COUNT(*) FROM post;

QUERY PLAN
-------------------------------------------------------------
 Aggregate  (cost=99.50..99.51 rows=1 width=0)
   -> Seq Scan on post  (cost=0.00..87.00 rows=5000 width=0)
```

SQL Server

The SQL Server Management Studio provides an execution plan viewer:

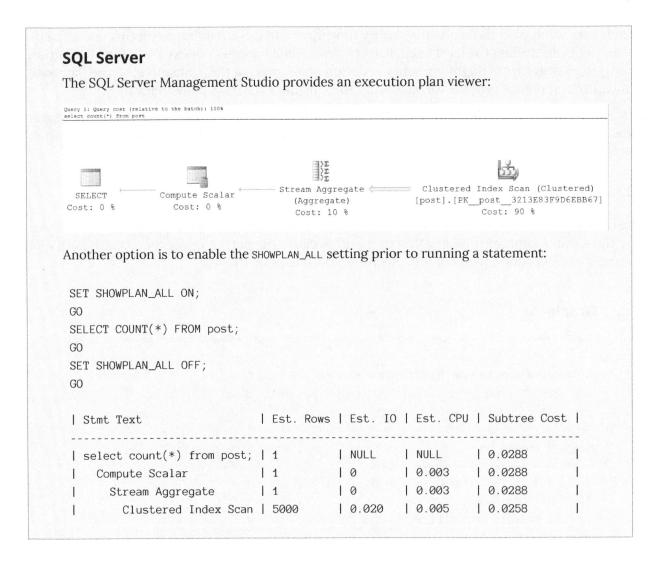

Another option is to enable the SHOWPLAN_ALL setting prior to running a statement:

```
SET SHOWPLAN_ALL ON;
GO
SELECT COUNT(*) FROM post;
GO
SET SHOWPLAN_ALL OFF;
GO
```

Stmt Text	Est. Rows	Est. IO	Est. CPU	Subtree Cost
select count(*) from post;	1	NULL	NULL	0.0288
Compute Scalar	1	0	0.003	0.0288
Stream Aggregate	1	0	0.003	0.0288
Clustered Index Scan	5000	0.020	0.005	0.0258

MySQL

The plan is displayed using EXPLAIN or EXPLAIN EXTENDED:

```
mysql> EXPLAIN EXTENDED SELECT COUNT(*) FROM post;
```

id	select type	table	type	key	key len	rows	filtered	Extra
1	SIMPLE	post	index	PRIMARY	8	5000	100.00	Using index

MySQL

When using MySQL 5.6.5[a] or later, you can make use of the JSON EXPLAIN format, which provides lots of information compared to the TRADITIONAL EXPLAIN format output.

```
mysql> EXPLAIN FORMAT=JSON select distinct title from post;
{
    "query_block": {
        "select_id": 1,
        "cost_info": {
            "query_cost": "1017.00"
        },
        "duplicates_removal": {
            "using_temporary_table": true,
            "using_filesort": false,
            "table": {
                "table_name": "post",
                "access_type": "ALL",
                "rows_examined_per_scan": 5000,
                "rows_produced_per_join": 5000,
                "filtered": "100.00",
                "cost_info": {
                    "read_cost": "17.00",
                    "eval_cost": "1000.00",
                    "prefix_cost": "1017.00",
                    "data_read_per_join": "3M"
                },
                "used_columns": [
                    "id",
                    "title"
                ]
            }
        }
    }
}
```

[a]https://dev.mysql.com/doc/refman/5.6/en/explain.html

4.1.3 Executor

From the Optimizer, the execution plan goes to the Executor where it is used to fetch the associated data and build the result set. The Executor makes use of the Storage Engine (for loading data according to the current execution plan) and the Transaction Engine (to enforce the current transaction data integrity guarantees).

Having a reasonably large in-memory buffer allows the database to reduce the I/O contention, therefore reducing transaction response time. The consistency model also has an impact on the overall transaction performance since locks may be acquired to ensure data integrity, and the more locking, the less the chance for parallel execution.

4.2 Caching performance gain

Before jumping into more details about *server-side* and *client-side* statement caching, it is better to visualize the net effect of reusing statements on the overall application performance. The following test calculates the number of queries a database engine can execute in a one-minute time span. To better emulate a non-trivial execution plan, the test executes a statement combining both table joining and query nesting.

```
SELECT p.title, pd.created_on
FROM    post p
LEFT JOIN post_details pd ON p.id = pd.id
WHERE  EXISTS (
    SELECT 1
    FROM    post_comment
    WHERE  post_id = p.id AND version = ?
)
```

Running it on four different database systems, the following throughput numbers are collected.

Table 4.1: Statement caching performance gain

Database System	No Caching Throughput (Statements Per Minute)	Caching Throughput (Statements Per Minute)	Percentage Gain
DB_A	419 833	507 286	20.83%
DB_B	194 837	303 100	55.56%
DB_C	116 708	166 443	42.61%
DB_D	15 522	15 550	0.18%

Most database systems can clearly benefit from reusing statements and, in some particular use cases, the performance gain is quite substantial.

 Statement caching plays a very important role in optimizing high-performance OLTP (Online transaction processing) systems.

4.3 Server-side statement caching

Because statement parsing and the execution plan generation are resource intensive operations, some database providers offer an execution plan cache. The statement string value is used as input to a hashing function, and the resulting value becomes the execution plan cache entry key. If the statement string value changes from one execution to the other, the database cannot reuse an already generated execution plan. For this purpose, dynamic-generated JDBC Statement(s) are not suitable for reusing execution plans.

Forced Parameterization

Some database systems offer the possibility of intercepting SQL statements at runtime so that all value literals are replaced with bind variables. This way, the newly parameterized statement can reuse an already cached execution plan.

To enable this feature, each database system offers a vendor-specific syntax.

Oracle

```
ALTER SESSION SET cursor_sharing=force;
```

SQL Server

```
ALTER DATABASE high_performance_java_persistence SET PARAMETERIZATION FORCED;
```

Server-side prepared statements allow the data access logic to reuse the same execution plan for multiple executions. A PreparedStatement is always associated with a single SQL statement, and bind parameters are used to vary the runtime execution context. Because PreparedStatement(s) take the SQL query at creation time, the database can precompile the associated SQL statement prior to executing it.

During the precompilation phase, the database validates the SQL statement and parses it into a syntax tree. When it comes to executing the `PreparedStatement`, the driver sends the actual parameter values, and the database can jump to compiling and running the actual execution plan.

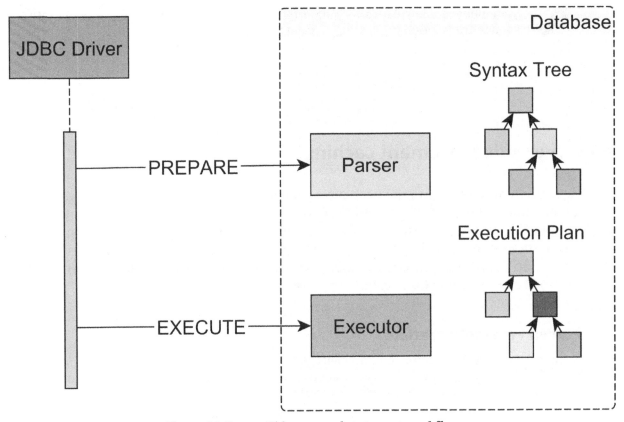

Figure 4.2: Server-Side prepared statement workflow

Conceptually, the prepare and the execution phases happen in separate database roundtrips. However, some database systems choose to optimize this process, therefore, multiplexing these two phases into a single database roundtrip.

Because of index selectivity, in the absence of the actual bind parameter values, the Optimizer cannot compile the syntax tree into an execution plan. Since a disk access is required for fetching every additional row-level data, indexing is suitable when selecting only a fraction of the whole table data. Most database systems take this decision based on the index selectivity of the current bind parameter values.

Because each disk access requires reading a whole block of data, accessing too many disparate blocks can actually perform worse than scanning the whole table (random access is slower than sequential scans).

For prepared statements, the execution plan can either be compiled on every execution or it can be cached and reused. Recompiling the plan can generate the best data access paths for any given bind variable set while paying the price of additional database resources usage. Reusing a plan can spare database resources, but it might not be suitable for every parameter value combination.

4.3.1 Bind-sensitive execution plans

Assuming a *task* table has a *status* column with three distinct values: TO_DO, DONE, and FAILED. The table has 100 000 rows, of which 1000 are TO_DO entries, 95 000 are DONE, and 4000 are FAILED records.

In database terminology, the number of rows returned by a given predicate is called cardinality and, for the *status* column, the cardinality varies from 1000 to 95 000.

$$C = \{1000, 4000, 95\,000\}$$

By dividing cardinality with the total number of rows, the predicate selectivity is obtained:

$$S = \frac{C}{N} \times 100 = \{1\%, 4\%, 95\%\}$$

The lower the selectivity, the fewer rows are matched for a given bind value and the more selective the predicate gets. The Optimizer tends to prefer sequential scans over index lookups for high selectivity percentages, to reduce the total number of disk-access roundtrips (especially when data is scattered among multiple data blocks).

When searching for DONE entries, the Optimizer chooses a table scan access path (the estimated number of selected rows is 95 080):

```
SQL> EXPLAIN SELECT * FROM task WHERE status = 'DONE' LIMIT 100;

Limit  (cost=0.00..1.88 rows=100 width=13)
->   Seq Scan on task  (cost=0.00..1791.00 rows=95080 width=13)
       Filter: ((status)::text = 'DONE'::text)
```

Otherwise, the search for TO_DO or FAILED entries is done through an index lookup:

```
SQL> EXPLAIN SELECT * FROM task WHERE status = 'TO_DO' LIMIT 100;

Limit  (cost=0.29..4.25 rows=100 width=13)
->   Index Scan using task_status_idx on task  (cost=0.29..36.16 rows=907)
       Index Cond: ((status)::text = 'TO_DO'::text)

SQL> EXPLAIN SELECT * FROM task WHERE status = 'FAILED' LIMIT 100;

Limit  (cost=0.29..3.86 rows=100 width=13)
->   Index Scan using task_status_idx on task  (cost=0.29..143.52 rows=4013)
       Index Cond: ((status)::text = 'FAILED'::text)
```

So, the execution plan depends on bind parameter value selectivity. If the selectivity is constant across the whole bind value domain, the execution plan will no longer be sensitive to parameter values. A *generic* execution plan is much easier to reuse than a bind-sensitive one.

The following section describes how some well-known database systems implement server-side prepared statements in relation to their associated execution plans.

Oracle

Every SQL statement goes through the Parser, where it is validated both syntactically and semantically. Next, a hashing function takes the SQL statement, and the resulting hash key is used for searching the Shared Pool for an existing execution plan.

In Oracle terminology, reusing an execution plan is called a *soft parse*. To reuse a plan, the SQL statement must be identical with a previously processed one (even the case sensitivity and whitespaces are taken into consideration).

If no execution plan is found, the statement will undergo a *hard parse*[a]. The Optimizer evaluates multiple execution plans and chooses the one with the lowest associated cost, which is further compiled into a *source tree* by the *Row Source Generator*. Whether reused (*soft parse*) or generated (*hard parse*), the source tree goes to the Executor, which fetches the associated result set.

Bind peeking

As previously mentioned, the Optimizer cannot determine an optimal access path in the absence of the actual bind values. For this reason, Oracle uses *bind peeking*[b] during the *hard parse* phase.

The first set of bind parameter values determines the selectivity of the cached execution plan. By now it is clear that this strategy is feasible for uniformly distributed data sets, and a single execution plan cannot perform consistently for bind-sensitive predicates.

As of 11g, Oracle has introduced adaptive cursor sharing so that a statement can utilize multiple execution plans. The execution plan is stored along with the selectivity metadata associated with the bind parameters used for generating this plan. An execution plan is reused only if its selectivity matches the one given by the current bind parameter values.

Both the execution plan cache and the adaptive cursor sharing are enabled by default, and, for highly concurrent OLTP systems, hard parsing should be avoided whenever possible. The plan cache allows database resources to be allocated to the execution part rather than being wasted on compiling, therefore improving response time.

 `PreparedStatement(s)` optimize the execution plan cache-hit rate and are therefore preferred over plain JDBC `Statement(s)`.

---

[a]https://docs.oracle.com/database/121/TGSQL/tgsql_sqlproc.htm#TGSQL175
[b]https://docs.oracle.com/database/121/TGSQL/tgsql_cursor.htm#TGSQL848

SQL Server

SQL Server always caches execution plans[a] for both JDBC `Statement(s)` and `PreparedStatement(s)`. The execution plans are stored in the *procedure cache* region, and they are evicted only when the in-memory storage starts running out of space.

Even if SQL Server supports plain statements *forced parameterization*, preparing statements remains the most effective way to increase the likelihood of an execution plan cache-hit.

 The catch is that all prepared statements should use the qualified object name, thus, the schema must always precede the table name.

So, instead of a query like this:

```
SELECT * FROM task WHERE status = ?;
```

the data access layer should always append the schema to all table names:

```
SELECT * FROM etl.task WHERE status = ?;
```

Without specifying the database object schema, the cache cannot determine which statistics to consider when analyzing the effectiveness of a given execution plan.

SQL Server inspects the actual parameter values during the first execution of a prepared statement. This process is called *parameter sniffing*, and its effectiveness is relative to predicate value distribution.

The database engine monitors statement execution times, and if the existing cached plan does not perform efficiently or if the underlying table structure or data distribution statistics undergo a conflicting change, then the database will recompile the execution plan according to the new parameter values.

For skewed data, reusing plans might be suboptimal, and recompiling plans on every execution could be a better alternative. To address the *parameter sniffing* limitations, SQL Server offers the `OPTION (RECOMPILE)` query hint[b], so the statement can bypass the cache and generate a fresh plan on every execution.

```
SELECT * FROM task WHERE status = ? OPTION(RECOMPILE);
```

---

[a]https://technet.microsoft.com/en-us/library/ms181055%28v=sql.100%29.aspx
[b]https://msdn.microsoft.com/en-us/library/ms181714.aspx

PostgreSQL

Prior to 9.2, a prepared statement was planned and compiled entirely during the prepare phase, so the execution plan was generated in the absence of the actual bind parameter values. Although it attempted to spare database resources, this strategy was very sensitive to skewed data. Since PostgreSQL 9.2, the prepare phase only parses and rewrites a statement, while the optimization and the planning phase are deferred until execution time. This way, the rewritten syntax tree is optimized according to the actual bind parameter values, and an optimal execution plan is generated.

For a singular execution, a plain statement requires only a one database roundtrip, while a prepared statement needs two (a prepare request and an execution call). To avoid the networking overhead, by default, JDBC PreparedStatement(s) do both the prepare and the execute phases over a single database request.

A client-side prepared statement must run at least 5 times for the driver to turn it into a server-side statement. The default execution count value is given by the prepareThreshold parameter, which is configurable as a connection property or through a driver-specific API[a].

After several executions, if the performance is not sensitive to bind parameter values, the Optimizer might choose to turn the plan into a generic one and cache it for reuse.

---

[a]https://jdbc.postgresql.org/documentation/publicapi/org/postgresql/PGStatement.html

MySQL

When preparing a statement, the MySQL Parser generates a syntax tree which is further validated and pre-optimized by a *resolution* mechanism. The syntax tree undergoes several data-insensitive transformations, and the final output is a *permanent tree*.

Since MySQL 5.7.4[a], all *permanent transformations* (rejoining orders or subquery optimizations) are done in the prepare phase, so the execution phase only applies data-sensitive transformations. MySQL does not cache execution plans, so every statement execution is optimized for the current bind parameter values, therefore avoiding data skew issues.

Because of some unresolved issues, since version 5.0.5[b], the MySQL JDBC driver only emulates server-side prepared statements. To switch to server-side prepared statements, both the useServerPrepStmts and the cachePrepStmts connection properties must be set to *true*.

Before activating this feature, it is better to check the latest Connector/J release notes and validate this feature is safe for using.

---

[a]http://mysqlserverteam.com/mysql-performance-schema-prepared-statements-instrumentation/
[b]http://dev.mysql.com/doc/relnotes/connector-j/en/news-5-0-5.html

4.4 Client-side statement caching

Not only the database side can benefit from caching statements, but also the JDBC driver can reuse already constructed statement objects. The main goals of the client-side statement caching can be summarized as follows:

- Reducing client-side statement processing, which, in turn, lowers transaction response time.
- Sparing application resources by recycling statement objects along with their associated database-specific metadata.

In high-performance OLTP applications, transactions tend to be very short, so even a minor response time reduction can make a difference in the overall transaction throughput.

Oracle implicit statement caching

Unlike server-side plan cache, the client one is confined to a database connection only. Since the SQL String becomes the cache entry key, PreparedStatement(s) and CallableStatement(s) have a better chance of getting reused. Therefore, the Oracle JDBC driver supports caching only for these two statement types. When enabling caching (disabled by default), the driver returns a logical statement, so when the client closes it, the logical statement goes back to the cache.

From a development point of view, there is an *implicit* statement caching mechanism as well as an *explicit* one. Both caching options share the same driver storage, which needs to be configured according to the current application requirements.

The implicit cache can only store statement *metadata*, which does not change from one execution to the other. Although it can be set for each individual Connection, it is convenient to configure it at the DataSource level (all connections inheriting the same caching properties):

```
connectionProperties.put("oracle.jdbc.implicitStatementCacheSize",
    Integer.toString(cacheSize));
dataSource.setConnectionProperties(connectionProperties);
```

Setting the implicitStatementCacheSize also enables the cache. By default, all executing statements are being implicitly cached, and this might not be desirable (some occasional queries might evict other frequently executed statements). To control the statement caching policy, JDBC defines the isPoolable() and setPoolable(boolean poolable) Statement methods:

```
if (statement.isPoolable()) {
    statement.setPoolable(false);
}
```

Oracle explicit statement caching

The explicit cache is configurable and managed through an Oracle-specific API. Prior to using it, it must be enabled and resized using the underlying `OracleConnection` reference.

```
OracleConnection oracleConnection = (OracleConnection) connection;
oracleConnection.setExplicitCachingEnabled(true);
oracleConnection.setStatementCacheSize(cacheSize);
```

When using the explicit cache, the data access controls which statements are cacheable, so there is no need for using the `setPoolable(boolean poolable)` method anymore. The following example demonstrates how to make use of the explicit caching mechanism.

```
PreparedStatement statement = oracleConnection
    .getStatementWithKey(SELECT_POST_REVIEWS_KEY);
if (statement == null)
    statement = connection.prepareStatement(SELECT_POST_REVIEWS);
try {
    statement.setInt(1, 10);
    statement.execute();
} finally {
    ((OraclePreparedStatement) statement).closeWithKey(SELECT_POST_REVIEWS_KEY);
}
```

The explicit caching relies on two main operations, which can be summarized as follows:

1. The `getStatementWithKey(String key)` method loads a statement from the cache. If no entry is found, the `PreparedStatement` must be manually created using standard JDBC API.
2. The `closeWithKey(String key)` method pushes the statement back into the pool.

 The vendor-specific API couples the data access code to the Oracle-specific API which hinders portability and it require a more complex data access logic (when accommodating multiple database systems).

Aside from caching *metadata*, the explicit cache also stores execution *state* and *data*. Although reusing more client-side constructs might improve performance even further, this strategy poses the risk of mixing previous and current execution contexts, so caution is advised.

SQL Server

Although the Microsoft SQL Server JDBC driver defines a `disableStatementPooling` property, as of writing (the 4.2 version), the statement cache cannot be enabled[a].

On the other hand, jTDS (the open source JDBC 3.0 implementation) offers statement caching on a per-connection basis. Being a JDBC 4.0-specific API, The `setPoolable(boolean poolable) Statement` method is not implemented in the 1.3.1 jTDS release. The cache has a default size of 500 entries which is also adjustable.

```
((JtdsDataSource) dataSource).setMaxStatements(cacheSize);
```

Even if jTDS has always focused on performance, the lack of a steady release schedule is a major drawback compared to the Microsoft driver.

---

[a]https://msdn.microsoft.com/en-us/library/ms378988%28v=sql.110%29.aspx

PostgreSQL

Since the PostgreSQL JDBC driver 9.4-1202[a] version, the client-side statements are cached, and their associated server-side statement keys are retained even after the initial `PreparedStatement(s)` is closed. As long as the current connection cache contains a given SQL statement, both the client-side `PreparedStatement` and the server-side object can be reused. The `setPoolable(boolean poolable)` method has no effect, and caching cannot be disabled on a per-statement basis.

The statement cache is controlled by the following connection properties:

- `preparedStatementCacheQueries` - the number of statements cached for each database connection. A value of 0 disables the cache, and server-side prepared statements are no longer available after the `PreparedStatement` is closed. The default value is 256.
- `preparedStatementCacheSizeMiB` - the statement cache has an upper memory bound, and the default value is 5 MB. A value of 0 disables the cache.

These properties can be set both as connection parameters[b] or as `DataSource` properties:

```
((PGSimpleDataSource) dataSource).setPreparedStatementCacheQueries(cacheSize);
((PGSimpleDataSource) dataSource).setPreparedStatementCacheSizeMiB(cacheSizeMb);
```

---

[a]https://jdbc.postgresql.org/documentation/changelog.html#version_9.4-1202
[b]https://jdbc.postgresql.org/documentation/head/connect.html#connection-parameters

MySQL

The statement caching is associated with a database connection, and it applies to all executing statements. In the 5.1.36 Connector/J driver version, the `setPoolable(boolean poolable)` method can disable caching for server-side statements only, the client-side ones being unaffected by this setting.

The client-side statement cache is configured using the following properties:

- `cachePrepStmts` - enables the client-side statement cache as well as the server-side statement validity checking. By default, the statement cache is disabled.
- `prepStmtCacheSize` - the number of statements cached for each database connection. The default cache size is 25.
- `prepStmtCacheSqlLimit` - the maximum length of a SQL statement allowed to be cached. The default maximum value is 256.

These properties can be set both as connection parameters[a] or at `DataSource` level:

```
((MysqlDataSource) dataSource).setCachePrepStmts(true);
((MysqlDataSource) dataSource).setPreparedStatementCacheSize(cacheSize);
((MysqlDataSource) dataSource).setPreparedStatementCacheSqlLimit(maxLength);
```

---

[a]http://dev.mysql.com/doc/connector-j/en/connector-j-reference-configuration-properties.html

5. ResultSet Fetching

Having discussed the SQL statement optimizations (batching and caching), it is time to move on to the response part of a query processing. Unlike the insert, update, and delete statements, which only return the affected row count, a JDBC select query returns a ResultSet instead.

The database Executor takes an execution plan and fetches data into a result set. Rows may be either extracted at once or upon being requested by the database client.

The SQL Standard defines both the result set and the cursor descriptor through the following properties:

- scrollability (the direction in which the result set can be iterated)
- sensitivity (when should data be fetched)
- updatability (available for cursors, it allows the client to modify records while traversing the result set)
- holdability (the result set scope in regard to a transaction lifecycle).

Following the standard specification, the JDBC ResultSet offers support for all the properties above.

Table 5.1: JDBC ResultSet properties

Property Name	Description
TYPE_FORWARD_ONLY	The result set can only be iterated from the first to the last element. This is the default *scrollability* value.
TYPE_SCROLL_INSENSITIVE	The result set takes a loading time snapshot which can be iterated both forward and backward.
TYPE_SCROLL_SENSITIVE	The result set is fetched on demand while being iterated without any direction restriction.
CONCUR_READ_ONLY	The result set is just a static data projection which does not allow row-level manipulation. This is the default *changeability* value.
CONCUR_UPDATABLE	The cursor position can be used to update or delete records, or even insert a new one.
CLOSE_CURSORS_AT_COMMIT	The result set is closed when the current transaction ends.
HOLD_CURSORS_OVER_COMMIT	The result set remains open even after the current transaction is committed.

5.1 ResultSet scrollability

The JDBC ResultSet can be traversed using an application-level cursor. The fetching mechanism is therefore hidden behind an iterator API, which decouples the application code from the data retrieval strategy. Some database drivers prefetch the whole result set on the client-side, while other implementations retrieve batches of data on a demand basis.

By default, the ResultSet uses a *forward-only* application-level cursor, which can be traversed only once, from the first position to last one. Although this is sufficient for most applications, JDBC also offers *scrollable* cursors, therefore allowing the row-level pointer to be positioned freely (in any direction and on every record).

The main difference between the two scrollable result sets lays in their *selectivity*. An *insensitive* cursor offers a static view of the current result set, so the data needs to be fetched entirely prior to being iterated. A *sensitive* cursor allows the result set to be fetched dynamically so it can reflect concurrent changes.

Oracle

Since the database engine does not offer support for scrollable result sets, the JDBC driver emulates it on top of a client-side caching mechanism[a]. As a consequence, the result set should not be too large as, otherwise, it can easily fill the client application memory.

 A sensitive scrollable result set is limited to selecting data from a single table only.

[a]https://docs.oracle.com/database/121/JJDBC/resltset.htm#JJDBC28615

SQL Server

All three cursor types are supported. An insensitive scroll generates a server-side database snapshot, which the client fetches in batches. The sensitive scroll uses a server-side updatable window and changes are synchronized only for the current processing window.

 The driver suggests using *read-only* cursors when there is no intent on updating the result set. The forward-only scroll delivers the best performance for small result sets[a].

PostgreSQL

By default, the result set is fetched entirely and cached on the client-side. Only the forward-only and the insensitive scroll are supported. For large result sets, fetching all records at once can put much pressure on both the database server resources and the client-side memory. For this purpose, PostgreSQL allows associating a result set to a database cursor[a] so records can be fetched on demand.

```
PreparedStatement statement = connection.prepareStatement(
    "SELECT title FROM post WHERE id BETWEEN ? AND ?"
);
statement.setFetchSize(100);
```

 Only the forward-only result set type can benefit from database-side cursors, and the statement fetch size must be set to a positive integer value.

---

[a]https://jdbc.postgresql.org/documentation/head/query.html

MySQL

Only the insensitive scroll type is supported, even when explicitly specifying a forward-only result set. Because MySQL does not support database cursors, the driver retrieves the whole result set and caches it on the client-side. Large result sets can be streamed[a] only if the statement type is both forward-only and read-only and the fetch size value is set to the lowest java.lang.Integer value.

```
PreparedStatement statement = connection.prepareStatement(
    "SELECT title FROM post WHERE id BETWEEN ? AND ?",
    ResultSet.TYPE_FORWARD_ONLY, ResultSet.CONCUR_READ_ONLY
);
statement.setFetchSize(Integer.MIN_VALUE);
```

 Streaming requires fetching one row at a time, which might incur multiple database roundtrips. Until the stream is closed, the connection cannot execute any other statement.

---

[a]http://dev.mysql.com/doc/connector-j/en/connector-j-reference-implementation-notes.html

5.2 ResultSet changeability

By default, the result set is just a read-only view of the underlying data projection. Inspired by database cursors, the JDBC standard offers updatable result sets, so the data access logic can modify records while iterating the application-level cursor.

Mixing reading and writing logic into a single database transaction reminds of two-tier architectures, where holding the result set, even in the user think time, was both common and acceptable.

For web applications, requests should be as short as possible, and most application-level transactions span over multiple web requests. The former request may use a read-only database transaction to fetch data and render it to the user, while the latter might use a read-write transaction to apply data modifications. In such scenario, an updatable result set is of little use, especially because holding it open (along with the underlying database connection) over multiple requests can really hurt application scalability.

The following test case verifies if a forward-only and read-only cursor performs better than a sensitive and updatable one. The test executes 10 000 statements, fetching 100 posts along with *details* and their associated 1000 comments.

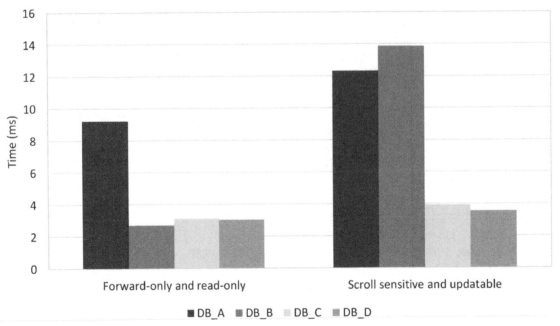

Figure 5.1: ResultSet cursor type

Every database system under test showed a slight improvement when using forward-only and read-only result sets.

 As a rule of thumb, if the current transaction does not require updating selected records, the forward-only and read-only default result set type might be the most efficient option. Even if it is a reminiscence from JDBC 1.0, the default result set is still the right choice in most situations.

5.3 ResultSet holdability

The JDBC 3.0 version added support for result set holdability and, unlike scrollability and updatability, the default value is implementation-specific.

Oracle

The default and the only supported holdability value is HOLD_CURSORS_OVER_COMMIT. An exception is thrown when trying to change this setting to any other value.

SQL Server

By default, the result set is kept open even after the current transaction is committed or rolled back. SQL Server supports the CLOSE_CURSORS_AT_COMMIT setting as well.

PostgreSQL

Unlike other database systems, the default holdability value is CLOSE_CURSORS_AT_COMMIT, but the driver also supports the HOLD_CURSORS_OVER_COMMIT setting.

MySQL

The default and the only supported holdability value is HOLD_CURSORS_OVER_COMMIT.

In a typical enterprise application, database connections are reused from one transaction to another, so holding a result set after a transaction ends is risky. Depending on the underlying database system and on the cursor type, a result set might allocate system resources, which, for scalability reasons, need to be released as soon as possible.

 Although the CLOSE_CURSORS_AT_COMMIT holdability option is not supported by all database engines, the same effect can be achieved by simply closing all acquired ResultSet(s) and their associated Statement objects.

5.4 Fetching size

The JDBC ResultSet acts as an application-level cursor, so whenever the statement is traversed, the result must be transferred from the database to the client. The transfer rate is controlled by the Statement fetch size.

```
statement.setFetchSize(fetchSize);
```

A custom fetch size gives the driver a hint as to the number of rows needed to be retrieved in a single database roundtrip. The default value of 0 leaves each database choose its driver-specific fetching policy.

Oracle

The default fetch size is set to 10 records, as a consequence of the JDBC driver memory model.

The Oracle 10i and 11g drivers pre-allocate a `byte[]` and a `char[]` buffers at statement creation time, whose lengths are given by the multiplication of the fetch size by the maximum memory footprint of each selected column. A `VARCHAR2(N)` column can accommodate at most N characters (or 2N bytes). Storing a field with a maximum size of 5 characters into a `VARCHAR2(4000)` column would pre-allocate 8000 bytes on the client-side, which is definitely a waste of memory.

 Avoiding memory allocation, by reusing existing buffers, is a very solid reason for employing statement caching. Only when using the implicit statement cache, the 10i and 11g drivers can benefit from recycling client-side memory buffers.

The 12c implementation[a] defers the buffer allocation until the result set is ready for fetching. This driver version uses two `byte[]` arrays instead, which are allocated lazily. Compared to the previous versions, the 12c memory footprint is greatly reduced since, instead of allocating the maximum possible data storage, the driver uses the actually extracted data size.

Although the optimal fetch size is application-specific, being influenced by the data size and the runtime environment concurrency topology, the Oracle JDBC driver specification recommends limiting the fetch size to at most 100 records.

Like with any other performance optimization, these indications are suggestions at best, and measuring application performance is the only viable way of finding the right fetch size.

---

[a]http://www.oracle.com/technetwork/database/application-development/jdbc-memory-management-12c-1964666.pdf

SQL Server

The SQL Server JDBC driver uses *adaptive buffering*[a], so the result set is fetched in batches, as needed. The size of a batch is therefore automatically controlled by the driver.

 Although enabled by default, adaptive buffering is limited to forward-only and read-only cursors. Both scrollable and updatable result sets operate on a single block of data, whose length is determined by the current statement fetch size.

---

[a]https://msdn.microsoft.com/en-us/library/bb879937%28v=sql.110%29.aspx

PostgreSQL

The entire result set is fetched at once[a] into client memory. The default fetch size requires only one database roundtrip, at the price of increasing the driver memory consumption. By changing fetch size, the result set is associated with a database cursor, allowing data to be fetched on demand.

[a]https://jdbc.postgresql.org/documentation/head/query.html

MySQL

Because of the network protocol design consideration[a], fetching the whole result set is the most efficient data retrieval strategy. The only streaming option requires processing one row at a time, and the number of database roundtrips is given by the read-ahead buffer configuration.

[a]http://dev.mysql.com/doc/connector-j/en/connector-j-reference-implementation-notes.html

The following graph captures the response time of four database systems when fetching 10 000 rows while varying the fetch size of the forward-only and read-only `ResultSet`.

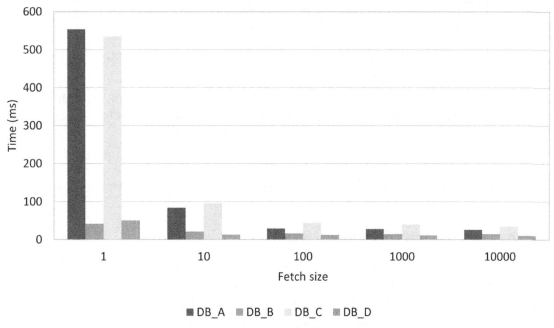

Figure 5.2: ResultSet fetch size

Fetching one row at a time requires 10 000 roundtrips, and the networking overhead impacts response time. Up to 100 rows, the fetch size plays an important role in lowering retrieval time (only 100 roundtrips), but beyond this point, the gain becomes less noticeable.

5.5 ResultSet size

Setting the appropriate fetching size can undoubtedly speed up the result set retrieval, as long as a statement fetches only the data required by the current business logic. All too often, unfortunately, especially with the widespread of ORM tools, the statement might select more data than necessary. This issue might be caused by selecting too many rows or too many columns, which are later discarded in the data access or the business layer.

5.5.1 Too many rows

Tables tend to grow (especially if the application gains more traction), and, with time, a moderate result set might easily turn into a performance bottleneck. These issues are often discovered in production systems, long after the application code was shipped.

A user interface can accommodate just as much info as the view allows displaying. For this reason, it is inefficient to fetch a whole result set if it cannot fit into the user interface. Pagination or dynamic scrolling are common ways of addressing this issue, and partitioning data sets becomes unavoidable.

Limiting result sets is common in batch processing as well. To avoid long-running transactions (which might put pressure on the database undo/redo logs), and to also benefit from parallel execution, a batch processor divides the current workload into smaller jobs. This way, a batch job can take only a subset of the whole processing data.

 When the result set size is limited by external factors, it makes no sense to select more data than necessary.

Without placing upper bounds, the result sets grow proportionally with the underlying table data. A large result set requires more time to be extracted and to be sent over the wire too.

Limiting queries can, therefore, ensure predictable response times and database resource utilization. The shorter the query processing time, the quicker the row-level locks are released, and the more scalable the data access layer becomes.

There are basically two ways of limiting a result set.

The former and the most efficient strategy is to include the row restriction clause in the SQL statement. This way, the Optimizer can better come up with an execution plan that is optimal for the current result set size (like selecting an index scan instead of a table scan).

The latter is to configure a maximum row count at the JDBC `Statement` level. Ideally, the driver can adjust the statement to include the equivalent result set size restriction as a SQL clause, but, most often, it only hints the database engine to use a database cursor instead.

5.5.1.1 SQL limit clause

SQL:2008

Although the SQL:2008 added support for limiting result sets, only starting from Oracle 12c[a], SQL Server 2012[b] and PostgreSQL 8.4[c], the standard syntax started being supported.

```
SELECT pc.id AS pc_id, p.title AS p_title
FROM post_comment pc
INNER JOIN post p ON p.id = pc.post_id
ORDER BY pc_id
OFFSET ? ROWS
FETCH FIRST (?) ROWS ONLY
```

 Surrounding the *row count* placeholder with parentheses is a workaround for a PostgreSQL database issue[d]. On SQL Server it works with or without the enclosing parentheses.

Older database versions or other database systems (e.g. MySQL 5.7) still rely on a vendor-specific syntax to restrict the result set size.

---

[a]https://docs.oracle.com/database/121/SQLRF/statements_10002.htm#SQLRF01702
[b]https://technet.microsoft.com/en-us/library/gg699618%28v=sql.110%29.aspx
[c]http://www.postgresql.org/docs/current/static/sql-select.html#SQL-LIMIT

Oracle

Unlike other relational databases, Oracle does not have a reserved keyword for restricting a query result set, but because each record is attributed a result set entry order number (given by the ROWNUM virtual column), the syntax for limiting a result set becomes:

```
SELECT *
FROM (
        SELECT pc.id AS pc_id, p.title AS p_title
        FROM post_comment pc
        INNER JOIN post p ON p.id = pc.post_id
        ORDER BY pc_id
)
WHERE ROWNUM <= ?
```

SQL Server

The TOP keyword has been the *de facto* way of restricting the result set size:

```
SELECT TOP (?) pc.id AS pc_id, p.title AS p_title
FROM post_comment pc
INNER JOIN post p ON p.id = pc.post_id
ORDER BY pc_id
```

PostgreSQL and MySQL

The LIMIT keyword places an upper bound on the result set size:

```
SELECT pc.id AS pc_id, p.title AS p_title
FROM post_comment pc
INNER JOIN post p ON p.id = pc.post_id
ORDER BY pc_id
LIMIT ?
```

5.5.1.2 JDBC max rows

The JDBC specification defines the maxRows[1] attribute which limits all ResultSet(s) for the current statement.

```
statement.setMaxRows(maxRows);
```

Unlike the SQL construct, the JDBC alternative is portable across all driver implementations. This can be very handy especially when the application needs to support multiple database systems.

According to the JDBC documentation, the driver is expected to discard the extra rows when the maximum threshold is reached.

From a data access performance perspective, dropping extra rows is a poor strategy because it wastes both database resources (CPU, I/O, Memory) as well as networking bandwidth.

---

[1]http://docs.oracle.com/javase/8/docs/api/java/sql/Statement.html#setMaxRows-int-

Oracle

When a `ResultSet` is being traversed, the client-side cursor fetches data in chunks (the fetch size attribute controlling the number of records in a chunk).

After each new batch retrieval, the total number of records is checked against the `maxRows` upper bound, and if the threshold is reached, the driver closes the networking stream.

The `maxRows` upper bound can, therefore, prevent the database and the client-side driver from wasting resources on fetching records the client does not even need. However, if the `maxRows` value is small, the Optimizer will not use indexes if the size of the scanned data set is rather large.

SQL Server

When the `Statement.setMaxRows(int maxRows)`[a] method is called, the driver calls the SET ROWCOUNT SQL command:

```
SET ROWCOUNT N
```

Unlike the TOP or FETCH SQL directives, the ROWCOUNT command is taken into consideration only during the execution phase, and it does not influence the plan generation. Because of this, the execution plan might not be optimized for the given result set size, so a table scan might be chosen over an index.

 The SQL Server documentation[b] recommends using the SQL directives over the SET ROWCOUNT command.

---

[a]https://msdn.microsoft.com/en-us/library/ms378838%28v=sql.110%29.aspx

PostgreSQL

The JDBC driver takes the `maxRows` statement attribute and sends it along with the query being executed. With this info, the Optimizer can choose an execution plan that is tailored for the given result set size, and it might even avoid some expensive operations like sorting the whole projection. The Extractor can also close the database cursor right after it fetched the desired number of records, therefore sparing both database and networking resources.

MySQL

The maxRows attribute is not sent to the database server, so neither the Optimizer nor the Extractor can benefit from this hint. While the JDBC driver would normally fetch all rows, by placing an upper bound on the result set size, the client-side can spare some networking overhead.

5.5.1.3 Less is more

The following test is going to demonstrate the performance improvement of limiting the result set size. The test data set consists of 100 000 *post* and 1 000 000 *comment* entries. In the first round, the entire result set is being fetched, and the response time is going to be proportional to the projection size. By limiting the result set to 100 records, either by using SQL or the JDBC maxSize setting, the response time is going to drop significantly.

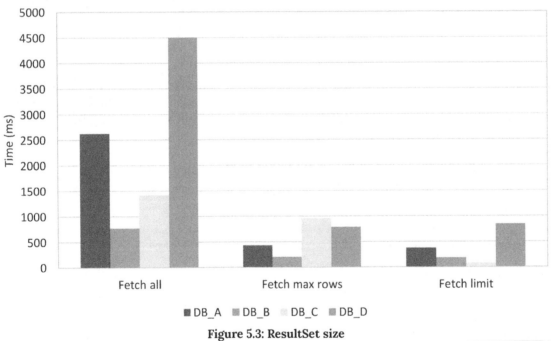

Figure 5.3: **ResultSet size**

The test results confirm the previous assumptions and the SQL level restriction proves to be the optimal strategy for limiting a result set. The maxRows driver implementation yields a surprisingly good result, especially when taking into consideration the JDBC specification on dropping extra records. Fetching a large result set puts much pressure on database resources, which does not only affect the current processing unit of work. Other concurrent transactions can also exhibit longer processing times, as a consequence of database resources shortage.

5.5.2 Too many columns

Not only fetching too many rows can cause performance issues but even extracting too many columns can increase the result set processing response time. The next test case is going to select 100 *posts* with *details* and their associated 1000 *comments*, using one of following two statements:

```
SELECT *
FROM post_comment pc
INNER JOIN post p ON p.id = pc.post_id
INNER JOIN post_details pd ON p.id = pd.id

SELECT pc.version
FROM post_comment pc
INNER JOIN post p ON p.id = pc.post_id
INNER JOIN post_details pd ON p.id = pd.id
```

The following graph depicts the execution times of fetching all columns, as opposed to extracting only a subset of the whole column projection.

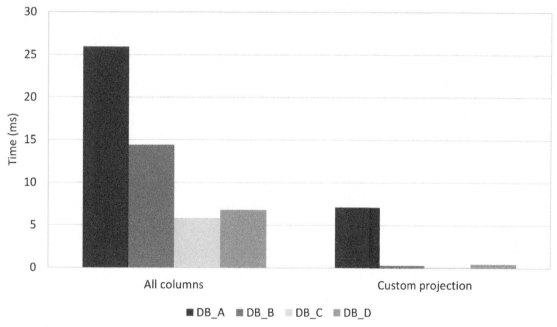

Figure 5.4: ResultSet projection size

This situation is more prevalent among ORM tools, as for populating entities entirely, all columns are needed to be selected. This might pass unnoticed when selecting just a few entities, but, for large result sets, this can turn into a noticeable performance issue.

 If a business case requires only a subset of all entity attributes, fetching extra columns will become a waste of database and application resources (CPU, Memory, I/O, Networking).

6. Transactions

A database system must allow concurrent access to the underlying data. However, shared data means that read and write operations must be synchronized to ensure that data integrity is not compromised.

To control concurrent modifications, the Java programming language defines the `synchronized` keyword for two purposes:

- It can restrict access to a shared `Object` (to preserve invariants), so only a `Thread` can execute a routine at any given time.
- It propagates changes from the current `Thread` local memory to the global memory that is available to all running threads of executions.

This behavior is typical for other concurrent programming environments and database systems are no different. In a relational database, the mechanism for ensuring data integrity is implemented on top of transactions.

A transaction is a collection of read and write operations that can either succeed or fail together, as a unit. All database statements must execute within a transactional context, even when the database client does not explicitly define its boundaries.

In 1981, Jim Gray first defined the properties of a database transaction in his famous paper: The transaction concept: virtues and limitations[1]. Both this paper and the first versions of the SQL standard (SQL-86 and SQL-89) only used three properties for defining a database transaction: *Atomicity*, *Consistency*, and *Durability*.

Along with other relation database topics, the transaction research has continued ever since, and so the SQL-92 version introduced the concept of *Isolation Levels*. These four properties have been assembled in the well-known ACID (*Atomicity, Consistency, Isolation, and Durability*) acronym that soon became synonym with relation database transactions.

Knowing how database transactions work is very important for two main reasons:

- effective data access (data integrity should not be compromised when aiming for high-performance)
- efficient data access (reducing contention can minimize transaction response time which, in turn, increases throughput).

The next sections detail each transaction property in relation to high-performance data processing.

---

[1]http://research.microsoft.com/en-us/um/people/gray/papers/theTransactionConcept.pdf

6.1 Atomicity

Atomicity is the property of grouping multiple operations into an all-or-nothing unit of work, which can succeed only if all individual operations succeed. For this reason, the database must be able to roll back all actions associated with every executed statement.

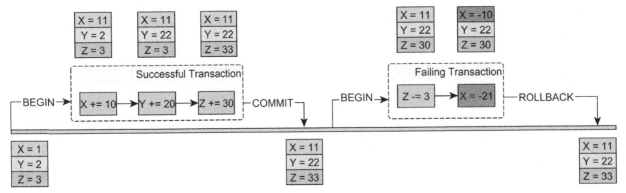

Figure 6.1: Atomic units of work

Write-write conflicts

Ideally, every transaction would have a completely isolated branch which could be easily discarded in case of a rollback. This scenario would be similar to how a *Version Control System* (e.g. *git*) implements branching. In case of conflicts, the Virtual Control System aborts the commit operation, and the client has to manually resolve the conflict. Unlike VCS tools, the relational database engine must manage conflicts without any human intervention.

For this reason, the database prevents write-write conflict situations, and only one transaction can write a record at any given time.

All statements are executed against the actual data structures (tables, indexes, in-memory buffers), only to be materialized at commit time. In case of rollback, the database must revert any pending changed datum to its previous state.

Oracle

The *undo tablespace*[a] stores the previous data versions in *undo segments*. Upon rolling back, the database engine searches the associated *undo segments* that can recreate the *before image* of every datum that was changed by the currently running transaction.

[a]https://docs.oracle.com/database/121/ADMIN/undo.htm#ADMIN11460

SQL Server

The *transaction log*[a] stores details about the currently running transactions and their associated modifications. The rollback process scans the *transaction log* backward to find the associated undo records. When the record is found, the database engine restores the before image of the affected datum.

 To prevent the transaction log from filling up, the log must be truncated on a regular basis. Long-running transactions can delay the truncation process, so that is another reason to avoid them as much as possible.

---

[a]https://msdn.microsoft.com/en-us/library/ms190925.aspx

PostgreSQL

Unlike other database systems, PostgreSQL does not use a dedicated append-only undo log. Because of its multi-version nature, every database object maintains its own version history. In the absence of the log seek-up phase, the rollback process becomes much lighter as it only requires to switch from one version to the other.

The downside is that the previous version space is limited in size, and so it must be reused. The process of reclaiming the storage occupied by old versions is called VACUUMING.

Each transaction has an associated XID[a], and newer transactions must have a greater XID number than all previous ones.

The transaction XID is a 32-bit number so it can accommodate over 4 billion transactions. In a high-performance application, the transaction lifespan is very short, and if the VACUUM process is disabled, this threshold may be reached. When the XID counter reaches its maximum value, it wraps around and start again from zero.

The transactions issued prior to the XID wraparound have their identifiers greater than newer transactions started after the XID counter reset. This anomaly can cause the system to perceive older transactions as they were started in the future, which can lead to very serious data integrity issues.

---

[a]http://www.postgresql.org/docs/9.4/static/routine-vacuuming.html

MySQL

The *undo log* is stored in the *rollback segment*[a] of the system tablespace.

Each *undo log* is split into two sections, one responsible for rolling back purposes and the other for reconstructing the before image. The first section can be wiped out right after the transaction is ended, while the other needs to linger for as long as any currently running query or other concurrent transactions need to see a previous version of the records in question.

Behind the scenes, MySQL runs a *purge* process that cleans up the storage occupied by deleted records, and it also reclaims the undo log segments that are no longer required.

 Long-running transactions delay the *purge* process execution, causing the undo log to grow very large, especially in write-heavy data access scenarios.

---

[a]https://dev.mysql.com/doc/refman/5.7/en/innodb-multi-versioning.html

6.2 Consistency

A modifying transaction can be seen as a state transformation, moving the database from one valid state to another. The relational database schema ensures that all primary modifications (insert/update/delete statements), as well as secondary ones (issued by triggers), obey certain rules on the underlying data structures:

- column types
- column length
- column nullability
- foreign key constraints
- unique key constraints
- custom *check* constraints.

Consistency is about validating the transaction state change so that all committed transactions leave the database in a proper state. If only one constraint gets violated, the entire transaction will be rolled back, and all modifications are going to be reverted.

Although the application must validate user input prior to crafting database statements, the application-level checks cannot span over other concurrent requests, possibly coming from different web servers. When the database is the primary integration point, the advantages of a strict schema become even more apparent.

MySQL

Traditionally, MySQL constraints are not strictly enforced[a], and the database engine replaces invalid values with predefined defaults:

- Out-of-range numeric values are set to either 0 or the maximum possible value.
- String values are trimmed to the maximum length.
- Incorrect Date/Time values are permitted (e.g. 2015-02-30).
- NOT NULL constraints are only enforced for single INSERT statements. For multi-row inserts, 0 replaces a null numeric value, and `''` is used for a null String.

Since the 5.0.2 version, *strict* constraints are possible if the database engine is configured to use a custom *sql mode*[b]:

```
SET GLOBAL sql_mode='POSTGRESQL,STRICT_ALL_TABLES';
```

Because the sql_mode resets on server startup, it is better to set it up in the MySQL configuration file:

```
[mysqld]
sql_mode = POSTGRESQL,STRICT_ALL_TABLES
```

[a]https://dev.mysql.com/doc/refman/5.7/en/constraint-invalid-data.html
[b]https://dev.mysql.com/doc/refman/5.7/en/sql-mode.html

Consistency as in CAP Theorem

According to the CAP theorem[a], when a distributed system encounters a network partition, the system must choose either *Consistency* (all changes are instantaneously applied to all nodes) or *Availability* (any node can accept a request), but not both. While in the definition of ACID, consistency is about obeying constraints, in the CAP theorem context, consistency refers to *linearizability*[b], which is an isolation guarantee instead.

[a]https://en.wikipedia.org/wiki/CAP_theorem
[b]http://www.bailis.org/blog/linearizability-versus-serializability/

6.3 Isolation

If there were only one user accessing the database, there would not be any risk of data conflicts. According to the Universal Scalability Law, if the sequential fraction of the data access patterns is less than 100%, the database system may benefit from parallelization.

By offering multiple concurrent connections, the transaction throughput can increase, and the database system can accommodate more traffic. However, parallelization imposes additional challenges as the database must interleave transactions in such a way that conflicts do not compromise data integrity. The execution order of all the currently running transaction operations is said to be *serializable* when its outcome is the same as if the underlying transactions were executed one after the other.

The serializable execution is, therefore, the only transaction isolation level that does not compromise data integrity while allowing a certain degree of parallelization. In 1981, Jim Gray described the largest airlines and banks as having 10 000 terminals and 100 active transactions, which explains why, up until SQL-92, serializable was the *de facto* transaction isolation level.

6.3.1 Concurrency control

To manage data conflicts, several concurrency control mechanisms have been developed throughout the years. There are two strategies for handling data collisions:

- Avoiding conflicts (e.g. *two-phase locking*) requires locking to control access to shared resources.
- Detecting conflicts (e.g. *Multi-Version Concurrency Control*) provides better concurrency, at the price of relaxing serializability and possibly accepting various data anomalies.

6.3.1.1 Two-phase locking

In 1976, Kapali Eswaran and Jim Gray (et al.) published The Notions of Consistency and Predicate Locks in a Database System[2] paper, which demonstrated that serializability can be obtained if all transactions used the *two-phase locking* (2PL) protocol.

Initially, all database systems employed 2PL for implementing serializable transactions, but, with time, many vendors have moved towards an MVCC (Multi-Version Concurrency Control) architecture. By default, SQL Server still uses locking for implementing the Serializability isolation level.

Because 2PL guarantees transaction serializability, it is very important to understand the price of maintaining strict data integrity on the overall application scalability and transaction performance.

---

[2]http://research.microsoft.com/en-us/um/people/gray/papers/On%20the%20Notions%20of%20Consistency%20and%20Predicate%20Locks%20in%20a%20Database%20System%20CACM.pdf

However, locking is not used only in 2PL implementations, and, to address both DML and DDL statement interaction and to minimize contention on shared resources, relational database systems use Multiple granularity locking[3].

Database objects are hierarchical in nature, a logical tablespace being mapped to multiple database files, which are built of data pages, each page containing multiple rows. For this reason, locks can be acquired on different database object types.

Locking on lower levels (e.g. rows) can offer better concurrency as it reduces the likelihood of contention. Because each lock takes resources, holding multiple lower-level locks can add up, so the database might decide to substitute multiple lower-level locks into a single upper-level one. This process is called *lock escalation*, and it trades off concurrency for database resources.

Each database system comes with its own lock hierarchy, but the most common types (even mentioned by the 2PL initial paper) remain the following ones:

- shared (read) lock, preventing a record from being written while allowing reads
- exclusive (write) lock, disallowing both read and write operations.

Locks alone are not sufficient for preventing conflicts. A concurrency control strategy must define how locks are being acquired and released because this also has an impact on transaction interleaving.

For this purpose, the 2PL protocol defines a lock management strategy for ensuring serializability. The 2PL protocol splits a transaction into two sections:

- expanding phase (locks are acquired, and no lock is released)
- shrinking phase (all locks are released, and no other lock is further acquired).

In lock-based concurrency control, all transactions must follow the 2PL protocol, as otherwise serializability might be compromised, resulting in data anomalies.

Transaction schedule

To provide recovery from failures, the transaction schedule (the sequence of all interleaved operations) must be strict. If a write operation, in a first transaction, happens-before a conflict occurring in a subsequent transaction, in order to achieve transaction *strictness*, the first transaction commit event must also happen before the conflict.

Because operations are properly ordered, strictness can prevent *cascading aborts (one transaction rollback triggering a chain of other transaction aborts, to preserve data consistency)*. Releasing all locks only after the transaction has ended (either commit or rollback) is a requirement for having a strict schedule.

---

[3]https://en.wikipedia.org/wiki/Multiple_granularity_locking

The following diagram shows how transaction interleaving is coordinated by 2PL:

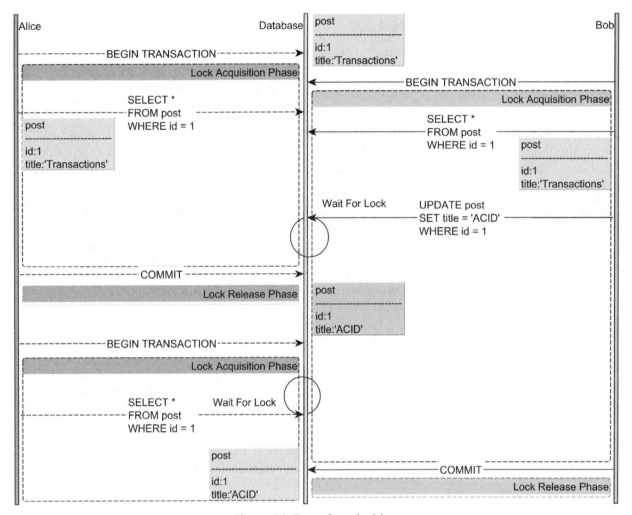

Figure 6.2: Two-phase locking

- Both *Alice* and *Bob* select a *post* record, both acquiring a shared lock on this record.
- When *Bob* attempts to update the *post* entry, his statement is blocked by the Lock Manager because *Alice* is still holding a shared lock on this database row.
- Only after *Alice's* transaction ends and all locks are being released, *Bob* can resume his update operation.
- *Bob's* update generates a lock upgrade, so the shared lock is replaced by an exclusive lock, which prevents any other concurrent read or write operation.
- *Alice* starts a new transaction and issues a select query for the same *post* entry, but the statement is blocked by the Lock Manager since *Bob* owns an exclusive lock on this record.
- After *Bob's* transaction is committed, all locks are released, and *Alice's* query can be resumed, so she gets the latest value of this database record.

Deadlocks

Using locking for controlling access to shared resources is prone to deadlocks, and the transaction scheduler alone cannot prevent their occurrences.

A deadlock happens when two concurrent transactions cannot make progress because each one waits for the other to release a lock. Because both transactions are in the lock acquisition phase, neither one releases a lock prior to acquiring the next one.

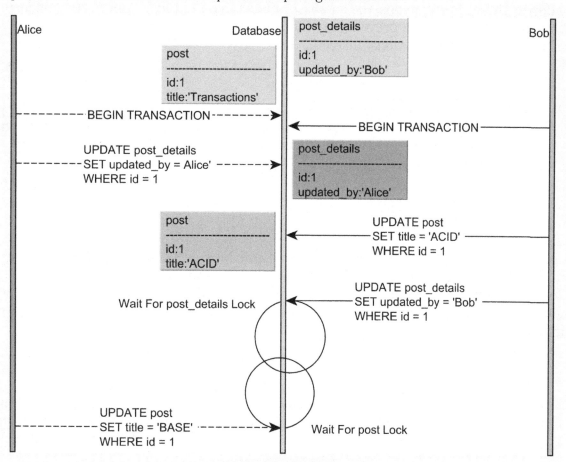

Figure 6.3: Dead lock

Preserving the lock order becomes the responsibility of the data access layer, and the database can only assist in recovering from a deadlock situation.

The database engine runs a separate process that scans the current conflict graph for lock-wait cycles (which are caused by deadlocks). When a cycle is detected, the database engine picks one transaction and aborts it, causing its locks to be released, so the other transaction can make progress.

6.3.1.2 Multi-Version Concurrency Control

Although locking can provide a serializable transaction schedule, the cost of lock contention can undermine both transaction response time and scalability. The response time can increase because transactions must wait for locks to be released, and long-running transactions can slow down the progress of other concurrent transactions as well. According to both Amdahl's Law and the Universal Scalability Law, concurrency is also affected by contention.

To address these shortcomings, the database vendors have opted for optimistic concurrency control mechanisms. If 2PL prevents conflicts, Multi-Version Concurrency Control (MVCC) uses a conflict detection strategy instead.

 The promise of MVCC is that readers do not block writers and writers do not block readers. The only source of contention comes from writers blocking other concurrent writers, which otherwise would compromise transaction rollback and atomicity.

To prevent blocking, the database can rebuild previous versions of a database record so an uncommitted change can be hidden away from incoming concurrent readers. The lack of locking makes it more difficult to implement a serializable schedule, so the database engine must analyze the current interleaving operations and detect anomalies that would compromise serializability.

Oracle

Oracle does not implement 2PL at all, relying on MVCC mechanism for managing concurrent data access. Every query gets a point-in-time data snapshot and, depending on the isolation level, the timestamp reference can be relative to the current statement or to the current transaction start time.

To rebuild previous record versions, Oracle uses the undo segments[a], which already contain all the necessary data required for rolling back an uncommitted change. The point-in-time is based on the System Change Number (SCN), which is a logical timestamp reference and, unlike physical time, is guaranteed to be incremented monotonically.

Apart from MVCC, Oracle also supports explicit locking as well, using the SELECT FOR UPDATE SQL syntax.

---

[a]https://docs.oracle.com/database/121/CNCPT/consist.htm#CNCPT221

SQL Server

By default, SQL Server uses locks for implementing all the isolation levels stipulated by the SQL standard.

For the *Read Committed* isolation level to take advantage of the MVCC model, the following configuration must be set first:

```
ALTER DATABASE high_performance_java_persistence
SET READ_COMMITTED_SNAPSHOT ON;
```

For a higher-level isolation, SQL Server offers the *Snapshot* isolation mode, which must be activated at the database level:

```
ALTER DATABASE high_performance_java_persistence
SET ALLOW_SNAPSHOT_ISOLATION ON;
```

Because Snapshot is a custom isolation level, it must also be set at the connection level prior to starting a new transaction:

```
SET TRANSACTION ISOLATION LEVEL SNAPSHOT;
GO
BEGIN TRANSACTION;
GO
COMMIT TRANSACTION;
GO
```

After enabling row versioning, the database can track record changes in the *tempdb* database.

When a row is either updated or deleted, the current row entry holds a reference back to the previous version, which is recorded in the version store, in the tempdb database. Rows are not deleted right away but only marked for deletion, the actual removal being done by the *Ghost cleanup task*. Old versions must be kept for as long as a currently running transaction might need them, which is specified by the transaction isolation level.

The Ghost cleanup task runs periodically and reclaims storage from old versions that are no longer necessary.

 A long-running transaction would require the database engine to keep some old version for a very long time, and, because version changes are chained in a linked list structure, restoring a very old version might becomes resource intensive.

PostgreSQL

Unlike all other database systems, PostgreSQL stores both the current rows and their previous versions (even the ones for the aborted transactions) in the actual database table. Like Oracle, PostgreSQL embraces the MVCC data access model, and it does not offer a 2PL transaction isolation implementation at all.

Each table row has two additional columns (*xmin* and *xmax*), which are used to control the visibility of various row versions. When a row is inserted, the current transaction identifier is stored in the xmin column.

Both the update and the delete operations end up creating a new row entry with a xmax column storing the current transaction identifier.

The *Vacuum* cleaner process runs regularly and reclaims storage occupied by deleted entries (and successfully committed) or by previous versions that are no longer required by the currently running transactions.

Although PostgreSQL is seen as a pure MVCC model, locking is still required to prevent write-write conflicts or for explicit locking[a]. SELECT FOR UPDATE is used to acquire an exclusive row-level lock, while SELECT FOR SHARE is for applying a shared lock instead.

---

[a]http://www.postgresql.org/docs/9.5/static/explicit-locking.html

MySQL

The InnoDB storage engine offers support for ACID transactions and uses MVCC for controlling access to shared resources. The InnoDB MVCC implementation is very similar to Oracle, and previous versions of database rows are stored in the rollback segment as well.

When a transaction demands a previous row version, MySQL must reconstruct it from rollback segments. Delete operations just mark an entry as being ready for deletion, and the *purge* thread is going to do the actual physical cleanup.

Both the transaction rollback and the previous row version restoring processes (required by a given transaction visibility guarantees) are very much the same thing.

Like other database systems, MySQL also offers explicit locking[a] for when MVCC is no longer satisfactory. A shared lock is acquired using SELECT LOCK IN SHARE MODE, while, for exclusive locks, the much more common SELECT FOR UPDATE syntax is being used.

---

[a]https://dev.mysql.com/doc/refman/5.7/en/innodb-locking-reads.html

6.3.2 Phenomena

For reasonable transaction throughput values, it makes sense to imply transaction *serializability*. As the incoming traffic grows, the price for strict data integrity becomes too high, and this is the primary reason for having multiple isolation levels. Relaxing serializability guarantees may generate data integrity anomalies, which are also referred as *phenomena*.

The SQL-92 standard introduced three phenomena that can occur when moving away from a serializable transaction schedule:

- *dirty read*
- *non-repeatable read*
- *phantom read.*

In reality, there are other phenomena that can occur due to transaction interleaving, as the famous paper *A Critique of ANSI SQL Isolation Levels*[4] describes:

- *dirty write*
- *read skew*
- *write skew*
- *lost update.*

Choosing a certain isolation level is a trade-off between increasing concurrency and acknowledging the possible anomalies that might occur.

Scalability is undermined by contention and coherency costs. The lower the isolation level, the less locking (or multi-version transaction abortions), and the more scalable the application gets.

However, a lower isolation level allows more phenomena, and the data integrity responsibility is shifted from the database side to the application logic, which must ensure that it takes all measures to prevent or mitigate any such data anomaly.

Before jumping to isolation levels, it is better to understand what's behind each particular phenomenon and how it can affect data integrity. When choosing a given transaction isolation level, understanding phenomena becomes fundamental to taking the right decision,

---

[4]http://research.microsoft.com/apps/pubs/default.aspx?id=69541

6.3.2.1 Dirty write

A dirty write happens when two concurrent transactions are allowed to modify the same row at the same time. As previously mentioned, all changes are applied to the actual database object structures, which means that the second transaction simply overwrites the first transaction pending change.

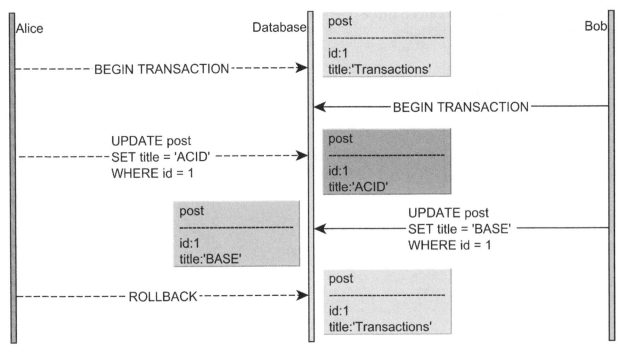

Figure 6.4: Dirty write

If the two transactions commit, one transaction will silently overwrite the other transaction, causing a *lost update*. Another problem arises when the first transaction wants to roll back. The database engine would have to choose one of the following action paths:

- It can restore the row to its previous version (as it was before the first transaction changed it), but then it overwrites the second transaction uncommitted change.
- It can acknowledge the existence of a newer version (issued by the second transaction), but then, if the second transaction has to roll back, its previous version will become the uncommitted change of the first transaction.

If the database engine did not prevent dirty writes, guaranteeing rollbacks would not be possible. Because atomicity cannot be implemented in the absence of reliable rollbacks, all database systems must, therefore, prevent dirty writes.

Although the SQL standard does not mention this phenomenon, even the lowest isolation level (*Read Uncommitted*) can prevent it.

6.3.2.2 Dirty read

As previously mentioned, all database changes are applied to the actual data structures (memory buffers, data blocks, indexes). A dirty read happens when a transaction is allowed to read the uncommitted changes of some other concurrent transaction. Taking a business decision on a value that has not been committed is risky because uncommitted changes might get rolled back.

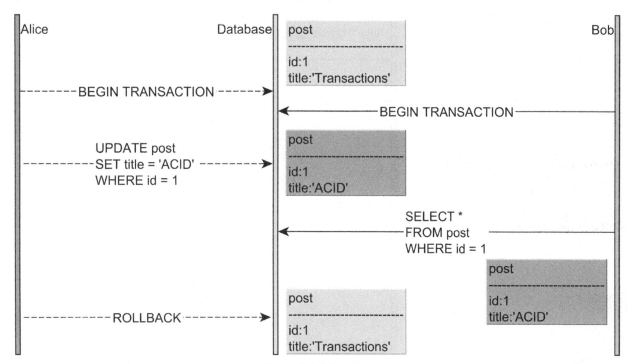

Figure 6.5: Dirty read

This anomaly is only permitted by the Read Uncommitted isolation level, and, because of the serious impact on data integrity, most database systems offer a higher default isolation level.

To prevent dirty reads, the database engine must hide uncommitted changes from all other concurrent transactions. Each transaction is allowed to see its own changes because otherwise the read-your-own-writes consistency guarantee is compromised.

A naive approach would be to lock uncommitted rows, but this would not be practical at all. If a long-running transaction acquired such a lock, no other transaction would be able to read that record until the lock is released.

Since the undo log already captures the previous version of every uncommitted record, the database engine can use it to restore the previous value in other concurrent transaction queries. Because this mechanism is used by all other isolation levels (Read Committed, Repeatable Read, Serializable), most database systems optimize the before image restoring process (lowering its overhead on the overall application performance).

Read Uncommitted is rarely needed (non-strict reporting queries where dirty reads are acceptable), so Read Committed is usually the lowest practical isolation level.

6.3.2.3 Non-repeatable read

If one transaction reads a database row without applying a shared lock on the newly fetched record, then a concurrent transaction might change this row before the first transaction has ended.

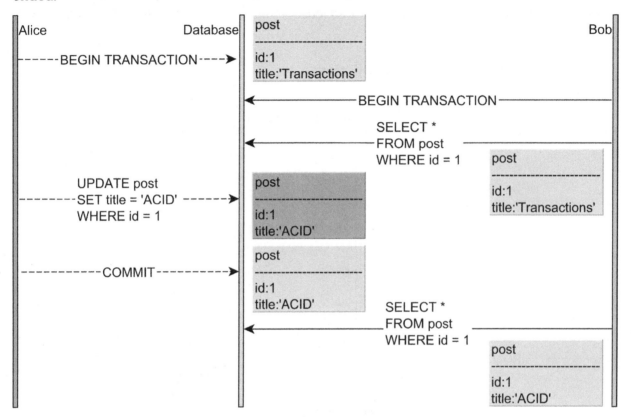

Figure 6.6: Non-repeatable read

This phenomenon is problematic when the current transaction makes a business decision based on the first value of the given database row (a client might order a product based on a stock quantity value that is no longer a positive integer).

Most database systems have moved to a Multi-Version Concurrency Control model, and shared locks are no longer mandatory for preventing non-repeatable reads. By verifying the current row version, a transaction can be aborted if a previously fetched record has changed in the meanwhile.

Repeatable Read and Serializable prevent this anomaly by default. With Read Committed, it is possible to avoid non-repeatable (fuzzy) reads if the shared locks are acquired explicitly (e.g. SELECT FOR SHARE).

Some ORM frameworks (e.g. JPA/Hibernate) offer application-level repeatable reads. The first snapshot of any retrieved entity is cached in the currently running *Persistence Context*. Any successive query returning the same database row is going to use the very same object that was previously cached. This way, the fuzzy reads may be prevented even in Read Committed isolation level.

6.3.2.4 Phantom read

If a transaction makes a business decision based on a set of rows satisfying a given predicate, without range locks, a concurrent transaction might insert a record matching that particular predicate.

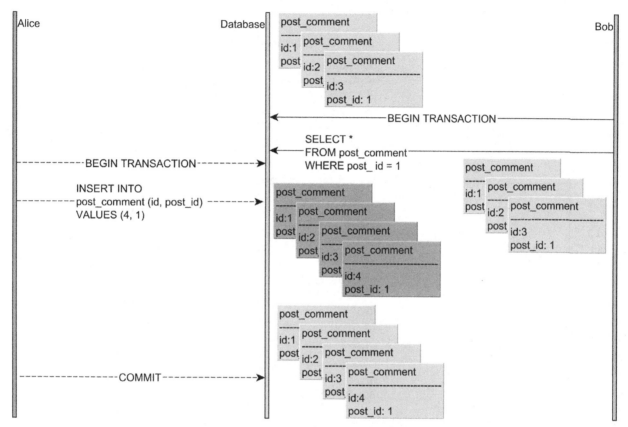

Figure 6.7: Phantom read

The SQL standard says that Phantom Read occurs if two consecutive query executions render different results because a concurrent transaction has modified the range of records in between the two calls. Although providing consistent reads is a mandatory requirement for serializability, that is not sufficient. For instance, one buyer might purchase a product without being aware of a better offer that was added right after the user has finished fetching the offer list.

The 2PL-based Serializable isolation prevents Phantom Reads through the use of predicate locking. On the other hand, MVCC database engines address the Phantom Read anomaly by returning consistent snapshots. However, a concurrent transaction can still modify the range of records that was read previously. Even if the MVCC database engine introspects the transaction schedule, the outcome is not always the same with a 2PL-based implementation. One such example is when the second transaction issues an insert without reading the same range of records as the first transaction. In this particular use case, some MVCC database engines will not end up rolling back the first transaction.

6.3.2.5 Read skew

Read skew is a lesser known anomaly that involves a constraint on more than one database tables. In the following example, the application requires the *post* and the *post_details* be updated in sync. Whenever a *post* record changes, its associated *post_details* must register the user who made the current modification.

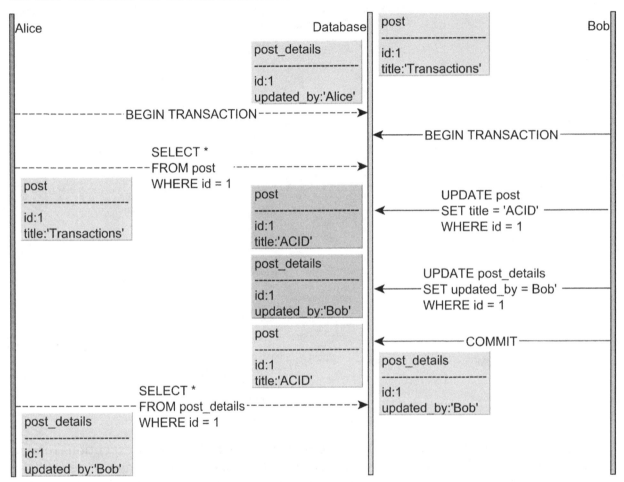

Figure 6.8: Read skew

In between selecting the *post* and the *post_details* rows, a second transaction sneaks in and manages to update both records. The first transaction sees an older version of the *post* row and the latest version of the associated *post_details*. Because of this read skew, the first transaction assumes that this particular *post* was updated by *Bob*, although, in fact, it is an older version updated by *Alice*.

Like with non-repeatable reads, there are two ways to avoid this phenomenon:

- The first transaction can acquire shared locks on every read, therefore preventing the second transaction from updating these records.
- The first transaction can be aborted upon validating the commit constraints (when using an MVCC implementation of the Repeatable Read or Serializable isolation levels).

6.3.2.6 Write skew

Like read skew, this phenomenon involves disjoint writes over two different tables that are constrained to be updated as a unit. Whenever the *post* row changes, the client must update the *post_details* with the user making the change.

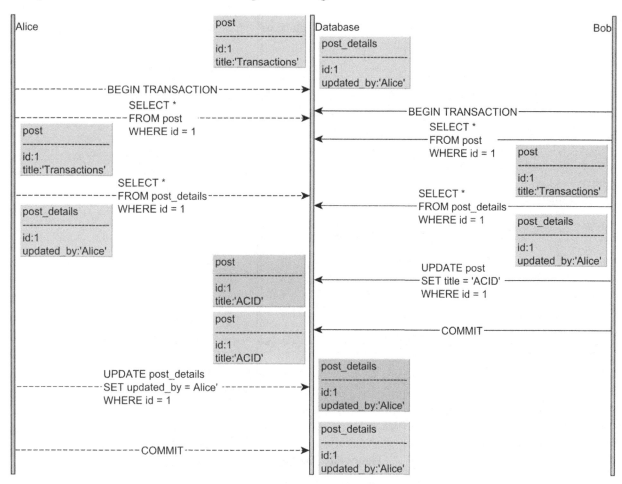

Figure 6.9: Write skew

Both *Alice* and *Bob* selects the *post* and its associated *post_details* record. If write skew is allowed, *Alice* and *Bob* can update these two records separately, therefore breaking the constraint.

Like with non-repeatable reads, there are two ways to avoid this phenomenon:

- The first transaction can acquire shared locks on both entries, therefore preventing the second transaction from updating these records.
- The database engine can detect that another transaction has changed these records, and so it can force the first transaction to roll back (under an MVCC implementation of Repeatable Read or Serializable).

6.3.2.7 Lost update

This phenomenon happens when a transaction reads a row while another transaction modifies it prior to the first transaction to finish. In the following example, *Bob's* update is silently overwritten by *Alice*, who is not aware of the record update.

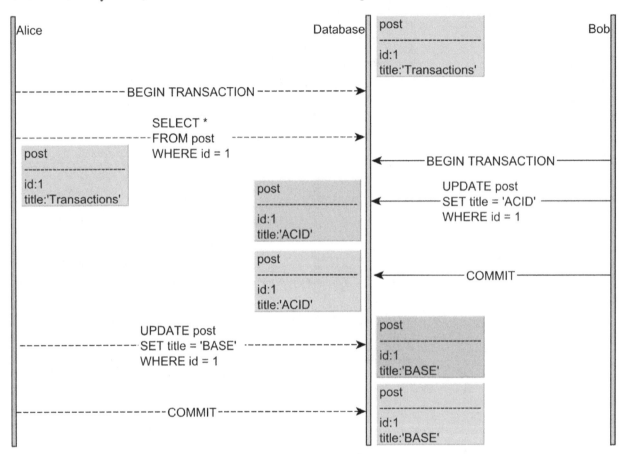

Figure 6.10: Lost update

This anomaly can have serious consequences on data integrity (a buyer might purchase a product without knowing the price has just changed), especially because it affects Read Committed, the default isolation level in many database systems.

Traditionally, Repeatable Read protected against lost updates since the shared locks could prevent a concurrent transaction from modifying an already fetched record. With MVCC, the second transaction is allowed to make the change, while the first transaction is aborted when the database engine detects the row version mismatch (during the first transaction commit).

Most ORM tools, such as Hibernate, offer application-level optimistic locking, which automatically integrates the row version whenever a record modification is issued. On a row version mismatch, the update count is going to be zero, so the application can roll back the current transaction, as the current data snapshot is stale.

6.3.3 Isolation levels

As previously stated, Serializable is the only isolation level to provide a truly ACID transaction interleaving. However, serializability comes at a price as locking introduces contention, which, in turn, limits concurrency and scalability. Even in multi-version concurrency models, serializability may require aborting too many transactions that are affected by phenomena.

For this purpose, the SQL-92 version introduced multiple isolation levels, and the database client has the option of balancing concurrency against data correctness. Each isolation level is defined in terms of the minimum number of phenomena that it must prevent, and so the SQL standard introduces the following transaction isolation levels:

Table 6.1: Standard isolation levels

Isolation Level	Dirty read	Non-repeatable read	Phantom read
Read Uncommitted	Yes	Yes	Yes
Read Committed	No	Yes	Yes
Repeatable Read	No	No	Yes
Serializable	No	No	No

Without an explicit setting, the JDBC driver uses the default isolation level, which can be introspected using the `getDefaultTransactionIsolation()`[5] method of the `DatabaseMetaData` object:

```
int level = connection.getMetaData().getDefaultTransactionIsolation();
```

The default isolation level can be changed using the `setTransactionIsolation(int level)`[6] `Connection` method.

```
connection.setTransactionIsolation(Connection.TRANSACTION_SERIALIZABLE);
```

> Even if ACID properties imply a serializable schedule, most relational database systems use a lower default isolation level instead:
>
> - Read Committed (Oracle, SQL Server, PostgreSQL)
> - Repeatable Read (MySQL).

The following sections go through each particular transaction isolation level and demonstrate the actual list of phenomena that are prevented by a given database system.

---

[5]http://docs.oracle.com/javase/8/docs/api/java/sql/DatabaseMetaData.html#getDefaultTransactionIsolation--
[6]http://docs.oracle.com/javase/8/docs/api/java/sql/Connection.html#setTransactionIsolation-int-

6.3.3.1 Read Uncommitted

Table 6.2: Read Uncommitted phenomena occurrence

Phenomena	SQL Server	PostgreSQL	MySQL
Dirty Write	No	No	No
Dirty Read	Yes	No	Yes
Non-Repeatable Read	Yes	Yes	Yes
Phantom Read	Yes	Yes	Yes
Read Skew	Yes	Yes	Yes
Write Skew	Yes	Yes	Yes
Lost Update	Yes	Yes	Yes

Oracle

Dirty reads are not allowed, and so the lowest isolation level is Read Committed.

The JDBC driver will even throw an exception if the client tries to set the Read Uncommitted isolation on the current `Connection`.

SQL Server

Read Uncommitted only protects against dirty writes, all other phenomena being allowed. When using Read Uncommitted, there is no exclusive lock associated with a given SQL modification, so uncommitted changes are available to other concurrent transactions even before they get committed. If the risk of dirty reads can be assumed, avoiding exclusive locks may speed up reporting queries, especially when scanning large amounts of data.

For lock-based concurrency control mechanisms, Read Uncommitted is worth considering if the risk of dirty reads is a much smaller issue than locking a large portion of a database table. Because MVCC avoids reader-writer and writer-reader locking, it might not exhibit a considerable performance enhancement from permitting dirty reads.

PostgreSQL

Like Oracle, PostgreSQL does not allow dirty reads, the lowest isolation level being Read Committed.

 When choosing Read Uncommitted, the JDBC driver silently falls back to Read Committed.

MySQL

Although it uses MVCC, InnoDB implements Read Uncommitted so that dirty reads are permitted. As an optimization, each query is spared from rebuilding the previously committed versions (using the rollback segments) of the currently scanned records (in case they have been recently modified).

6.3.3.2 Read Committed

Read Committed is one of the most common isolation levels, and it behaves consistently across multiple relational database systems or various concurrency control models.

Many database systems choose Read Committed as the default isolation level because it delivers the best performance while preventing fatal anomalies such as dirty writes and dirty reads. However, performance has its price as Read Committed permits many anomalies that might lead to data corruption.

Table 6.3: Read Committed phenomena occurrence

Phenomena	Oracle	SQL Server	SQL Server MVCC	PostgreSQL	MySQL
Dirty Write	No	No	No	No	No
Dirty Read	No	No	No	No	No
Non-Repeatable Read	Yes	Yes	Yes	Yes	Yes
Phantom Read	Yes	Yes	Yes	Yes	Yes
Read Skew	Yes	Yes	Yes	Yes	Yes
Write Skew	Yes	Yes	Yes	Yes	Yes
Lost Update	Yes	Yes	Yes	Yes	Yes

Oracle

Every statement has a start timestamp, which is used to create a database snapshot relative to this particular point-in-time. This way, writers can still update the currently selected records, and the database can simply reconstruct the previous versions that were available when the query started. Subsequent query executions can return different row versions, so non-repeatable reads are permitted.

When two transactions attempt to update the same record, the first one locks the record to prevent dirty writes. The second transaction must wait until the first transaction releases the lock (either commit or rollback), and the statement filtering criteria are reevaluated against latest data.

PostgreSQL

Like Oracle, every query sees a database snapshot as of the beginning of the currently running query. Because shared locks are not used to protect previously read records from being modified, Read Committed allows a large spectrum of data anomalies.

Exclusive locks prevent write-write conflicts, so when two transactions update the same record, the second one waits for the first transaction to release its locks. When the second transaction resumes its execution, if the filtering criteria are still relevant, it might overwrite the first transaction modifications, therefore causing lost updates.

MySQL

Query-time snapshots are used to isolate statements from other concurrent transactions. When explicitly acquiring shared or exclusive locks or when issuing update or delete statements (which acquire exclusive locks to prevent dirty writes), if the selected rows are filtered by unique search criteria (e.g. primary key), the locks can be applied to the associated index entries.

Prior to 5.7[a], if the modifying statements used a range filter and the search criteria took advantage of a unique index scan, then the database could use a gap or a next-key lock (therefore protecting against phantom reads as well). Statement-based replication is not available for Read Committed, so the application must use the row-based binary logging instead.

---

[a]https://dev.mysql.com/doc/refman/5.7/en/set-transaction.html#idm140311316367072

99

> **SQL Server**
>
> By default, SQL statements use shared locks to prevent other transactions from modifying the currently fetched records. The locks are released by the time the query finishes executing. When activating Read Committed Snapshot Isolation, the database does not use shared locks anymore, and each query selects the row version as it was when the query started.

6.3.3.3 Repeatable Read

One of the least compliant isolation levels, Repeatable Read implementation details leak into its phenomena prevention spectrum:

Table 6.4: Repeatable Read phenomena occurrence

Phenomena	SQL Server	PostgreSQL	MySQL
Dirty Write	No	No	No
Dirty Read	No	No	No
Non-Repeatable Read	No	No	No
Phantom Read	Yes	No	No
Read Skew	No	No	No
Write Skew	No	Yes	Yes
Lost Update	No	No	Yes

> **Oracle**
>
> The Repeatable Read isolation is not supported at all, and the JDBC driver will throw an exception if the client tries to set it explicitly.

> **SQL Server**
>
> For every row the client reads, the current transaction acquires a shared lock that prevents any other transaction from concurrently modifying it. The shared locks are released when the transaction either commits or rolls back.

PostgreSQL

The Repeatable Read is implemented using Snapshot Isolation[a], so not only fuzzy reads are prevented, but even phantom reads are prohibited as well. Instead of using locking, the PostgreSQL MVCC implementation allows conflicts to occur, but it aborts any transaction whose guarantees do not hold anymore.

[a]https://en.wikipedia.org/wiki/Snapshot_isolation

MySQL

Every transaction can only see rows as if they were when the current transaction started. This prevents non-repeatable reads, but it still allows lost updates and write skews.

6.3.3.4 Serializable

Serializable is supposed to provide a transaction schedule, whose outcome, even in spite of statement interleaving, is equivalent to a serial execution.

Even if the concurrency control mechanism is lock-based or it manages multiple record versions, it must prevent all phenomena to ensure serializable transactions. Preventing all phenomena mentioned by the SQL standard (dirty reads, non-repeatable reads and phantom reads) is not enough, and Serializable must protect against lost update, read skew and write skew as well.

In practice, the concurrency control implementation details leak, and not all relational database systems provide a truly Serializable isolation level (some data integrity anomalies might still occur).

Table 6.5: Serializable phenomena occurrence

Phenomena	Oracle	SQL Server	SQL Server MVCC	PostgreSQL	MySQL
Dirty Write	No	No	No	No	No
Dirty Read	No	No	No	No	No
Non-Repeatable Read	No	No	No	No	No
Phantom Read	No	No	No	No	No
Read Skew	No	No	No	No	No
Write Skew	Yes	No	Yes	No	No
Lost Update	No	No	No	No	No

Oracle

The Serializable isolation level is, in fact, an MVCC implementation of the Snapshot Isolation concurrency control mechanism. Like the Repeatable Read isolation in PostgreSQL, Oracle cannot prevent write skews, meaning it cannot provide a truly serializable transaction.

SQL Server

The Serializable isolation level is based on 2PL, and all phenomena are therefore prevented. The MVCC-based Snapshot Isolation is close to Oracle Serializable and PostgreSQL Repeatable Read, and so it allows write skews.

PostgreSQL

To overcome the Snapshot Isolation limitations, PostgreSQL has developed the Serializable Snapshot Isolation (SSI), which provides true serializable transactions. Because SSI is still an MVCC implementation, PostgreSQL monitors the transaction schedule and detects *possible* serializability anomalies.

The current implementation may detect *false positives*[a], and some transactions might get aborted even if they did not really break transaction serializability. Only the Precisely Serializable Snapshot Isolation (PSSI) model can eliminate all false positives, but the performance penalty being too high, the database implementers stuck to SSI instead.

_____

[a]http://drkp.net/papers/ssi-vldb12.pdf

MySQL

The Serializable isolation builds on top of Repeatable Read with the difference that every record that gets selected is protected with a shared lock as well. The lock-based approach allows MySQL to prevent the write skew phenomena, which is prevalent among many Snapshot Isolation implementations.

6.4 Durability

When purchasing an airlinc ticket, the money is withdrawn from the bank account, and a seat is reserved for the given buyer. Assuming that, right after the ticket is purchased, the airline reservation system crashes, all the previously processed transactions must hold true even after the system restarts. If the system does not enforce this requirement, the registered ticket might vanish, and the buyer is possibly left with a debited account and no ticket at all.

> Durability ensures that all committed transaction changes become permanent.

Durability allows system recoverability, and, to some extent, it is similar to the rolling back mechanism.

> ### What about undo logs?
>
> To support transaction rollbacks and to rebuild previous versions in MVCC systems, the database system already records the current modifications (including uncommitted changes) in the undo log. However, recoverability needs committed changes only, and, because the obsolete undo segments might be frequently recycled, the undo log alone is not suitable for recoverability.

When a transaction is committed, the database persists all current changes in an append-only, sequential data structure commonly known as the *redo log*.

> ### Oracle
>
> The *redo log*[a] consists of multiple redo records, each one containing *change vectors*, which capture the actual data block changes. For performance reasons, the redo records are stored in a buffer, and the Log Writer flushes the in-memory records to the current active redo log file. At any given time, Oracle has, at least, two redo files, but only one of them is active and available for collecting the log buffer entries. When a transaction is committed, the database flushes the buffer and changes become persisted.
>
> If the buffer fills, Oracle will flush it along with any uncommitted changes, which can be removed if their associated transaction is rolled back.
>
> ───────────
> [a]https://docs.oracle.com/database/121/ADMIN/onlineredo.htm#ADMIN11302

SQL Server

Unlike Oracle, SQL Server combines both the undo and the redo log into a single data structure called *transaction log*. By default, when a transaction is committed, all the associated transaction log entries are flushed to the disk before returning the control back to the client.

SQL Server 2014 added support for configurable durability[a]. The log entry flushing can be delayed, which can provide better I/O utilization and lower transaction response times. If the system crashes, all the unflushed log entries will be wiped out from memory. Asynchronous flushing is, therefore, appropriate only when data loss is tolerated.

[a]https://msdn.microsoft.com/en-us/library/dn449490.aspx

PostgreSQL

Statement changes are captured in the *Write-Ahead Log (WAL)*[a]. The log entries are buffered in memory and flushed on every transaction commit.

Because their state can be restored from the WAL during recovery, the cached data pages and index entries need not be flushed for every transaction (therefore optimizing I/O utilization). Ever since 9.1[b], PostgreSQL supports configurable durability, so the WAL can also be flushed asynchronously.

[a]http://www.postgresql.org/docs/9.5/static/wal-intro.html
[b]http://www.postgresql.org/docs/9.5/static/non-durability.html

MySQL

All the *redo log* entries associated with a single transaction are stored in the *mini transaction buffer* and flushed at once into the *global redo buffer*. The global buffer is flushed to disk during commit. By default, there are two log files which are used alternatively.

Flushing is done synchronously by default, but it can be switched to an asynchronous mode via the innodb_flush_log_at_trx_commit[a] parameter.

[a]http://dev.mysql.com/doc/refman/5.7/en/innodb-parameters.html#sysvar_innodb_flush_log_at_trx_commit

Since durability is very important for business operations, it is better to stick to the synchronous flushing mechanism.

Delaying durability guarantees becomes a valid option only when data loss is tolerated by business requirements and the redo log flushing is a real performance bottleneck.

6.5 Read-only transactions

The JDBC `Connection` defines the `setReadOnly(boolean readOnly)`[7] method which can be used to *hint* the driver to apply some database optimizations for the upcoming read-only transactions. This method should not be called in the middle of a transaction because the database system cannot turn a read-write transaction into a read-only one (a transaction must start as read-only from the very beginning).

Oracle

According to the JDBC driver documentation[a], the database server does not support read-only transaction optimizations. Even when the read-only `Connection` status is set to `true`, modifying statements are still permitted, and the only way to restrict such statements is to execute the following SQL command:

```
connection.setAutoCommit(false);
try(CallableStatement statement = connection.prepareCall(
    "BEGIN SET TRANSACTION READ ONLY; END;")) {
    statement.execute();
}
```

The `SET TRANSACTION READ ONLY` command must run after disabling the auto-commit status, as otherwise it is only applied for this particular statement only.

[a]https://docs.oracle.com/database/121/JJDBC/apxtips.htm#JJDBC28956

---

[7]http://docs.oracle.com/javase/8/docs/api/java/sql/Connection.html#setReadOnly%28boolean%29

SQL Server

Like Oracle, the read-only `Connection` does not propagate to the database engine, and the only way to disable SQL modifications is to use a separate account, restricted to viewing data only.

Setting the `ApplicationIntent=ReadOnly`[a] connection property does not prevent the JDBC driver from executing modifying statements on a read-only `Connection`. This property has the purpose of routing read-write and read-only connections to replica nodes instead.

---

[a]https://msdn.microsoft.com/en-us/library/gg471494.aspx

PostgreSQL

An exception is thrown when executing a modifying statement on a `Connection` whose read-only status was set to `true`.

The database engine optimizes read-only transactions, so the false-positives anomaly rate is reduced for the Serializable isolation level, and it allows *deferrable* serializable snapshots[a]. A deferrable snapshot is activated when executing SET TRANSACTION SERIALIZABLE READ ONLY DEFERRABLE. The current transaction must wait for a safe snapshot to become available, which can be executed without the risk of being aborted by a non-serializable anomaly. If the default read-write Serializable transactions are problematic when accessing large volumes of data, the deferrable snapshots might be a better alternative for long-running transactions.

---

[a]http://arxiv.org/pdf/1208.4179.pdf

MySQL

If a modifying statement is executed when the `Connection` is set to read-only, the JDBC driver will throw an exception.

InnoDB can optimize read-only transactions[a] because it can skip the transaction ID generation as it is not required for read-only transactions.

---

[a]https://dev.mysql.com/doc/refman/5.7/en/innodb-performance-ro-txn.html

6.5.1 Read-only transaction routing

Setting up a database replication environment is useful for both high-availability (a Slave can replace a crashing Master) and traffic splitting. In a Master-Slave replication topology, the Master node accepts both read-write and read-only transactions, while Slave nodes only take read-only traffic.

Oracle

The Oracle ADG (Active Data Guard) allows an enterprise application to distribute read-write traffic to the Primary node and read-only transactions to a Standby database. WebLogic Server GridLink Data Source[a] provides failover and load balancing capabilities over Oracle ADG.

[a]http://www.oracle.com/technetwork/middleware/weblogic/learnmore/1534212

SQL Server

The database Availability Group must be configured to use read-only routing, in which case the redirection is based on the `ApplicationIntent` connection property. This means that the application requires separate `DataSource(s)` for read-write and read-only connections, and transaction routing must initiate in the application service layer.

PostgreSQL

The JDBC driver defines two connection properties[a] for load balancing purposes: `loadBalanceHosts` (which is disabled by default) and `targetServerType` (`master` or `preferSlave`). To enable transaction routing, the application must do the routing itself using separate `DataSource(s)`.

[a]https://jdbc.postgresql.org/documentation/head/connect.html

MySQL

The `com.mysql.jdbc.ReplicationDriver`[a] supports transaction routing on a Master-Slave topology, the decision being made on the `Connection` read-only status basis.

[a]https://dev.mysql.com/doc/connector-j/en/connector-j-master-slave-replication-connection.html

Even if the JDBC driver does not support Master-Slave routing, the application can do it using multiple DataSource instances. This design cannot rely on the read-only status of the underlying Connection since the routing must take place before a database connection is fetched.

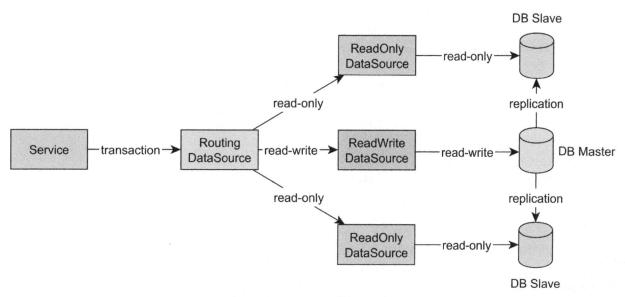

Figure 6.11: Transaction routing

If the transaction manager supports declarative read-only transactions, the routing decision can be taken based on the current transaction read-only preference. Otherwise, the routing must be done manually in each service layer component, and so a read-only transaction uses a read-only DataSource or a read-only JPA Persistence Context.

6.6 Transaction boundaries

Every database statement executes in the context of a database transaction, even if the client does not explicitly set transaction boundaries. While there might be single statement transactions (usually a read-only query), when the unit of work consists of multiple SQL statements, the database should wrap them all in a single unit of work.

By default, every Connection starts in *auto-commit* mode, each statement being executed in a separate transaction. Unfortunately, it does not work for multi-statement transactions as it moves atomicity boundaries from the logical unit of work to each individual statement.

 Auto-commit should be avoided as much as possible, and, even for single statement transactions, it is good practice to mark the transaction boundaries explicitly.

In the following example, a sum of money is transferred between two bank accounts. The balance must always be consistent, so if an account gets debited, the other one must always be credited with the same amount of money.

```
try(Connection connection = dataSource.getConnection();
    PreparedStatement transferStatement = connection.prepareStatement(
        "UPDATE account SET balance = ? WHERE id = ?"
    )) {
    transferStatement.setLong(1, Math.negateExact(cents));
    transferStatement.setLong(2, fromAccountId);
    transferStatement.executeUpdate();

    transferStatement.setLong(1, cents);
    transferStatement.setLong(2, toAccountId);
    transferStatement.executeUpdate();
}
```

Because of the auto-commit mode, if the second statement failed, only those particular changes could be rolled back, the first statement being already committed cannot be reverted anymore.

The default auto-commit mode must be disabled and the transaction has to be managed manually. The transaction is committed if every statement runs successfully and a rollback is triggered on a failure basis. With this in mind, the previous example should be rewritten as follows:

```
try(Connection connection = dataSource.getConnection()) {
    connection.setAutoCommit(false);
    try(PreparedStatement transferStatement = connection.prepareStatement(
        "UPDATE account SET balance = ? WHERE id = ?"
    )) {
        transferStatement.setLong(1, Math.negateExact(cents));
        transferStatement.setLong(2, fromAccountId);
        transferStatement.executeUpdate();

        transferStatement.setLong(1, cents);
        transferStatement.setLong(2, toAccountId);
        transferStatement.executeUpdate();

        connection.commit();
    } catch (SQLException e) {
        connection.rollback();
        throw e;
    }
}
```

The astute reader might notice that the previous example breaks the *Single responsibility principle* since the Data Access Object (DAO) method mixes both transaction management and data access logic. Transaction management is a cross-cutting concern, making it a good candidate for being moved to a separate common library. This way, the transaction management logic resides in one place, and a lot of duplicated code can be removed from the DAO methods. One way to extract the transaction management logic is to use the *Template method pattern*:

```
public void transact(Consumer<Connection> callback) {
    Connection connection = null;
    try {
        connection = dataSource.getConnection();
        callback.accept(connection);
        connection.commit();
    } catch (Exception e) {
        if (connection != null) {
            try {
                connection.rollback();
            } catch (SQLException ex) {
                throw new DataAccessException(e);
            }
        }
        throw (e instanceof DataAccessException ?
            (DataAccessException) e : new DataAccessException(e));
    } finally {
        if(connection != null) {
            try {
                connection.close();
            } catch (SQLException e) {
                throw new DataAccessException(e);
            }
        }
    }
}
```

 Transactions should never be abandoned on failure, and it is mandatory to initiate a transaction rollback (to allow the database to revert any uncommitted changes and release any lock as soon as possible).

With this utility in hand, the previous example can be simplified to:

```
transact((Connection connection) -> {
    try(PreparedStatement transferStatement = connection.prepareStatement(
        "UPDATE account SET balance = ? WHERE id = ?"
    )) {
        transferStatement.setLong(1, Math.negateExact(cents));
        transferStatement.setLong(2, fromAccountId);
        transferStatement.executeUpdate();

        transferStatement.setLong(1, cents);
        transferStatement.setLong(2, toAccountId);
        transferStatement.executeUpdate();
    } catch (SQLException e) {
        throw new DataAccessException(e);
    }
});
```

Although better than the first code snippet, separating data access logic and transaction management is not sufficient.

The transaction boundaries are still rigid, and, to include multiple data access method in a single database transaction, the Connection object has to be carried out as a parameter to every single DAO method.

Declarative transactions can better address this issue by breaking the strong coupling between the data access logic and the transaction management code. Transaction boundaries are marked with metadata (e.g. annotations) and a separate transaction manager abstraction is in charge of coordinating transaction logic.

Java EE and JTA

Declarative transactions become a necessity for distributed transactions. When Java EE (Enterprise Edition) first emerged, application servers hosted both web applications and middleware integration services, which meant that the Java EE container needed to coordinate multiple DataSource(s) or even JMS (Java Messaging) queues.

Following the X/Open XA architecture, JTA (Java Transaction API) powers the Java EE distributed transactions requirements.

6.6.1 Distributed transactions

The difference between local and global transactions is that the former uses a single resource manager, while the latter operates on multiple heterogeneous resource managers. The ACID guarantees are still enforced on each individual resource, but a global transaction manager is mandatory to orchestrate the distributed transaction outcome.

All transactional resource adapters are registered by the global transaction manager, which decides when a resource is allowed to commit or rollback. The Java EE managed resources become accessible through JNDI (Java Naming and Directory Interface) or CDI (Contexts and Dependency Injection).

Spring provides a transaction management abstraction layer which can be configured to either use local transactions (JDBC or RESOURCE_LOCAL[8] JPA) or global transactions through a stand-alone JTA transaction manager. The dependency injection mechanism auto-wires managed resources into Spring beans.

6.6.1.1 Two-phase commit

JTA makes use of the two-phase commit (2PC) protocol to coordinate the atomic resource commitment in two steps: a *prepare* and a *commit* phase.

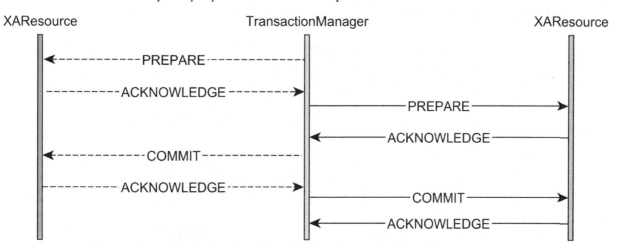

Figure 6.12: Two-phase commit protocol

In the former phase, a resource manager takes all the necessary actions to prepare the transaction for the upcoming commit. Only if all resource managers successfully acknowledge the preparation step, the transaction manager proceeds with the commit phase. If one resource does not acknowledge the prepare phase, the transaction manager will proceed to roll back all current participants.

If all resource managers acknowledge the commit phase, the global transaction will end successfully.

---

[8]http://docs.oracle.com/javaee/7/api/javax/persistence/spi/PersistenceUnitTransactionType.html#RESOURCE_
LOCAL

If one resource fails to commit (or times out), the transaction manager will have to retry this operation in a background thread until it either succeeds or reports the incident for manual intervention.

The one-phase commit (1PC) optimization

Because Java EE uses JTA transactions exclusively, the extra coordination overhead of the additional database roundtrip may hurt performance in a high-throughput application environment. When a transaction enlists only one resource adapter (designating a single resource manager), the transaction manager can skip the prepare phase, and either execute the commit or the rollback phase. With this optimization, the distributed transaction behaves similarly to how JDBC `Connection(s)` manage local transactions.

The `XAResource.commit(Xid xid, boolean onePhase`[a] method takes a `boolean` flag, which the transaction manager sets to *true* to hint the associated resource adapter to initiate the 1PC optimization.

[a]https://docs.oracle.com/javaee/7/api/javax/transaction/xa/XAResource.html#commit-javax.transaction.xa.Xid-boolean-

---

6.6.2 Declarative transactions

Transaction boundaries are usually associated with a Service layer, which uses one or more DAO to fulfill the business logic. The transaction *propagates* from one component to the other within the service-layer transaction boundaries.

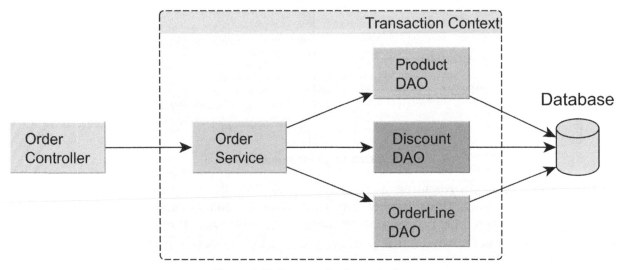

Figure 6.13: Transaction boundaries

The declarative transaction model is supported by both Java EE and Spring. Transaction boundaries are controlled through similar propagation strategies, which define how boundaries are inherited or disrupted at the borderline between the outermost component (in the current call stack) and the current one (waiting to be invoked).

Propagation

To configure the transaction propagation strategy for EJB components, Java EE defines the `@TransactionAttribute`[a] annotation. Since Java EE 7, even non-EJB components can now be enrolled in a transactional context if they are augmented with the `@Transactional`[b] annotation.

In Spring, transaction propagation (like any other transaction properties) is configurable via the `@Transactional`[c] annotation.

---

[a]http://docs.oracle.com/javaee/7/api/javax/ejb/TransactionAttribute.html
[b]http://docs.oracle.com/javaee/7/api/javax/transaction/Transactional.html
[c]https://docs.spring.io/spring/docs/current/javadoc-api/org/springframework/transaction/annotation/Transactional.html#propagation--

Table 6.6: Transaction propagation strategies

Propagation	Java EE	Spring	Description
REQUIRED	Yes	Yes	This is the default propagation strategy, and it only starts a transaction unless the current thread is not already associated with a transaction context
REQUIRES_NEW	Yes	Yes	Any currently running transaction context is suspended and replaced by a new transaction
SUPPORTS	Yes	Yes	If the current thread already runs inside a transaction, this method will use it. Otherwise, it executes outside of a transaction context
NOT_SUPPORTED	Yes	Yes	Any currently running transaction context is suspended, and the current method is run outside of a transaction context
MANDATORY	Yes	Yes	The current method runs only if the current thread is already associated with a transaction context
NESTED	No	Yes	The current method is executed within a nested transaction if the current thread is already associated with a transaction. Otherwise, a new transaction is started.
NEVER	No	Yes	The current method must always run outside of a transaction context, and, if the current thread is associated with a transaction, an exception will be thrown.

Declarative exception handling

Since the transaction logic wraps around the underlying service and data access logic call chain, the exception handling must also be configured declaratively. By default, both Java EE and Spring roll back on system exceptions (any `RuntimeException`) and commit on application exceptions (checked exceptions).

In Java EE, the rollback policy can be customized using the `@ApplicationException`[a] annotation.

Spring allows each transaction to customize the rolling back policy[b] by listing the exception types triggering a transaction failure.

---

[a]http://docs.oracle.com/javaee/7/api/javax/ejb/ApplicationException.html

[b]https://docs.spring.io/spring/docs/current/javadoc-api/org/springframework/transaction/annotation/Transactional.html#rollbackFor--

Declarative read-only transactions

Java EE does not support read-only transactions to be marked declaratively.

Spring offers the transactional read-only attribute[a], which can propagate to the underlying JPA provider (to optimize the `EntityManager` flushing mechanism) and to the current associated JDBC `Connection`.

---

[a]https://docs.spring.io/spring/docs/current/javadoc-api/org/springframework/transaction/annotation/Transactional.html#readOnly--

Declarative isolation levels

The Java EE does not offer support for configurable isolation levels, so it is up to the underlying `DataSource` to define it for all database connections.

Spring supports transaction-level isolation levels[a] when using the `JpaTransactionManager`[b]. For JTA transactions, the `JtaTransactionManager`[c] follows the Java EE standard and disallows overriding the default isolation level. As a workaround, the Spring framework provides extension points, so the application developer can customize the default behavior and implement a mechanism to set isolation levels on a transaction basis.

---

[a]https://docs.spring.io/spring/docs/current/javadoc-api/org/springframework/transaction/annotation/Transactional.html#isolation--

[b]https://docs.spring.io/spring/docs/current/javadoc-api/org/springframework/orm/jpa/JpaTransactionManager.html

[c]https://docs.spring.io/spring/docs/current/javadoc-api/org/springframework/transaction/jta/JtaTransactionManager.html

6.7 Application-level transactions

So far, the book focused on database transactions to enforce ACID properties. However, from the application perspective, a business workflow might span over multiple physical database transactions, in which case the database ACID guarantees are not sufficient anymore. A logical transaction may be composed of multiple web requests, including user think time, for which reason it can be visualized as a *long conversation*.

In the following example, *Alice* and a background process are concurrently modifying the same database record.

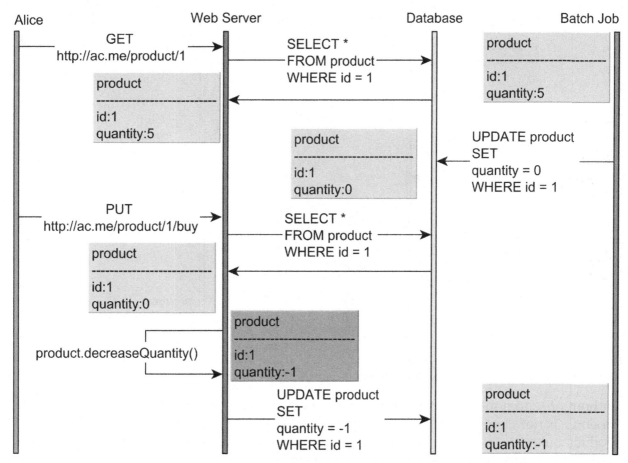

Figure 6.14: Stateless conversation losing updates

Because *Alice* logical transaction encloses two separate web requests, each one associated with a separate database transaction, without an additional concurrency control mechanism, even the strongest isolation level cannot prevent the lost update phenomena.

Spanning a database transaction over multiple web requests is prohibitive since locks would be held during user think time, therefore hurting scalability. Even with MVCC, the cost of maintaining previous versions (that can lead to a large version graph) can escalate and affect both performance and concurrency. Application-level transactions require application-level concurrency control mechanisms.

HTTP is stateless by nature and, for very good reasons, stateless applications are easier to scale than stateful ones. However, application-level transactions cannot be stateless, as otherwise newer requests would not continue from where the previous request was left. Preserving state across multiple web requests allows building a conversational context, providing application-level repeatable reads guarantees.

In the next diagram, *Alice* uses a stateful conversational context, but, in the absence of a record versioning system, it is still possible to lose updates.

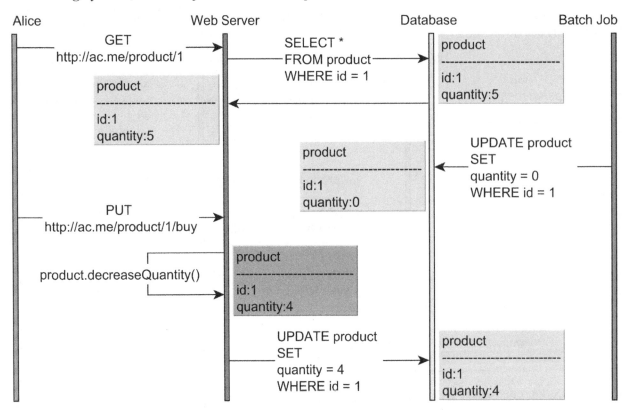

Figure 6.15: Stateful conversation losing updates

Without *Alice* to notice, the batch process resets the product quantity. Thinking the product version has not changed, *Alice* attempts to purchase one item which decreases the previous product quantity by one. In the end, *Alice* has simply overwritten the batch processor modification, and data integrity has been compromised.

So the application-level repeatable reads are not self-sufficient (this argument is true for database isolation levels as well). To prevent lost updates, a concurrency control mechanism becomes mandatory.

6.7.1 Pessimistic and optimistic locking

Isolation levels entail implicit locking, whether it involves physical locks (like 2PL) or data anomaly detection (MVCC). To coordinate state changes, application-level concurrency control makes use of explicit locking, which comes in two flavors: pessimistic and optimistic locking.

6.7.1.1 Pessimistic locking

As previously explained, most database systems already offer the possibility of manually requesting shared or exclusive locks. This concurrency control is said to be *pessimistic* because it assumes that conflicts are bound to happen, and so they must be prevented accordingly.

As locks can be released in a timely fashion, exclusive locking is appropriate during the last database transaction of a given long conversation. This way, the application can guarantee that, once locks are acquired, no other transaction can interfere with the currently locked resources.

 Acquiring locks on critical records can prevent non-repeatable reads, lost updates, as well as read and write skew phenomena.

6.7.1.2 Optimistic locking

Undoubtedly a misnomer (albeit rather widespread), optimistic locking does not incur any locking at all. A much better name would be optimistic concurrency control since it uses a totally different approach to managing conflicts than pessimistic locking.

MVCC is an optimistic concurrency control strategy since it assumes that contention is unlikely to happen, and so it does not rely on locking for controlling access to shared resources. The optimistic concurrency mechanisms detect anomalies and resort to aborting transactions whose invariants no longer hold.

While the database knows exactly which row versions have been issued in a given time interval, the application is left to maintaining a *happens-before* event ordering. Each database row must have an associated version, which is locally incremented by the logical transaction. Every modifying SQL statement (update or delete) uses the previously loaded version as an assumption that the row has not been changed in the meanwhile.

Because even the lowest isolation level can prevent write-write conflicts, only one transaction is allowed to update a row version at any given time. Since the database already offers monotonic updates, the row versions can also be incremented monotonically, and the application can detect when an updating record has become stale.

The optimistic locking concurrency algorithm looks like this:

- When a client reads a particular row, its version comes along with the other fields.
- Upon updating a row, the client filters the current record by the version it has previously loaded.

```
UPDATE product
SET (quantity, version) = (4, 2)
WHERE id = 1 AND version = 1
```

- If the statement update count is zero, the version was incremented in the meanwhile, and the current transaction now operates on a stale record version.

The previous example can be adjusted to take advantage of this optimistic concurrency control mechanism. This time, the product is versioned, and both the web application and the batch processor data access logic are using the row versions to coordinate the *happens-before* update ordering.

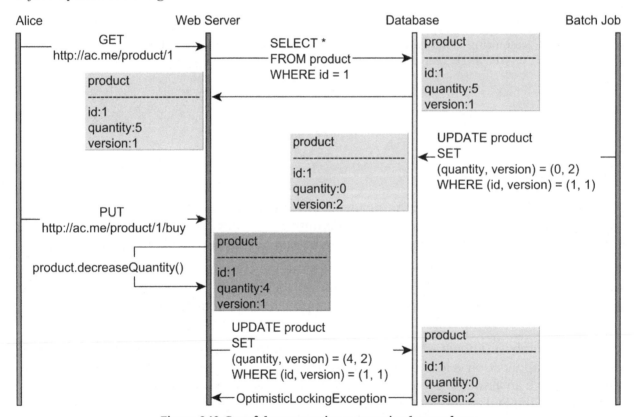

Figure 6.16: Stateful conversation preventing lost updates

Both *Alice* and the batch processor try to increment the product version optimistically. The batch processor can successfully update the product quantity since the SQL statement filtering criteria matches the actual database record version.

When *Alice* tries to update the product, the database returns a zero update count, and, this way, she is notified about the concurrent update that happened in the meanwhile.

The lost update can be prevented because the application can abort the current transaction when being notified of the stale record versions.

II JPA and Hibernate

7. Why JPA and Hibernate matter

Although JDBC does a very good job of exposing a common API that hides the database vendor-specific communication protocol, it suffers from the following shortcomings:

- The API is undoubtedly verbose, even for trivial tasks.
- Batching is not transparent from the data access layer perspective, requiring a specific API than its non-batched statement counterpart.
- Lack of built-in support for explicit locking and optimistic concurrency control.
- For local transactions, the data access is tangled with transaction management semantics.
- Fetching joined relations requires additional processing to transform the ResultSet into Domain Models or DTO (Data Transfer Object) graphs.

Although the primary goal of an ORM (Object-Relational Mapping) tool is to automatically translate object state transitions into SQL statements, this chapter aims to demonstrate that Hibernate can address all the aforementioned JDBC shortcomings.

Java Persistence history

The EJB 1.1 release offered a higher-level persistence abstraction through scalable enterprise components, known as Entity Beans. Although the design looked good on paper, in reality, the heavyweight RMI-based implementation proved to be disastrous from a performance perspective. Neither the EJB 2.0 support for *local interfaces* could revive the Entity Beans popularity, and, due to high-complexity and vendor-specific implementation details, most projects chose JDBC instead.

Hibernate was born out of all the frustration of using the Entity Bean developing model. As an open-source project, Hibernate managed to gain a lot of popularity, and so it soon became the *de facto* Java persistence framework.

In response to all the criticism associated with Entity Bean persistence, the Java Community Process advanced a lightweight POJO-based approach, and the JDO specification was born. Although JDO is data source agnostic, being capable of operating with both relation databases as well as NoSQL or even flat files, it never managed to hit mainstream popularity. For this reason, the Java Community Process decided that EJB3 would be based on a new specification, inspired by Hibernate and TopLink, and JPA (Java Persistence API) became the standard Java persistence technology.

The morale of this is that persistence is a very complex topic, and it demands a great deal of knowledge of both the database and the data access usage patterns.

7.1 The impedance mismatch

When a relational databasc is manipulated through an object-oriented program, the two different data representations start conflicting.

In a relational database, data is stored in tables, and the relational algebra defines how data associations are formed. On the other hand, an object-oriented programming (OOP) language allows objects to have both state and behavior, and bidirectional associations are permitted.

The burden of converging these two distinct approaches has generated much tension, and it has been haunting enterprise systems for a very long time.

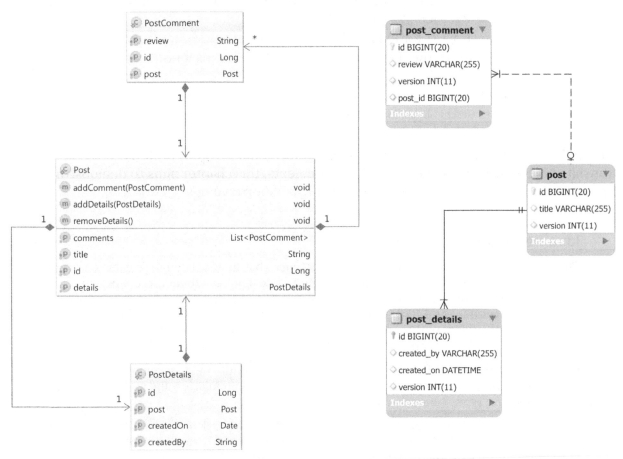

Figure 7.1: Object/Relational Mapping

The above diagram portrays the two different schemas that the data access layer needs to correlate. While the database schema is driven by the SQL standard specification, the Domain Model comes with an object-oriented schema representation as well.

The Domain Model encapsulates the business logic specifications and captures both data structures and the behavior that governs business requirements. OOP facilitates Domain Modeling, and many modern enterprise systems are implemented on top of an object-oriented programming language.

Because the underlying data resides in a relational database, the Domain Model must be adapted to the database schema and the SQL-driven communication protocol. The ORM design pattern helps to bridge these two different data representations and close the technological gap between them. Every database row is associated with a Domain Model object (*Entity* in JPA terminology), and so the ORM tool can translate the entity state transitions into DML statements.

From an application development point of view, this is very convenient since it is much easier to manipulate Domain Model relationships rather than visualizing the business logic through its underlying SQL statements.

7.2 JPA vs. Hibernate

JPA is only a specification. It describes the interfaces that the client operates with and the standard object-relational mapping metadata (Java annotations or XML descriptors). Beyond the API definition, JPA also explains (although not exhaustively) how these specifications are ought to be implemented by the JPA providers. JPA evolves with the Java EE platform itself (Java EE 6 featuring JPA 2.0 and Java EE 7 introducing JPA 2.1).

Hibernate was already a full-featured Java ORM implementation by the time the JPA specification was released for the first time. Although it implements the JPA specification, Hibernate retains its native API for both backward compatibility and to accommodate non-standard features.

Even if it is best to adhere to the JPA standard, in reality, many JPA providers offer additional features targeting a high-performance data access layer requirements. For this purpose, Hibernate comes with the following non-JPA compliant features:

- extended identifier generators (hi/lo, pooled, pooled-lo)
- transparent prepared statement batching
- customizable CRUD (`@SQLInsert`, `@SQLUpdate`, `@SQLDelete`) statements
- static/dynamic entity/collection filters (e.g. `@FilterDef`, `@Filter`, `@Where`)
- mapping attributes to SQL fragments (e.g. `@Formula`)
- immutable entities (e.g. `@Immutable`)
- more flush modes (e.g. `FlushMode.MANUAL`, `FlushMode.ALWAYS`)
- querying the second-level cache by the natural key of a given entity
- entity-level cache concurrency strategies
  (e.g. `Cache(usage = CacheConcurrencyStrategy.READ_WRITE)`)
- versioned bulk updates through HQL
- exclude fields from optimistic locking check (e.g. `@OptimisticLock(excluded = true)`)
- versionless optimistic locking (e.g. `OptimisticLockType.ALL`, `OptimisticLockType.DIRTY`)
- support for skipping (without waiting) pessimistic lock requests
- support for Java 8 Date and Time and `stream()`
- support for multitenancy

If JPA is the interface, Hibernate is one implementation and implementation details always matter from a performance perspective.

The JPA implementation details leak and ignoring them might hinder application performance or even lead to data inconsistency issues. As an example, the following JPA attributes have a peculiar behavior, which can surprise someone who is familiar with the JPA specification only:

- The FlushModeType.AUTO[1] does not trigger a flush for native SQL queries like it does for JPQL or Criteria API.
- The FetchType.EAGER[2] might choose a SQL join or a secondary select whether the entity is fetched directly from the `EntityManager` or through a JPQL (Java Persistence Query Language) or a Criteria API query.

That is why this book is focused on how Hibernate manages to implement both the JPA specification and its non-standard native features (that are relevant from an efficiency perspective).

Portability concerns

Like other non-functional requirements, portability is a feature, and there is still a widespread fear of embracing database-specific or framework-specific features. In reality, it is more common to encounter enterprise applications facing data access performance issues than having to migrate from one technology to the other (be it a relation database or a JPA provider).

The lowest common denominator of many RDBMS is a superset of the SQL-92 standard (although not entirely supported either). SQL-99 supports Common Table Expressions, but MySQL 5.7 does not. Although SQL-2003 defines the MERGE operator, PostgreSQL 9.5 favored the UPSERT operation instead. By adhering to a SQL-92 syntax, one could achieve a higher degree of database portability, but the price of giving up database-specific features can take a toll on application performance. Portability can be addressed either by subtracting non-common features or through specialization. By offering different implementations, for each supported database system (like the jOOQ framework does), portability can still be achieved.

The same argument is valid for JPA providers too. By layering the application, it is already much easier to swap JPA providers, if there is even a compelling reason for switching one mature JPA implementation with another.

---

[1]https://docs.oracle.com/javaee/7/api/javax/persistence/FlushModeType.html
[2]https://docs.oracle.com/javaee/7/api/javax/persistence/FetchType.html#EAGER

7.3 Schema ownership

Because of data representation duality, there has been a rivalry between taking ownership of the underlying schema. Although theoretically, both the database and the Domain Model could drive the schema evolution, for practical reasons, the schema belongs to the database.

An enterprise system might be too large to fit into a single application, so it is not uncommon to split in into multiple subsystems, each one serving a specific goal. As an example, there can be front-end web applications, integration web services, email schedulers, full-text search engines and back-end batch processors that need to load data into the system. All these subsystems need to use the underlying database, whether it is for displaying content to the users or dumping data into the system.

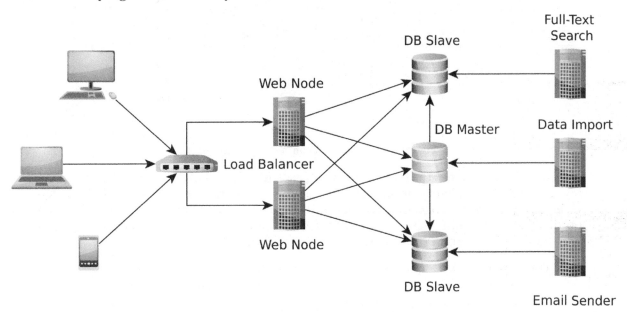

Figure 7.2: Database-centric integration

Although it might not fit any enterprise system, having the database as a central integration point can still be a choice for many reasonable size enterprise systems.

The relational database concurrency models offer strong consistency guarantees, therefore having a significant advantage to application development. If the integration point does not provide transactional semantics, it will be much more difficult to implement a distributed concurrency control mechanism.

Most database systems already offer support for various replication topologies, which can provide more capacity for accommodating an increase in the incoming request traffic. Even if the demand for more data continues to grow, the hardware is always getting better and better (and cheaper too), and database vendors keep on improving their engines to cope with more data.

For these reasons, having the database as an integration point is still a relevant enterprise system design consideration.

The distributed commit log

For very large enterprise systems, where data is split among different providers (relational database systems, caches, Hadoop, Spark), it is no longer possible to rely on the relational database to integrate all disparate subsystems.

In this case, Apache Kafka[a] offers a fault-tolerant and scalable append-only log structure, which every participating subsystem can read and write concurrently.

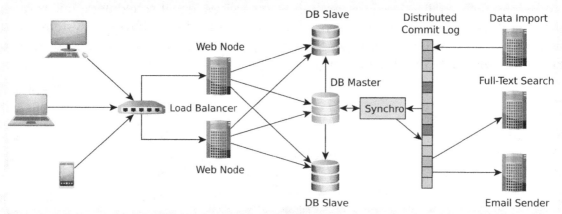

Figure 7.3: Distributed commit log integration

The commit log becomes the integration point, each distributed node individually traversing it and maintaining client-specific pointers in the sequential log structure. This design resembles a database replication mechanism, and so it offers durability (the log is persisted on disk), write performance (append-only logs do not require random access) and read performance (concurrent reads do not require blocking) as well.

---

[a]http://kafka.apache.org/

No matter what architecture style is chosen, there is still need to correlate the transient Domain Model with the underlying persistent data.

The data schema evolves along the enterprise system itself, and so the two different schema representations must remain congruent at all times.

Even if the data access framework can auto-generate the database schema, the schema must be migrated incrementally, and all changes need to be traceable in the VCS (Version Control System) as well. Along with table structure, indexes and triggers, the database schema is, therefore, accompanying the Domain Model source code itself. A tool like Flywaydb[3] can automate the database schema migration, and the system can be deployed continuously, whether it is a test or a production environment.

---

[3]http://flywaydb.org/

The schema ownership goes to the database, and the data access layer must assist the Domain Model to communicate with the underlying data.

7.4 Entity state transitions

JPA shifts the developer mindset from SQL statements to entity state transitions. An entity can be in one of the following states:

Table 7.1: JPA entity states

State	Description
New (Transient)	A newly created entity which is not mapped to any database row is considered to be in the New or Transient state. Once it becomes managed, the Persistence Context issues an insert statement at flush time.
Managed (Persistent)	A Persistent entity is associated with a database row, and it is being managed by the currently running Persistence Context. State changes are detected by the *dirty checking* mechanism and propagated to the database as update statements at flush time.
Detached	Once the currently running Persistence Context is closed, all the previously managed entities become detached. Successive changes are no longer tracked, and no automatic database synchronization is going to happen.
Removed	A removed entity is only scheduled for deletion, and the actual database delete statement is executed during Persistence Context flushing.

The Persistence Context captures entity state changes, and, during flushing, it translates them into SQL statements. The JPA `EntityManager`[4] and the Hibernate `Session`[5] (which includes additional methods for moving an entity from one state to the other) interfaces are gateways towards the underlying Persistence Context, and they define all the entity state transition operations.

---

[4]http://docs.oracle.com/javaee/7/api/javax/persistence/EntityManager.html#persist-java.lang.Object-
[5]https://docs.jboss.org/hibernate/orm/current/javadocs/org/hibernate/Session.html

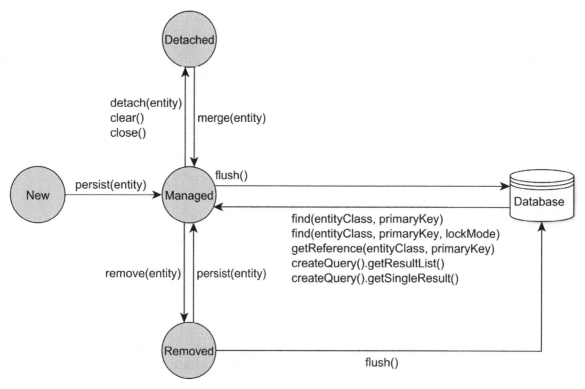

Figure 7.4: JPA entity state transitions

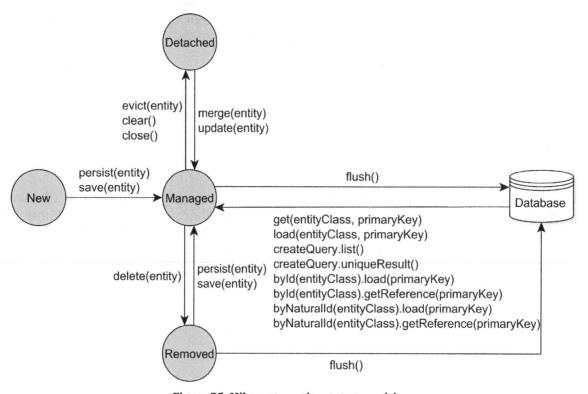

Figure 7.5: Hibernate entity state transitions

7.5 Write-based optimizations

SQL injection prevention

By managing the SQL statement generation, the JPA tool can assist in minimizing the risk of SQL injection attacks. The less the chance of manipulating SQL String statements, the safer the application can get. The risk is not completely eliminated because the application developer can still recur to concatenating SQL or JPQL fragments, so rigor is advised.

 Hibernate uses PreparedStatement(s) exclusively, so not only it protects against SQL injection, but the data access layer can better take advantage of server-side and client-side statement caching as well.

Auto-generated DML statements

The enterprise system database schema evolves with time, and the data access layer must mirror all these modifications as well.

Because the JPA provider auto-generates insert and update statements, the data access layer can easily accommodate database table structure modifications. By updating the entity model schema, Hibernate can automatically adjust the modifying statements accordingly.

This applies to changing database column types as well. If the database schema needs to migrate a postal code from an INT database type to a VARCHAR(6), the data access layer will need only to change the associated Domain Model attribute type from an Integer to a String, and all statements are going to be automatically updated. Hibernate defines a highly customizable JDBC-to-database type mapping system, and the application developer can override a default type association, or even add support for new database types (that are not currently supported by Hibernate).

The entity fetching process is automatically managed by the JPA implementation, which auto-generates the select statements of the associated database tables. This way, JPA can free the application developer from maintaining entity selection queries as well.

Hibernate allows customizing all the CRUD statements, in which case the application developer is responsible for maintaining the associated DML statements.

Although it takes care of the entity selection process, most enterprise systems need to take advantage of the underlying database querying capabilities. For this reason, whenever the database schema changes, all the native SQL queries need to be updated manually (according to their associated business logic requirements).

Write-behind cache

The Persistence Context acts as a transactional write-behind cache, deferring entity state flushing up until the last possible moment.

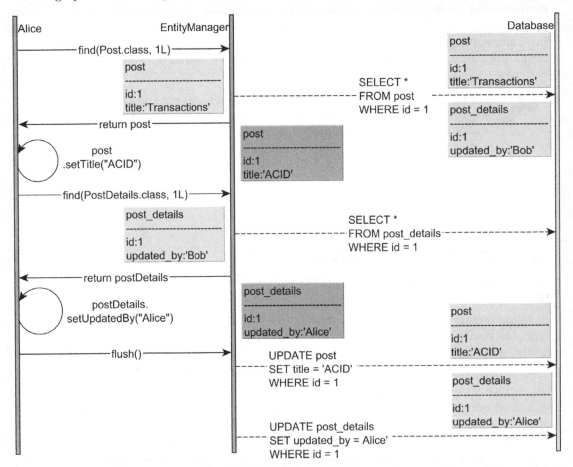

Figure 7.6: Persistence Context

Because every modifying DML statement requires locking (to prevent dirty writes), the write behind cache can reduce the database lock acquisition interval, therefore increasing concurrency.

 However, caches introduce consistency challenges, and the Persistence Context requires a flush prior to executing any JPQL or native SQL query, as otherwise it might break the read-your-own-write consistency guarantee.

As detailed in the following chapters, Hibernate does not automatically flush pending changes when a native query is about to be executed, and the application developer must explicitly instruct what database tables are needed to be synchronized.

Transparent statement batching

Since all changes are being flushed at once, Hibernate may benefit from batching JDBC statements. Batch updates can be enabled transparently, even after the data access logic has been implemented. Most often, performance tuning is postponed until the system is already running in production, and switching to batching statements should not require a considerable development effort.

 With just one configuration, Hibernate can execute all prepared statements in batches.

Application-level concurrency control

As previously explained, no database isolation level can protect against losing updates when executing a multi-request long conversation. JPA supports both optimistic and pessimistic locking.

The JPA optimistic locking mechanism allows preventing lost updates because it imposes a *happens-before* event ordering. However, in multi-request conversations, optimistic locking requires maintaining old entity snapshots, and JPA makes it possible through *Extended Persistence Contexts* or detached entities.

 A Java EE application server can preserve a given Persistence Context across several web requests, therefore providing application-level repeatable reads. However, this strategy is not free since the application developer must make sure the Persistence Context is not bloated with too many entities, which, apart from consuming memory, it can also affect the performance of the Hibernate default dirty checking mechanism.

Even when not using Java EE, the same goal can be achieved using detached entities, which provide fine-grained control over the amount of data needed to be preserved from one web request to the other. JPA allows merging detached entities, which rebecome managed and automatically synchronized with the underlying database system.

JPA also supports a pessimistic locking query abstraction, which comes in handy when using lower-level transaction isolation modes.

 Hibernate has a native pessimistic locking API, which brings support for timing out lock acquisition requests or skipping already acquired locks.

7.6 Read-based optimizations

Following the SQL standard, the JDBC ResultSet is a tabular representation of the underlying fetched data. The Domain Model being constructed as an entity graph, the data access layer must transform the flat ResultSet into a hierarchical structure.

Although the goal of the ORM tool is to reduce the gap between the object-oriented Domain Model and its relational counterpart, it is very important to remember that the source of data is not an in-memory repository, and the fetching behavior influences the overall data access efficiency.

 The database cannot be abstracted out of this context, and pretending that entities can be manipulated just like any other plain objects is very detrimental to application performance. When it comes to reading data, the impedance mismatch becomes even more apparent, and, for performance reasons, it is mandatory to keep in mind the SQL statements associated with every fetching operation.

In the following example, the *posts* records are fetched along with all their associated *comments*. Using JDBC, this task can be accomplished using the following code snippet:

```
doInJDBC(connection -> {
    try (PreparedStatement statement = connection.prepareStatement(
        "SELECT * " +
        "FROM post AS p " +
        "JOIN post_comment AS pc ON p.id = pc.post_id " +
        "WHERE " +
        "   p.id BETWEEN ? AND ? + 1"
    )) {
        statement.setInt(1, id);
        statement.setInt(2, id);
        try (ResultSet resultSet = statement.executeQuery()) {
            List<Post> posts = toPosts(resultSet);
            assertEquals(expectedCount, posts.size());
        }
    } catch (SQLException e) {
        throw new DataAccessException(e);
    }
});
```

When joining *many-to-one* or *one-to-one* associations, each ResultSet record corresponds to a pair of entities, so both the parent and the child can be resolved in each iteration. For *one-to-many* or *many-to-many* relationships, because of how the SQL join works, the ResultSet contains a duplicated parent record for each associated child.

Constructing the hierarchical entity structure requires manual ResultSet transformation, and, to resolve duplicates, the parent entity references are stored in a Map structure.

```java
List<Post> toPosts(ResultSet resultSet) throws SQLException {
    Map<Long, Post> postMap = new LinkedHashMap<>();
    while (resultSet.next()) {
        Long postId = resultSet.getLong(1);
        Post post = postMap.get(postId);
        if(post == null) {
            post = new Post(postId);
            postMap.put(postId, post);
            post.setTitle(resultSet.getString(2));
            post.setVersion(resultSet.getInt(3));
        }
        PostComment comment = new PostComment();
        comment.setId(resultSet.getLong(4));
        comment.setReview(resultSet.getString(5));
        comment.setVersion(resultSet.getInt(6));
        post.addComment(comment);
    }
    return new ArrayList<>(postMap.values());
}
```

The JDBC 4.2 PreparedStatement supports only positional parameters, and the first ordinal starts from 1. JPA allows named parameters as well, which are especially useful when a parameter needs to be referenced multiple times, so the previous example can be rewritten as follows:

```java
doInJPA(entityManager -> {
    List<Post> posts = entityManager.createQuery(
        "select distinct p " +
        "from Post p " +
        "join fetch p.comments " +
        "where " +
        "   p.id BETWEEN :id AND :id + 1", Post.class)
    .setParameter("id", id)
    .getResultList();
    assertEquals(expectedCount, posts.size());
});
```

In both examples, the object-relation transformation takes place either implicitly or explicitly. In the JDBC use case, the associations must be manually resolved, while JPA does it automatically (based on the entity schema).

The fetching responsibility

Besides mapping database columns to entity attributes, the entity associations can also be represented in terms of object relationships. More, the fetching behavior can be hard-wired to the entity schema itself, which is most often a terrible thing to do.

Fetching multiple one-to-many or many-to-many associations is even more problematic because they might require a Cartesian Product, therefore affecting performance. Controlling the hard-wired schema fetching policy is cumbersome as it prevents overriding an eager retrieval with a lazy loading mechanism.

 Each business use case has different data access requirements, and one policy cannot anticipate all possible use cases, so the fetching strategy should always be set up on a query basis.

Prefer projections for read-only views

Although it is very convenient to fetch entities along with all their associated relationships, it is better to take into consideration the performance impact as well. As previously explained, fetching too much data is not suitable because it increases the transaction response time.

In reality, not all use cases require loading entities, and not all read operations need to be served by the same fetching mechanism. Sometimes a custom projection (selecting only a few columns from an entity) is much more suitable, and the data access logic can even take advantage of database-specific SQL constructs that might not be supported by the JPA query abstraction.

 As a rule of thumb, fetching entities is suitable when the logical transaction requires modifying them, even if that only happens in a successive web request. With this is mind, it is much easier to reason on which fetching mechanism to employ for a given business logic use case.

The second-level cache

If the Persistence Context acts as a transactional write-behind cache, its lifetime will be bound to that of a logical transaction. For this reason, the Persistence Context is also known as the first-level cache, and so it cannot be shared by multiple concurrent transactions.

On the other hand, the second-level cache is associated with an `EntityManagerFactory`, and all Persistence Contexts have access to it. The second-level cache can store entities as well as entity associations (one-to-many and many-to-many relationships) and even entity query results. Because JPA does not make it mandatory, each provider takes a different approach to caching (as opposed to EclipseLink, by default, Hibernate disables the second-level cache).

Most often, caching is a trade-off between consistency and performance. Because the cache becomes another source of truth, inconsistencies might occur, and they can be prevented only when all database modifications happen through a single `EntityManagerFactory` or a synchronized distributed caching solution. In reality, this is not practical since the application might be clustered on multiple nodes (each one with its own `EntityManagerFactory`) and the database might be accessed by multiple applications.

 Although the second-level cache can mitigate the entity fetching performance issues, it requires a distributed caching implementation, which might not elude the networking penalties anyway.

7.7 Wrap-up

Bridging two highly-specific technologies is always a difficult problem to solve. When the enterprise system is built on top of an object-oriented language, the object-relational impedance mismatch becomes inevitable. The ORM pattern aims to close this gap although it cannot completely abstract it out.

In the end, all the communication flows through JDBC and every execution happens in the database engine itself. A high-performance enterprise application must resonate with the underlying database system, and the ORM tool must not disrupt this relationship.

Just like the problem it tries to solve, Hibernate is a very complex framework with many subtleties that require a thorough knowledge of both database systems, JDBC, and the framework itself. This chapter is only a summary, meant to present JPA and Hibernate into a different perspective that prepares the reader for high-performance object-relational mapping. There is no need to worry if some topics are not entirely clear because the upcoming chapters analyze all these concepts in greater detail.

8. Connection Management and Monitoring

As previously explained in the JDBC Connection Management chapter, for performance reasons, database connections are better off reused. Because JPA providers generate SQL statements on behalf of users, it is very important to monitor this process and acknowledge its outcome. This chapter explains the Hibernate connection provider mechanism and ways to monitor statement execution.

8.1 JPA connection management

Like the whole Java EE suite, the JPA 1.0 specification was very much tied to enterprise application servers. In a Java EE container, all database connections are managed by the application server which provides connection pooling, monitoring, and JTA capabilities.

Once configured, the Java EE `DataSource` can be located through JNDI. In the `persistence.xml` configuration file, the application developer must supply the JNDI name of the associated JTA or RESOURCE_LOCAL `DataSource`. The `transaction-type` attribute must also match the data source transaction capabilities.

```
<persistence-unit name="persistenceUnit" transaction-type="JTA">
    <provider>org.hibernate.jpa.HibernatePersistenceProvider</provider>
    <jta-data-source>java:global/jdbc/flexypool</jta-data-source>
</persistence-unit>
```

A `RESOURCE_LOCAL` transaction must use a `non-jta-data-source` DataSource.

```
<persistence-unit name="persistenceUnit" transaction-type="RESOURCE_LOCAL">
    <provider>org.hibernate.jpa.HibernatePersistenceProvider</provider>
    <non-jta-data-source>java:/comp/env/jdbc/hsqldb</non-jta-data-source>
</persistence-unit>
```

While for a Java EE application it is perfectly fine to rely on the application server for providing a full-featured `DataSource` reference, stand-alone applications are usually configured using dependency injection rather than JNDI.

From the JPA implementation perspective, the `DataSource` can be either configured externally or by the JPA provider itself. Most often, configuring an external `DataSource` is still the preferred alternative as it gives more flexibility in decorating the connection providing mechanism (e.g. logging, monitoring).

JPA providers can fetch connections through the underlying JDBC `Driver` since JPA 2.0 has standardized the database connection configuration properties:

Table 8.1: JPA connection properties

Property	Description
javax.persistence.jdbc.driver	Driver full class name (e.g. `org.hsqldb.jdbc.JDBCDriver`)
javax.persistence.jdbc.url	Driver Url (e.g. `jdbc:hsqldb:mem:test`)
javax.persistence.jdbc.user	Database user's name
javax.persistence.jdbc.password	Database user's password

Unfortunately, these properties alone are not sufficient because most enterprise applications need connection pooling and monitoring capabilities anyway. For this reason, JPA connection management is still an implementation-specific topic, and the upcoming sections dive into the connection provider mechanism employed by Hibernate.

8.2 Hibernate connection providers

Hibernate needs to operate both in Java EE and stand-alone environments, and the database connectivity configuration can be done either declaratively or programmatically. To accommodate JDBC `Driver` connections as well as RESOURCE_LOCAL and JTA `DataSource` configurations, Hibernate defines its own connection factory abstraction, represented by the `org.hibernate.engine.jdbc.connections.spi.ConnectionProvider` interface:

```
public interface ConnectionProvider extends Service, Wrapped {

    public Connection getConnection() throws SQLException;

    public void closeConnection(Connection connection) throws SQLException;

    public boolean supportsAggressiveRelease();
}
```

Because the connection provider might influence transaction response time, each provider is analyzed from a high-performance OLTP system perspective.

8.2.1 DriverManagerConnectionProvider

Hibernate picks this provider when being given the aforementioned JPA 2.0 connection properties or the Hibernate-specific configuration counterpart:

- `hibernate.connection.driver_class`
- `hibernate.connection.url`
- `hibernate.connection.username`
- `hibernate.connection.password`.

 Although it fetches database connections through the underlying `DriverManager`, this provider tries to avoid the connection acquisition overhead by using a trivial pooling implementation. The Hibernate documentation does not recommend using the `DriverManagerConnectionProvider` in a production setup.

8.2.2 C3P0ConnectionProvider

C3p0[1] is a mature connection pooling solution that has proven itself in many production environments, and, using the underlying JDBC connection properties, Hibernate can replace the built-in connection pool with a c3p0 `DataSource`. To activate this provider, the application developer must supply at least one configuration property starting with the `hibernate.c3p0` prefix:

```
<property name="hibernate.c3p0.max_size" value="5"/>
```

C3p0 (released in 2001) and Apache DBCP[2] (released in 2002) are the oldest and the most deployed stand-alone Java connection pooling solutions. Later in 2010, BoneCP[3] emerged as a high-performance alternative for c3p0 and Apache DBCP.

Nowadays, the BoneCP GitHub page says it is been deprecated in favor of HikariCP[4].

---

[1]http://www.mchange.com/projects/c3p0/
[2]https://commons.apache.org/proper/commons-dbcp/
[3]https://github.com/wwadge/bonecp
[4]https://github.com/brettwooldridge/HikariCP

As of writing, the most attractive Java connection pools are HikariCP, Vibur DBCP[5], and Apache DBCP2. HikariCP and Vibur DBCP offer built-in Hibernate connection providers.

8.2.3 HikariCPConnectionProvider

Hibernate 5 supports HikariCP (one of the fastest connection pools) via the following dependency:

```
<dependency>
    <groupId>org.hibernate</groupId>
    <artifactId>hibernate-hikaricp</artifactId>
    <version>${hibernate.version}</version>
</dependency>
```

By specifying the `hibernate.connection.provider_class` property, the application developer can override the default connection provider mechanism:

```
<property name="hibernate.connection.provider_class"
    value="org.hibernate.hikaricp.internal.HikariCPConnectionProvider"/>
```

Unlike `DriverManagerConnectionProvider` or `C3P0ConnectionProvider`, HikariCP requires specific configuration properties[6]:

Table 8.2: HikariCP connection properties

Property	Description
hibernate.hikari.dataSourceClassName	Driver full class name
hibernate.hikari.dataSource.url	Driver Url
hibernate.hikari.dataSource.user	Database user's name
hibernate.hikari.dataSource.password	Database user's password
hibernate.hikari.maximumPoolSize	Maximum pool size

---

[5]https://github.com/vibur/vibur-dbcp
[6]https://github.com/brettwooldridge/HikariCP

8.2.4 DatasourceConnectionProvider

This provider is chosen when the JPA configuration file defines a `non-jta-data-source` or a `jta-data-source` element, or when supplying a `hibernate.connection.datasource` configuration property.

Unlike other providers, this one is compatible with JTA transactions, which are mandatory in Java EE.

Spring works with both stand-alone JTA transaction managers (e.g. Bitronix or Atomikos) and Java EE `DataSource(s)`, and, because it offers the best control over the actual `DataSource` configuration, the `DatasourceConnectionProvider` is the preferred choice (even for HikariCP).

8.2.5 Connection release modes

Hibernate defers the database connection acquisition until the current transaction has to execute its first SQL statement (either triggered by a read or a write operation). This optimization allows Hibernate to reduce the physical transaction interval, therefore increasing the chance of getting a connection from the pool.

The connection release strategy is controlled through the `hibernate.connection.release_mode` property which can take the following values:

Table 8.3: Connection release modes

Value	Description
after_transaction	Once acquired, the database connection is released only after the current transaction either commits or rolls back.
after_statement	The connection is released after each statement execution and reacquired prior to running the next statement. Although not required by either JDBC or JTA specifications, this strategy is meant to prevent application servers from mistakenly detecting[7] a connection leak between successive EJB (Enterprise Java Beans) calls
auto	This is the default value, and for RESOURCE_LOCAL transactions, it uses the `after_transaction` mode, while for JTA transactions it falls back to `after_statement`.

---

[7]http://lists.jboss.org/pipermail/hibernate-dev/2006-December/000903.html

For JTA transactions, the default mode might be too strict since not all Java EE application servers exhibit the same behavior for managing transactional resources. This way, it is important to check if database connections can be closed outside of the EJB component that triggered the connection acquisition event. Spring-based enterprise systems do not use Enterprise Java Beans, and, even when using a stand-alone JTA transaction manager, the after_transaction connection release mode might be just fine.

It is somehow intuitive that the after_statement mode incurs some performance penalty associated with the frequent acquisition/releasing connection cycles. For this reason, the following test measures the connection acquisition overhead when using Bitronix in a Spring application context. Each transaction executes the same statement (fetching the current timestamp) for a given number of times (represented on the x-axis). The y-axis captures the recorded transaction response times for both after_statement and after_transaction connection release modes.

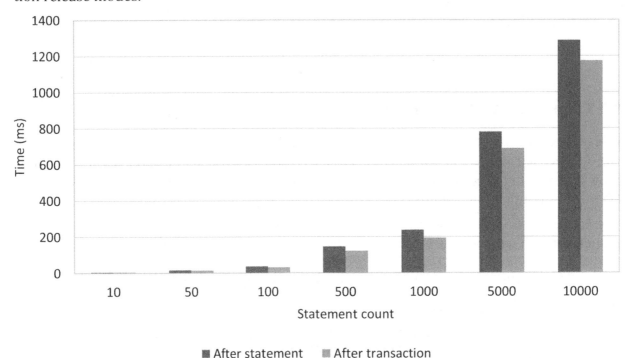

Figure 8.1: Connection release mode

The more statements a transaction executes, the greater the penalty of reacquiring the associated database connection from the underlying connection pool. To better visualize the connection acquisition overhead, the test runs up to 10 000 statements, even if this number is probably too high for the typical OLTP transaction.

Ideally, database transactions should be as short as possible, and the number of statements should not be too high either. This requirement stems from the fact that the number of pooled connections is limited and locks are better released sooner than later.

The `after_transaction` connection release mode is more efficient than the default JTA `after_statement` strategy, and so it should be used if the JTA transaction resource management logic does not interfere with this connection releasing strategy.

8.3 Monitoring connections

As previously concluded, using an externally configured `DataSource` is preferred because the actual `DataSource` can be decorated with connection pooling, monitoring and logging capabilities. Because that is exactly how FlexyPool[8] works too, the following diagram captures the `DataSource` proxying mechanism:

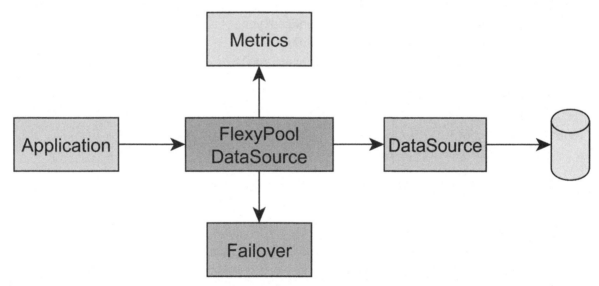

Figure 8.2: FlexyPool architecture

Instead of getting the actual `DataSource` instance, the data access layer gets a proxy reference. The proxy intercepts connection acquisition and releasing requests, and, this way, it can monitor its usage.

When using Spring, setting up FlexyPool is fairly easy because the application has total control over the `DataSource` configuration.

In Java EE, database connections should always be fetched from a managed `DataSource`, and one simple way of integrating FlexyPool is to extend the default `DatasourceConnectionProviderImpl` and substitute the original `DataSource` with the `FlexyPoolDataSource`.

For this reason, FlexyPool comes with the following Hibernate connection provider:

---

[8]https://github.com/vladmihalcea/flexy-pool

```
public class FlexyPoolHibernateConnectionProvider
    extends DatasourceConnectionProviderImpl {

    private transient FlexyPoolDataSource<DataSource> flexyPoolDataSource;

    @Override
    public void configure(Map props) {
        super.configure(props);
        flexyPoolDataSource = new FlexyPoolDataSource<>(getDataSource());
    }

    @Override
    public Connection getConnection() throws SQLException {
        return flexyPoolDataSource.getConnection();
    }

    @Override
    public boolean isUnwrappableAs(Class unwrapType) {
        return super.isUnwrappableAs(unwrapType) ||
            getClass().isAssignableFrom(unwrapType);
    }

    @Override
    public void stop() {
        flexyPoolDataSource.stop();
        super.stop();
    }
}
```

To use the `FlexyPoolHibernateConnectionProvider`, the application must configure the `hibernate.connection.provider_class` property:

```
<property
 name="hibernate.connection.provider_class"
 value="com.vladmihalcea.flexypool.adaptor.FlexyPoolHibernateConnectionProvider"
/>
```

8.3.1 Hibernate statistics

Hibernate has a built-in statistics collector which gathers notifications related to database connections, `Session` transactions and even second-level caching usage. The `StatisticsImplementor` interface defines the contract for intercepting various Hibernate internal events:

Figure 8.3: Hibernate `StatisticsImplementor` interface

There is a great variety of metrics Hibernate can collect on user's behalf, but, for performance reasons, the statistics mechanism is disabled by default.

To enable the statistics gathering mechanism, the following property must be configured first:

```
<property name="hibernate.generate_statistics" value="true"/>
```

Once statistics are being collected, in order to print them into the current application log, the following logger configuration must be set up:

```
<logger
    name="org.hibernate.engine.internal.StatisticalLoggingSessionEventListener"
    level="info" />
```

With these two settings in place, whenever a Hibernate Session (Persistence Context) ends, the following report is displayed in the currently running log.

```
37125102 nanoseconds spent acquiring 10000 JDBC connections;
25521714 nanoseconds spent releasing 10000 JDBC connections;
95242323 nanoseconds spent preparing 10000 JDBC statements;
923615040 nanoseconds spent executing 10000 JDBC statements;
```

The default statistics collector just counts the number of times a certain callback method was called, and, if that is not satisfactory, the application developer can supply its own custom StatisticsImplementor implementation.

Dropwizard Metrics

In a high-throughput transaction system, the amount of metric data needed to be recorded can be overwhelming, so storing all these values into memory is not practical at all.

To reduce the memory footprint, the Dropwizard Metrics[a] project uses various *reservoir sampling*[b] strategies, which either employ a fixed-size sampler or a time-based sampling window.

Not only it supports a great variety of metrics (e.g. timers, histograms, gauges), but Dropwizard Metrics can use multiple reporting channels as well (e.g. SLF4J, JMX, Ganglia, Graphite).

 For all these reasons, it is better to use a mature framework such as Dropwizard Metrics instead of building a custom implementation from scratch.

---

[a]https://github.com/dropwizard/metrics
[b]https://en.wikipedia.org/wiki/Reservoir_sampling

8.3.1.1 Customizing statistics

Although the built-in metrics are rather informative, Hibernate is not limited to the default statistics collector mechanism which can be completely customized.

In the upcoming example, the statistics collector also provides the following metrics:

- the distribution of physical transaction time (the interval between the moment a connection is first acquired and when it gets released)
- a histogram of the number of connections acquisition requests during the lifespan of any given transaction (due to the after_statement release mode).

The StatisticsReport class provides metric storage and report generation features on top of Dropwizard Metrics:

```java
public class StatisticsReport {

    private final Logger LOGGER = LoggerFactory.getLogger(getClass());

    private MetricRegistry metricRegistry = new MetricRegistry();

    private Histogram connectionCountHistogram = metricRegistry.
        histogram("connectionCountHistogram");

    private Timer transactionTimer = metricRegistry.
        timer("transactionTimer");

    private Slf4jReporter logReporter = Slf4jReporter
            .forRegistry(metricRegistry)
            .outputTo(LOGGER)
            .build();

    public void transactionTime(long nanos) {
        transactionTimer.update(nanos, TimeUnit.NANOSECONDS);
    }

    public void connectionsCount(long count) {
        connectionCountHistogram.update(count);
    }

    public void generate() {
        logReporter.report();
    }
}
```

The StatisticsImplementor interface defines the contract between the Hibernate internal API and the various custom statistics gathering implementations. For simplicity sake, the following StatisticsImplementor interface implementation extends the default ConcurrentStatisticsImpl class, as it only needs to override the connect and endTransaction methods.

```java
public class TransactionStatistics extends ConcurrentStatisticsImpl {
    private static final ThreadLocal<AtomicLong> startNanos =
        new ThreadLocal<AtomicLong>() {
        @Override protected AtomicLong initialValue() {
            return new AtomicLong();
        }
    };
    private static final ThreadLocal<AtomicLong> connectionCounter =
        new ThreadLocal<AtomicLong>() {
        @Override protected AtomicLong initialValue() {
            return new AtomicLong();
        }
    };
    private StatisticsReport report = new StatisticsReport();

    @Override public void connect() {
        connectionCounter.get().incrementAndGet();
        startNanos.get().compareAndSet(0, System.nanoTime());
        super.connect();
    }

    @Override public void endTransaction(boolean success) {
        try {
            report.transactionTime(System.nanoTime() - startNanos.get().get());
            report.connectionsCount(connectionCounter.get().get());
            report.generate();
        } finally {
            startNanos.remove();
            connectionCounter.remove();
        }
        super.endTransaction(success);
    }
}
```

The StatisticsImplementor is a singleton instance, therefore the ThreadLocal counters must be reset after a transaction is ended. When a transaction ends, the report is generated, and both the physical transaction time and the number of connection requests, issued during a particular transaction, are flushed to the log.

Because a Persistence Context can run multiple concurrent transactions, the report is generated at the end of each individual transaction.

To use a custom StatisticsImplementor instance, Hibernate requires a StatisticsFactory supplied as a configuration property. Taking a SessionFactoryImplementor parameter, the StatisticsImplementor building process has access to the Hibernate configuration data as well.

```
public class TransactionStatisticsFactory implements StatisticsFactory {
    @Override public StatisticsImplementor buildStatistics(
        SessionFactoryImplementor sessionFactory) {
        return new TransactionStatistics();
    }
}
```

The hibernate.stats.factory configuration property must contain the fully qualified name of the StatisticsFactory implementation class:

```
<property name="hibernate.stats.factory" value="com.vladmihalcea.book.hpjp.hiber\
nate.statistics.TransactionStatisticsFactory" />
```

When running the previous JTA connection release mode example along with this custom statistics collector, the following output is being displayed:

```
type=HISTOGRAM, name=connectionCounterHistogram, count=107,
min=1, max=10000, mean=162.41, stddev=1096.69,
median=1.0, p75=1.0, p95=50.0, p98=1000.0, p99=5000.0, p999=10000.0

type=TIMER, name=transactionTimer, count=107,
min=0.557524, max=1272.75, mean=27.16, stddev=152.57,
median=0.85, p75=1.24, p95=41.25, p98=283.50, p99=856.19, p999=1272.75,
mean_rate=36.32, rate_unit=events/second, duration_unit=milliseconds
```

 For a high-performance data access layer, statistics and metrics becomes mandatory requirements. The Hibernate statistics mechanism is a very powerful tool, allowing the development team to get a better insight into Hibernate inner workings.

8.4 Statement logging

An ORM tool can automatically generate DML statements, and it is the application developer responsibility to validate both their effectiveness as well as their overall performance impact. Deferring the SQL statement validation until the data access layer starts showing performance issues is risky, and it can even impact development cost. For this reason, SQL statement logging becomes relevant from the early stages of application development.

 When a business logic is implemented, the Definition of Done should include a review of all the associated data access layer operations. Following this rule can save much hassle when the enterprise system is deployed into production.

Although the JPA 2.1 does not feature a standard configuration property for logging SQL statements, most JPA implementations support this feature through framework-specific setups. For this purpose, Hibernate defines the following configuration properties:

Table 8.4: Connection release modes

Property	Description
hibernate.show_sql	Prints SQL statements to the console
hibernate.format_sql	Formats SQL statements before being logged or printed to the console
hibernate.use_sql_comments	Adds comments to the automatically generated SQL statement

Using the System console for logging is bad practice, a logging framework (e.g. Logback or Log4j) being a better alternative for it supports configurable appenders and logging levels.

 Because it prints to the console, the hibernate.show_sql property should be avoided.

Hibernate logs all SQL statements on a debug level in the org.hibernate.SQL logging hierarchy.

To enable statement logging, the following Logback logger must be added to the associated configuration file:

```
<logger name="org.hibernate.SQL" level="debug"/>
```

Because Hibernate uses `PreparedStatement(s)` exclusively, the bind parameter values are not available when the statement gets printed into the log:

```
INSERT INTO post (title, version, id) VALUES (?, ?, ?)
```

 Although bind parameters might be logged separately (e.g. `org.hibernate.type.descriptor.sql`), the most straight-forward way of logging SQL statements along with their runtime bind parameter values is to use an external `DataSource` proxy. Because the proxy intercepts all statement executions, the bind parameter values can be introspected and printed as well.

8.4.1 Statement formatting

By default, every SQL statement, no matter how long, is written as a single line of text. To increase readability, Hibernate can transform SQL statements in a human-readable format that spans over multiple log lines. This feature can be activated by setting the following configuration property:

```
<property name="hibernate.format_sql" value="true" />
```

With this setting in place, the previous statement can be formatted as follows:

```
insert
    into
        post
        (title, version, id)
    values
        (?, ?, ?)
```

Although formatting statements can improve readability, this setting is only suitable for the development phase. In a production system, logs are often parsed and aggregated in a centralized system, and the multi-line statement format can impact the log parsing mechanism. Once aggregated, logged queries can be formatted prior to being displayed in the application performance monitoring user interface.

The `hibernate.format_sql` property applies to logged statements only, and it does not propagate to the underlying JDBC `Driver` (SQL statements are still sent as single lines of text).

This way, the statement formatting does not have any effect when statements are logged through an external `DataSource` proxy.

8.4.2 Statement-level comments

Besides formatting, Hibernate can explain the statement generation process by appending SQL-level comments into the statement body. This feature allows the application developer to get a better understanding of the following processes:

- the entity state transition that triggered the currently executing statement
- the reason for choosing a join when fetching a given result set
- the explicit locking mechanism employed by the current statement.

By default, Hibernate does not append any SQL comment in the automatically generated statements, and, to enable this mechanism, the following Hibernate property must be configured:

```
<property name="hibernate.use_sql_comments" value="true" />
```

When persisting a `Post` entity, Hibernate explains the entity state transition associated with this particular statement through the following comment:

```
/* insert com.vladmihalcea.book.hpjp.util.providers.BlogEntityProvider$Post */
INSERT INTO post (title, version, id) VALUES (?, ?, ?)
```

As opposed to SQL statement formatting, SQL comments are generated not only during logging as they propagate to the underlying `Driver` as well.

Although it might be a useful technique for debugging purposes, in a production environment, it is better to leave it disabled, to reduce the database request networking overhead.

8.4.3 Logging parameters

Either the JDBC `Driver` or the `DataSource` must be proxied to intercept statement executions and log them along with the actual parameter values. Besides statement logging, a JDBC proxy can provide other cross-cutting features like long-running query detection or custom statement execution listeners.

8.4.3.1 DataSource-proxy

A lesser-known JDBC logging framework, datasource-proxy[9] provides support for custom JDBC statement execution listeners. In Java EE, not all application servers allow configuring an external `DataSource`, as they rely on their own custom implementations that bind the user supplied JDBC `Driver`. Because it can only decorate a `DataSource`, datasource-proxy might not be suitable for all Java EE environments.

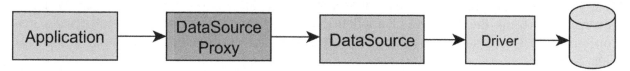

Figure 8.4: **DataSource-Proxy Architecture**

On the other hand, the programmatic configuration support fits the Java-based configuration approach taken by most modern Spring applications:

```
@Bean
public DataSource dataSource() {
    SLF4JQueryLoggingListener loggingListener = new SLF4JQueryLoggingListener();
    loggingListener.setQueryLogEntryCreator(new InlineQueryLogEntryCreator());
    return ProxyDataSourceBuilder
        .create(actualDataSource())
        .name(DATA_SOURCE_PROXY_NAME)
        .listener(loggingListener)
        .build();
}
```

---

[9]https://github.com/ttddyy/datasource-proxy

In the following example, datasource-proxy is used to log a batch insert of three `Prepared-Statement(s)`. Although normally a batch is printed in a single line of log, the output was split into multiple lines to fit the current page layout.

```
Name:DATA_SOURCE_PROXY, Time:6, Success:True,
Type:Prepared, Batch:True, QuerySize:1, BatchSize:3,
Query:["insert into post (title, version, id) values (?, ?, ?)"],
Params:[(Post no. 0, 0, 0), (Post no. 1, 0, 1), (Post no. 2, 0, 2)]
```

Not only the bind parameter values are now present, but, because they are grouped all together, it is very easy to visualize the batching mechanism too.

 With the custom statement listener support, datasource-proxy allows building a query count validator to assert the auto-generated statement count and, therefore, prevent N+1 query problems during the development phase.

8.4.3.2 P6Spy

P6Spy[10] was released in 2002, in an era when J2EE application servers were ruling the world of enterprise systems. Because Java EE application servers do not allow programmatic `DataSource` configuration, P6Spy supports a declarative configuration approach (through a `spy.properties` file).

P6Spy offers support for proxying both a JDBC `Driver` (which is suitable for Java EE applications) or a JDBC `DataSource` (supported by some Java EE containers and common practice for Spring enterprise applications).

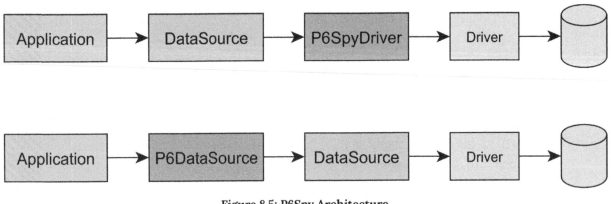

Figure 8.5: P6Spy Architecture

---

[10]https://github.com/p6spy/p6spy

Running the previous example gives the following output (formatting was also applied):

```
p6spy - 1448122491807|0|batch|connection 7|
        insert into post (title, version, id) values (?, ?, ?)|
        insert into post (title, version, id) values ('Post no. 0', 0, 0)
p6spy - 1448122491807|0|batch|connection 7|
        insert into post (title, version, id) values (?, ?, ?)|
        insert into post (title, version, id) values ('Post no. 1', 0, 1)
p6spy - 1448122491807|0|batch|connection 7|
        insert into post (title, version, id) values (?, ?, ?)|
        insert into post (title, version, id) values ('Post no. 2', 0, 2)
p6spy - 1448122491812|5|statement|connection 7|
        insert into post (title, version, id) values (?, ?, ?)|
        insert into post (title, version, id) values ('Post no. 2', 0, 2)
```

In the order of their occurrence, the output is built out of the following columns:

Table 8.5: P6Spy output

Field	Description
Timestamp	The statement execution timestamp
Execution time	The statement execution duration (in milliseconds)
Category	The current statement category (e.g. statement, batch)
Connection	The database connection identifier (as assigned by P6Spy)
Original statement	The original statement that was intercepted by P6Spy
Formatted statement	The statement with all parameter placeholders replaced with the actual bind values

The first three lines are associated with adding statements to the batch, while the fourth line is logging the actual batch execution (which also explains the *execution time* column value).

One very useful configuration is the outagedetection property, which can detect long-running statements.

9. Mapping Types and Identifiers

JPA addresses the Object/Relational mismatch by associating Java object types to database structures Assuming there is a `task` database table having four columns (e.g. `id`,`created_by`, `created_on`, and `status`), the JPA provider must map it to Domain Model consisting of two Java class (e.g. `Task` and `Change`).

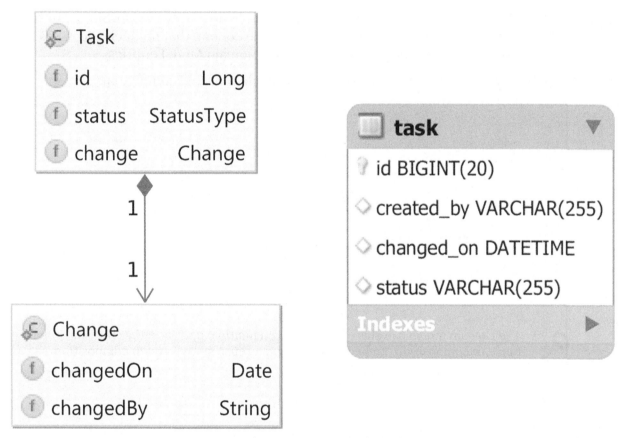

Figure 9.1: Type Mapping

JPA uses three main Object-Relational mapping elements: *type*, *embeddable*, and *entity*. In the previous diagram, the `Task` object is an entity, while the `Change` object is an embeddable type.

Both the entity and the embeddable group multiple Domain Model attributes by relying on Hibernate `Type(s)` to associate database column types with Java value objects (e.g. `String`, `Integer`, `Date`). The major difference between an entity and an embeddable is the presence of an identifier, which is used to associate a database table unique key (usually the primary key) with a Domain Model object attribute.

Although it is common practice to map all database columns, this is not a strict requirement. Sometimes it is more practical to use a root entity and several sub-entities, so each business case fetches just as much info as needed (while still benefiting from entity state management).

Identifiers are mandatory for entity elements, and an embeddable type is forbidden to have an identity of its own. Knowing the database table and the column that uniquely identifies any given row, Hibernate can correlate database rows with Domain Model entities.

An embeddable type groups multiple attributes in a single reusable component.

```
@Embeddable
public class Change {
    @Column(name = "changed_on")
    private Date changedOn;

    @Column(name = "created_by")
    private String changedBy;
}
```

 The Domain Model can share state between multiple entities either by using inheritance or composition. Embeddable types can reuse state through composition.

The composition association[1], defined by UML, is the perfect analogy for the relationship between an entity and an embeddable. When an entity includes an embeddable type, all its attributes become part of the owner entity.

The embeddable object cannot define its own identifier because otherwise, the entity has more than one identities. Lacking an identifier, the embeddable object cannot be managed by a Persistence Context, and its state is controlled by its parent entity.

Because they can have a significant impact on the overall application performance, the rest of the chapter discusses types and identifiers in greater detail.

---

[1]https://en.wikipedia.org/wiki/Object_composition

9.1 Types

For every supported database type, JDBC defines a `java.sql.JDBCType` enumeration. Since it builds on top of JDBC, Hibernate does the mapping between JDBC types and their associated Java counterparts (primitives or Objects).

9.1.1 Primitive types

Table 9.1: Primitive Types

Hibernate type	JDBC type	Java type
BooleanType	BIT	boolean, Boolean
NumericBooleanType	INTEGER (e.g. 0, 1)	boolean, Boolean
TrueFalseType	CHAR (e.g. 'F', 'f', 'T', 't')	boolean, Boolean
YesNoType	CHAR (e.g. 'N', 'n', 'Y', 'y')	boolean, Boolean
ByteType	TINYINT	byte, Byte
ShortType	SMALLINT	short, Short
CharacterType	CHAR	char, Character
CharacterNCharType	NCHAR	char, Character
IntegerType	INTEGER	int, Integer
LongType	BIGINT	long, Long
FloatType	FLOAT	float, Float
DoubleType	DOUBLE	double, Double
CharArrayType	VARCHAR	char[], Character[]

From one database system to another, the boolean type can be represented either as a BIT, BYTE, BOOLEAN or CHAR database type, so defines four Type(s) to resolve the boolean primitive type.

 Only non-nullable database columns can be mapped to Java primitives (boolean, byte, short, char, int, long, float, double). For mapping nullable columns, it is better to use the primitive wrappers instead (Boolean, Byte, Short, Char, Integer, Long, Float, Double).

9.1.2 String types

A Java `String` can consume as much memory as the Java Heap has available. On the other hand, database systems define both limited-size types (VARCHAR and NVARCHAR) and unlimited ones (TEXT, NTEXT, BLOB, and NCLOB).

To accommodate this mapping discrepancy, Hibernate defines the following `Type(s)`:

Table 9.2: String Types

Hibernate type	JDBC type	Java type
StringType	VARCHAR	String
StringNVarcharType	NVARCHAR	String
TextType	LONGVARCHAR	String
NTextType	LONGNVARCHAR	String
MaterializedClobType	CLOB	String
MaterializedNClobType	NCLOB	String

9.1.3 Date and Time types

When it comes to time, there are multiple Java or database representations, which explains the vast number of time-related Hibernate `Type(s)`.

Table 9.3: Date and Time Types

Hibernate type	JDBC type	Java type
DateType	DATE	Date
TimeType	TIME	Time
TimestampType	TIMESTAMP	Timestamp, Date
DbTimestampType	TIMESTAMP	Timestamp, Date
CalendarType	TIMESTAMP	Calendar, GregorianCalendar
CalendarDateType	DATE	Calendar, GregorianCalendar
CalendarTimeType	TIME	Calendar, GregorianCalendar
TimeZoneType	VARCHAR	TimeZone

 Handling time is tricky because of various time zones, leap seconds and daylight saving conventions. Storing timestamps in UTC (Coordinated Universal Time) and doing time zone transformations in the data layer is common practice.

9.1.4 Numeric types

Oracle can represent numbers up to 38 digits, therefore only fitting in a `BigInteger` or a `BigDecimal` (`java.lang.Long` and `java.lang.Double` can only store up to 8 bytes).

Table 9.4: Numeric Types

Hibernate type	JDBC type	Java type
BigIntegerType	NUMERIC	BigInteger
BigDecimalType	NUMERIC	BigDecimal

9.1.5 Binary types

For binary types, most database systems offer multiple storage choices (e.g. RAW, VARBINARY, BYTEA, BLOB, CLOB). In Java, the data access layer can use an array of byte(s), a JDBC `Blob` or `Clob`, or even a `Serializable` type, if the Java object was marshaled prior to being saved to the database.

Table 9.5: Binary Types

Hibernate type	JDBC type	Java type
BinaryType	VARBINARY	byte[], Byte[]
BlobType	BLOB	Blob
ClobType	CLOB	Clob
NClobType	NCLOB	Clob
MaterializedBlobType	BLOB	byte[], Byte[]
ImageType	LONGVARBINARY	byte[], Byte[]
SerializableType	VARBINARY	Serializable
SerializableToBlobType	BLOB	Serializable

9.1.6 UUID types

There are various ways of persisting a Java UUID (Universally Unique Identifier), and, based on the memory footprint, the most efficient storage types are the database-specific UUID column types.

Table 9.6: UUID Types

Hibernate type	JDBC type	Java type
UUIDBinaryType	BINARY	UUID
UUIDCharType	VARCHAR	UUID
PostgresUUIDType	OTHER	UUID

When not natively supported, a BINARY type requires fewer bytes than a VARCHAR, so the associated index has a smaller memory footprint too.

9.1.7 Other types

Hibernate can also map Java Enum(s), Class, URL, Locale and Currency too.

Table 9.7: Other Types

Hibernate type	JDBC type	Java type
EnumType	CHAR, LONGVARCHAR, VARCHAR INTEGER, NUMERIC, SMALLINT, TINYINT, BIGINT, DECIMAL, DOUBLE, FLOAT	Enum
ClassType	VARCHAR	Class
CurrencyType	VARCHAR	Currency
LocaleType	VARCHAR	Locale
UrlType	VARCHAR	URL

9.1.8 Custom types

Not only that it has a very rich set of data types, but PostgreSQL allows adding custom types as well (using the CREATE DOMAIN[2] DDL statement). Choosing the appropriate database type for each Domain Model field can really make a difference in terms of data access performance. Although there is a great variety of built-in Type(s), the application developer is not limited to the off-the-shelf ones only, and new Type(s) can be added without too much effort.

In the following example, the business logic requires monitoring access to an enterprise application. For this purpose, the data access layer stores the IP (Internet Protocol) addresses of each logged-in user.

Assuming this internal application uses the IPv4 protocol only, the IP addresses are stored in the Classless Inter-Domain Routing format (e.g. 192.168.123.231/24). PostgreSQL can store IPv4 addresses either in a cidr or inet type, or it can use a VARCHAR(18) column type.

The VARCHAR(18) column requires 18 characters, and, assuming a UTF-8 encoding, each IPv4 address needs at most 18 bytes. The smallest size address (e.g. 0.0.0.0/0) taking 9 characters, the VARCHAR(18) approach requires between 9 and 18 characters for each IPv4 address.

---

[2]http://www.postgresql.org/docs/9.5/static/sql-createdomain.html

The inet type is specially designed for IPv4 and IPv6 network addresses, and it also supports various network address specific operators (e.g. <, >, &&), as well as other address transforming functions (e.g. host(inet), netmask(inet)). As opposed to the VARCHAR(18) approach, the inet type requires only 7 bytes for each IPv4 address.

For it has a more compact size (the index can better fit into memory) and supporting many specific operators, the inet type is a much more attractive choice. Although, by default, Hibernate does not support inet types, adding a custom Hibernate Type is a straightforward task. The IPv4 address is encapsulated in its own wrapper, which can also define various address manipulation functions too.

```
public class IPv4 implements Serializable {

    private final String address;

    public IPv4(String address) {
        this.address = address;
    }

    public String getAddress() {
        return address;
    }

    @Override public boolean equals(Object o) {
        if (this == o) return true;
        if (o == null || getClass() != o.getClass()) return false;
        return Objects.equals(address, IPv4.class.cast(o).address);
    }

    @Override public int hashCode() {
        return Objects.hash(address);
    }

    public InetAddress toInetAddress() throws UnknownHostException {
        return Inet4Address.getByName(address);
    }
}
```

When an entity wants to change an IPv4 field, it must provide a new object instance. An immutable type is much easier to handle since its internal state does not change throughout the currently running Persistence Context.

All custom types must implement the UserType interface, and, since the ImmutableType takes care
of most UserType implementation details, the IPv4Type can focus on type-specific conversation
logic.

```
public class IPv4Type extends ImmutableType<IPv4> {

    public IPv4Type() {
        super(IPv4.class);
    }

    @Override public int[] sqlTypes() { return new int[]{ Types.OTHER}; }

    @Override public IPv4 get(ResultSet rs, String[] names,
        SessionImplementor session, Object owner) throws SQLException {
        String ip = rs.getString(names[0]);
        return (ip != null) ? new IPv4(ip) : null;
    }

    @Override public void set(PreparedStatement st, IPv4 value, int index,
        SessionImplementor session) throws SQLException {
        if (value == null) {
            st.setNull(index, Types.OTHER);
        } else {
            PGobject holder = new PGobject();
            holder.setType("inet");
            holder.setValue(value.getAddress());
            st.setObject(index, holder);
        }
    }
}
```

The get() method is used to map the inet field to an IPv4 object instance, while the set() is
used for transforming the IPv4 object to the PostgreSQL JDBC driver inet equivalent.

 Types.OTHER is used for mapping database types not supported by JDBC.

```java
public abstract class ImmutableType<T> implements UserType {
    private final Class<T> clazz;

    protected ImmutableType(Class<T> clazz) { this.clazz = clazz; }

    @Override public Object nullSafeGet(ResultSet rs, String[] names,
        SessionImplementor session, Object owner) throws SQLException {
        return get(rs, names, session, owner);
    }

    @Override public void nullSafeSet(PreparedStatement st, Object value,
        int index, SessionImplementor session) throws SQLException {
        set(st, clazz.cast(value), index, session);
    }

    @Override public Class<T> returnedClass() { return clazz; }

    @Override public boolean equals(Object x, Object y) {
        return Objects.equals(x, y);
    }

    @Override public int hashCode(Object x) { return x.hashCode(); }

    @Override public Object deepCopy(Object o) { return o; }

    @Override public boolean isMutable() { return false; }

    @Override public Serializable disassemble(Object o) {
        return (Serializable) o;
    }

    @Override public Object assemble(Serializable o, Object owner) { return o; }

    @Override
    public Object replace(Object o, Object target, Object owner) { return o; }

    protected abstract T get(ResultSet rs, String[] names,
        SessionImplementor session, Object owner) throws SQLException;

    protected abstract void set(PreparedStatement st, T value, int index,
        SessionImplementor session) throws SQLException;
}
```

The @Type annotation instructs Hibernates to use the IPv4Type for mapping the IPv4 field.

```
@Entity
public class Event {

    @Id @GeneratedValue
    private Long id;

    @Type(type = "com.vladmihalcea.book.hpjp.hibernate.type.IPv4Type")
    @Column(name = "ip", columnDefinition = "inet")
    private IPv4 ip;

    public Event() {}

    public Event(String address) {
        this.ip = new IPv4(address);
    }

    public Long getId() {
        return id;
    }

    public IPv4 getIp() {
        return ip;
    }

    public void setIp(String address) {
        this.ip = new IPv4(address);
    }
}
```

GiST operators

PostgreSQL 9.4 added GiST operator support[a] for inet and cidr column types. To enable this feature, a GiST index with the inet_ops operator class must be created on the associated inet columns.

```
CREATE INDEX ON event USING gist (ip inet_ops)
```

[a]http://www.postgresql.org/docs/9.4/static/gist-builtin-opclasses.html

Managing Event(s) is easy when Hibernate takes care of the underlying type conversation.

```
final AtomicReference<Event> eventHolder = new AtomicReference<>();

doInJPA(entityManager -> {
    entityManager.persist(new Event());
    Event event = new Event("192.168.0.231");
    entityManager.persist(event);
    eventHolder.set(event);
});

doInJPA(entityManager -> {
    Event event = entityManager.find(Event.class, eventHolder.get().getId());
    event.setIp("192.168.0.123");
});
```

Running the previous example generates the following SQL statements:

```
INSERT INTO event (ip, id) VALUES (NULL(OTHER), 1)
INSERT INTO event (ip, id) VALUES (`192.168.0.231`, 2)

SELECT e0_.id as id1_0_0_, e0_.ip as ip2_0_0_
FROM event e0_
WHERE e0_.id = 2

UPDATE event SET ip=`192.168.0.123` WHERE id = 2
```

One of the best aspects of using database-specific types is getting access to advanced querying capabilities. Because the GiST index allows inet_ops operators, the following query can be used to check if an Event was generated for a given subnetwork:

```
Event matchingEvent = (Event) entityManager.createNativeQuery(
    "SELECT {e.*} " +
    "FROM event e " +
    "WHERE " +
    "   e.ip && CAST(:network AS inet) = TRUE", Event.class)
.setParameter("network", "192.168.0.1/24")
.getSingleResult();

assertEquals("192.168.0.123", matchingEvent.getIp().getAddress());
```

9.2 Identifiers

All database tables must have a primary key column, so each row can be uniquely identified (the primary key must be both UNIQUE and NOT NULL).

> Although the SQL standard does not impose primary keys to be immutable, it is more practical[a] to avoid changing them.
>
> _____
> [a]https://asktom.oracle.com/pls/asktom/f?p=100:11:0::::P11_QUESTION_ID:5773459616034

The primary key can have a meaning in the real world, in which case it is a *natural* key, or it can be generated synthetically, in which case it is called a *surrogate* identifier.

For natural keys, unicity is enforced by a real-world unique sequence generator (e.g. National Identification Numbers, Social Security Numbers, Vehicle Identification Numbers). In reality, natural unique numbers might pose problems when the unique constraints do not hold true anymore. For example, a National Identification Number might yield unique numbers, but if the enterprise system must accommodate users coming from multiple countries, it is possible that two different countries assigned the same identifier.

The natural key can be composed of one or multiple columns. Compound natural keys might incur an additional performance penalty because multi-column joins are slower than single-column ones, and multi-column indexes have a bigger memory footprint too.

Natural keys must be sufficiently long to accommodate as many identifiers as the system needs throughout its lifecycle. Because primary keys are often indexed, the longer the key, the more memory an index entry requires. Each joined table includes a foreign key mirroring the parent primary key, and foreign keys are frequently indexed as well.

> ### Index memory impact
>
> Fixed-size non-numerical keys (e.g. CHAR, VARCHAR) are less efficient than numerical ones (e.g. INTEGER, BIGINT) both for joining (a simple key performs better than a compound one) or indexing (the more compact the data type, the less memory space is required by an associated index).
>
> A CHAR(17) natural key (e.g. Vehicle Identification Number) requires 17 characters (17 bytes when using ASCII characters and a UTF-8 encoding) as opposed to 4 bytes (32 bit INTEGER) or 8 bytes (64 bit BIGINT).

Surrogate keys are generated independently of the current row data, so table column constraints may evolve with time (changing a user birthday or email address). The surrogate key can be generated by a numerical sequence generator (e.g. a database identity column or a sequence), or it can be constructed by a pseudorandom number generator (e.g. GUID[3] or UUID[4]). Both the numerical and UUID keys have both pros and cons.

The UUID is defined by the RFC 4122[5] standard and it is stored as a 128-bit sequence. The GUID term refers to any globally unique identifier, which might comprise other non-standard implementations. For consistency, this chapter further refers to unique identifiers as UUID.

A UUID takes 128 bits, which is four times more than an INTEGER and twice as BIGINT. On the other hand, a UUID number has less chance of a conflict in a Multi-Master database replication topology. To avoid such conflicts, many relational database systems increment the identity or sequence numbers in steps, each node getting its own offset. Because UUIDs are not sequential, they induce fragmentation, and that can really affect the performance of clustered indexes.

Requiring less space and being more index-friendly, numerical sequences are preferred over UUID keys.

9.2.1 UUID identifiers

Nevertheless, some enterprise systems use UUID primary keys, so it is worth knowing what Hibernate types work best for this task. The UUID key can either be generated by the application using the java.util.UUID class or it can be assigned by the database system.

If the database system does not have a built-in UUID type, a BINARY(16) column type is preferred. Although a CHAR(32) column could also store the UUID textual representation, the additional space overhead makes it a less favorable pick.

---

[3]http://en.wikipedia.org/wiki/Globally_Unique_Identifier

[4]http://en.wikipedia.org/wiki/Universally_Unique_Identifier

[5]https://www.ietf.org/rfc/rfc4122.txt

Oracle

There is no UUID type in Oracle, so a RAW(16) column must be used instead. The SYS_GUID()[a] database function can generate a globally unique identifier.

---
[a]http://docs.oracle.com/database/121/SQLRF/functions202.htm#SQLRF06120

SQL Server

The uniqueidentifier[a] data type is used for storing GUID identifiers. The NEWID()[b] function can generate a UUID compatible with the RFC 4122 standard.

Because by default SQL Server uses clustered indexes for primary keys, to avoid the fragmentation effect, the NEWSEQUENTIALID()[c] function can assign pseudo-sequential UUID numbers (greater than previously generated ones). This guarantee is kept as long as the Windows server is not restarted.

---
[a]https://msdn.microsoft.com/en-us/library/ms187942.aspx
[b]https://msdn.microsoft.com/en-us/library/ms190348.aspx
[c]https://msdn.microsoft.com/en-us/library/ms189786.aspx

PostgreSQL

The UUID type[a] can store RFC 4122 compliant unique identifiers. The database does not offer a built-in UUID generation function, so the identifier must be generated by the data access layer.

---
[a]http://www.postgresql.org/docs/9.5/static/datatype-uuid.html

MySQL

The UUID must be stored in a BINARY(16) column type. The UUID()[a] functions can generate a 128-bit unique identifier. Because the UUID() function might cause problems for statement-based replication, passing the generated identifier as a variable[b] is a workaround to this limitation.

---
[a]http://dev.mysql.com/doc/refman/5.7/en/miscellaneous-functions.html#function_uuid
[b]https://dev.mysql.com/doc/refman/5.7/en/replication-features-functions.html

For generating UUID identifiers, Hibernate offers three generators (*assigned, uuid, uuid2*), which we'll be discussed in greater detail in the following sections.

9.2.1.1 The assigned generator

By simply omitting the @GeneratedValue[6] annotation, Hibernate falls back to the assigned identifier, which allows the data access layer to control the identifier generation process. The following example maps a java.util.UUID identifier to a BINARY(16) column type:

```
@Entity @Table(name = "post")
public class Post {

    @Id @Column(columnDefinition = "BINARY(16)")
    private UUID id;

    public Post() {}

    public Post(UUID id) {
        this.id = id;
    }
}
```

When persisting a *post*, Hibernate generates the following insert statement:

```
INSERT INTO post (id) VALUES
([86, 10, -104, 26, 60, -115, 79, 78, -118, -45, 64, 94, -64, -40, 66, 100])
```

The UUIDBinaryType translates the java.util.UUID to an array of byte(s) that is stored in the associated BINARY(16) column type.

 Because the identifier is generated in the data access layer, the database server is freed from this responsibility, and so it can allocate its resources to other data processing tasks.

Hibernate can also generate a UUID identifier on behalf of the application developer, as described in the following two sections.

---

[6]https://docs.oracle.com/javaee/7/api/javax/persistence/GeneratedValue.html

9.2.2 The legacy UUID generator

The UUID hex generator[7] is registered under the `uuid` name and generates hexadecimal UUID string representations. Using a 8-8-4-8-4 byte layout, the UUID hex generator is not compliant with the RFC 4122 standard, which uses a 8-4-4-4-12 byte format. The following code snippet depicts the `UUIDHexGenerator` mapping and the associated insert statement.

```
@Entity @Table(name = "post")
public class Post {

    @Id @Column(columnDefinition = "CHAR(32)")
    @GeneratedValue(generator = "uuid")
    @GenericGenerator(name = "uuid", strategy = "uuid")
    private String id;
}
```

```
INSERT INTO post (id) VALUES (402880e451724a820151724a83d00000)
```

9.2.2.1 The newer UUID generator

The newer UUID generator[8] is RFC 4122 compliant (variant 2) and is registered under the `uuid2` name (working with `java.lang.UUID`, `byte[]` and `String` Domain Model object types). Compared to the previous use case, the mapping and the test case look as follows:

```
@Entity @Table(name = "post")
public class Post {

    @Id @Column(columnDefinition = "BINARY(16)")
    @GeneratedValue(generator = "uuid2")
    @GenericGenerator(name = "uuid2", strategy = "uuid2")
    private UUID id;
}
```

```
INSERT INTO post (id) VALUES
([77, 2, 31, 83, -45, -98, 70, 40, -65, 40, -50, 30, -47, 16, 30, 124])
```

---

[7]https://docs.jboss.org/hibernate/orm/current/javadocs/org/hibernate/id/UUIDHexGenerator.html
[8]https://docs.jboss.org/hibernate/orm/current/javadocs/org/hibernate/id/UUIDGenerator.html

Being RFC 4122 compliant and able to operate with BINARY column type, the UUIDGenerator is preferred over the legacy UUIDHexGenerator.

9.2.3 Numerical identifiers

As previously explained, a numerical surrogate key is usually preferred since it takes less space and indexes work better with sequential identifiers. To generate numerical identifiers, most database systems offer either identity (or auto_increment) columns or sequence objects.

JPA defines the GenerationType[9] enumeration for all supported identifier generator types:

- IDENTITY is for mapping the entity identifier to a database identity column.
- SEQUENCE allocates identifiers by calling a given database sequence.
- TABLE is for relational databases that do not support sequences (e.g. MySQL 5.7), the *table* generator emulating a database sequence by using a separate table.
- AUTO decides the identifier generation strategy based on the current database dialect.

 As explained in the JDBC part, database sequences work better with batch updates and allow various application-side optimization techniques as well.

9.2.3.1 Identity generator

The identity column type (included in the SQL:2003[10] standard) is supported by Oracle 12c[11], SQL Server[12] and MySQL (AUTO_INCREMENT)[13], and it allows an INTEGER or a BIGINT column to be auto-incremented on demand.

The incrementation process is very efficient since it uses a lightweight locking mechanism, as opposed to the more heavyweight transactional course-grain locks. The only drawback is that the newly assigned value can only be known after executing the actual insert statement.

---

[9]https://docs.oracle.com/javaee/7/api/javax/persistence/GenerationType.html
[10]http://en.wikipedia.org/wiki/SQL:2003
[11]http://docs.oracle.com/database/121/SQLRF/statements_7002.htm#SQLRF55657
[12]http://msdn.microsoft.com/en-us/library/ms186775.aspx
[13]http://dev.mysql.com/doc/refman/5.7/en/example-auto-increment.html

---

Batch updates

Because Hibernate separates the id generation from the actual entity insert statement, entities using the identity generator may not participate in JDBC batch updates. Hibernate issues the insert statement during the `persist()` method call, therefore breaking the transactional write-behind caching semantic used for entity state transitions.

Even if some JDBC drivers allow fetching the associated generated keys when executing a batch update, Hibernate still needs an improvement in this regard.

The identity generator can be mapped as follows:

```
@Entity @Table(name = "post")
public class Post {

    @Id
    @GeneratedValue(strategy = GenerationType.IDENTITY)
    private Long id;
}
```

The following example demonstrates how the transaction write-behind caching model is circumvented by the identity column semantics. Although disabled by default, JDBC batching was enabled to compare results between identity and sequence generators.

```
doInJPA(entityManager -> {
    for (int i = 0; i < batchSize; i++) {
        entityManager.persist(new Post());
    }
    LOGGER.debug("Flush is triggered at commit-time");
});
```

Executing the previous test case generates the following output.

```
INSERT INTO post (id) VALUES (DEFAULT)
INSERT INTO post (id) VALUES (DEFAULT)

DEBUG - Flush is triggered at commit-time
```

Because the associated entity identifier can only be known after the insert statement is executed, Hibernate triggers the entity state transition prior to flushing the currently running Persistence Context.

9.2.3.2 Sequence generator

A sequence is a database object that generates consecutive numbers. Defined by the SQL:2003 standard, database sequences are supported by Oracle, SQL Server 2012 and PostgreSQL, and, compared to identity columns, sequences offer the following advantages:

- The same sequence can be used to populate multiple columns, even across tables.
- Values may be preallocated to improve performance.
- Allowing incremental steps, sequences can benefit from application-level optimization techniques.
- Because the sequence call can be decoupled from the actual insert statement, Hibernate does not disable JDBC batch updates.

To demonstrate the difference between the identity and the sequence identifier generators, the previous example is changed to use a database sequence this time.

```
@Entity @Table(name = "post")
public class Post {

    @Id
    @GeneratedValue(strategy=GenerationType.SEQUENCE)
    private Long id;
}
```

Running the previous test case generates the following output:

```
CALL NEXT VALUE FOR hibernate_sequence
CALL NEXT VALUE FOR hibernate_sequence

DEBUG - Flush is triggered at commit-time

INSERT INTO post (id) VALUES (1, 2)
```

When executing the `persist()` method, Hibernate calls the associated database sequence and fetches an identifier for the newly persisted entity. The actual insert statement is postponed until flush time, which allows Hibernate to take advantage of JDBC batching.

9.2.3.3 Table generator

Because of the mismatch between the identifier generator and the transactional write-behind cache, JPA offers an alternative sequence-like generator that works even when sequences are not natively supported.

A database table is used to hold the latest sequence value, and row-level locking is employed to prevent two concurrent connections from acquiring the same identifier value.

Escaping transactional row-level locking

A database sequence is a non-transactional object because the sequence value allocation happens outside of the transactional context associated with the database connection requesting a new identifier. Database sequences use dedicated locks to prevent concurrent transactions from acquiring the same value, but locks are released as soon as the counter is incremented. This design ensures minimal contention even when the sequence is used concomitantly by multiple concurrent transactions.

Using a database table as a sequence is challenging, as, to prevent two transactions from getting the same sequence value, row-level locking must be used. However, unlike the sequence object locks, the row-level lock is transactional, and, once acquired, it can only be released when the current transaction ends (either committing or rolling back). This would be a terrible scalability issue because a long-running transaction would prevent any other transaction from acquiring a new sequence value.

To cope with this limitation, a separate database transaction is used for fetching a new sequence value. This way, the row-level lock associated with incrementing the sequence counter value can be released as soon as the sequence update transaction ends.

For local transactions, a new transaction means fetching another database connection and committing it after executing the sequence processing logic. This can put additional pressure on the underlying connection pool, especially if there is already a significant contention for database connections.

In a JTA environment, the currently running transaction must be suspended, and the sequence value is fetched in a separate transaction. The JTA transaction manager has to do additional work to accommodate the transaction context switch, and that can also have an impact on the overall application performance.

 Without any application-level optimization, the row-level locking approach can become a performance bottleneck if the sequence logic is called way too often.

To continue the previous example, the *post* uses the table generator this time:

```
@Entity @Table(name = "post")
public class Post {

    @Id
    @GeneratedValue(strategy=GenerationType.TABLE)
    private Long id;
}
```

The following output is obtained when inserting a new *post*:

```
SELECT tbl.next_val
FROM hibernate_sequences tbl
WHERE tbl.sequence_name=default
FOR UPDATE

INSERT INTO hibernate_sequences (sequence_name, next_val)
VALUES (default, 1)

UPDATE hibernate_sequences SET next_val=2
WHERE next_val=1 AND sequence_name=default

SELECT tbl.next_val
FROM hibernate_sequences tbl
WHERE tbl.sequence_name=default
FOR UPDATE

UPDATE hibernate_sequences SET next_val=3
WHERE next_val=2 AND sequence_name=default

DEBUG - Flush is triggered at commit-time

INSERT INTO post (id) values (1, 2)
```

The table generator benefits from JDBC batching, but every table sequence update incurs three steps:

- The lock statement is executed to ensure that the same sequence value is not allocated for two concurrent transactions.
- The current value is incremented in the data access layer.
- The new value is saved back to the database and the secondary transaction is committed to release the row-level lock.

Unlike identity columns and sequences, which can increment the sequence in a single request, the table generator entails a significant performance overhead. For this reason, Hibernate comes with a series of optimizers which can improve performance for both sequence and table generators.

 Although it is a portable identifier generation strategy, the table generator introduces a serializable execution (the row-level lock), which can hinder scalability. Compared to this application-level sequence generation technique, identity columns and sequences are highly optimized for high concurrency scenarios and should be the preferred choice anyway.

9.2.3.4 Optimizers

As previously mentioned, both the sequence and the table identifier generator have multiple implementations which can improve the performance of the identifier generation process. The sequence and table generators can be split into two categories:

- Legacy implementations (being deprecated since Hibernate 5.0) like SequenceGenerator, SequenceHiLoGenerator and MultipleHiLoPerTableGenerator.
- Newer and more efficient implementations such as SequenceStyleGenerator and TableGenerator.

These two categories are not compatible, and the application developer must either choose the legacy identifiers or the enhanced ones. Prior to Hibernate 5.0, the legacy identifier generators were provided by default and the application developer could switch to the newer ones by setting the following configuration property:

```
<property name="hibernate.id.new_generator_mappings" value="true"/>
```

Hibernate 5 has decided to drop support for the legacy identifiers and to use the enhanced ones by default.

Among the legacy identifier generators, the SequenceGenerator did not offer any optimization, as every new identifier value would require a call to the underlying database sequence. On the other hand, the SequenceHiLoGenerator and the MultipleHiLoPerTableGenerator offered a *hi/lo* optimization mechanism aimed to reduce the number of calls to a database server. Although these generators are deprecated, the legacy *hi/lo* algorithm is still a valid optimizer even for the newer identifier generators.

9.2.3.4.1 The hi/lo algorithm

The hi/lo algorithm splits the sequences domain into *hi* groups. A *hi* value is assigned synchronously, and every *hi* group is given a maximum number of *lo* entries, that can by assigned off-line without worrying about identifier value conflicts.

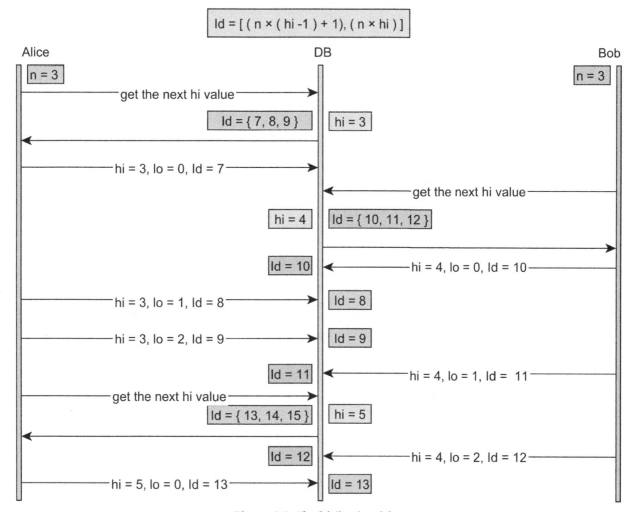

Figure 9.2: The hi/lo algorithm

1. The *hi* token is assigned either by the database sequence or the table generator, so two consecutive calls are guaranteed to see monotonically increasing values.
2. Once a *hi* token is retrieved, the *increment size (n - the number of *lo* entries)* defines the range of identifier values a transaction can safely allocate. The identifiers range is bounded by the following interval: $Id = [n \times (hi - 1) + 1, n \times hi]$ and the allocation is done as follows:
   - the current group values start from $n \times (hi - 1) + 1$
   - the *lo* value is taken from the following interval: {$$} [0, n - 1] {$$}
   - by adding the *lo* value to the initial group value, a unique identifier is obtained.
3. When all *lo* values are used, a new *hi* value is fetched, and the cycle continues.

The following example shows how the hi/lo algorithm works in practice. The entity is mapped as follows:

```
@Entity
public class Post {

    @Id
    @GeneratedValue(strategy = GenerationType.SEQUENCE, generator = "hilo")
    @GenericGenerator(
        name = "hilo",
        strategy = "org.hibernate.id.enhanced.SequenceStyleGenerator",
        parameters = {
            @Parameter(name = "sequence_name", value = "sequence"),
            @Parameter(name = "initial_value", value = "1"),
            @Parameter(name = "increment_size", value = "3"),
            @Parameter(name = "optimizer", value = "hilo")
        }
    )
    private Long id;
}
```

Because the increment size is 3, the following test inserts 4 entities to show the number of database sequence calls.

```
doInJPA(entityManager -> {
    for(int i = 0; i < 4; i++) {
        Post post = new Post();
        entityManager.persist(post);
    }
});
```

Running the previous test generates the following output:

```
CALL NEXT VALUE FOR hilo_seqeunce
CALL NEXT VALUE FOR hilo_seqeunce

INSERT INTO post (id) VALUES (1)
INSERT INTO post (id) VALUES (2)
INSERT INTO post (id) VALUES (3)
INSERT INTO post (id) VALUES (4)
```

The first sequence call is for the first three values, while the second one is generated when reaching the forth entity that needs to be persisted. The more inserts a transaction requires, the better the performance gain from reducing the number of database sequence calls.

Unfortunately, this optimizer has a major limitation. Because the database sequence only assigns group values, all database clients must be aware of this algorithm. If the DBA must insert a row in the table above, he must use the hi/lo algorithm to determine the range of values that she can safely use.

For this reason, Hibernate offers other optimizer algorithms that are interoperable with external clients, unaware of the application-level optimization technique in use.

9.2.3.4.2 The default sequence identifier generator

The JPA identifier generator strategy only specifies the identifier type and not the algorithm used for generating such identifiers.

For the sequence generator, considering the following JPA mapping:

```
@Id
@GeneratedValue(generator = "sequence", strategy=GenerationType.SEQUENCE)
@SequenceGenerator(name = "sequence", allocationSize = 3)
private Long id;
```

Hibernate chooses the SequenceHiLoGenerator when the hibernate.id.new_generator_mappings configuration property is false. This was the default setting for Hibernate 3 and 4. The legacy SequenceHiLoGenerator uses the hi/lo algorithm, and, if the allocation size is greater than one, database interoperability could be compromised (every insert must be done according to the hi/lo algorithm rules).

If the aforementioned configuration property is true (the default setting for Hibernate 5), then the JPA mapping above will use the SequenceStyleGenerator instead.

Unlike its previous predecessor, the SequenceStyleGenerator uses configurable identifier optimizer strategies, and the application developer can even supply its own optimization implementation.

9.2.3.4.3 The default table identifier generator

Just like with sequences, the JPA table generator mapping can use a legacy or an enhanced generator, depending on the current Hibernate configuration settings:

```
@Id
@GeneratedValue(generator = "table", strategy=GenerationType.TABLE)
@TableGenerator(name = "table", allocationSize = 3)
private Long id;
```

If the `hibernate.id.new_generator_mappings` configuration property is false, then Hibernate will choose the `MultipleHiLoPerTableGenerator`. This generator requires a single table for managing multiple identifiers, and just like `SequenceHiLoGenerator`, it also uses the hi/lo algorithm by default.

When the enhanced identifier generators are activated, Hibernate uses the `TableGenerator` instead, which can also take configurable optimizer strategies.

For both the enhanced sequence and the table identifier generator, Hibernate comes with the following built-in optimizers:

Table 9.8: Hibernate identifier optimizers

Optimizer type	Implementation class	Description
none	NoopOptimizer	Every identifier is fetched using a new roundtrip to the database
hi/lo	HiLoOptimizer	It allocates identifiers by using the legacy hi/lo algorithm
pooled	PooledOptimizer	It is an enhanced version of the hi/lo algorithm which is interoperable with other systems unaware of this identifier generator
pooled-lo	PooledLoOptimizer	It is a variation of the pooled optimizer, the database sequence value representing the *lo* value instead of the *hi* one

By default, the `SequenceStyleGenerator` and `TableGenerator` identifier generators uses the `pooled` optimizer. If the `hibernate.id.optimizer.pooled.prefer_lo` configuration property is set to true, Hibernate will use the `pooled-lo` optimizer by default.

Both the `pooled` and the `pooled-lo` encode the database sequence value into the identifier range boundaries, so allocating a new value using the actual database sequence call does not interfere with the identifier generator allocation process.

9.2.3.4.4 The pooled optimizer

The pooled optimizer can be configured as follows:

```
@Entity
public class Post {

    @Id
    @GeneratedValue(strategy = GenerationType.SEQUENCE, generator = "pooled")
    @GenericGenerator(
        name = "pooled",
        strategy = "org.hibernate.id.enhanced.SequenceStyleGenerator",
        parameters = {
            @Parameter(name = "sequence_name", value = "sequence"),
            @Parameter(name = "initial_value", value = "1"),
            @Parameter(name = "increment_size", value = "3"),
            @Parameter(name = "optimizer", value = "pooled")
        }
    )
    private Long id;
}
```

The increment size gives the range of values allocated by the sequence generator with one database roundtrip. Although it is inefficient to flush the Persistence Context after every persist method call, in this test, the flush outlines when the database sequence was called.

```
doInJPA(entityManager -> {
    for (int i = 0; i < 5; i++) {
        entityManager.persist(new Post());
        entityManager.flush();
    }
    entityManager.unwrap(Session.class).doWork(connection -> {
        try(Statement statement = connection.createStatement()) {
            statement.executeUpdate(
                "INSERT INTO post VALUES NEXT VALUE FOR sequence"
            );
        }
    });
    for (int i = 0; i < 3; i++) {
        entityManager.persist(new Post());
        entityManager.flush();
    }
});
```

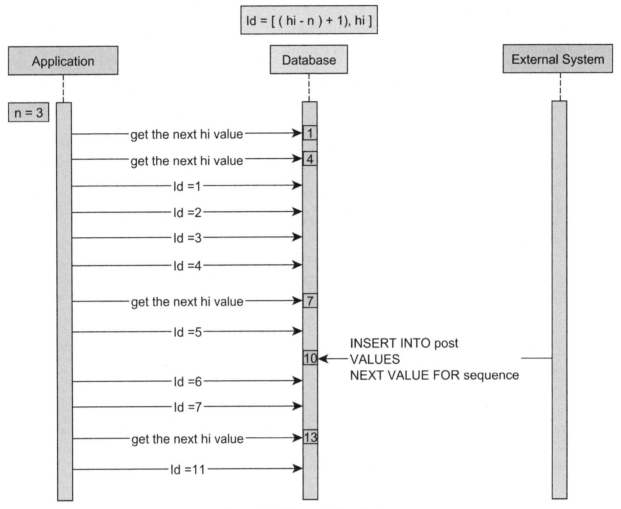

Figure 9.3: The pooled optimizer

If increment size (n) is the number of identifiers within a range, the pooled optimizer will generate identifiers with the following formula: $Id = [(hi - n) + 1, hi]$.

- The first sequence call generates the *lo* value and the second one determines the *hi* value, so the first range of identifiers is {2, 3, 4}.
- When adding the 5th entity, the pooled optimizer calls the sequence again and obtains the next *hi* value, the next identifier range being {5, 6, 7}.
- After inserting the 5th entity, an external system adds a *post* row and assigns the primary key with the value returned by the sequence call.
- The Hibernate application thread resumes and inserts the identifiers 6 and 7.
- The 8th entity requires a new sequence call, and so a new range is allocated {11, 12, 13}.

9.2.3.4.5 The pooled-lo optimizer

By changing the previous mapping to use the `pooled-lo` optimizer, the identifier generation changes as follows:

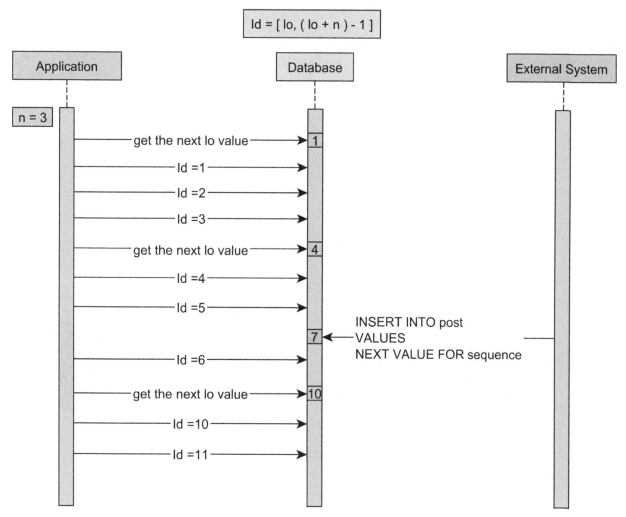

Figure 9.4: The pooled-lo optimizer

If increment size (n) is the number of identifiers within a range, the pooled-lo optimizer will generate identifiers with the following formula: $Id = [lo, (lo + n) - 1]$.

- The first sequence call generates the *lo* value, so the first range of identifiers is {1, 2, 3}.
- When adding the 4th entity, the pooled-lo optimizer calls the sequence and obtains the next *lo* value, the next identifier range being {4, 5, 6}.
- After inserting the 5th entity, an external system adds a *post* row and assigns the primary key with the value returned by the sequence call.
- The Hibernate application thread resumes and inserts the identifier 6.
- The 7th entity requires a new sequence call, and so a new range is allocated {10, 11, 12}.

9.2.3.5 Optimizer gain

To visualize the performance gain of using sequence and table generator optimizers, the following test measures the identifier allocation time when inserting 50 *post* entities and while varying the increment size (1, 5, 10, and 50).

9.2.3.5.1 Sequence generator performance gain

When using a sequence generator with the default pooled optimizer, the following 99th percentile is being recorded:

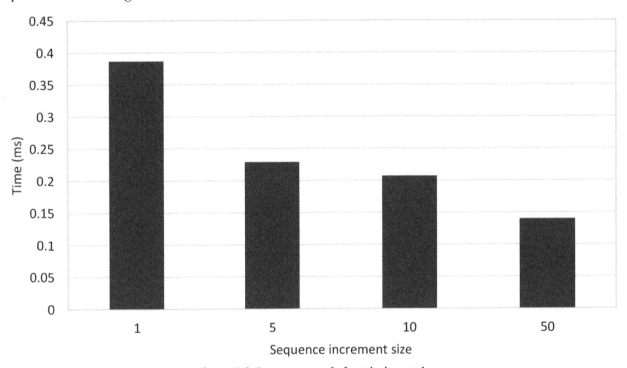

Figure 9.5: Sequence pooled optimizer gain

Database sequences are fast, but, even so, the pooled optimizer manages to reduce the identifier generation time considerably.

For write-intensive applications, the increment size needs to be adjusted according to the number of rows being inserted in one transaction.

9.2.3.5.2 Table generator performance gain

The same test suite is run against a table generator with a pooled optimizer, and the increment size also varies between 1, 5, 10, and 50. Because of the row-level locking and the extra database connection switch overhead, the table generator is less efficient than a database sequence.

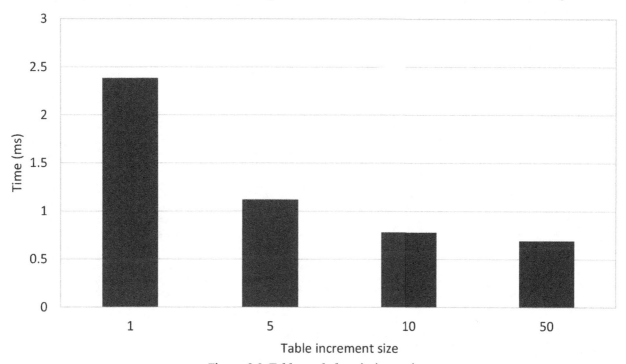

Figure 9.6: Table pooled optimizer gain

Just like with the database sequence, the pooled optimizer managed to reduce the time it took for assigning a new entity identifier.

9.2.3.6 Identifier generator performance

To evaluate the concurrency cost of each identifier generators, the following test measures the time it takes to insert 100 post entities when multiple running threads are involved. JDBC batching is enabled, and the connection pool is adjusted to accommodate the maximum number of database connection required (e.g. 32).

 In reality, the application might not be configured with so many database connections, and the table generator connection acquisition cost might be even higher.

The first relational database system under test supports identity columns, so it is worth measuring how the identifier and the table generator compete. Unlike the previous test, this one measures the total time taken for inserting all entities, and not just the identifier allocation time interval.

Each test iteration increases contention by allocating more worker threads that need to execute the same database insert load.

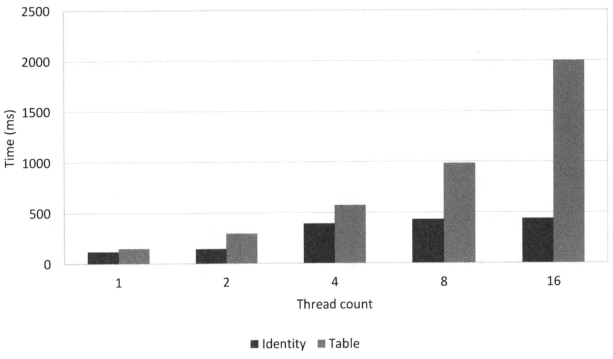

Figure 9.7: Identity vs. Table

Even if it cannot benefit from JDBC batching, the identity generator still manages to outperform the table generator, which uses a pooled optimizer with an increment size of 100.

 The more threads are used, the less efficient the table generator becomes. On the other hand, identity columns scale much better with more concurrent transactions.

Even if does not support JDBC batching, native identity columns are still a valid choice, and, in future, Hibernate might even support batch inserts for those as well.

The gap between the sequence and the table generator is even higher because, just like the table generator, the sequence generator can also take advantage of the pooled optimizer as well as JDBC batch inserts.

Running the same test against a relational database supporting sequences, the following results are being recorded:

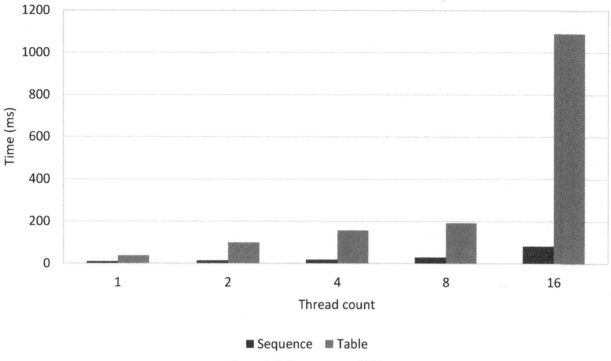

Figure 9.8: Sequence vs. Table

The performance impact of the table generator becomes noticeable in high concurrent environments, where the row-level locking and the database connection switch introduces a serial execution.

Because they use lightweight synchronization mechanisms, database sequences scale better than row-level locking concurrency control mechanisms.

Database sequences are the most efficient Hibernate identifier choice, allowing sequence call optimizers and without compromising JDBC batching.

10. Relationships

In a relational database, associations are formed by correlating rows belonging to different tables. A relationship is established when a child table defines a foreign key referencing the primary key of its parent table. Every database association is built on top of foreign keys, resulting three table relationship types:

- *one-to-many* is the most common relationship, and it associates a row from a parent table to multiple rows in a child table.
- *one-to-one* is a variation of the *one-to-many* relationship with an additional uniqueness constraint on the child-side foreign key.
- *many-to-many* requires a junction table containing two foreign keys that reference two different parent tables.

The following diagram depicts all these three table relationships:

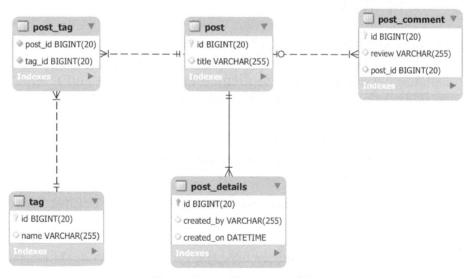

Figure 10.1: Table relationships

The post table has a one-to-many relationship with the post_comment table because a post row might be referenced by multiple comments. The one-to-many relationship is established through the post_id column which has a foreign key referencing the post table primary key. Because a post_comment cannot exist without a post, the post is the parent-side while the post_comment is the child-side.

The post table has a one-to-one relationship with the post_details. Like the one-to-many association, the one-to-one relationship involves two tables and a foreign key. The foreign key has a uniqueness constraint, so only one child row can reference a parent record.

The post and the tag are both independent tables and neither one is a child of the other. A post can feature several tag(s), while a tag can also be associated with multiple post(s). This is a typical many-to-many association, and it requires a junction table to resolve the child-side of these two parent entities. The junction table requires two foreign keys referencing the two parent tables.

 The foreign key is, therefore, the most important construct in building a table relationship, and, in a relation database, the child-side controls a table relationship.

In a relational database, the foreign key is associated with the child-side only. For this reason, the parent-side has no knowledge of any associated child relationships, and, from a mapping perspective, table relationships are always unidirectional (the child foreign key references the parent primary key).

10.1 Relationship types

When mapping a JPA entity, besides the underlying table columns, the application developer can map entity relationships either in one direction or in a bidirectional way. This is another impedance mismatch between the object-oriented Domain Model and relational database system because, when using an ORM tool, the parent and the child-side can reference each other.

A relationship is unidirectional if only one entity side maps the table relationship and is bidirectional if the table relationship can be navigated in both directions (either from the entity parent-side or the child-side).

To properly represent both sides of an entity relationship, JPA defines four association mapping constructs:

- @ManyToOne represents the child-side (where the foreign key resides) in a database one-to-many table relationship.
- @OneToMany is associated with the parent-side of a one-to-many table relationship.
- @ElementCollection defines a one-to-many association between an entity and multiple value types (basic or embeddable).
- @OneToOne is used for both the child-side and the parent-side in a one-to-one table relationship.
- @ManyToMany mirrors a many-to-many table relationship.

Because the entity relationship choice has a considerable impact on the overall application performance, this chapter analyzes the data access operation efficiency of all these JPA associations.

Mapping collections

In a relational database, all table relationships are constructed using foreign keys and navigated through SQL queries. JPA allows mapping both the foreign key side (the child entity has a reference to its parent), as well as the parent side (the parent entity has one or more child entities).

Although `@OneToMany`, `@ManyToMany` or `@ElementCollection` are convenient from a data access perspective (entity state transitions can be cascaded from parent entities to children), they are definitely not free of cost. The price for reducing data access operations is paid in terms of result set fetching flexibility and performance. A JPA collection, either of entities or value types (basic or embeddables), binds a parent entity to a query that usually fetches all the associated child records. Because of this, the entity mapping becomes sensitive to the number of child entries.

If the children count is relatively small, the performance impact of always retrieving all child entities might be unnoticeable. However, if the number of child records grows too large, fetching the entire children collection may become a performance bottleneck. Unfortunately, the entity mapping is done during the early phases of a project development, and the development team might be unaware of the number of child records a production system exhibits.

Not just the mere size can be problematic, but also the number of attributes of the child entity. Because entities are usually fetched as a whole, the result set is, therefore, proportional to the number of columns the child table contains. Even if a collection is fetched lazily, Hibernate might still require to fully load each entity when the collection is accessed for the first time. Although Hibernate supports extra lazy collection fetching, this is only a workaround and does not address the root problem.

Alternatively, every collection mapping can be replaced by a data access query, which can use a SQL projection that is tailored to the data requirements of each business use case. This way, the query can take business case specific filtering criteria. Although JPA 2.1 does not support dynamic collection filtering, Hibernate offers Persistence Context-bound collection `Filters`.

 When handling large data sets, it is good practice to limit the result set size, both for UI (to increase responsiveness) or batch processing tasks (to avoid long running transactions). Just because JPA offers supports collection mapping, it does not mean they are mandatory for every domain model mapping. Until there is a clear understanding of the number of child records (or if there is even need to fetch child entities entirely), it is better to postpone the collection mapping decision. For high-performance systems, a data access query is often a much more flexible alternative.

10.2 @ManyToOne

The @ManyToOne relationship is the most common JPA association, and it maps exactly to the one-to-many table relationship. When using a @ManyToOne association, the underlying foreign key is controlled by the child-side, no matter the association is unidirectional or bidirectional.

This section focuses on unidirectional @ManyToOne relationships only, the bidirectional case being further discussed with the @OneToMany relationship. In the following example, the Post entity represents the parent-side, while the PostComment is the child-side.

As already mentioned, the JPA entity relationship diagram matches exactly the one-to-many table relationship.

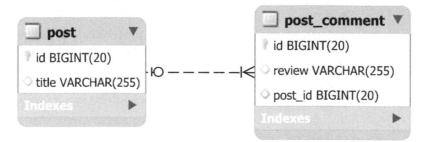

Figure 10.2: The one-to-many table relationship

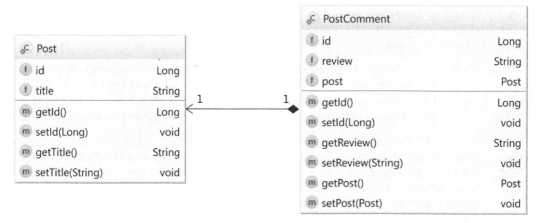

Figure 10.3: @ManyToOne relationship

Instead of mapping the post_id foreign key column, the PostComment uses a @ManyToOne relationship to the parent Post entity. The PostComment can be associated with an existing Post object reference, and the PostComment can also be fetched along with the Post entity.

```
@ManyToOne
@JoinColumn(name = "post_id")
private Post post;
```

Hibernate translates the internal state of the @ManyToOne Post object reference to the post_id foreign key column value.

If the @ManyToOne attribute is set to a valid Post entity reference:

```
Post post = entityManager.find(Post.class, 1L);
PostComment comment = new PostComment("My review");
comment.setPost(post);
entityManager.persist(comment);
```

Hibernate will generate an inscrt statement populating the post_id column with the identifier of the associated Post entity.

```
INSERT INTO post_comment (post_id, review, id) VALUES (1, 'My review', 2)
```

If the Post attribute is later set to null:

```
comment.setPost(null);
```

The post_id column will also be updated with a NULL value:

```
UPDATE post_comment SET post_id = NULL, review = 'My review' WHERE id = 2
```

Because the @ManyToOne association controls the foreign key directly, the automatically generated DML statements are very efficient.

Actually, the best-performing JPA associations always rely on the child-side to translate the JPA state to the foreign key column value.

This is one of the most important rules in JPA relationship mapping, and it will be further emphasized for @OneToMany, @OneToOne and even @ManyToMany associations.

10.3 @OneToMany

While the @ManyToOne association is the most natural mapping of the one-to-many table relationship, the @OneToMany association can also mirror this database relationship, but only when being used as a bidirectional mapping. A unidirectional @OneToMany association uses an additional junction table, which no longer fits the one-to-many table relationship semantics.

10.3.1 Bidirectional @OneToMany

The bidirectional @OneToMany association has a matching @ManyToOne child-side mapping that controls the underlying one-to-many table relationship. The parent-side is mapped as a collection of child entities.

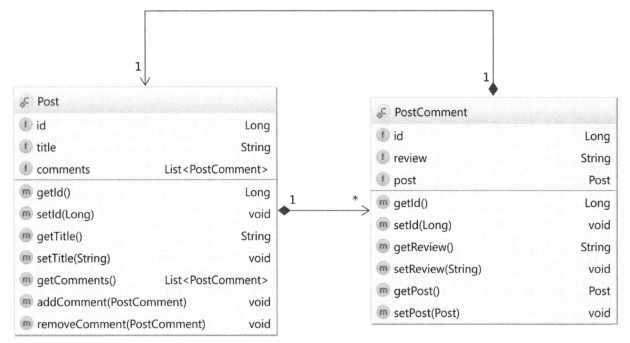

Figure 10.4: Bidirectional @OneToMany relationship

In a bidirectional association, only one side can control the underlying table relationship. For the bidirectional @OneToMany mapping, it is the child-side @ManyToOne association in charge of keeping the foreign key column value in sync with the in-memory Persistence Context. This is the reason why the bidirectional @OneToMany relationship must define the mappedBy attribute, indicating that it only mirrors the @ManyToOne child-side mapping.

```
@OneToMany(mappedBy = "post", cascade = CascadeType.ALL, orphanRemoval = true)
private List<PostComment> comments = new ArrayList<>();
```

 Even if the child-side is in charge of synchronizing the entity state changes with the database foreign key column value, a bidirectional association must always have both the parent-side and the child-side in sync.

To synchronize both ends, it is practical to provide parent-side helper methods that add/remove child entities.

```
public void addComment(PostComment comment) {
    comments.add(comment);
    comment.setPost(this);
}

public void removeComment(PostComment comment) {
    comments.remove(comment);
    comment.setPost(null);
}
```

One of the major advantages of using a bidirectional association is that entity state transitions can be cascaded from the parent entity to its children. In the following example, when persisting the parent Post entity, all the PostComment child entities are persisted as well.

```
Post post = new Post("First post");

PostComment comment1 = new PostComment("My first review");
post.addComment(comment1);
PostComment comment2 = new PostComment("My second review");
post.addComment(comment2);

entityManager.persist(post);
```

```
INSERT INTO post (title, id) VALUES ('First post', 1)
INSERT INTO post_comment (post_id, review, id) VALUES (1, 'My first review', 2)
INSERT INTO post_comment (post_id, review, id) VALUES (1, 'My second review', 3)
```

When removing a comment from the parent-side collection:

```
post.removeComment(comment1);
```

The orphan removal attribute instructs Hibernate to generate a delete DML statement on the targeted child entity:

```
DELETE FROM post_comment WHERE id = 2
```

Equality-based entity removal

The helper method for the child entity removal relies on the underlying child object equality for matching the collection entry that needs to be removed.

If the application developer does not choose to override the default `equals` and `hashCode` methods, the `java.lang.Object` identity-based equality is going to be used. The problem with this approach is that the application developer must supply a child entity object reference that is contained in the current child collection.

Sometimes child entities are loaded in one web request and saved in a `HttpSession` or a Stateful Enterprise Java Bean. Once the Persistence Context, which loaded the child entity is closed, the entity becomes detached. If the child entity is sent for removal into a new web request, the child entity must be reattached or merged into the current Persistence Context. This way, if the parent entity is loaded along with its child entities, the removal operation will work properly since the removing child entity is already managed and contained in the children collection.

If the entity has not changed, reattaching this child entity will be redundant and so the `equals` and the `hashCode` methods must be overridden to express equality in terms of a unique business key. In case the child entity has a `@NaturalId` or a unique attribute set, the `equals` and the `hashCode` methods can be implemented on top of that. Assuming the `PostComment` entity has the following two columns whose combination render a unique business key, the equality contract can be implemented as follows:

```
private String createdBy;

@Temporal(TemporalType.TIMESTAMP)
private Date createdOn = new Date();

@Override
public boolean equals(Object o) {
    if (this == o) return true;
    if (o == null || getClass() != o.getClass()) return false;
    PostComment that = (PostComment) o;
    return Objects.equals(createdBy, that.createdBy) &&
            Objects.equals(createdOn, that.createdOn);
}

@Override
public int hashCode() {
    return Objects.hash(createdBy, createdOn);
}
```

Identifier-based equality

The java.lang.Object.equals[a] method Javadoc demands the strategy be *reflexive*, *symmetric*, *transitive*, and *consistent*.

While the first three equality properties (*reflexive*, *symmetric*, *transitive*) are easier to achieve, especially with the `java.util.Objects`[b] equals and hashCode utilities, *consistency* requires more diligence.

 For a JPA or Hibernate entity, *consistency* means that the equality result is *reflexive*, *symmetric* and *transitive* across all entity state transitions (e.g. new/transient, managed, detached, removed).

If the entity has a `@NaturalId` attribute, then ensuring *consistency* is simple since the natural key is assigned even from the transient state, and this attribute never changes afterward. However, not all entities have a natural key to use for equality checks, so another table column must be used instead.

Luckily, most database tables have a primary key, which uniquely identifies each row of a particular table. The only caveat is to ensure *consistency* across all entity state transitions.

A naive implementation would look like this:

```
@Entity
public class Post {

    @Id @GeneratedValue
    private Long id;

    @Override
    public boolean equals(Object o) {
        if (this == o) return true;
        if (!(o instanceof Post)) return false;
        return Objects.equals(id, ((Post) o).id);
    }

    @Override
    public int hashCode() {
        return Objects.hash(id);
    }
}
```

---

[a]https://docs.oracle.com/javase/8/docs/api/java/lang/Object.html#equals-java.lang.Object-
[b]https://docs.oracle.com/javase/7/docs/api/java/util/Objects.html

Now, when running the following test case:

```
Set<Post> tuples = new HashSet<>();
tuples.add(entity);
assertTrue(tuples.contains(entity));

doInJPA(entityManager -> {
    entityManager.persist(entity);
    entityManager.flush();
    assertTrue(tuples.contains(entity));
});
```

The final assertion will fail because the entity can no longer be found in the Set collection since the new identifier value is associated with a different Set bucket than the one where the entity got stored in.

To fix it, the equals and hashCode methods must be changed as follows:

```
@Override
public boolean equals(Object o) {
    if (this == o) return true;
    if (!(o instanceof Post)) return false;
    return id != null && id.equals(((Post) o).id);
}


@Override
public int hashCode() {
    return 31;
}
```

When the entity identifier is null, equality can only be guaranteed for the same object references. Otherwise, no transient object is equal to any other transient or persisted object. That's why the equals method above skips the identifier check if the current object has a null identifier value.

Using a constant hashCode value solves the previous bucket-related problem associated with Set(s) or Map(s) because, this time, only a single bucket is going to be used. Although in general, using a single Set bucket is not very efficient for large collection of objects, in this particular use case, this workaround is valid since managed collections should be rather small to be efficient. Otherwise, fetching a @OneToMany Set with thousands of entities is orders of magnitude more costly than the one-bucket search penalty.

When using List(s), the constant hashCode value is not an issue at all, and, for bidirectional collections, the Hibernate-internal PersistentList(s) are more efficient than PersistentSet(s).

The bidirectional @OneToMany association generates efficient DML statements because the @ManyToOne mapping is in charge of the table relationship. Because it simplifies data access operations as well, the bidirectional @OneToMany association is worth considering when the size of the child records is relatively low.

10.3.2 Unidirectional @OneToMany

The unidirectional @OneToMany association is very tempting because the mapping is simpler than its bidirectional counterpart. Because there is only one side to take into consideration, there is no need for helper methods and the mapping does not feature a mappedBy attribute either.

```
@OneToMany(cascade = CascadeType.ALL, orphanRemoval = true)
private List<PostComment> comments = new ArrayList<>();
```

Unfortunately, in spite its simplicity, the unidirectional @OneToMany association is less efficient than the unidirectional @ManyToOne mapping or the bidirectional @OneToMany association.

Against any intuition, the unidirectional @OneToMany association does not map to a one-to-many table relationship. Because there is no @ManyToOne side to control this relationship, Hibernate uses a separate junction table to manage the association between a parent row and its child records.

Figure 10.5: The @OneToMany table relationship

The table post_post_comment has two foreign key columns, which reference both the parent-side row (the Post_id column is a foreign key to the post table primary key) and the child-side entity (the comments_id references the primary key of the post_comment table).

Without going into analyzing the associated data access operations, it is obvious that joining three tables is less efficient than joining just two. Because there are two foreign keys, there need to be two indexes (instead of one), so the index memory footprint increases. However, since this is a regular table mapping for a many-to-many relationship, the extra table and the increased memory footprint are not even the biggest performance issue. The algorithm for managing the collection state is what makes any unidirectional @OneToMany association less attractive.

Considering there is a `Post` entity with two `PostComment` child records, obtained by running the following example:

```
Post post = new Post("First post");

post.getComments().add(new PostComment("My first review"));
post.getComments().add(new PostComment("My second review"));
post.getComments().add(new PostComment("My third review"));

entityManager.persist(post);
```

While for a bidirectional `@OneToMany` association there were three child rows being added, the unidirectional association requires three additional inserts for the junction table records.

```
INSERT INTO post (title, id) VALUES ('First post', 1)
INSERT INTO post_comment (review, id) VALUES ('My first review', 2)
INSERT INTO post_comment (review, id) VALUES ('My second review', 3)
INSERT INTO post_comment (review, id) VALUES ('My third review', 4)
INSERT INTO post_post_comment (Post_id, comments_id) VALUES (1, 2)
INSERT INTO post_post_comment (Post_id, comments_id) VALUES (1, 3)
INSERT INTO post_post_comment (Post_id, comments_id) VALUES (1, 4)
```

When removing the first element of the collection:

```
post.getComments().remove(0);
```

Hibernate generates the following DML statements:

```
DELETE FROM post_post_comment WHERE Post_id = 1
INSERT INTO post_post_comment (Post_id, comments_id) VALUES (1, 3)
INSERT INTO post_post_comment (Post_id, comments_id) VALUES (1, 4)
DELETE FROM post_comment WHERE id = 2
```

First, all junction table rows associated with the parent entity are deleted, and then the remaining in-memory records are added back again. The problem with this approach is that instead of a single junction table remove operation, the database has way more DML statements to execute.

Another problem is related to indexes. If there is an index on each foreign key column (which is the default for many relational databases), the database engine must delete the associated index entries only to add back the remaining ones. The more elements a collection has, the less efficient a remove operation gets.

The unidirectional @OneToMany relationship is less efficient both for reading data (three joins are required instead of two), as for adding (two tables must be written instead of one) or removing (entries are removed and added back again) child entries.

10.3.3 Ordered unidirectional @OneToMany

If the collection can store the index of every collection element, the unidirectional @OneToMany relationship may benefit for some element removal operations. First, an @OrderColumn annotation must be defined along the @OneToMany relationship mapping:

```
@OneToMany(cascade = CascadeType.ALL, orphanRemoval = true)
@OrderColumn(name = "entry")
private List<PostComment> comments = new ArrayList<>();
```

At the database level, the entry column is included in the junction table.

Figure 10.6: The unidirectional @OneToMany with an @OrderColumn

It is better not to mistake the @OrderColumn with the @OrderBy JPA annotation. While the former allows the JPA provider to materialize the element index into a dedicated database column so that the collection is sorted using an ORDER BY clause, the latter does the sorting at runtime based on the ordering criteria provided by the @OrderBy annotation.

Considering there are three PostComment entities added for a given Post parent entity:

```
post.getComments().add(new PostComment("My first review"));
post.getComments().add(new PostComment("My second review"));
post.getComments().add(new PostComment("My third review"));
```

The index of every collection element is going to be stored in the entry column of the junction table:

```
INSERT INTO post_comment (review, id) VALUES ('My first review', 2)
INSERT INTO post_comment (review, id) VALUES ('My second review', 3)
INSERT INTO post_comment (review, id) VALUES ('My third review', 4)
INSERT INTO post_post_comment (Post_id, entry, comments_id) VALUES (1, 0, 2)
INSERT INTO post_post_comment (Post_id, entry, comments_id) VALUES (1, 1, 3)
INSERT INTO post_post_comment (Post_id, entry, comments_id) VALUES (1, 2, 4)
```

When removing elements from the tail of the collection:

```
post.getComments().remove(2);
```

Hibernate only requires a single junction table delete statement:

```
DELETE FROM post_post_comment WHERE Post_id = 1 and entry = 2
DELETE FROM post_comment WHERE id = 4
```

Unfortunately, this optimization does not hold for entries that are not located towards the head of the collection, so when deleting the first element:

```
post.getComments().remove(0);
```

Hibernate deletes all child elements associated with this parent entity, and then it updates the remaining database entries to preserve the same element ordering as the in-memory collection snapshot:

```
DELETE FROM post_post_comment WHERE Post_id=1 and entry=1
UPDATE post_post_comment set comments_id = 3 WHERE Post_id = 1 and entry = 0
DELETE FROM post_comment WHERE id = 2
```

If the unidirectional @OneToMany collection is used like a stack and elements are always removed from the collection tail, the remove operations will be more efficient when using an @OrderColumn. But the closer an element is to the head of the list, the more update statements must be issued, and the additional updates have an associated performance overhead.

10.3.3.1 @ElementCollection

Although it is not an entity association type, the @ElementCollection is very similar to the unidirectional @OneToMany relationship. To represent collections of basic types (e.g. String, int, BigDecimal) or embeddable types, the @ElementCollection must be used instead. If the previous associations involved multiple entities, this time, there is only a single Post entity with a collection of String comments.

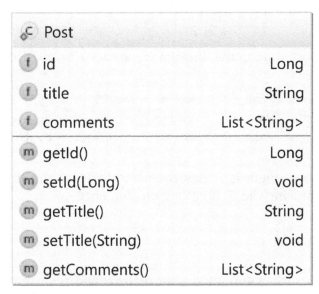

Figure 10.7: The @ElementCollection relationship

The mapping for the comments collection looks as follows:

```
@ElementCollection
private List<String> comments = new ArrayList<>();
```

Value types inherit the persistent state from their parent entities, so their lifecycle is also bound to the owner entity. Any operation against the entity collection is going to be automatically materialized into a DML statement.

When it comes to adding or removing child records, the `@ElementCollection` behaves like a unidirectional `@OneToMany` relationship, annotated with `CascadeType.ALL` and `orphanRemoval`.

From a database perspective, there is one child table holding both the foreign key column and the collection element value.

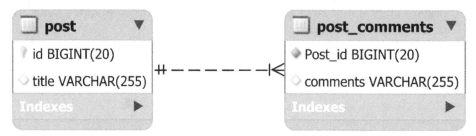

Figure 10.8: The @ElementCollection table relationship

To persist three comments, the data access layer only has to add them to the parent entity collection:

```
post.getComments().add("My first review");
post.getComments().add("My second review");
post.getComments().add("My third review");
```

Hibernate issues the insert statements during Persistence Context flushing:

```
INSERT INTO Post_comments (Post_id, comments) VALUES (1, 'My first review')
INSERT INTO Post_comments (Post_id, comments) VALUES (1, 'My second review')
INSERT INTO Post_comments (Post_id, comments) VALUES (1, 'My third review')
```

Unfortunately, the remove operation uses the same logic as the unidirectional `@OneToMany` association, so when removing the first collection element:

```
post.getComments().remove(0);
```

Hibernate deletes all the associated child-side records and re-inserts the in-memory ones back into the database table:

```
DELETE FROM Post_comments WHERE Post_id = 1
INSERT INTO Post_comments (Post_id, comments) VALUES (1, 'My second review')
INSERT INTO Post_comments (Post_id, comments) VALUES (1, 'My third review')
```

In spite its simplicity, the `@ElementCollection` is not very efficient for element removal. Just like unidirectional `@OneToMany` collections, the `@OrderColumn` can optimize the removal operation for entries located near the collection tail.

10.3.4 @OneToMany with @JoinColumn

JPA 2.0 added support for mapping the @OneToMany association with a @JoinColumn so that it can map the one-to-many table relationship. With the @JoinColumn, the @OneToMany association controls the child table foreign key, so there is no need for a junction table.

On the JPA side, the class diagram is identical to the aforementioned unidirectional @OneToMany relationship, and the only difference is the JPA mapping which takes the additional @JoinColumn:

```
@OneToMany(cascade = CascadeType.ALL, orphanRemoval = true)
@JoinColumn(name = "post_id")
private List<PostComment> comments = new ArrayList<>();
```

When adding three PostComment entities, Hibernate generates the following SQL statements:

```
post.getComments().add(new PostComment("My first review"));
post.getComments().add(new PostComment("My second review"));
post.getComments().add(new PostComment("My third review"));
```

```
INSERT INTO post_comment (review, id) VALUES ('My first review', 2)
INSERT INTO post_comment (review, id) VALUES ('My second review', 3)
INSERT INTO post_comment (review, id) VALUES ('My third review', 4)
UPDATE post_comment SET post_id = 1 WHERE id = 2
UPDATE post_comment SET post_id = 1 WHERE id = 3
UPDATE post_comment SET post_id = 1 WHERE id = 4
```

Besides the regular insert statements, Hibernate issues three update statements for setting the post_id column on the newly inserted child records. The update statements are generated by the Hibernate-internal CollectionRecreateAction which tries to preserve the element order whenever the collection state changes. In this particular case, the CollectionRecreateAction should not be scheduled for execution, however, as of writing (Hibernate 5.2.3), this issue still replicates.

Although, from a performance perspective, it is an improvement over the regular @OneToMany mapping, in practice, it is still not as efficient as a regular bidirectional @OneToMany association.

When deleting the last element of the collection:

```
post.getComments().remove(2);
```

Hibernate generates the following SQL statements:

```
UPDATE post_comment SET post_id = null WHERE post_id = 1 AND id = 4
DELETE from post_comment WHERE id = 4
```

Again, there is an additional update statement associated with the child removal operation. When a child entity is removed from the parent-side collection, Hibernate sets the child table foreign key column to null. Afterward, the orphan removal logic kicks in, and it triggers a delete statement against the disassociated child entity.

Unlike the regular @OneToMany association, the @JoinColumn alternative is consistent in regard to the collection entry position that is being removed. So, when removing the first element of the collection:

```
post.getComments().remove(0);
```

Hibernate still generates an additional update statement:

```
UPDATE post_comment SET post_id = null WHERE post_id = 1 AND id = 2
DELETE from post_comment WHERE id = 2
```

Bidirectional @OneToMany with @JoinColumn relationship

The @OneToMany with @JoinColumn association can also be turned into a bidirectional relationship, but it requires instructing the child-side to avoid any insert and update synchronization:

```
@ManyToOne
@JoinColumn(name = "post_id", insertable = false, updatable = false)
private Post post;
```

The redundant update statements are generated for both the unidirectional and the bidirectional association, so the most efficient foreign key mapping is the @ManyToOne association.

10.3.5 Unidirectional `@OneToMany Set`

All the previous examples were using `List(s)`, but Hibernate supports `Set(s)` as well. For the next exercise, the `PostComment` entity uses the following mapping:

```java
@Entity(name = "PostComment") @Table(name = "post_comment")
public class PostComment {

    @Id @GeneratedValue
    private Long id;

    private String slug;

    private String review;

    public PostComment() {
        byte[] bytes = new byte[8];
        ByteBuffer.wrap(bytes).putDouble(Math.random());
        slug = Base64.getEncoder().encodeToString(bytes);
    }

    public PostComment(String review) {
        this();
        this.review = review;
    }

    //Getters and setters omitted for brevity

    @Override
    public boolean equals(Object o) {
        if (this == o) return true;
        if (o == null || getClass() != o.getClass()) return false;
        PostComment comment = (PostComment) o;
        return Objects.equals(slug, comment.slug);
    }

    @Override
    public int hashCode() {
        return Objects.hash(slug);
    }
}
```

This time, the `PostComment` entity uses a `slug` attribute which provide a way to uniquely identify each comment belonging to a given `Post` entity.

Because the PostComment references are going to be stored in a java.util.Set, it is best to override the equals and hashCode Object methods according to the entity business key. In this particular example, the PostComment does not have any meaningful business key, so the slug attribute is used for the equality checks.

The parent Post entity has a unidirectional @OneToMany association that uses a java.util.Set:

```
@OneToMany(cascade = CascadeType.ALL, orphanRemoval = true)
private Set<PostComment> comments = new HashSet<>();
```

When adding three PostComment entities:

```
post.getComments().add(new PostComment("My first review"));
post.getComments().add(new PostComment("My second review"));
post.getComments().add(new PostComment("My third review"));
```

Hibernate generates the following SQL statements:

```
INSERT INTO post_comment (review, slug, id)
VALUES ('My second review', 'P+HLCF25scI=', 2)
INSERT INTO post_comment (review, slug, id)
VALUES ('My first review', 'P9y8OGLTCyg=', 3)
INSERT INTO post_comment (review, slug, id)
VALUES ('My third review', 'P+fWF+Ck/LY=', 4)

INSERT INTO post_post_comment (Post_id, comments_id) VALUES (1, 2)
INSERT INTO post_post_comment (Post_id, comments_id) VALUES (1, 3)
INSERT INTO post_post_comment (Post_id, comments_id) VALUES (1, 4)
```

The remove operation is much more effective this time because the collection element order needs not be enforced anymore.

When removing the PostComment child entities:

```
for(PostComment comment: new ArrayList<>(post.getComments())) {
    post.getComments().remove(comment);
}
```

Hibernate generates one statement for removing the junction table entries and three delete statements for the associated post_comment records.

```
DELETE FROM post_post_comment WHERE Post_id = 1

DELETE FROM post_comment WHERE id = 2
DELETE FROM post_comment WHERE id = 3
DELETE FROM post_comment WHERE id = 4
```

To avoid using a secondary table, the @OneToMany mapping can use the @JoinColumn annotation.

```
@OneToMany(cascade = CascadeType.ALL, orphanRemoval = true)
@JoinColumn(name = "post_id")
private Set<PostComment> comments = new HashSet<>();
```

Upon inserting three PostComment entities, Hibernate generates the following statements:

```
INSERT INTO post_comment (review, slug, id)
VALUES ('My third review', 'P8pcnLprqcQ=', 2)
INSERT INTO post_comment (review, slug, id)
VALUES ('My second review', 'P+Gau1+Hhxs=', 3)
INSERT INTO post_comment (review, slug, id)
VALUES ('My first review', 'P+kr9LOQTK0=', 4)

UPDATE post_comment SET post_id = 1 WHERE id = 2
UPDATE post_comment SET post_id = 1 WHERE id = 3
UPDATE post_comment SET post_id = 1 WHERE id = 4
```

When deleting all three PostComment entities, the generated statements look like this:

```
UPDATE post_comment SET post_id = null WHERE post_id = 1

DELETE FROM post_comment WHERE id = 2
DELETE FROM post_comment WHERE id = 3
DELETE FROM post_comment WHERE id = 4
```

 Although it is an improvement over the unidirectional unordered or ordered List, the unidirectional Set is still less efficient than the bidirectional @OneToMany association.

10.4 @OneToOne

From a database perspective, the one-to-one association is based on a foreign key that is constrained to be unique. This way, a parent row can be referenced by at most one child record only.

In JPA, the @OneToOne relationship can be either unidirectional or bidirectional.

10.4.1 Unidirectional @OneToOne

In the following example, the Post entity represents the parent-side, while the PostDetails is the child-side of the one-to-one association.

As already mentioned, the JPA entity relationship diagram matches exactly the one-to-one table relationship.

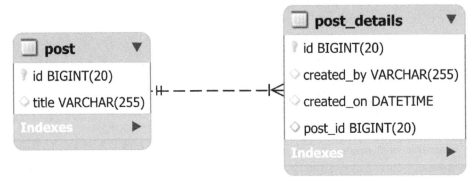

Figure 10.9: The one-to-one table relationship

Even from the Domain Model side, the unidirectional @OneToOne relationship is strikingly similar to the unidirectional @ManyToOne association.

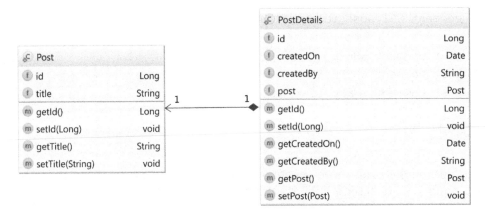

Figure 10.10: The unidirectional @OneToOne relationship

The mapping is done through the @OneToOne annotation, which, just like the @ManyToOne mapping, might also take a @JoinColumn as well.

```
@OneToOne
@JoinColumn(name = "post_id")
private Post post;
```

The unidirectional @OneToOne association controls the associated foreign key, so, when the post attribute is set:

```
Post post = entityManager.find(Post.class, 1L);
PostDetails details = new PostDetails("John Doe");
details.setPost(post);
entityManager.persist(details);
```

Hibernate populate the foreign key column with the associated post identifier:

```
INSERT INTO post_details (created_by, created_on, post_id, id)
VALUES ('John Doe', '2016-01-08 11:28:21.317', 1, 2)
```

Even if this is a unidirectional association, the Post entity is still the parent-side of this relationship. To fetch the associated PostDetails, a JPQL query is needed:

```
PostDetails details = entityManager.createQuery(
    "select pd " +
    "from PostDetails pd " +
    "where pd.post = :post", PostDetails.class)
.setParameter("post", post)
.getSingleResult();
```

If the Post entity always needs its PostDetails, a separate query might not be desirable. To overcome this limitation, it is important to know the PostDetails identifier prior to loading the entity.

One workaround would be to use a @NaturalId, which might not require a database access if the entity is stored in the second-level cache. Fortunately, there is even a simpler approach which is also portable across JPA providers as well. The JPA 2.0 specification added support for derived identifiers, making possible to link the PostDetails identifier to the post table primary key.

This way, the post_details table primary key can also be a foreign key referencing the post table identifier.

The `PostDetails` `@OneToOne` mapping is changed as follows:

```
@OneToOne
@MapsId
private Post post;
```

This time, the table relationship does not feature any additional foreign key column since the `post_details` table primary key references the `post` table primary key:

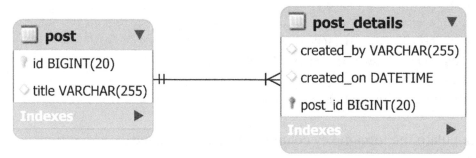

Figure 10.11: The shared key one-to-one

Because `PostDetails` has the same identifier as the parent `Post` entity, it can be fetched without having to write a JPQL query.

```
PostDetails details = entityManager.find(PostDetails.class, post.getId());
```

The shared primary key efficiency

First of all, the shared primary key approach reduces the memory footprint of the child-side table indexes since it requires a single indexed column instead of two. The more records a child table has, the better the improvement gain for reducing the number of indexed columns.

More, the child entity can now be simply retrieved from the second-level cache, therefore preventing a database hit. In the previous example, because the child entity identifier was not known, a query was inevitable. To optimize the previous use case, the *query cache* would be required as well, but the query cache is not without issues either.

 Because of the reduced memory footprint and enabling the second-level cache direct retrieval, the JPA 2.0 *derived identifier* is the preferred `@OneToOne` mapping strategy. The shared primary key is not limited to unidirectional associations, being available for bidirectional `@OneToOne` relationships as well.

10.4.2 Bidirectional @OneToOne

A bidirectional @OneToOne association allows the parent entity to map the child-side as well:

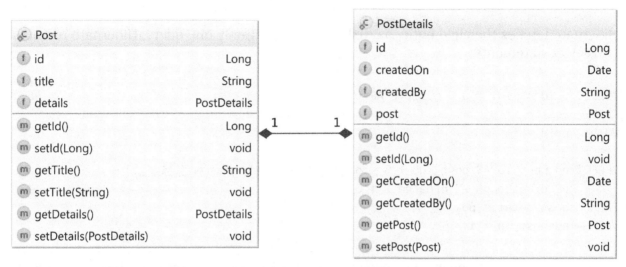

Figure 10.12: The bidirectional @OneToOne relationship

The parent-side defines a mappedBy attribute because the child-side (which can still share the primary key with its parent) is still in charge of this JPA relationship:

```
@OneToOne(mappedBy = "post", cascade = CascadeType.ALL, fetch = FetchType.LAZY)
private PostDetails details;
```

Because this is a bidirectional relationship, the Post entity must ensure that both sides of this relationship are set upon associating a PostDetails entity:

```
public void setDetails(PostDetails details) {
    this.details = details;
    details.setPost(this);
}
```

Unlike the parent-side @OneToMany relationship where Hibernate can simply assign a proxy even if the child collection is empty, the @OneToOne relationship must decide if to assign the child reference to null or to an Object, be it the actual entity object type or a runtime Proxy.

This is an issue that affects the parent-side @OneToOne association, while the child-side, which has an associated foreign key column, knows whether the parent reference should be null or not. For this reason, the parent-side must execute a secondary query to know if there is a mirroring foreign key reference on the child-side.

Even if the association is lazy, when fetching a Post entity:

```
Post post = entityManager.find(Post.class, 1L);
```

Hibernate fetches the child entity as well, so, instead of only one query, Hibernate requires two select statements:

```
SELECT p.id AS id1_0_0_, p.title AS title2_0_0_
FROM   post p
WHERE  p.id = 1


SELECT pd.post_id AS post_id3_1_0_, pd.created_by AS created_1_1_0_,
       pd.created_on AS created_2_1_0_
FROM   post_details pd
WHERE  pd.post_id = 1
```

If the application developer only needs parent entities, the additional child-side secondary queries will be executed unnecessarily, and this might affect application performance. The more parent entities are needed to be retrieved, the more obvious the secondary queries performance impact gets.

Limitations

Even if the foreign key is NOT NULL and the parent-side is aware about its non-nullability through the optional attribute (e.g. @OneToOne(mappedBy = "post", fetch = FetchType.LAZY, optional = false)), Hibernate still generates a secondary select statement.

For every managed entity, the Persistence Context requires both the entity type and the identifier, so the child identifier must be known when loading the parent entity, and the only way to find the associated post_details primary key is to execute a secondary query. Because the child identifier is known when using @MapsId, in future, HHH-10771[a] should address the secondary query issue.

 Bytecode enhancement is the only viable workaround. However, it only works if the parent side is annotated with @LazyToOne(LazyToOneOption.NO_PROXY) and the child side is not using @MapsId. Because it's simpler and more predictable, the unidirectional @OneToOne relationship is often preferred.

---

[a]https://hibernate.atlassian.net/browse/HHH-10771

10.5 @ManyToMany

The @ManyToMany relationship is the trickiest of all JPA relationships as the remaining of this chapter demonstrates. Like the @OneToOne relationship, the @ManyToMany association can be either unidirectional or bidirectional. From a database perspective, the @ManyToMany association mirrors a many-to-many table relationship:

Figure 10.13: The many-to-many table relationship

10.5.1 Unidirectional @ManyToMany

In the following example, it makes sense to have the Post entity map the @ManyToMany relationship since there is not much need for navigating this association from the Tag relationship side (although we can still do it with a JPQL query).

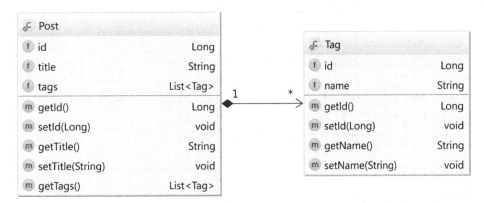

Figure 10.14: The unidirectional @ManyToMany relationship

In the Post entity, the @ManyToMany unidirectional association is mapped as follows:

```
@ManyToMany(cascade = { CascadeType.PERSIST, CascadeType.MERGE } )
@JoinTable(name = "post_tag",
    joinColumns = @JoinColumn(name = "post_id"),
    inverseJoinColumns = @JoinColumn(name = "tag_id")
)
private List<Tag> tags = new ArrayList<>();
```

When adding several entities:

```
Post post1 = new Post("JPA with Hibernate");
Post post2 = new Post("Native Hibernate");

Tag tag1 = new Tag("Java");
Tag tag2 = new Tag("Hibernate");

post1.getTags().add(tag1);
post1.getTags().add(tag2);
post2.getTags().add(tag1);

entityManager.persist(post1);
entityManager.persist(post2);
```

Hibernate manages to persist both the Post and the Tag entities along with their junction records.

```
INSERT INTO post (title, id) VALUES ('JPA with Hibernate', 1)
INSERT INTO post (title, id) VALUES ('Native Hibernate', 4)

INSERT INTO tag (name, id) VALUES ('Java', 2)
INSERT INTO tag (name, id) VALUES ('Hibernate', 3)

INSERT INTO post_tag (post_id, tag_id) VALUES (1, 2)
INSERT INTO post_tag (post_id, tag_id) VALUES (1, 3)
INSERT INTO post_tag (post_id, tag_id) VALUES (4, 2)
```

Cascading

For @ManyToMany associations, CascadeType.REMOVE does not make too much sense when both sides represent independent entities. In this case, removing a Post entity should not trigger a Tag removal because the Tag can be referenced by other posts as well. The same arguments apply to orphan removal since removing an entry from the tags collection should only delete the junction record and not the target Tag entity.

 For both unidirectional and bidirectional associations, it is better to avoid the CascadeType.REMOVE mapping. Instead of CascadeType.ALL, the cascade attributes should be declared explicitly (e.g. CascadeType.PERSIST, CascadeType.MERGE).

But just like the unidirectional `@OneToMany` association, problems arise when it comes to removing the junction records:

```
post1.getTags().remove(tag1);
```

Hibernate deletes all junction rows associated with the `Post` entity whose `Tag` association is being removed and inserts back the remaining ones:

```
DELETE FROM post_tag WHERE post_id = 1

INSERT INTO post_tag (post_id, tag_id) VALUES (1, 3)
```

10.5.2 Bidirectional `@ManyToMany`

The bidirectional `@ManyToMany` relationship can be navigated from both the `Post` and the `Tag` side.

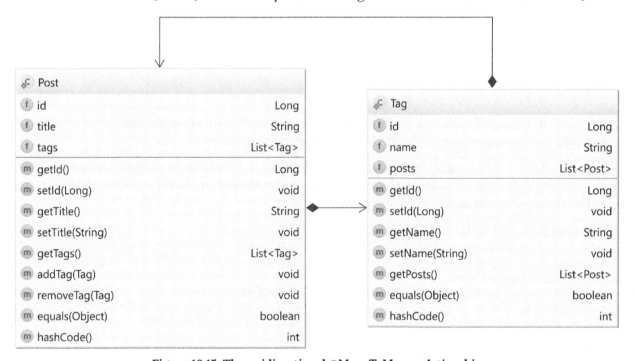

Figure 10.15: The unidirectional @ManyToMany relationship

While in the one-to-many and many-to-one associations the child-side is the one holding the foreign key, for a many-to-many table relationship both ends are parent-sides and the junction table plays the child-side role.

Because the junction table is hidden when using the default `@ManyToMany` mapping, the application developer must choose an owning and a `mappedBy` side.

In this example, the Post retains the same mapping as shown in the unidirectional @ManyToMany section, while the Tag entity adds a mappedBy side:

```
@ManyToMany(mappedBy = "tags")
private List<Post> posts = new ArrayList<>();
```

Like any other bidirectional associations, both sides must in sync, so the helper methods are being added here as well. For a @ManyToMany association, the helper methods must be added to the entity that is more likely to interact with. In this example, the business logic manages Post(s) rather than Tag(s), so the helper methods are added to the Post entity:

```
public void addTag(Tag tag) {
    tags.add(tag);
    tag.getPosts().add(this);
}

public void removeTag(Tag tag) {
    tags.remove(tag);
    tag.getPosts().remove(this);
}
```

Both Post and Tag entities have unique attributes which can simplify the entity removal operation even when mixing detached and managed entities.

While adding an entity into the @ManyToMany collection is efficient since it requires a single SQL insert into the junction table, the entity disassociation suffers from the same issue as the unidirectional @ManyToMany relationship does.

When changing the order of the elements:

```
post1.getTags().sort(
    Collections.reverseOrder(Comparator.comparing(Tag::getId))
);
```

Hibernate deletes all associated junction entries and reinsert them back again, as imposed by the unidirectional *bag* semantics:

```
DELETE FROM post_tag WHERE post_id = 1

INSERT INTO post_tag (post_id, tag_id) VALUES (1, 3)
INSERT INTO post_tag (post_id, tag_id) VALUES (1, 2)
```

Hibernate manages each side of a @ManyToMany relationship like a unidirectional @OneToMany association between the parent-side (e.g. Post or the Tag) and the hidden child-side (e.g. the post_tag table post_id or tag_id foreign keys). This is the reason why the entity removal or changing their order resulted in deleting all junction entries and reinserting them by mirroring the in-memory Persistence Context.

10.5.3 The @OneToMany alternative

Just like the unidirectional @OneToMany relationship can be optimized by allowing the child-side to control this association, the @ManyToMany mapping can be transformed so that the junction table is mapped to an entity.

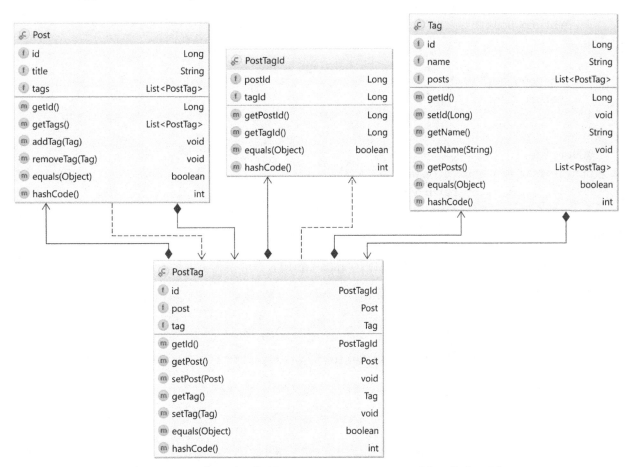

Figure 10.16: The @OneToMany as a many-to-many table relationship

The PostTag entity has a composed identifier made out of the post_id and tag_id columns.

```java
@Embeddable
public class PostTagId implements Serializable {

    private Long postId;

    private Long tagId;

    public PostTagId() {}

    public PostTagId(Long postId, Long tagId) {
        this.postId = postId;
        this.tagId = tagId;
    }

    public Long getPostId() {
        return postId;
    }

    public Long getTagId() {
        return tagId;
    }

    @Override
    public boolean equals(Object o) {
        if (this == o) return true;
        if (o == null || getClass() != o.getClass()) return false;
        PostTagId that = (PostTagId) o;
        return Objects.equals(postId, that.postId) &&
                Objects.equals(tagId, that.tagId);
    }

    @Override
    public int hashCode() {
        return Objects.hash(postId, tagId);
    }
}
```

Using these columns, the `PostTag` entity can map the `@ManyToOne` sides as well:

```java
@Entity
@Table(name = "post_tag")
public class PostTag {

    @EmbeddedId
    private PostTagId id;

    @ManyToOne
    @MapsId("postId")
    private Post post;

    @ManyToOne
    @MapsId("tagId")
    private Tag tag;

    private PostTag() {}

    public PostTag(Post post, Tag tag) {
        this.post = post;
        this.tag = tag;
        this.id = new PostTagId(post.getId(), tag.getId());
    }

    //Getters and setters omitted for brevity

    @Override
    public boolean equals(Object o) {
        if (this == o) return true;
        if (o == null || getClass() != o.getClass()) return false;
        PostTag that = (PostTag) o;
        return Objects.equals(post, that.post) &&
                Objects.equals(tag, that.tag);
    }

    @Override
    public int hashCode() {
        return Objects.hash(post, tag);
    }
}
```

The Post entity maps the bidirectional @OneToMany side of the post @ManyToOne association:

```
@OneToMany(mappedBy = "post", cascade = CascadeType.ALL, orphanRemoval = true)
private List<PostTag> tags = new ArrayList<>();
```

The Tag entity maps the bidirectional @OneToMany side of the tag @ManyToOne association:

```
@OneToMany(mappedBy = "tag", cascade = CascadeType.ALL, orphanRemoval = true)
private List<PostTag> posts = new ArrayList<>();
```

This way, the bidirectional @ManyToMany relationship is transformed in two bidirectional @OneToMany associations.

The removeTag helper method is much more complex because it needs to locate the PostTag associated with the current Post entity and the Tag that is being disassociated.

```
public void removeTag(Tag tag) {
    for (Iterator<PostTag> iterator = tags.iterator(); iterator.hasNext(); ) {
        PostTag postTag = iterator.next();
        if (postTag.getPost().equals(this) && postTag.getTag().equals(tag)) {
            iterator.remove();
            postTag.getTag().getPosts().remove(postTag);
            postTag.setPost(null);
            postTag.setTag(null);
            break;
        }
    }
}
```

The PostTag equals and hashCode methods rely on the Post and Tag equality semantics. The Post entity uses the title as a business key, while the Tag relies on its name column uniqueness constraint.

When rerunning the entity removal example featured in the unidirectional @ManyToMany section:

```
post1.removeTag(tag1);
```

Hibernate issues a single delete statement, therefore targeting a single PostTag junction record:

```
DELETE FROM post_tag WHERE post_id = 1 AND tag_id = 3
```

Changing the junction elements order has not effect this time:

```
post1.getTags().sort((postTag1, postTag2) ->
    postTag2.getId().getTagId().compareTo(postTag1.getId().getTagId())
)
```

This is because the `@ManyToOne` side only monitors the foreign key column changes and the internal collection state is not taken into consideration. To materialize the order of elements, the `@OrderColumn` must be used instead:

```
@OneToMany(mappedBy = "post", cascade = CascadeType.ALL, orphanRemoval = true)
@OrderColumn(name = "entry")
private List<PostTag> tags = new ArrayList<>();
```

The `post_tag` junction table features an `entry` column storing the collection element order. When reversing the element order, Hibernate updates the `entry` column:

```
UPDATE post_tag SET entry = 0 WHERE post_id = 1 AND tag_id = 4
UPDATE post_tag SET entry = 1 WHERE post_id = 1 AND tag_id = 3
```

 The most efficient JPA relationships are the ones where the foreign key side is controlled by a child-side `@ManyToOne` or `@OneToOne` association. For this reason, the many-to-many table relationship is best mapped with two bidirectional `@OneToMany` associations. The entity removal and the element order changes are more efficient than the default `@ManyToMany` relationship and the junction entity can also map additional columns (e.g. `created_on`, `created_by`).

11. Inheritance

Java, like any other object-oriented programming language, makes heavy use of inheritance and polymorphism. Inheritance allows defining class hierarchies that offer different implementations of a common interface.

Conceptually, the Domain Model defines both data (e.g. persisted entities) and behavior (business logic). Nevertheless, inheritance is more useful for varying behavior rather than reusing data (composition is much more suitable for sharing structures). Even if the data (persisted entities) and the business logic (transactional services) are decoupled, inheritance can still help varying business logic (e.g. Visitor pattern[1]).

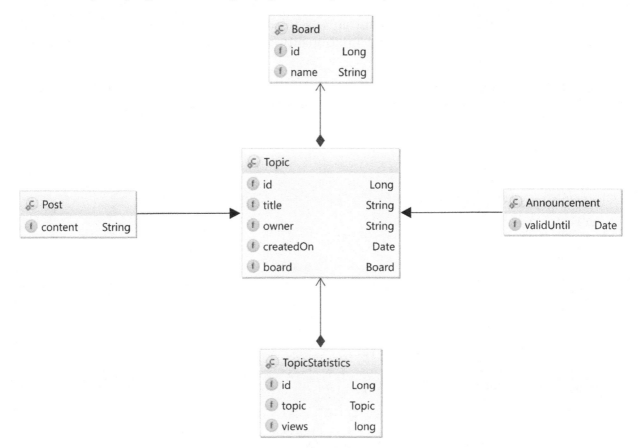

Figure 11.1: Domain Model Inheritance

---

[1]https://en.wikipedia.org/wiki/Visitor_pattern

The root entity of this Domain Model is the Board entity because, either directly or indirectly, all the other entities are associated with a Board

```
@Entity @Table(name = "board")
public class Board {

    @Id @GeneratedValue
    private Long id;

    private String name;

    //Getters and setters omitted for brevity
}
```

The end user can submit either a Post or an Announcement on a particular Board. Because the Post and the Announcement share the same functionality (differing only in data), they both inherit from a Topic base class.

The Topic class defines a relationship to a Board entity, hence the Post and the Announcement entities can also be associated with a Board instance.

```
@Entity @Table(name = "topic")
public class Topic {

    @Id @GeneratedValue
    private Long id;

    private String title;

    private String owner;

    @Temporal(TemporalType.TIMESTAMP)
    private Date createdOn = new Date();

    @ManyToOne(fetch = FetchType.LAZY)
    private Board board;

    //Getters and setters omitted for brevity
}
```

Both the Post and the Announcement entities extend the Topic class and define their own specific attributes.

```
@Entity @Table(name = "post")
public class Post extends Topic {

    private String content;

    //Getters and setters omitted for brevity
}

@Entity @Table(name = "announcement")
public class Announcement extends Topic {

    @Temporal(TemporalType.TIMESTAMP)
    private Date validUntil;

    //Getters and setters omitted for brevity
}
```

The TopicStatistics is at the bottom of this Domain Model as it is only needed for monitoring purposes, without being directly associated with the main business logic. Because statistics are needed for both Post and Announcement entities, the TopicStatistics defines a Topic entity association.

```
@Entity @Table(name = "topic_statistics")
public class TopicStatistics {

    @Id @GeneratedValue
    private Long id;

    @OneToOne @JoinColumn(name = "id") @MapsId
    private Topic topic;

    private long views;

    //Getters and setters omitted for brevity
}
```

Another approach would be to add this relationship into the `Topic` class, and the `topic` rows would then reference the `topic_statistics` records. For the sake of demonstrating how entity association polymorphism works, the `TopicStatistics` was chosen to be the child-side.

As natural as this Domain Model may be represented in an object-oriented programming language, transposing it to a relational database is anything but straightforward. Although SQL-99 added support for type inheritance, this feature is seldom implemented. Therefore, relational database systems are relying on tuples and relational algebra for representing and manipulating data. For this reason, mapping inheritance in a relational database is one of the most obvious object-relational impedance mismatches.

Without native support from the database system, inheritance can only be emulated through table relationships. In the *Patterns of Enterprise Application Architecture* book, Martin Fowler defines three ways of mapping inheritance into a relational database:

- Single Table Inheritance[2], which uses a single database table to represent all classes in a given inheritance hierarchy.
- Class Table Inheritance[3], which maps each class to a table, and the inheritance association is resolved through table joins.
- Concrete Table Inheritance[4], where each table defines all fields that are either defined in the subclass or inherited from a superclass.

The JPA specification defines all these three inheritance mapping models through the following strategies:

- `InheritanceType.SINGLE_TABLE`
- `InheritanceType.JOINED`
- `InheritanceType.TABLE_PER_CLASS`.

JPA also covers the case when inheritance is only available in the Domain Model, without being mirrored into the database (e.g. `@MappedSuperclass`).

Whenever the data access layer implements a functionality without support from the underlying database system, care must be taken to ensure that application performance is not compromised. This chapter aims to analyze what trade-offs are required for employing inheritance as well as its impact on application performance.

---

[2]http://martinfowler.com/eaaCatalog/singleTableInheritance.html
[3]http://martinfowler.com/eaaCatalog/classTableInheritance.html
[4]http://martinfowler.com/eaaCatalog/concreteTableInheritance.html

11.1 Single table

The single table inheritance is the default JPA strategy, funneling a whole inheritance Domain Model hierarchy into a single database table.

To employ this strategy, the Topic entity class must be mapped with one of the following annotations:

- @Inheritance (being the default inheritance model, it is not mandatory to supply the strategy when using single table inheritance).
- @Inheritance(strategy = InheritanceType.SINGLE_TABLE).

The Post and the Announcement entities do not need any extra mapping (the Java inheritance semantics being sufficient).

Preserving the same layout as depicted in the Domain Model class diagram, the table relationships associated with this inheritance strategy look like this:

Figure 11.2: Single table

The topic table contains columns associated with the Topic base class as well as columns related to attributes from Post and Announcement entities.

In the following example, one Post and one Announcement entities are going to be persisted along with their associated @OneToOne TopicStatistics relations.

```
Post post = new Post();
post.setOwner("John Doe");
post.setTitle("Inheritance");
post.setContent("Best practices");
post.setBoard(board);

entityManager.persist(post);

Announcement announcement = new Announcement();
announcement.setOwner("John Doe");
announcement.setTitle("Release x.y.z.Final");
announcement.setValidUntil(Timestamp.valueOf(LocalDateTime.now().plusMonths(1)));
announcement.setBoard(board);

entityManager.persist(announcement);

TopicStatistics postStatistics = new TopicStatistics(post);
postStatistics.incrementViews();
entityManager.persist(postStatistics);

TopicStatistics announcementStatistics = new TopicStatistics(announcement);
announcementStatistics.incrementViews();
entityManager.persist(announcementStatistics);
```

Both the Post and the Announcement entities are saved in the topic table whose primary key is shared with the topic_statistics table.

```
INSERT INTO topic (board_id, createdOn, owner, title, content, DTYPE, id)
VALUES (1, '2016-01-17 09:22:22.11', 'John Doe', 'Inheritance',
    'Best practices', 'Post', 1)

INSERT INTO topic (board_id, createdOn, owner, title, validUntil, DTYPE, id)
VALUES (1, '2016-01-17 09:22:22.11', 'John Doe', 'Release x.y.z.Final',
    '2016-02-17 09:22:22.114', 'Announcement', 2)

INSERT INTO topic_statistics (views, id) VALUES (1, 2)

INSERT INTO topic_statistics (views, id) VALUES (1, 3)
```

One advantage of using inheritance in the Domain Model is the support for polymorphic queries. When the application developer issues a select query against the Topic entity:

```
List<Topic> topics = entityManager.createQuery(
    "select t from Topic t where t.board.id = :boardId", Topic.class)
.setParameter("boardId", 1L)
.getResultList();
```

Hibernate goes to the topic table, and, after fetching the result set, it maps every row to its associated subclass instance (e.g. Post or Announcement) by analyzing the discriminator column (e.g. DTYPE) value.

```
SELECT t.id AS id2_1_, t.board_id AS board_id8_1_, t.createdOn AS created03_1_,
    t.owner AS owner4_1_, t.title AS title5_1_, t.content AS content6_1_,
    t.validUntil AS validUnt7_1_, t.DTYPE AS DTYPE1_1_
FROM topic t
WHERE t.board_id = 1
```

Domain Model inheritance allows base class entity associations to be automatically resolved upon being retrieved. When loading a TopicStatistics along with its Topic relation:

```
TopicStatistics statistics = entityManager.createQuery(
    "select s from TopicStatistics s join fetch s.topic t where t.id = :topicId"
    , TopicStatistics.class)
.setParameter("topicId", topicId)
.getSingleResult();
```

Hibernate joins the topic_statistics and the topic tables so that it can create a TopicStatistics entity with an actual Post or Announcement attribute object reference.

```
SELECT
    ts.id AS id1_2_0_, t.id AS id2_1_1_, ts.views AS views2_2_0_,
    t.board_id AS board_id8_1_1_, t.createdOn AS created03_1_1_,
    t.owner AS owner4_1_1_, t.title AS title5_1_1_, t.content AS content6_1_1_,
    t.validUntil AS validUnt7_1_1_, t.DTYPE AS DTYPE1_1_1_
FROM topic_statistics ts
INNER JOIN topic t ON ts.id = t.id
WHERE t.id = 2
```

Even if not practical in this particular example, @OneToMany associations are also possible.

The `Board` entity can map a bidirectional `@OneToMany` relationship as follows:

```
@OneToMany(mappedBy = "board")
private List<Topic> topics = new ArrayList<>();
```

Fetching the collection lazily generates a separate select statement, identical to the aforementioned `Topic` entity query. When fetching the collection eagerly, Hibernate requires a single table join.

```
Board board = entityManager.createQuery(
    "select b from Board b join fetch b.topics where b.id = :id", Board.class)
.setParameter("id", id)
.getSingleResult();
```

```
SELECT b.id AS id1_0_0_, t.id AS id2_1_1_, b.name AS name2_0_0_,
    t.board_id AS board_id8_1_1_, t.createdOn AS createdO3_1_1_,
    t.owner AS owner4_1_1_, t.title AS title5_1_1_, t.content AS content6_1_1_,
    t.validUntil AS validUnt7_1_1_, t.DTYPE AS DTYPE1_1_1_,
    t.board_id AS board_id8_1_0__, t.id AS id2_1_0__
FROM board b
INNER JOIN topic t ON b.id = t.board_id
WHERE b.id = 1
```

Performance and data integrity considerations

Since only one table is used for storing entities, both reads and writes are fast. Even when using a `@ManyToOne` or a `@OneToOne` base class association, Hibernate needs a single join between parent and child tables. The `@OneToMany` base class entity relationship is also efficient since it either generates a secondary select or a single table join.

Because all subclass attributes are collocated in a single table, NOT NULL constraints are not allowed for columns belonging to subclasses. Being automatically inherited by all subclasses, the base class attributes may be non-nullable. From a data integrity perspective, this limitation defeats the purpose of Consistency (guaranteed by the ACID properties).

Nevertheless, the data integrity rules can be enforced through database trigger procedures or CHECK constraints (a column non-nullability is accounted based on the class discriminator value). Another approach is to move the check into the data access layer. Bean Validation can validate `@NotNull` attributes at runtime. JPA also defines callback methods (e.g. `@PrePersist`, `@PreUpdate`) as well as entity listeners (e.g. `@EntityListeners`) which can throw an exception when a non-null constraint is violated.

11.1.1 Data integrity constraints

The SQL standard defines the CHECK constraint which can be used to apply a row-level verification for each table record that is inserted. Depending on the underlying database, the CHECK constraint can be enforced (e.g. Oracle, SQL Server, PostgreSQL) or ignored (e.g. MySQL[5]).

For the aforementioned database tables, the content column must never be null if the underlying record is a Post, and the validUntil column should not be null if the database row represents an Announcement entity. Luckily, the default DTYPE column specifies the entity type associated with each particular table row.

To ensure the aforementioned data integrity rules, the following CHECK constraints needs to be added:

```
ALTER TABLE Topic ADD CONSTRAINT post_content_check CHECK (
    CASE WHEN DTYPE = 'Post'
        THEN CASE WHEN content IS NOT NULL THEN 1 ELSE 0 END
        ELSE 1
    END = 1
)

ALTER TABLE Topic ADD CONSTRAINT announcement_validUntil_check CHECK (
    CASE WHEN DTYPE = 'Announcement'
        THEN CASE WHEN validUntil IS NOT NULL THEN 1 ELSE 0 END
        ELSE 1
    END = 1
)
```

With these CHECK constraints in place, when trying to insert a Post entity without a content:

```
entityManager.persist(new Post());
```

PostgreSQL generates the following error message:

```
INSERT INTO topic (board_id, createdOn, owner, title, content, DTYPE, id)
VALUES ((NULL(BIGINT), '2016-07-15 13:45:16.705', NULL(VARCHAR), NULL(VARCHAR),
        NULL(VARCHAR), 'Post', 4)

-- SQL Error: 0, SQLState: 23514
-- new row for relation "topic" violates check constraint "post_content_check"
```

---

[5]http://dev.mysql.com/doc/refman/5.7/en/create-table.html

For MySQL, the same result can be achieved with a TRIGGER instead.

```
CREATE
TRIGGER post_content_check BEFORE INSERT
ON Topic
FOR EACH ROW
BEGIN
    IF NEW.DTYPE = 'Post'
    THEN
        IF NEW.content IS NULL
        THEN
            signal sqlstate '45000'
            set message_text = 'Post content cannot be NULL';
        END IF;
    END IF;
END;

CREATE
TRIGGER announcement_validUntil_check BEFORE INSERT
ON Topic
FOR EACH ROW
BEGIN
    IF NEW.DTYPE = 'Announcement'
    THEN
        IF NEW.validUntil IS NULL
        THEN
            signal sqlstate '45000'
            set message_text = 'Announcement validUntil cannot be NULL';
        END IF;
    END IF;
END;
```

When running the previous Post insert, MySQL generates the following output:

```
INSERT INTO topic (board_id, createdOn, owner, title, content, DTYPE, id)
VALUES ((NULL(BIGINT), '2016-07-15 13:50:51.989', NULL(VARCHAR), NULL(VARCHAR),
        NULL(VARCHAR), 'Post', 4)

-- SQL Error: 1644, SQLState: 45000
-- Post content cannot be NULL
```

Although a little bit verbose, the CHECK and TRIGGER constraints are very useful to ensure data integrity when using single table inheritance.

11.2 Join table

The join table inheritance resembles the Domain Model class diagram since each class is mapped to an individual table. The subclass tables have a foreign key column referencing the base class table primary key.

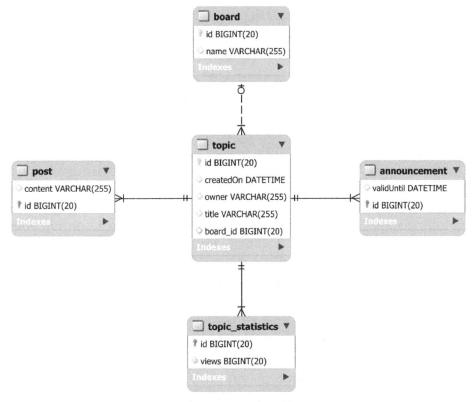

Figure 11.3: Join table

To use this inheritance strategy, the `Topic` entity must be annotated with:

```
@Inheritance(strategy = InheritanceType.JOINED)
```

The `Post` and the `Announcement` entities can use a `@PrimaryKeyJoinColumn` mapping to define the base class foreign key column.

By default, the subclass table primary key column is used as a foreign key as well.

When persisting the same entities defined in the single table section, Hibernate generates the following SQL statements:

```
INSERT INTO topic (board_id, createdOn, owner, title, id)
VALUES (1, '2016-01-17 09:27:10.694', 'John Doe', 'Inheritance', 1)

INSERT INTO post (content, id) VALUES ('Best practices', 1)

INSERT INTO topic (board_id, createdOn, owner, title, id)
VALUES (1, '2016-01-17 09:27:10.694', 'John Doe', 'Release x.y.z.Final', 2)

INSERT INTO announcement (validUntil, id) VALUES ('2016-02-17 09:27:10.698', 2)

INSERT INTO topic_statistics (views, id) VALUES (1, 2)

INSERT INTO topic_statistics (views, id) VALUES (1, 3)
```

The base class information goes into the topic table while the subclass content goes in the post or the announcement tables. When fetching all Topic entities associated with a specific Board:

```
List<Topic> topics = entityManager.createQuery(
    "select t from Topic t where t.board.id = :boardId", Topic.class)
.setParameter("boardId", 1L)
.getResultList();
```

Hibernate must join the base class with each individual subclass table.

```
SELECT
    t.id AS id1_3_,
    t.board_id AS board_id5_3_,
    t.createdOn AS created02_3_,
    t.owner AS owner3_3_,
    t.title AS title4_3_,
    t1_.content AS content1_2_,
    t2_.validUntil AS validUnt1_0_,
    CASE WHEN t1_.id IS NOT NULL THEN 1
        WHEN t2_.id IS NOT NULL THEN 2
        WHEN t.id IS NOT NULL THEN 0
    END AS clazz_
FROM topic t
LEFT OUTER JOIN post t1_ ON t.id = t1_.id
LEFT OUTER JOIN announcement t2_ ON t.id = t2_.id
WHERE t.board_id = 1
```

When loading a `TopicStatistics` entity along with its `Topic` association:

```
TopicStatistics statistics = entityManager.createQuery(
    "select s from TopicStatistics s join fetch s.topic t where t.id = :topicId"
    , TopicStatistics.class)
.setParameter("topicId", topicId)
.getSingleResult();
```

Hibernate must join four tables to construct the desired result set:

```
SELECT
    ts.id AS id1_4_0_,
    t.id AS id1_3_1_,
    ts.views AS views2_4_0_,
    t.board_id AS board_id5_3_1_,
    t.createdOn AS createdO2_3_1_,
    t.owner AS owner3_3_1_,
    t.title AS title4_3_1_,
    t1_.content AS content1_2_1_,
    t2_.validUntil AS validUnt1_0_1_,
    CASE WHEN t1_.id IS NOT NULL THEN 1
        WHEN t2_.id IS NOT NULL THEN 2
        WHEN t.id IS NOT NULL THEN 0
    END AS clazz_1_
FROM topic_statistics ts
INNER JOIN topic t ON ts.id = t.id
LEFT OUTER JOIN post t1_ ON t.id = t1_.id
LEFT OUTER JOIN announcement t2_ ON t.id = t2_.id
WHERE t.id = 2
```

Considering that the `Board` entity defines a `@OneToMany` `Topic` association:

```
@OneToMany(mappedBy = "board")
private List<Topic> topics = new ArrayList<>();
```

Fetching the collection lazily generates a separate select statement, identical to the previous `Topic` entity query.

When fetching the collection eagerly:

```
Board board = entityManager.createQuery(
    "select b from Board b join fetch b.topics where b.id = :id", Board.class)
.setParameter("id", id)
.getSingleResult();
```

Hibernate requires three joins to fetch all topic-related information.

```
SELECT
    b.id AS id1_1_0_, t.id AS id1_3_1_, b.name AS name2_1_0_,
    t.board_id AS board_id5_3_1_, t.createdOn AS created02_3_1_,
    t.owner AS owner3_3_1_, t.title AS title4_3_1_,
    t1_.content AS content1_2_1_, t2_.validUntil AS validUnt1_0_1_,
    CASE WHEN t1_.id IS NOT NULL THEN 1
         WHEN t2_.id IS NOT NULL THEN 2
         WHEN t.id IS NOT NULL THEN 0
    END AS clazz_1_,
    t.board_id AS board_id5_3_0__, t.id AS id1_3_0__
FROM board b
INNER JOIN topic t ON b.id = t.board_id
LEFT OUTER JOIN post t1_ ON t.id = t1_.id
LEFT OUTER JOIN announcement t2_ ON t.id = t2_.id
WHERE b.id = 1
```

Performance considerations

Unlike single table inheritance, the joined table strategy allows nullable subclass attribute columns.

When writing data, Hibernate requires two insert statements for each subclass entity, so there's a performance impact compared to single table inheritance. The index memory footprint also increases because instead of a single table primary key, the database must index the base class and all subclasses primary keys.

When reading data, polymorphic queries require joining the base class with all subclass tables, so, if there are n subclasses, Hibernate will need N+1 joins. The more joins, the more difficult it is for the database to calculate the most efficient execution plan.

11.3 Table-per-class

The table-per-class inheritance model has a table layout similar to the joined table strategy, but, instead of storing base class columns in the `topic` table, each subclass table also stores columns from the `topic` table. There is no foreign key between the `topic` and the `post` or `announcement` subclass tables, and there is no foreign key in the `topic_statistics` table either.

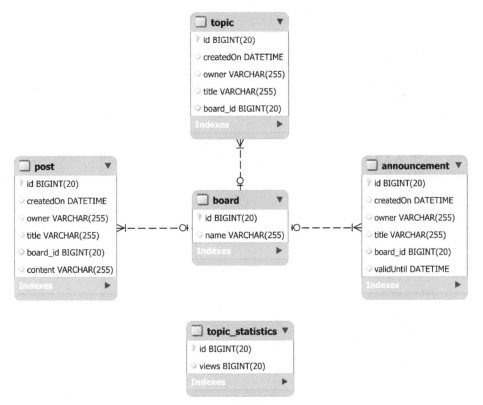

Figure 11.4: Table-per-class

To use this inheritance strategy, the `Topic` must be annotated with `@Inheritance(strategy = InheritanceType.TABLE_PER_CLASS)`.

Inserting the `Post` and the `Announcement` entities defined in the single table inheritance section generates the following SQL statements:

```
INSERT INTO post (board_id, createdOn, owner, title, content, id)
VALUES (1, '2016-01-17 09:31:12.018', 'John Doe', 'Inheritance',
        'Best practices', 2)

INSERT INTO announcement (board_id, createdOn, owner, title, validUntil, id)
VALUES (1, '2016-01-17 09:31:12.018', 'John Doe', 'Release x.y.z.Final',
        '2016-02-17 09:31:12.023', 3)
```

```
INSERT INTO topic_statistics (views, id) VALUES (1, 2)

INSERT INTO topic_statistics (views, id) VALUES (1, 3)
```

Unlike the joined table inheritance, each persisted subclass entity requires a single insert statement.

When fetching all `Topic` entities associated with a specific `Board`:

```
List<Topic> topics = entityManager.createQuery(
    "select t from Topic t where t.board.id = :boardId", Topic.class)
.setParameter("boardId", 1L)
.getResultList();
```

Hibernate uses UNION ALL to fetch rows from the base class and every subclass table in this particular inheritance tree.

```
SELECT
    t.id AS id1_3_,
    t.board_id AS board_id5_3_,
    t.createdOn AS created02_3_,
    t.owner AS owner3_3_,
    t.title AS title4_3_,
    t.content AS content1_2_,
    t.validUntil AS validUnt1_0_,
    t.clazz_ AS clazz_
FROM (
    SELECT id, createdOn, owner, title, board_id,
        CAST(NULL AS VARCHAR(100)) AS content,
        CAST(NULL AS TIMESTAMP) AS validUntil, 0 AS clazz_
    FROM topic
    UNION ALL
    SELECT id, createdOn, owner, title, board_id, content,
        CAST(NULL AS TIMESTAMP) AS validUntil, 1 AS clazz_
    FROM post
    UNION ALL
    SELECT id, createdOn, owner, title, board_id,
        CAST(NULL AS VARCHAR(100)) AS content, validUntil, 2 AS clazz_
    FROM announcement ) t
WHERE  t.board_id = 1
```

When loading a `TopicStatistics` while also fetching its associated `Topic` relation, Hibernate must use `UNION ALL` for the inheritance tables to construct the desired result set:

```
TopicStatistics statistics = entityManager.createQuery(
    "select s from TopicStatistics s join fetch s.topic t where t.id = :topicId"
    , TopicStatistics.class)
.setParameter("topicId", topicId)
.getSingleResult();
```

```
SELECT
    ts.id AS id1_4_0_, t.id AS id1_3_1_, ts.views AS views2_4_0_,
    t.board_id AS board_id5_3_1_, t.createdOn AS createdO2_3_1_,
    t.owner AS owner3_3_1_, t.title AS title4_3_1_, t.content AS content1_2_1_,
    t.validUntil AS validUnt1_0_1_, t.clazz_ AS clazz_1_
FROM topic_statistics ts
INNER JOIN (
    SELECT id, createdOn, owner, title, board_id,
        CAST(NULL AS VARCHAR(100)) AS content,
        CAST(NULL AS TIMESTAMP) AS validUntil, 0 AS clazz_
    FROM topic
    UNION ALL
    SELECT id, createdOn, owner, title, board_id,
        content,
        CAST(NULL AS TIMESTAMP) AS validUntil, 1 AS clazz_
    FROM post
    UNION ALL
    SELECT id, createdOn, owner, title, board_id,
        CAST(NULL AS VARCHAR(100)) AS content,
        validUntil, 2 AS clazz_
    FROM announcement
) t ON ts.id = t.id
WHERE t.id = 2
```

The identity generator is not allowed with this strategy because rows belonging to different subclasses would share the same identifier, therefore conflicting in polymorphic @ManyToOne or @OneToOne associations.

Considering that the `Board` entity defines a `@OneToMany Topic` association:

```
@OneToMany(mappedBy = "board")
private List<Topic> topics = new ArrayList<>();
```

Fetching the collection lazily generates a separate select statement, identical to the previous `Topic` entity query.

When fetching the `topics` collection eagerly:

```
Board board = entityManager.createQuery(
    "select b from Board b join fetch b.topics where b.id = :id", Board.class)
.setParameter("id", id)
.getSingleResult();
```

Hibernate requires a join with the result of unifying all three topic-related tables.

```
SELECT
    b.id AS id1_1_0_, t1.id AS id1_3_1_, b.name AS name2_1_0_,
    t1.board_id AS board_id5_3_1_, t1.createdOn AS createdO2_3_1_,
    t1.owner AS owner3_3_1_, t1.title AS title4_3_1_,
    t1.content AS content1_2_1_, t1.validUntil AS validUnt1_0_1_,
    t1.clazz_ AS clazz_1_, t1.board_id AS board_id5_3_0__, t1.id AS id1_3_0__
FROM board b
INNER JOIN (
    SELECT id, createdOn, owner, title, board_id,
        CAST(NULL AS VARCHAR(100)) AS content,
        CAST(NULL AS TIMESTAMP) AS validUntil, 0 AS clazz_
    FROM topic
    UNION ALL
    SELECT id, createdOn, owner, title, board_id,
        content,
        CAST(NULL AS TIMESTAMP) AS validUntil, 1 AS clazz_
    FROM post
    UNION ALL
    SELECT id, createdOn, owner, title, board_id,
        CAST(NULL AS VARCHAR(100)) AS content,
        validUntil, 2 AS clazz_
    FROM announcement
) t1 ON b.id = t1.board_id
WHERE b.id = 1
```

Performance considerations

While write operations are faster than in the joined table strategy, the read operations are only efficient when querying against the actual subclass entities. Polymorphic queries can have a considerable performance impact because Hibernate must select all subclass tables and use UNION ALL to build the whole inheritance tree result set. As a rule of thumb, the more subclass tables, the less efficient the polymorphic queries get.

11.4 Mapped superclass

If the `Topic` class is not required to be a stand-alone entity, it will be more practical to leave inheritance out of the database. This way, the `Topic` can be made `abstract` and marked with the `@MappedSuperclass` annotation so that JPA can acknowledge the inheritance model on the entity-side only.

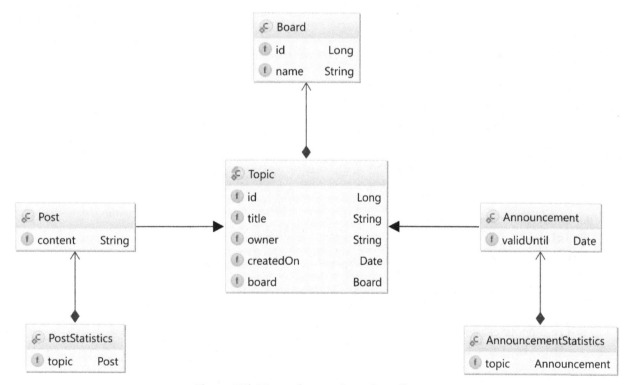

Figure 11.5: Mapped superclass class diagram

Having a single `TopicStatistics` entity with a `@OneToOne` `Topic` association is no longer possible because the `Topic` class is not an entity. This way, each `Topic` subclass must define its own statistics associations (e.g. `PostStatistics`, `AnnouncementStatistics`).

The PostStatistics and the AnnouncementStatistics entities looks as follows:

```java
@Entity @Table(name = "post_statistics")
public class PostStatistics
    extends TopicStatistics<Post> {

    @OneToOne
    @JoinColumn(name = "id")
    @MapsId
    private Post topic;

    private PostStatistics() {}

    public PostStatistics(Post topic) {
        this.topic = topic;
    }

    @Override
    public Post getTopic() {
        return topic;
    }
}

@Entity @Table(name = "announcement_statistics")
public class AnnouncementStatistics
    extends TopicStatistics<Announcement> {

    @OneToOne
    @JoinColumn(name = "id")
    @MapsId
    private Announcement topic;

    private AnnouncementStatistics() {}

    public AnnouncementStatistics(Announcement topic) {
        this.topic = topic;
    }

    @Override
    public Announcement getTopic() {
        return topic;
    }
}
```

To retain the inheritance semantics, the base class attributes are going to be merged with the subclass ones, so the associated subclass entity table contains both. This is similar to the table-per-class inheritance strategy, with the distinction that the base class is not mapped to a database table (hence, it cannot be used in polymorphic queries or associations).

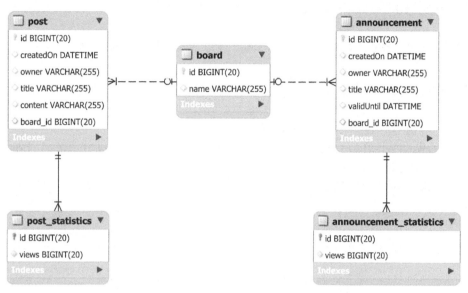

Figure 11.6: Mapped superclass

The post and the announcement tables feature columns that were inherited from the Topic base class. When persisting the same Post and Announcement entities and saving statistics using the newly defined entity classes:

```
TopicStatistics postStatistics = new PostStatistics(post);
postStatistics.incrementViews();
entityManager.persist(postStatistics);

TopicStatistics announcementStatistics =
    new AnnouncementStatistics(announcement);
announcementStatistics.incrementViews();
entityManager.persist(announcementStatistics);
```

Hibernate generates the following SQL statements:

```
INSERT INTO post (board_id, createdOn, owner, title, content, id )
VALUES (1, '2016-01-17 09:11:07.525', 'John Doe', 'Inheritance',
    'Best practices', 1)
```

```
INSERT INTO announcement (board_id, createdOn, owner, title, validUntil, id)
VALUES (1, '2016-01-17 09:11:07.525', 'John Doe', 'Release x.y.z.Final',
    '2016-02-17 09:11:07.529', 2)

INSERT INTO post_statistics (views, id) VALUES (1, 1)

INSERT INTO announcement_statistics (views, id) VALUES (1, 2)
```

Querying for statistics require specifying the actual `Topic` subclass statistics:

```
PostStatistics statistics = entityManager.createQuery(
    "select s from PostStatistics s join fetch s.topic t where t.id = :postId",
        PostStatistics.class)
.setParameter("postId", postId)
.getSingleResult();
```

This entity query generates a single SQL join statement:

```
SELECT
    s.id AS id1_4_0_,
    p.id AS id1_3_1_,
    s.views AS views2_4_0_,
    p.board_id AS board_id6_3_1_,
    p.createdOn AS createdO2_3_1_,
    p.owner AS owner3_3_1_,
    p.title AS title4_3_1_,
    p.content AS content5_3_1_
FROM post_statistics s
INNER JOIN post p ON s.id = p.id
WHERE p.id = 1
```

Polymorphic queries against the `Topic` class are not permitted and the `Board` entity cannot define a `@OneToMany` `Topic` collection either.

Performance considerations

Although polymorphic queries and associations are no longer permitted, the `@MappedSuperclass` yields very efficient read and write operations. Like single and table-per-class inheritance, write operations require a single insert statement and only one table is used for reading data.

Inheritance best practices

All the inheritance mapping models above require trading something in order to accommodate the impedance mismatch between the relational database system and the object-oriented Domain Model.

The default single table inheritance performs the best in terms of reading and writing data, but it forces the application developer to overcome the column nullability limitation. This strategy is useful when the database can provide support for trigger procedures, and the number of subclasses is relatively small.

The join table is worth considering when the number of subclasses is higher, and the data access layer does not require polymorphic queries. When the number of subclass tables is large, polymorphic queries require many joins, and fetching such a result set has a noticeable impact on application performance. This issue can be mitigated by restricting the result set (e.g. pagination), but that only applies to queries and not to @OneToMany or @ManyToMany associations. On the other hand, polymorphic @ManyToOne and @OneToOne associations are fine since, in spite of joining multiple tables, the result set can have at most one record only.

Table-per-class is the least effective when it comes to polymorphic queries or associations. If each subclass is stored in a separate database table, the @MappedSuperclass Domain Model inheritance might often be a better alternative.

 Although a powerful concept, Domain Model inheritance should be used sparingly and only when the benefits supersede trade-offs.

12. Flushing

As explained in the write-based optimizations section, the Persistence Context acts as a transactional write-behind cache. The Hibernate `Session` is commonly referred to as the first-level cache since every managed entity is stored in a `Map`, and, once an entity is loaded, any successive request serves it from the cache, therefore avoiding a database roundtrip.

However, aside from caching entities, the Persistence Context acts as an entity state transition buffer. Both the `EntityManager` and the Hibernate `Session` expose various entity state management methods:

- The `persist` method takes a transient entity and makes it managed.
- The `merge` method copies the internal state of a detached entity onto a freshly loaded entity instance.
- Hibernate also supports reattaching entity instances (e.g. `update`, `saveOrUpdate` or `lock`) which, unlike `merge`, does not require fetching a new entity reference copy.
- To remove an entity, the `EntityManager` defines the `remove` method, while Hibernate offers a `delete` method.

Like any write-behind cache, the Persistence Context requires flushing in order to synchronize the in-memory persistent state with the underlying database. At flush time, Hibernate can detect if a managed entity has changed since it was loaded and trigger a table row update. This process is called dirty checking, and it greatly simplifies data access layer operations.

So, when using JPA, the application developer can focus on entity state changes, and the Persistence Context takes care of the underlying DML statements. This way, the data access layer logic is expressed using Domain Model state transitions, rather than through insert, update, or delete SQL statements.

This approach is very convenient for several reasons:

- Entity state changes being buffered, the Persistence Context can delay their execution, therefore minimizing the row-level lock interval, associated with every database write operation.
- Being executed at once, the Persistence Context can use JDBC batch updates to avoid executing each statement in a separate database roundtrip.

However, having an intermediate write-behind cache is not without challenges and the Persistence Context can be subject to data inconsistencies. Since efficiency is meaningless if effectiveness is being compromised, this chapter aims to analyze the inner-workings of the flushing mechanism, so the application developer knows how to optimize it without affecting data consistency.

12.1 Flush modes

The Persistence Context can be flushed either manually or automatically.

Both `EntityManager` and the Hibernate native `Session` interface define the `flush()` method for triggering the synchronization between the in-memory Domain Model and the underlying database structures. Even so, without an automatic flushing mechanism, the application developer would have to remember to flush prior to running a query or before a transaction commit.

Triggering a flush before executing a query guarantees that in-memory changes are visible to the currently executing query, therefore preventing *read-your-own-writes* consistency issues.

Flushing the Persistence Context right before a transaction commit ensures that in-memory changes are durable. Without this synchronization, the pending entity state transitions would be lost once the current Persistence Context is closed.

For this purpose, JPA and Hibernate define automatic flush modes which, from a data access operation perspective, are more convenient than the manual flushing alternative.

JPA defines two automatic flush mode types:

- `FlushModeType.AUTO` is the default mode and triggers a flush before every query (JPQL or native SQL query) execution and prior to committing a transaction.
- `FlushModeType.COMMIT` only triggers a flush before a transaction commit.

Hibernate defines four flush modes:

- `FlushMode.AUTO` is the default Hibernate API flushing mechanism, and, while it flushes the Persistence Context on every transaction commit, it does not necessarily trigger a flush before every query execution.
- `FlushMode.ALWAYS` flushes the Persistence Context prior to every query (HQL or native SQL query) and before a transaction commit.
- `FlushMode.COMMIT` triggers a Persistence Context flush only when committing the currently running transaction.
- `FlushMode.MANUAL` disables the automatic flush mode, and the Persistence Context can only be flushed manually.

While the `FlushModeType.COMMIT` and `FlushMode.COMMIT` are equivalent, the JPA `FlushModeType.AUTO` is closer to `FlushMode.ALWAYS` than to the Hibernate `FlushModeType.AUTO` (unlike `FlushMode.ALWAYS`, `FlushModeType.AUTO` does not trigger a flush on every executing query).

FlushMode.AUTO SQL query consistency

The default Hibernate-specific `FlushMode.AUTO` employs a smart flushing mechanism. When executing an HQL query, Hibernate inspects what tables the current query is about to scan, and it triggers a flush only if there is a pending entity state transition matching the query table space. This optimization aims to reduce the number of flush calls and delay the first-level cache synchronization as much as possible.

Unfortunately, this does not work for native SQL queries. Because Hibernate does not have a parser for every database-specific query language, it cannot determine the database tables associated with a given native SQL query. However, instead of flushing before every such query, Hibernate relies on the application developer to instruct what table spaces need to be synchronized.

To guarantee SQL query consistency, the application developer can switch to `FlushMode.ALWAYS` (either at the `Session` level or on a query basis)

```
List<ForumCount> result = session.createSQLQuery(
    "SELECT b.name as forum, COUNT (p) as count " +
    "FROM post p " +
    "JOIN board b on b.id = p.board_id " +
    "GROUP BY forum")
.setFlushMode(FlushMode.ALWAYS)
.setResultTransformer( Transformers.aliasToBean(ForumCount.class))
.list();
```

Another alternative is to explicitly set the table spaces affected by the native query:

```
List<ForumCount> result = session.createSQLQuery(
    "SELECT b.name as forum, COUNT (p) as count " +
    "FROM post p " +
    "JOIN board b on b.id = p.board_id " +
    "GROUP BY forum")
.addSynchronizedEntityClass(Board.class)
.addSynchronizedEntityClass(Post.class)
.setResultTransformer( Transformers.aliasToBean(ForumCount.class))
.list();
```

 Only the Hibernate native API (e.g. `Session`) uses the smart flushing mechanism. When using the Java Persistence API (e.g. `EntityManager`), Hibernate flushes before every JPQL or native SQL query.

12.2 Events and the action queue

Internally, each entity state change has an associated event (e.g. `PersistEvent`, `MergeEvent`, `DeleteEvent`, etc) which is handled by an event listener (e.g. `DefaultPersistEventListener`, `DefaultMergeEventListener`, `DefaultDeleteEventListener`).

 Hibernate allows the application developer to substitute the default event listeners with custom implementations.

The Hibernate event listeners translate the entity state transition into an internal `EntityAction` that only gets executed at flush time. For this reason, Hibernate defines the following entity actions:

- When a transient entity becomes persistent, Hibernate generates either an `EntityInsertAction` or an `EntityIdentityInsertAction`, therefore triggering a SQL insert statement at flush time. For the identity generator strategy, Hibernate must immediately execute the insert statement because the entity identifier value must be known upfront.
- During flushing, for every modified entity, an `EntityUpdateAction` is generated which, when executed, triggers a SQL update statement.
- When an entity is marked as removed, Hibernate generates an `EntityDeleteAction`. During flushing, the associations marked with orphan removal can also generate an `OrphanRemovalAction` if a child-side entity is being dereferenced. These two actions trigger a database delete statement.

Because the Persistence Context can manage multiple entities, the pending entity actions are stored in the `ActionQueue` and executed at flush time.

 Entity state transitions can be cascaded from parent entities to children, in which case the original parent entity event is propagated to child entities. For example, when cascading the persist entity state transition, Hibernate behaves as if the application developer has manually called the `persist` method on every child entity.

12.2.1 Flush operation order

Towards the end of the Persistence Context flush, when all `EntityAction(s)` are in place, Hibernate executes them in a very strict order.

1. `OrphanRemovalAction`
2. `EntityInsertAction` and `EntityIdentityInsertAction`
3. `EntityUpdateAction`
4. `CollectionRemoveAction`
5. `CollectionUpdateAction`
6. `CollectionRecreateAction`
7. `EntityDeleteAction`.

The following exercise demonstrates why knowing the flush operation plays a very important role in designing the data access layer actions. Considering the following `Post` entity:

```
@Entity
@Table(name = "post", uniqueConstraints =
    @UniqueConstraint(name = "slug_uq", columnNames = "slug"))
public class Post {

    @Id
    @GeneratedValue
    private Long id;

    private String title;

    private String slug;

    //Getters and setters omitted for brevity
}
```

Assuming the database already contains this `post` record:

```
Post post = new Post();
post.setTitle("High-Performance Java Persistence");
post.setSlug("high-performance-java-persistence");

entityManager.persist(post);
```

When removing a Post and persisting a new one with the same slug:

```
Post post = entityManager.find(Post.class, postId);
entityManager.remove(post);

Post newPost = new Post();
newPost.setTitle("High-Performance Java Persistence Book");
newPost.setSlug("high-performance-java-persistence");
entityManager.persist(newPost);
```

Hibernate throws a ConstraintViolationException:

```
INSERT INTO post (slug, title, id) VALUES (`high-performance-java-persistence`,
    `High-Performance Java Persistence Book`, 2)
```

```
SqlExceptionHelper - integrity constraint violation:
unique constraint or index violation; SLUG_UQ table: POST
```

Even if the remove method is called before persist, the flush operation order executes the insert statement first and a constraint violation is thrown because there are two rows with the same slug value.

To override the default flush operation order, the application developer can trigger a manual flush after the remove method call:

```
Post post = entityManager.find(Post.class, postId);
entityManager.remove(post);
entityManager.flush();

Post newPost = new Post();
newPost.setTitle("High-Performance Java Persistence Book");
newPost.setSlug("high-Performance-java-persistence");
entityManager.persist(newPost);
```

This time, the statement order matches that of the data access operations:

```
DELETE FROM post WHERE id = 1
INSERT INTO post (slug, title, id) VALUES (`high-Performance-java-persistence`,
    `High-Performance Java Persistence Book`, 2)
```

Hibernate only retains the data access operation order among actions of the same type. Even if the manual flush fixes this test case, in practice, an update is much more efficient than a pair of an insert and a delete statements.

12.3 Dirty Checking

Whenever an entity changes its state from transient to managed, Hibernate issues a SQL insert statement. When the entity is marked as removed, a SQL delete statement is issued.

Unlike insert and delete, the update statement does not have an associated entity state transition. When an entity becomes managed, the Persistence Context tracks its internal state and, during flush time, a modified entity is translated to an update statement.

12.3.1 The default dirty checking mechanism

By default, when an entity is loaded, Hibernate saves a snapshot of persisted data in the currently running Persistence Context. The persisted data snapshot is represented by an `Object` array that is very close to the underlying table row values. At flush time, every entity attribute is matched against its loading time value:

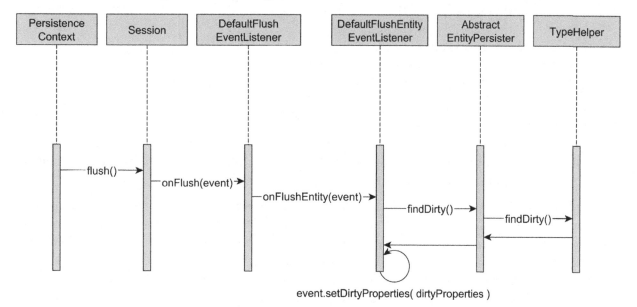

Figure 12.1: Default dirty checking mechanism

The number of individual *dirty checks* is given by the following formula:

$$N = \sum_{k=1}^{n} p_k$$

- n - the number of managed entities
- p - the number of entity attributes.

Even if only one entity attribute changed, Hibernate would still have to go through all managed entities in the current Persistence Context. If the number of managed entities is fairly large, the default dirty checking mechanism might have a significant impact on CPU resources.

12.3.1.1 Controlling the Persistence Context size

Since the entity loading time snapshot is held separately, the Persistence Context requires twice as much memory to store a managed entity.

If the application developer does not need to update the selected entities, a read-only transaction will be much more suitable. From a Persistence Context perspective, a read-only transaction should use a read-only Session. By default, the Session loads entities in read-write mode, but this strategy can be customized either at the Session level or on a query basis:

```
//session-level configuration
Session session = entityManager.unwrap(Session.class);
session.setDefaultReadOnly(true);


//query-level configuration
List<Post> posts = entityManager.createQuery(
    "select p from Post p", Post.class)
.setHint(QueryHints.HINT_READONLY, true)
.getResultList();
```

When entities are loaded in read-only mode, there is no loading time snapshot being taken and the dirty checking mechanism is disabled for these entities.

This optimization addresses both memory and CPU resources. Since the persistent data snapshot is not stored anymore, the Persistence Context consumes half the memory required by a default read-write Session. Having fewer objects to manage, the Garbage Collector requires fewer CPU resources when it comes to reclaiming the memory of a closed Persistence Context. Flushing the Persistence Context is also faster and requires fewer CPU resources since the read-only entities are no longer dirty-checked.

When doing batch processing, it is very important to keep the Persistence Context size within bounds. One approach is to periodically *flush* and *clear* the Persistence Context. To avoid the issues associated with a long-running database transaction (e.g. locks being held for long periods of times, database memory consumption), the Java Persistence API allows a Persistence Context to span over multiple database transactions. This way, each batch job iteration clears the Persistence Context, commits the underlying transaction, and starts a new one for the next iteration.

```
EntityManager entityManager = null;
EntityTransaction transaction = null;
try {
    entityManager = entityManagerFactory().createEntityManager();

    transaction = entityManager.getTransaction();
    transaction.begin();

    for ( int i = 0; i < entityCount; ++i ) {
        Post post = new Post( String.format( "Post %d", i ) );
        entityManager.persist( post );
        if ( i % batchSize == 0 ) {
            entityManager.flush();
            entityManager.clear();

            transaction.commit();
            transaction.begin();
        }
    }

    transaction.commit();
} catch (RuntimeException e) {
    if ( transaction != null && transaction.isActive()) {
        transaction.rollback();
    }
    throw e;
} finally {
    if (entityManager != null) {
        entityManager.close();
    }
}
```

Another approach is to split the load into multiple smaller batch jobs and possibly process them concurrently. This way, long-running transactions are avoided and the Persistence Context has to manage only a limited number of entities.

The Persistence Context should be kept as small as possible. As a rule of thumb, only the entities that need to be modified should ever become managed. Read-only transactions should either use DTO projections or fetch entities in read-only mode.

12.3.2 Bytecode enhancement

Although Hibernate has supported bytecode enhancement for a long time, prior to Hibernate 5, the dirty checking mechanism was not taking advantage of this feature. Hibernate 5 has re-implemented the bytecode instrumentation mechanism, and now it is possible to avoid the reflection-based dirty checking mechanism. The bytecode enhancement can be done at compile-time, runtime or during deployment. The compile-time alternative is preferred for the following reasons:

- The enhanced classes can be covered by unit tests.
- The Java EE application server or the stand-alone container (e.g. Spring) can bootstrap faster because there's no need to instrument classes at runtime or deploy-time.
- Class loading issues are avoided since the application server does not have to take care of two versions of the same class (the original and the enhanced one).

The Hibernate tooling project comes with bytecode enhancement plugins for both Maven and Gradle. For Maven, the following plugin must be configured in the pom.xml file:

```xml
<plugin>
    <groupId>org.hibernate.orm.tooling</groupId>
    <artifactId>hibernate-enhance-maven-plugin</artifactId>
    <version>${hibernate.version}</version>
    <executions>
        <execution>
            <configuration>
                <enableDirtyTracking>true</enableDirtyTracking>
            </configuration>
            <goals>
                <goal>enhance</goal>
            </goals>
        </execution>
    </executions>
</plugin>
```

The bytecode enhancement plugin supports three instrumentation options which must be explicitly enabled during configuration:

- lazy initialization (allows entity attributes to be fetched lazily)
- dirty tracking (the entity tracks its own attribute changes)
- association management (allows automatic sides synchronization for bidirectional associations).

After the Java classes are compiled, the plugin goes through all entity classes and modifies their bytecode according to the instrumentation options chosen during configuration.

When enabling the *dirty tracking* option, Hibernate tracks attribute changes through the $$_hibernate_tracker attribute. Every setter method also calls the $$_hibernate_trackChange method to register the change.

```
@Transient
private transient DirtyTracker $$_hibernate_tracker;

public void $$_hibernate_trackChange(String paramString) {
    if (this.$$_hibernate_tracker == null) {
        this.$$_hibernate_tracker = new SimpleFieldTracker();
    }
    this.$$_hibernate_tracker.add(paramString);
}
```

Considering the following original Java entity class setter method:

```
public void setTitle(String title) {
    this.title = title;
}
```

Hibernate transforms it to the following bytecode representation:

```
public void setTitle(String title) {
    if(!EqualsHelper.areEqual(this.title, title)) {
        this.$$_hibernate_trackChange("title");
    }
    this.title = title;
}
```

When the application developer calls the setTitle method with an argument that differs from the currently stored title, the change is going to be recorded in the $$_hibernate_tracker class attribute.

During flushing, Hibernate inspects the $$_hibernate_hasDirtyAttributes method to validate if an entity was modified. The $$_hibernate_getDirtyAttributes method returns the names of all changed attributes.

```
public boolean $$_hibernate_hasDirtyAttributes() {
    return $$_hibernate_tracker != null && !$$_hibernate_tracker.isEmpty();
}

public String[] $$_hibernate_getDirtyAttributes() {
    if($$_hibernate_tracker == null) {
        $$_hibernate_tracker = new SimpleFieldTracker();
    }
    return $$_hibernate_tracker.get();
}
```

To validate the bytecode enhancement performance gain, the following test measures the dirty tracking time for 10, 20, 50, and 100 Post entity hierarchies (each Post is associated with one PostDetails, two PostComment and two Tag entities). Each iteration modifies six attributes: the Post title, the PostDetails creation date and owner, the PostComment review and the Tag name.

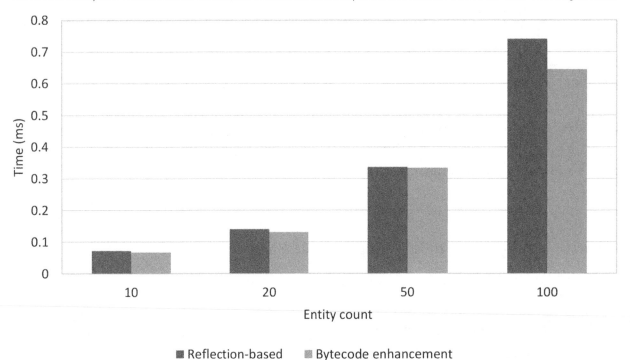

Figure 12.2: Bytecode enhancement performance gain

Both dirty checking mechanisms are very fast, and, compared to how much it takes to run a database query, the in-memory attribute modification tracking is insignificant. Up to 50 Post entities, the reflection-based and the bytecode enhancement dirty checking mechanisms perform comparably.

Although bytecode enhancement dirty tracking can speed up the Persistence Context flushing mechanism, if the size of the Persistence Context is rather small, the improvement will not be that significant.

The entity snapshot is still saved in the Persistence Context even when using bytecode enhancement because the persisted data might be used for the second-level cache entries. For this reason, keeping the Persistence Context in reasonable boundaries stays true no matter the dirty tracking mechanism in use.

13. Batching

As explained in the JDBC Batch Updates chapter, grouping multiple statements can reduce the number of database roundtrips, therefore, lowering transaction response time.

When it comes to translating entity state transitions, Hibernate uses only `PreparedStatement(s)` for the automatically generated insert, update, and delete DML operations. This way, the application is protected against SQL injection attacks, and the data access layer can better take advantage of JDBC batching and statement caching.

With plain JDBC, batch updates require programmatic configuration because, instead of calling `executeUpdate`, the application developer must use the `addBatch` and `executeBatch` methods. Unfortunately, performance tuning is sometimes done only after the application is deployed into production, and switching to batching JDBC statements requires significant code changes.

By default, Hibernate doesn't use JDBC batch updates, so when inserting 5 `Post` entities:

```
for (int i = 0; i < 3; i++) {
    entityManager.persist(new Post(String.format("Post no. %d", i + 1)));
}
```

Hibernate executes five insert statements, each one in a separate database roundtrip:

```
INSERT INTO post (title, id) VALUES (Post no. 1, 1)
INSERT INTO post (title, id) VALUES (Post no. 2, 2)
INSERT INTO post (title, id) VALUES (Post no. 3, 3)
```

Unlike JDBC, Hibernate can switch to batched `PreparedStatement(s)` with just one configuration property, and no code change is required:

```
<property name="hibernate.jdbc.batch_size" value="5"/>
```

 The `hibernate.jdbc.batch_size` configuration is applied globally for all `Session(s)`.

Session-level JDBC batching

Hibernate 5.2 adds support for Session-level JDBC batching. Prior to this release, there was no way to customize the JDBC batch size on a per-business use case basis. However, this feature is really useful since not all business use cases have the save data persistence requirements.

The JDBC batch size can be set programmatically on a Hibernate Session as follows:

```
doInJPA(entityManager -> {
    entityManager.unwrap(Session.class).setJdbcBatchSize(10);

    for ( long i = 0; i < entityCount; ++i ) {
        Post post = new Post();
        post.setTitle(String.format("Post nr %d", i));
        entityManager.persist(post);
    }
});
```

If the EntityManager uses a PersistenceContextType.EXTENDED scope, it is good practice to reset the custom JDBC batch size before existing the current business method:

```
@PersistenceContext(type = PersistenceContextType.EXTENDED)
private EntityManager entityManager;

@TransactionAttribute(value=REQUIRED)
public void savePosts() {
    entityManager.unwrap(Session.class).setJdbcBatchSize(10);
    try {
        for ( long i = 0; i < entityCount; ++i ) {
            Post post = new Post();
            post.setTitle(String.format("Post nr %d", i));
            entityManager.persist(post);
        }
        entityManager.flush();
    } finally {
        entityManager.unwrap(Session.class).setJdbcBatchSize(null);
    }
}
```

By setting the Session-level JDBC batch size to null, Hibernate is going to use the SessionFactory configuration (e.g. hibernate.jdbc.batch_size) the next time the EXTENDED EntityManager gets reused.

13.1 Batching insert statements

After setting the batch size property, when rerunning the previous test case, Hibernate generates a single insert statement:

```
Query:  ["INSERT INTO post (title, id) VALUES (?, ?)"],
Params: [('Post no. 1', 1), ('Post no. 2', 2), ('Post no. 3', 3)]
```

Identity columns and JDBC batching

If the Post identifier used an identity column, Hibernate would disable batched inserts.

```
INSERT INTO post (id, title) VALUES (default, 'Post no. 1')
INSERT INTO post (id, title) VALUES (default, 'Post no. 2')
INSERT INTO post (id, title) VALUES (default, 'Post no. 3')
```

Once an entity becomes managed, the Persistence Context needs to know the entity identifier to construct the first-level cache entry key, and, for identity columns, the only way to find the primary key value is to execute the insert statement.

 This restriction does not apply to update and delete statements which can still benefit from JDBC batching even if the entity uses the identity strategy.

Assuming the Post entity has a @OneToMany association with the PostComment entity, and the persist event is cascaded from the Post entity to its PostComment children:

```
@OneToMany(cascade = CascadeType.ALL, mappedBy = "post", orphanRemoval = true)
private List<PostComment> comments = new ArrayList<>();
```

When persisting three Post(s) along with their PostComment child entities:

```
for (int i = 0; i < 3; i++) {
    Post post = new Post(String.format("Post no. %d", i));
    post.addComment(new PostComment("Good"));
    entityManager.persist(post);
}
```

Hibernate executes one insert statement for each persisted entity:

```
INSERT INTO post (title, id) VALUES ('Post no. 0', 1)
INSERT INTO post_comment (post_id, review, id) VALUES (1, 'Good', 2)

INSERT INTO post (title, id) VALUES ('Post no. 1', 3)
INSERT INTO post_comment (post_id, review, id) VALUES (3, 'Good', 4)

INSERT INTO post (title, id) VALUES ('Post no. 2', 5)
INSERT INTO post_comment (post_id, review, id) VALUES (5, 'Good', 6)
```

Even if the JDBC batching is enabled, Hibernate still executes each statement separately. This is because JDBC batching requires executing the same PreparedStatement, and, since the parent and the child entity persist operations are interleaved, the batch must be flushed prior to proceeding with an entity of different type.

To fix this, the inserts must be ordered while still maintaining the parent-child referential integrity rules. For this purpose, Hibernate offers the following configuration property:

```
<property name="hibernate.order_inserts" value="true"/>
```

With this setting in place, Hibernate can benefit from JDBC batching once more:

```
INSERT INTO post (title, id)
VALUES (Post no. 0, 1), (Post no. 1, 3), (Post no. 2, 5)

INSERT INTO post_comment (post_id, review, id)
VALUES (1, Good, 2), (3, Good, 4), (5, Good, 6)
```

13.2 Batching update statements

Once the hibernate.jdbc.batch_size configuration property is set up, JDBC batching applies to SQL update statements too. Running the following test case:

```
List<Post> posts = entityManager.createQuery(
    "select p from Post p ", Post.class)
.getResultList();

posts.forEach(post -> post.setTitle(post.getTitle().replaceAll("no", "nr")));
```

Hibernate generates only one SQL update statement:

```
Query:  ["UPDATE post SET title = ? WHERE id = ?"],
Params: [('Post nr. 1', 1), ('Post nr. 2', 2), ('Post nr. 3', 3)]
```

Just like it was the case for batching insert statements, when updating entities of different types:

```
List<PostComment> comments = entityManager.createQuery(
    "select c " +
    "from PostComment c " +
    "join fetch c.post ", PostComment.class)
.getResultList();

comments.forEach(comment -> {
    comment.setReview(comment.getReview().replaceAll("Good", "Very good"));
    Post post = comment.getPost();
    post.setTitle(post.getTitle().replaceAll("no", "nr"));
});
```

Hibernate flushes the batched `PreparedStatement` before switching to an entity of a different type:

```
Query:  ["UPDATE post_comment SET post_id = ?, review = ? WHERE id = ?"],
Params: [(1, 'Very good', 2)]

Query:  ["UPDATE post SET title = ? WHERE id = ?"],
Params: [('Post nr. 0', 1)]

Query:  ["UPDATE post_comment SET post_id = ?, review = ? WHERE id = ?"],
Params: [(3, 'Very good', 4)]

Query:  ["UPDATE post SET title = ? WHERE id = ?"],
Params: [('Post nr. 1', 3)]

Query:  ["UPDATE post_comment SET post_id = ?, review = ? WHERE id = ?"],
Params: [(5, 'Very good', 6)]

Query:  ["UPDATE post SET title = ? WHERE id = ?"],
Params: [('Post nr. 2', 5)]
```

Analogous to ordering inserts, Hibernate offers the possibility of reordering batch updates as well:

```
<property name="hibernate.order_updates" value="true"/>
```

With this configuration in place, when rerunning the previous example, Hibernate generates only two update statements:

```
Query:   ["UPDATE post SET title = ? WHERE id = ?"],
Params:  [('Post nr. 0', 1), ('Post nr. 1', 3), ('Post nr. 2', 5)]

Query:   ["UPDATE post_comment SET post_id = ?, review = ? WHERE id = ?"],
Params:  [(1, 'Very good', 2), (3, 'Very good', 4), (5, 'Very good', 6)]
```

Batching versioned data

An entity is versioned if the @Version annotation is associated with a numerical or a timestamp attribute. The presence of the @Version attribute activates the implicit optimistic locking mechanism for update and delete statements. When the entity is updated or deleted, Hibernate includes the entity version in the where clause of the currently executing SQL statement. If the entity was modified by a concurrent transaction, the version of the underlying table row would not match the one supplied by the current running statement. The update count returned by an update or a delete statement reports the numbers of rows affected by the statement in question, and, if the count value is zero (or even less), a StaleObjectStateException is thrown.

Prior to Hibernate 5, JDBC batching was disabled for versioned entities during update and delete operations. This limitation was due to some JDBC drivers inability of correctly returning the update count of the affected table rows when enabling JDBC batching.

Validating the underlying JDBC driver support is fairly simple. Once the hibernate.jdbc.batch_-versioned_data property is activated, if there is no optimistic locking exception being mistakenly thrown during a non-concurrent batch update, then the driver supports versioned JDBC batching.

Since Hibernate 5, the hibernate.jdbc.batch_versioned_data configuration property is enabled by default, and it is disabled when using a pre-12c Oracle dialect (e.g. Oracle 8i, Oracle 9i, Oracle 10g). Because the Oracle 12c JDBC driver manages to return the actual update count even when using batching, the Oracle12cDialect sets the hibernate.jdbc.batch_versioned_data property to true.

   For Hibernate 3 and 4, the hibernate.jdbc.batch_versioned_data should be enabled if the JDBC driver supports this feature.

13.3 Batching delete statements

Considering that the `hibernate.jdbc.batch_size` configuration property is set, when running the following test case:

```
List<Post> posts = entityManager.createQuery(
    "select p " +
    "from Post p ", Post.class)
.getResultList();

posts.forEach(entityManager::remove);
```

Hibernate will generate a single `PreparedStatement`:

```
Query:  ["DELETE FROM post WHERE id = ?"],
Params: [(1), (2), (3)]
```

If the `Post` entity has a `@OneToMany PostComment` association, and since `CascadeType.REMOVE` is inherited from the `CascadeType.ALL` attribute, when the `Post` entity is removed, the associated `PostComment` child entities will be removed as well.

```
List<Post> posts = entityManager.createQuery(
    "select p " +
    "from Post p " +
    "join fetch p.comments ", Post.class)
.getResultList();

posts.forEach(entityManager::remove);
```

Even if the JDBC batching setting is enabled, Hibernate still issues each delete statement separately.

```
DELETE FROM post_comment WHERE id = 2
DELETE FROM post WHERE id = 1

DELETE FROM post_comment WHERE id = 4
DELETE FROM post WHERE id = 3

DELETE FROM post_comment WHERE id = 6
DELETE FROM post WHERE id = 5
```

> Once the HHH-10483[a] is resolved, Hibernate will support delete statement ordering.
>
> The `hibernate.jdbc.batch_versioned_data` property applies to batched deletes just like for update statements.
>
> ---
> [a]https://hibernate.atlassian.net/browse/HHH-10483

Fortunately, there are multiple workarounds to this issue. Instead of relying on `Cascade-Type.REMOVE`, the child entities can be manually removed before deleting the parent entities.

```
for (Post post : posts) {
    for (Iterator<PostComment> commentIterator = post.getComments().iterator();
            commentIterator.hasNext(); ) {
        PostComment comment = commentIterator.next();
        comment.setPost(null);
        commentIterator.remove();
    }
}
entityManager.flush();
posts.forEach(entityManager::remove);
```

Prior to deleting the `Post` entities, the Persistence Context is flushed to force the `PostComment` delete statements to be executed. This way, the Persistence Context does not interleave the SQL delete statements of the removing `Post` and `PostComment` entities.

```
Query:   ["DELETE FROM post_comment WHERE id = ?"],
Params:  [(2), (4), (6)

Query:   ["DELETE FROM post WHERE id = ?"],
Params:  [(1), (3), (5)]
```

A more efficient alternative is to execute a bulk HQL delete statement instead. First, the `PostComment` collection mapping must be modified to remove the `orphanRemoval`, as well as the `CascadeType.REMOVE` setting.

```
@OneToMany(cascade = {CascadeType.PERSIST, CascadeType.MERGE}, mappedBy = "post")
private List<PostComment> comments = new ArrayList<>();
```

Without removing the orphanRemoval and the CascadeType.REMOVE setting, Hibernate will issue a select statement for every child entity that gets removed. Not only the SQL statements are more effective (due to batching), but the flushing is also faster since the Persistence Context doesn't have to propagate the remove action.

With this new mapping in place, the remove operation can be constructed as follows:

```
List<Post> posts = entityManager.createQuery(
    "select p " +
    "from Post p ", Post.class)
.getResultList();

entityManager.createQuery(
    "delete " +
    "from PostComment c " +
    "where c.post in :posts")
.setParameter("posts", posts)
.executeUpdate();

posts.forEach(entityManager::remove);
```

This time, Hibernate generates only two statements. The child entities are deleted using a single bulk delete statement, while the parent entities are removed using a batched PreparedStatement.

```
Query:  ["DELETE FROM post_comment WHERE post_id in (? , ? , ?)"],
Params: [(1, 3, 5)]

Query:  ["DELETE FROM post WHERE id = ?"],
Params: [(1), (3), (5)]
```

The most efficient approach is to rely on database-level cascading. For this purpose, the post_comment table should be modified so that the post_id foreign key defines a DELETE CASCADE directive.

```
ALTER TABLE post_comment ADD CONSTRAINT fk_post_comment_post
FOREIGN KEY (post_id) REFERENCES post ON DELETE CASCADE
```

This way, the deletion operation can be reduced to simply removing the Post entities:

```
List<Post> posts = entityManager.createQuery(
    "select p " +
    "from Post p ", Post.class)
.getResultList();

posts.forEach(entityManager::remove);
```

Running the Post removal operation generates only one batched PreparedStatement:

```
Query:   ["DELETE FROM post WHERE id = ?"],
Params:  [(1), (3), (5)]
```

Because the Hibernate Session is unaware of the table rows being deleted on the database side, it is good practice to avoid fetching the associations that will be removed by the database.

```
List<Post> posts = entityManager.createQuery(
    "select p " +
    "from Post p ", Post.class)
.getResultList();

List<PostComment> comments = entityManager.createQuery(
    "select c " +
    "from PostComment c " +
    "where c.post in :posts", PostComment.class)
.setParameter("posts", posts)
.getResultList();

posts.forEach(entityManager::remove);
comments.forEach(comment -> comment.setReview("Excellent"));
```

When running the test case above, Hibernate generates the following SQL statements:

```
Query:   ["UPDATE post_comment SET post_id=?, review=? WHERE id=?"],
Params:  [(1, 'Excellent', 2), (3, 'Excellent', 4), (5, 'Excellent', 6)]

Query:   ["DELETE FROM post WHERE id=?"],
Params:  [(1), (3), (5)]
```

Luckily, the EntityDeleteAction is the last action being executed during flushing, so, even if the PostComment(s) are changed, the update statement is executed before the parent deletion.

But if the Persistence Context is flushed before changing the `PostComment` entities:

```
List<Post> posts = entityManager.createQuery(
    "select p " +
    "from Post p ", Post.class)
.getResultList();

List<PostComment> comments = entityManager.createQuery(
    "select c " +
    "from PostComment c " +
    "where c.post in :posts", PostComment.class)
.setParameter("posts", posts)
.getResultList();

posts.forEach(entityManager::remove);

entityManager.flush();

comments.forEach(comment -> comment.setReview("Excellent"));
```

An `OptimisticLockException` will be thrown because the associated table rows cannot be found anymore.

```
Query:  ["DELETE FROM post WHERE id=?"],
Params: [(1), (3), (5)]

Query:  ["UPDATE post_comment SET post_id=?, review=? WHERE id=?"],
Params: [(1, 'Excellent', 2), (3, 'Excellent', 4), (5, 'Excellent', 6)]

o.h.e.j.b.i.BatchingBatch - HHH000315: Exception executing batch
[Batch update returned unexpected row count from update [0];
actual row count: 0; expected: 1]
```

Because the row count value is zero, Hibernate assumes that the records were modified by some other concurrent transaction and it throws the exception to notify the upper layers of the data consistency violation.

14. Fetching

While in SQL data is represented as tuples, the object-oriented Domain Model uses graphs of entities. Hibernate takes care of the object-relational impedance mismatch, allowing the data access operations to be expressed in the form of entity state transitions.

It is definitely much more convenient to operate on entity graphs and let Hibernate translate state modifications to SQL statements, but convenience has its price. All the automatically generated SQL statements need to be validated, not only for effectiveness but for ensuring their efficiency as well.

With JDBC, the application developer has full control over the underlying SQL statements, and the select clause dictates the amount of data being fetched. Because Hibernate hides the SQL statement generation, fetching efficiency is not as transparent as with JDBC. More, Hibernate makes it very easy to fetch an entire entity graph with a single query, and too-much-fetching is one of the most common JPA-related performance issues.

To make matters worse, many performance issues can go unnoticed during development because the testing data set might be too small, in comparison to the actual production data. For this purpose, this chapter goes through various Java Persistence fetching strategies, and it explains which ones are suitable for a high-performance data-driven application.

As explained in the JDBC ResultSet Fetching chapter, fetching too many rows or columns can greatly impact the data access layer performance, and Hibernate is no different.

Hibernate can fetch a given result set either as a projection or as a graph of entities. The former is similar to JDBC and allows transforming the `ResultSet` into a list of DTO (Data Transfer Objects). The latter is specific to ORM tools, and it leverages the automatic persistence mechanism.

Unfortunately too often, this distinction is being forgotten, and data projections are unnecessarily replaced by entity queries. There are multiple reasons why entity queries are not a universal solution for reading data:

1. If a graph of entities has been loaded, but only a subset of the whole graph is used during UI rendering, the unused data will become a waste of database resources, network bandwidth, and server resources (objects need to be created and then reclaimed by the Java Garbage Collector without serving any purpose).
2. Entity queries are more difficult to paginate especially if they contain child collections.
3. The automatic dirty checking and the optimistic locking mechanisms are only relevant when data is meant to be modified.

So, projections are ideal when rendering subsets of data (e.g. read-only tables, auto-scrolling selectors), while entity queries are useful when the user wants to edit the fetched entities (e.g. forms, im-place editing).

When loading a graph of entities, the application developer must pay attention to the amount of data being fetched and also the number of statements being executed.

> As a rule of thumb, a transaction should fetch just as much data as required by the currently executing business logic. Fetching more data than necessary can increase response time and waste resources.
>
> Fetching entity graphs is useful when the data access layer needs to modify the currently loading entities.

14.1 DTO projection

While Hibernate allows fetching projections as an `Object` array, it is much more convenient to materialize the `ResultSet` in a DTO projection. Unlike returning an `Object[]`, the DTO projection is type-safe.

Considering the following `PostCommentSummary` DTO type:

```java
public class PostCommentSummary {

    private Number id;
    private String title;
    private String review;

    public PostCommentSummary(Number id, String title, String review) {
        this.id = id;
        this.title = title;
        this.review = review;
    }

    public PostCommentSummary() {}

    public Number getId() { return id; }

    public String getTitle() { return title; }

    public String getReview() { return review; }
}
```

When executing the following PostCommentSummary projection query:

```
List<PostCommentSummary> summaries = entityManager.createQuery(
    "select new " +
    "   com.vladmihalcea.book.hpjp.hibernate.fetching.PostCommentSummary( " +
    "        p.id, p.title, c.review ) " +
    "from PostComment c " +
    "join c.post p")
.getResultList();
```

Hibernate is only selecting the columns that are needed for building a PostCommentSummary instance.

```
SELECT p.id AS col_0_0_, p.title AS col_1_0_, c.review AS col_2_0_
FROM   post_comment c
INNER JOIN post p ON c.post_id = p.id
```

14.1.1 DTO projection pagination

Selecting too much data is a common cause of performance-related issues. A UI can display as much as the screen resolution allows it, and paginating data sets allows the UI to request only the info that is needed to be displayed in the current view. Pagination is also a safety measure since it sets an upper boundary on the amount of data that is fetched at once, and this is especially relevant when the tables being scanned tend to grow with time.

Pagination is a good choice even for batch processing because it limits the transaction size, therefore avoiding long-running transactions.

As explained in the JDBC ResultSet limit clause section, the SQL:2008 ResultSet pagination syntax hast started being supported since Oracle 12c, SQL Server 2012, and PostgreSQL 8.4, and many relational database systems still use a vendor-specific SQL syntax for offset pagination.

> In the SQL Performance Explained[a] book, Markus Winand explains why *keyset* pagination scales better than the default offset pagination mechanism. Unfortunately, Hibernate 5.1 does not support it, and the Keyset pagination requires executing a native SQL query instead.
>
> As long as the filtering criteria are highly-selective so that the scanning result set is relatively small, the offset pagination performs reasonably well.
>
> ―――――――――――
> [a]http://sql-performance-explained.com/

For the offset pagination, JPA can insulate the data access layer from database-specific syntax quirks. First, the ResultSet size can be limited by calling setMaxResults which Hibernate translates to a `Dialect`-specific statement syntax. While it would have been much easier for Hibernate to use the `setMaxRows` method of the underlying JDBC `Statement`, the database-specific query syntax is desirable since it can also influence the database execution plan.

When running the following projection query on a PostgreSQL database:

```
List<PostCommentSummary> summaries = entityManager.createQuery(
    "select new " +
    "   com.vladmihalcea.book.hpjp.hibernate.fetching.PostCommentSummary( " +
    "       p.id, p.title, c.review ) " +
    "from PostComment c " +
    "join c.post p " +
    "order by p.id")
.setFirstResult(pageStart)
.setMaxResults(pageSize)
.getResultList();
```

Hibernate generates the select statement as follows:

```
SELECT p.id AS col_0_0_, p.title AS col_1_0_, c.review AS col_2_0_
FROM   post_comment c
INNER JOIN post p ON c.post_id = p.id
ORDER BY p.id
LIMIT  10 OFFSET 20
```

In this particular example, the `LIMIT` and the `OFFSET` PostgreSQL directives are used to control the window of data that needs to be fetched by the currently executing query.

ORDER BY

Without the ORDER BY clause, the order of rows in a result set is not deterministic. However, in the pagination use case, the fetched record order need to be preserved whenever moving from one page to another. According to the SQL standard, only the ORDER BY clause can guarantee a deterministic result set order because records are sorted after being extracted.

 In the context of pagination, the ORDER BY clause needs to be applied on a column or a set of columns that are guarded by a unique constraint.

14.1.2 Native query DTO projection

DTO projections can be fetched with native queries as well. When using JPA, to fetch a list of PostCommentSummary objects with an SQL query, a @NamedNativeQuery with a @SqlResultSetMapping is required:

```java
@NamedNativeQuery(name = "PostCommentSummary",
    query =
        "SELECT p.id as id, p.title as title, c.review as review " +
        "FROM post_comment c " +
        "JOIN post p ON c.post_id = p.id " +
        "ORDER BY p.id",
    resultSetMapping = "PostCommentSummary"
)
@SqlResultSetMapping(name = "PostCommentSummary",
    classes = @ConstructorResult(
        targetClass = PostCommentSummary.class,
        columns = {
            @ColumnResult(name = "id"),
            @ColumnResult(name = "title"),
            @ColumnResult(name = "review")
        }
    )
)
```

To execute the above SQL query, the createNamedQuery method must be used:

```java
List<PostCommentSummary> summaries = entityManager.createNamedQuery(
        "PostCommentSummary")
.setFirstResult(pageStart)
.setMaxResults(pageSize)
.getResultList();
```

Hibernate generating the following paginated SQL query:

```sql
SELECT p.id as id, p.title as title, c.review as review
FROM   post_comment c
JOIN post p ON c.post_id = p.id
ORDER BY p.id
LIMIT  10 OFFSET 20
```

While JPQL might be sufficient in many situations, there might be times when a native SQL query is the only reasonable alternative because, this way, the data access layer can take advantage of the underlying database querying capabilities.

A much simpler alternative is to use the Hibernate-native API which allows transforming the `ResultSet` to a DTO through Java Reflection:

```
List<PostCommentSummary> summaries = session.createSQLQuery(
    "SELECT p.id as id, p.title as title, c.review as review " +
    "FROM post_comment c " +
    "JOIN post p ON c.post_id = p.id " +
    "ORDER BY p.id")
.setFirstResult(pageStart)
.setMaxResults(pageSize)
.setResultTransformer(
    new AliasToBeanResultTransformer(PostCommentSummary.class))
.list();
```

Although JPA 2.1 supports Constructor Expressions for JPQL queries as previously illustrated, there is no such alternative for native SQL queries.

Fortunately, Hibernate has long been offering this feature through the `ResultTransformer` mechanism which not only provides a way to return DTO projections, but it allows to customize the result set transformation, like when needing to build an hierarchical DTO structure.

To fully grasp why sometimes native queries become a necessity, the next example uses a hierarchical model that needs to be ranked across the whole tree structure. For this reason, in the following example, a post comment score ranking system is going to be implemented.

The goal of such a system is to provide the user a way to view only the most relevant comments, therefore, allowing him to ignore comments that have a low score.

The post comment score system is going to use the following database table:

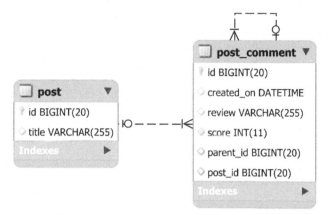

Figure 14.1:Post comment score ranking system tables

There is a one-to-many table relationship between post and post_comment. However, because users can also reply to comments, the post_comment table has also a one-to-one self-join table relationship.

The self-join association is commonly used for representing tree-like structures in a relational database. Additionally, each post_comment has a score which indicates its relevance.

The application in question needs to display the top-ranked comment hierarchies associated with a given post. The ranking can be calculated either in the data access layer or in the database, so it is worth comparing the performance impact of each of these two solutions.

The first approach uses application-level comment ranking, and, to minimize the fetching impact, a DTO projection is used to retrieve all records that need to be aggregated hierarchically.

```
List<PostCommentScore> postCommentScores = entityManager.createQuery(
    "select new " +
    " com.vladmihalcea.book.hpjp.hibernate.query.recursive.PostCommentScore(" +
    " pc.id, pc.parent.id, pc.review, pc.createdOn, pc.score ) " +
    "from PostComment pc " +
    "where pc.post.id = :postId ")
.setParameter("postId", postId)
.getResultList();
```

The associated SQL query looks as follows:

```
SELECT
    pc.id AS col_0_0_, pc.parent_id AS col_1_0_, pc.review AS col_2_0_,
    pc.created_on AS col_3_0_, pc.score AS col_4_0_
FROM  post_comment pc
WHERE pc.post_id = 1
```

The PostCommentScore DTO looks like this:

```java
public class PostCommentScore {

    private Long id;
    private Long parentId;
    private String review;
    private Date createdOn;
    private long score;

    private List<PostCommentScore> children = new ArrayList<>();

    public PostCommentScore(Number id, Number parentId, String review,
        Date createdOn, Number score) {
        this.id = id.longValue();
        this.parentId = parentId != null ? parentId.longValue() : null;
        this.review = review;
        this.createdOn = createdOn;
        this.score = score.longValue();
    }

    public PostCommentScore() {}

    //Getters and setters omitted for brevity

    public long getTotalScore() {
        long total = getScore();
        for(PostCommentScore child : children) {
            total += child.getTotalScore();
        }
        return total;
    }

    public List<PostCommentScore> getChildren() {
        List<PostCommentScore> copy = new ArrayList<>(children);
        copy.sort(Comparator.comparing(PostCommentScore::getCreatedOn));
        return copy;
    }

    public void addChild(PostCommentScore child) {
        children.add(child);
    }
}
```

Once the `PostCommentScore` list is fetched from the database, the data access layer must extract the top-ranking comment hierarchies. For this, the sorting must be done in-memory.

```
1   List<PostCommentScore> roots = new ArrayList<>();
2
3   Map<Long, PostCommentScore> postCommentScoreMap = new HashMap<>();
4   for(PostCommentScore postCommentScore : postCommentScores) {
5       Long id = postCommentScore.getId();
6       if (!postCommentScoreMap.containsKey(id)) {
7           postCommentScoreMap.put(id, postCommentScore);
8       }
9   }
10  for(PostCommentScore postCommentScore : postCommentScores) {
11      Long parentId = postCommentScore.getParentId();
12      if(parentId == null) {
13          roots.add(postCommentScore);
14      } else {
15          PostCommentScore parent = postCommentScoreMap.get(parentId);
16          parent.addChild(postCommentScore);
17      }
18  }
19  roots.sort(
20      Comparator.comparing(PostCommentScore::getTotalScore).reversed()
21  );
22  if(roots.size() > rank) {
23      roots = roots.subList(0, rank);
24  }
```

The in-memory ranking process can be summarized as follows:

- Lines 4-10: Because the query does not use an ORDER BY clause, there is no ordering guarantee. Grouping `PostCommentScore` entries by their identifier must be done prior to reconstructing the hierarchy.
- Lines 12-20: The hierarchy is built out of the flat `PostCommentScore` list. The `PostCommentScore` map is used to locate each `PostCommentScore` parent entry.
- Lines 22-24: The `PostCommentScore` roots are sorted by their total score.
- Lines 26-28: Only the top-ranking entries are kept and handed to the business logic.

For many developers, this approach might be the first option to consider when implementing such a task. Unfortunately, this method does not scale for large `ResultSet(s)` because fetching too much data and sending it over the network is going to have a significant impact on application performance. If a `post` becomes very popular, the number of `post_comment` rows can easily skyrocket, and the system might start experiencing performance issues.

By moving the score ranking processing in the database, the ResultSet can be limited to a maximum size before being returned to the data access layer. Summing scores for all comments belonging to the same post_comment root requires Recursive CTE queries and Window Functions, therefore, the following example uses PostgreSQL, and the database ranking logic looks like this:

```
List<PostCommentScore> postCommentScores = entityManager.createNativeQuery(
    "SELECT id, parent_id, root_id, review, created_on, score " +
    "FROM ( " +
    "    SELECT " +
    "        id, parent_id, root_id, review, created_on, score, " +
    "        dense_rank() OVER (ORDER BY total_score DESC) rank " +
    "    FROM ( " +
    "        SELECT " +
    "            id, parent_id, root_id, review, created_on, score, " +
    "            SUM(score) OVER (PARTITION BY root_id) total_score " +
    "        FROM (" +
    "          WITH RECURSIVE post_comment_score(id, root_id, post_id, " +
    "              parent_id, review, created_on, score) AS (" +
    "              SELECT " +
    "                  id, id, post_id, parent_id, review, created_on, score" +
    "              FROM post_comment " +
    "              WHERE post_id = :postId AND parent_id IS NULL " +
    "              UNION ALL " +
    "              SELECT pc.id, pcs.root_id, pc.post_id, pc.parent_id, " +
    "                  pc.review, pc.created_on, pc.score " +
    "              FROM post_comment pc " +
    "              INNER JOIN post_comment_score pcs ON pc.parent_id = pcs.id " +
    "              WHERE pc.parent_id = pcs.id " +
    "          ) " +
    "          SELECT id, parent_id, root_id, review, created_on, score " +
    "          FROM post_comment_score " +
    "        ) score_by_comment " +
    "    ) score_total " +
    "    ORDER BY total_score DESC, id ASC " +
    ") total_score_group " +
    "WHERE rank <= :rank", "PostCommentScore")
.unwrap(SQLQuery.class)
.setParameter("postId", postId).setParameter("rank", rank)
.setResultTransformer(new PostCommentScoreResultTransformer())
.list();
```

As usual, a SQL query can be better understood if starting from the inner-most query:

- Lines 14-17: This query is the first one to be executed, and it selects the post_comment roots associated with the given post identifier.
- Line 18: The UNION ALL directive combines the previously generated result set with the current Recursive CTE projection.
- Lines 19-23: These lines represent the recursive step which, in this case, it joins the current post_comment rows with the previously scanned parents.
- Lines 12-13 and 24-26: The Recursive CTE is only a construct that needs to be explicitly called by a query. For this example, the post_comment hierarchy has a root_id which identifies all records belonging to the same comment root.
- Lines 8-11: and 27: This outer query is used to sum all scores for a given post_comment hierarchy. Unlike a regular GROUP BY clause, the Window Function allows aggregating the score without affecting the selected result set.
- Lines 4-7: and 28-29: This outer query is used to order the post_comment hierarchies by their overall score, and each hierarchy is given a top rank (e.g. 1, 2, 3).
- Lines 2-3: and 30-31: The outer-most query is only selecting the post_comment hierarchies that have a top rank higher than a given threshold.
- Line 32: The JPA Query is dereferenced to the underlying Hibernate-specific SQLQuery object.
- Line 34: Because the query was cast to an SQLQuery instance, the result can be transformed using the ResultTransformer utility.

Without using a ResultTransformer, Hibernate would return a List of PostCommentScore objects that need to be manually transformed into a tree structure, exactly like it was the case with the first DTO projection that was fetching all PostCommentScore records.

In the Recursive CTE use case, the result set is already ordered by the database so that the hierarchical structure can be constructed in a single iteration. This can also be done for the first example, but adding an ORDER BY directive is going to slow down the query execution significantly. When ORDER BY was added, the SQL query was 20 times slower even if the ordering was done by the entity identifier which was indexed by default.

For this reason, the first example did not feature a SQL ORDER BY clause, and the result set was, therefore, iterated twice. Compared to a SQL query, in-memory processing is blazing fast. For instance, processing around 35 000 PostCommentScore records takes around 2.5 milliseconds. On the other hand, fetching just 100 PostCommentScore(s) takes more than 3 milliseconds.

In PostgreSQL, CTE is treated as an optimization fence[a], so caution is advised.

[a]http://blog.2ndquadrant.com/postgresql-ctes-are-optimization-fences/

The `PostCommentScoreResultTransformer` looks as follows:

```
public class PostCommentScoreResultTransformer implements ResultTransformer {

    private Map<Long, PostCommentScore> postCommentScoreMap = new HashMap<>();

    private List<PostCommentScore> roots = new ArrayList<>();

    @Override
    public Object transformTuple(Object[] tuple, String[] aliases) {
        PostCommentScore commentScore = (PostCommentScore) tuple[0];
        Long parentId = commentScore.getParentId();
        if (parentId == null) {
            roots.add(commentScore);
        } else {
            PostCommentScore parent = postCommentScoreMap.get(parentId);
            if (parent != null) {
                parent.addChild(commentScore);
            }
        }
        postCommentScoreMap.putIfAbsent(commentScore.getId(), commentScore);
        return commentScore;
    }

    @Override
    public List transformList(List collection) {
        return roots;
    }
}
```

Having two options for the same data access logic requires a test to prove which one performs better. Considering that n is the number of root-level post_comment records, the following test creates comments on three levels, each upper level having twice as much entries as the immediate lower level, and the total number of post_comment entries is given by the following formula:

$$N = n + n \times \frac{n}{2} + n \times \frac{n}{2} \times \frac{n}{4}$$

To understand how each of these two options scales, the number of root-level post_comment entries varies from 4 to 8, 16, 24, 32, 48, and 64 records. By applying the mathematical formula above, the total number of post_comment records contained within one hierarchy can vary from 20 to 104, 656, 2040, 4640, 15024, and 34880 rows. Increasing the ResultSet size, the impact of fetching too much data becomes more and more apparent. On the other hand, even if it still needs to scan a lot of records, the database-level processing can avoid the fetching penalty.

The following graph captures the results when running these two score ranking data processing alternatives:

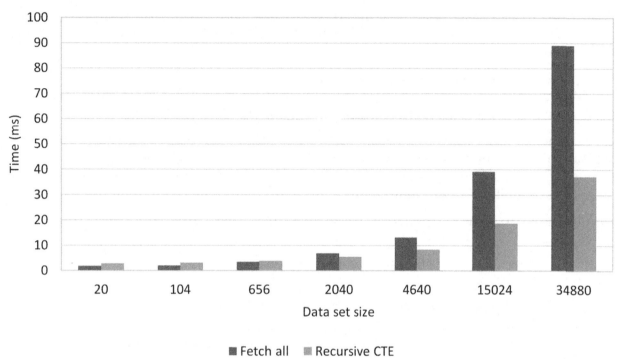

Figure 14.2: Fetching all records vs Recursive CTE

If the number of `post_comment` entries is low, the application-level processing will perform very well, even better than the Recursive CTE query. However, the larger the `ResultSet`, the more advantageous the database-processing alternative becomes. This graph is a good reminder that moving processing logic closer to the data set is a performance optimization that is worth considering.

Stored procedures

While SQL queries are ideal for fetching data projections, stored procedures and database functions can be very useful for processing data. Some complex database processing tasks can only be expressed through a procedure language (e.g. PL/SQL, T-SQL, PL/pgSQL) if the task requires mixing loops, conditional statements, arrays, or temporary tables.

Unlike SQL queries which are executed in the scope of the currently running transaction, stored procedure can also manipulate transaction boundaries. This can be very handy when trying to break an otherwise long-running transaction into smaller batches which can better fit the undo log memory buffers.

14.2 Query fetch size

When using JPA, the JDBC ResultSet is fully traversed and materialized into the expected query result. For this reason, the fetch size can only influence the number of database roundtrips required for fetching the entire ResultSet.

As explained in the JDBC Fetching Size section, when using SQL Server, PostgreSQL, or MySQL, the ResultSet is fetched in a single database roundtrip. For these three relational database systems, the default fetch size setting is often the right choice for JPA queries.

On the other hand, Oracle uses a default fetch size of only 10 records. Considering the previous pagination query, the page size being also 10, the default fetch size does not influence the number of database roundtrips. However, if the page size is 50, then Hibernate will require 5 roundtrips to fetch the entire ResultSet.

Luckily, Hibernate can control the fetch size either on a query basis or at the EntityManager-Factory level.

At the query level, the fetch size can be configured using the org.hibernate.fetchSize hint:

```
List<PostCommentSummary> summaries = entityManager.createQuery(
    "select new " +
    "    com.vladmihalcea.book.hpjp.hibernate.fetching.PostCommentSummary( " +
    "        p.id, p.title, c.review ) " +
    "from PostComment c " +
    "join c.post p")
.setFirstResult(pageStart)
.setMaxResults(pageSize)
.setHint(QueryHints.HINT_FETCH_SIZE, pageSize)
.getResultList();
```

The default fetch size can also be configured as a configuration property:

```
<property name="hibernate.jdbc.fetch_size" value="50"/>
```

 However, setting the default fetch size requires diligence because it affects every executing SQL query. Like with any other performance tuning setting, measuring the gain is the only way to determine if a settings makes sense or not.

14.3 Fetching entities

DTO projections are suitable for loading read-only data sets because they minimize the number of columns being fetched, and native queries can take advantage of the underlying database advanced querying capabilities. However, most enterprise applications need also modify data, and that is where DTO projections are no longer suitable for this task.

As explained at the beginning of this chapter, object-oriented queries predate entity state modifications. Hibernate supports the standard Java Persistence Query Language (JPQL) and the type-safe Criteria API. More, the Hibernate Query Language (HQL) extends JPQL, therefore offering more features that are not supported by the standard specification.

When an entity is loaded, it becomes managed by the currently running Persistence Context, and Hibernate can automatically detect changes and propagate them as SQL statements.

14.3.1 Direct fetching

The easiest way to load an entity is to call the `find` method of the Java Persistence `EntityManager` interface.

```
Post post = entityManager.find(Post.class, 1L);
```

The same can be achieved with the Hibernate native API:

```
Session session = entityManager.unwrap(Session.class);
Post post = session.get(Post.class, 1L);
```

When running either the `find` or the `get` method, Hibernate fires a `LoadEvent`. Without customizing event listeners, the `LoadEvent` is handled by the `DefaultLoadEventListener` class which tries to locate the entity as follows:

- First, Hibernate tries to find the entity in the currently running Persistence Context (the first-level cache). Once an entity is loaded, Hibernate always returns the same object instance on any successive fetching requests, no matter if it is a query or a direct fetching call. This mechanism guarantees application-level repeatable reads.
- If the entity is not found in the first-level cache and the second-level cache is enabled, Hibernate will try to fetch the entity from the second-level cache.
- If the second-level cache is disabled or the entity is not found in the cache, Hibernate will execute a SQL query to fetch the requested entity.

Not only the data access layer is much easier to implement this way, but Hibernate also offers strong data consistency guarantees. Backed by the application-level repeatable reads offered by the first-level cache, the built-in optimistic concurrency control mechanism can prevent *lost updates*, even across successive web requests.

While a SQL projection requires a database roundtrip to fetch the required data, entities can also be loaded from the second-level caching storage. By avoiding database calls, the entity caching mechanism can improve response time, while the database load can decrease as well.

14.3.1.1 Fetching a Proxy reference

Alternatively, direct fetching can also be done lazily. For this purpose, the `EntityManager` must return a Proxy which delays the SQL query execution until the entity is accessed for the first time.

This can be demonstrated with the following example:

```
Post post = entityManager.getReference(Post.class, 1L);
LOGGER.info("Loaded post entity");
LOGGER.info("The post title is '{}'", post.getTitle());
```

Hibernate generates the following logging sequence:

```
INFO - Loaded post entity

SELECT p.id AS id1_0_0_, p.title AS title2_0_0_
FROM   post p
WHERE  p.id = 1

INFO - The post title is 'Post nr. 1'
```

The `getReference` method call does not execute the SQL statement right away, so the `Loaded post entity` message is the first to be logged. When the `Post` entity is accessed by calling the `getTitle` method, Hibernate executes the select query and, therefore, loads the entity prior to returning the `title` attribute.

The same effect can be achieved with the Hibernate native API which offers two alternatives for fetching an entity Proxy:

```
Session session = entityManager.unwrap(Session.class);
Post post = session.byId(Post.class).getReference(1L);
```

```
Session session = entityManager.unwrap(Session.class);
Post post = session.load(Post.class, 1L);
```

> ## Populating a child-side parent association
>
> The child table row must set the foreign key column according to the parent record primary key value. However, the child entity mapping contains a reference to a parent object, and, if the parent entity is fetched with the find method, Hibernate is going to issue a select statement just for the sake of populating the underlying foreign key column value.
>
> If the current Persistence Context does not require to load the parent entity, the aforementioned select statement will be a waste of resources. For this purpose, the getReference method allows populating the parent attribute with a Proxy which Hibernate can use to set the underlying foreign key value even if the Proxy is uninitialized.

In the following example, a PostComment entity must be persisted with a reference to its parent Post entity.

```
Post post = entityManager.getReference(Post.class, 1L);

PostComment postComment = new PostComment("Excellent reading!");
postComment.setPost(post);

entityManager.persist(postComment);
```

Executing the above test case, Hibernate generates a single insert statement without fetching the Post entity:

```
INSERT INTO post_comment (post_id, review, id)
VALUES (1, 'Excellent reading!', 2)
```

14.3.1.2 Natural identifier fetching

Hibernate offers the possibility of loading an entity by its natural identifier (business key). The natural id can be either a single column or a combination of multiple columns that uniquely identifies a given database table row.

In the following example, the `Post` entity defines a `slug` attribute which serves as a natural identifier.

```
@Entity
@Table(name = "post")
public class Post {

    @Id
    @GeneratedValue
    private Long id;

    private String title;

    @NaturalId
    @Column(nullable = false, unique = true)
    private String slug;

    //Getters and setters omitted for brevity
}
```

Fetching an entity by its natural key is done as follows:

```
Session session = entityManager.unwrap(Session.class);
Post post = session.bySimpleNaturalId(Post.class).load(slug);
```

Behind the scenes, Hibernate executes the following SQL statements:

```
SELECT p.id AS id1_0_
FROM   post p
WHERE  p.slug = 'high-performance-java-persistence'

SELECT p.id AS id1_0_0_, p.slug AS slug2_0_0_, p.title AS title3_0_0_
FROM   post p
WHERE  p.id = 1
```

The natural identifier direct fetching mechanism defines a `getReference` method which, just like its JPA Proxy loading counterpart, returns an entity Proxy.

```
Post post = session.bySimpleNaturalId(Post.class).getReference(slug);
```

> **Caching**
>
> If the second-level cache is enabled, Hibernate can avoid executing the second query by loading the entity directly from the cache. Hibernate can also cache the natural identifier (e.g. `@NaturalIdCache`) associated with a given entity identifier, therefore preventing the first query as well.

14.3.2 Query fetching

With a simple API and having support for bypassing the database entirely by loading entities from the second-level cache, the direct fetching mechanism is a very convenient entity loading mechanism.

On the downside, direct fetching is limited to loading a single entity and only by its identifier or natural key. If the data access layer wants to load multiple entities satisfying a more complex filtering criteria, an entity query will become mandatory.

In the following example, a JPQL query is used to load all `Post` entities that have a non-nullable `slug` attribute.

```
List<Post> posts = entityManager.createQuery(
    "select p " +
    "from Post p " +
    "where p.slug is not null", Post.class)
.getResultList();
```

Executing the JPQL query above, Hibernate generates the following SQL query:

```
SELECT p.id AS id1_0_, p.slug AS slug2_0_, p.title AS title3_0_
FROM   post p
WHERE  p.slug IS NOT NULL
```

Loading by the entity natural key can be done through an entity query as well:

```
Post post = entityManager.createQuery(
    "select p from Post p where p.slug = :slug", Post.class)
.setParameter("slug", slug)
.getSingleResult();
```

And, as opposed to direct fetching API, the entity query alternative requires a single SQL statement:

```
SELECT p.id AS id1_0_, p.slug AS slug2_0_, p.title AS title3_0_
FROM    post p
WHERE   p.slug = 'high-performance-java-persistence'
```

Not only that it can take more filtering criteria, but the query can be constructed programmatically and in a type-safe manner as well. For this purpose, the following example is going to filter Post entities by their title attribute using an incoming titlePattern argument.

If the titlePattern is null, the underlying SQL statement will contain an IS NULL directive. Otherwise, the query must use a LIKE filtering criteria.

```
CriteriaBuilder builder = entityManager.getCriteriaBuilder();
CriteriaQuery<Post> criteria = builder.createQuery(Post.class);
Root<Post> fromPost = criteria.from(Post.class);

Predicate titlePredicate = titlePattern == null ?
    builder.isNull(fromPost.get(Post_.title)) :
    builder.like(fromPost.get(Post_.title), titlePattern);

criteria.where(titlePredicate);
List<Post> posts = entityManager.createQuery(criteria).getResultList();
```

Metamodel API

In the previous example, the title attribute is accessed through the Post entity Metamodel (e.g. Post_.title). The Post_ class is auto-generated during build-time by the org.hibernate.jpamodelgen.JPAMetaModelEntityProcessor Hibernate utility, and it provides a type-safe alternative to locating entity attributes.

Unlike using String attribute identifiers, the Metamodel API can generate a compilation error if an attribute name is changed without updating all Criteria API queries as well. When using an IDE, the Metamodel API allows entity attributes to be auto-discovered, therefore simplifying Criteria API query development.

 Although Hibernate features a native Criteria query implementation, it is better to use the Java Persistence Criteria API which supports the Metamodel API as well.

14.3.3 Fetching associations

All the previous entity queries were rather simple since only one entity type was resulting from the query execution. However, Java Persistence allows fetching associations as well, and this feature is a double-edged sword because it makes it very easy to select more data than a business case might require.

In the database, relationships are represented using foreign keys. To fetch a child association, the database could either join the parent and the child table in the same query, or the parent and the child can be extracted with distinct select statements.

In the object-oriented Domain Model, associations are either object references (e.g. `@ManyToOne`, `@OneToOne`) or collections (e.g. `@OneToMany`, `@ManyToMany`). From a fetching perspective, an association can either be loaded eagerly or lazily.

An eager association is bound to its declaring entity so, when the entity is fetched, the association must be fetched prior to returning the result back to the data access layer. The association can be loaded either through table joining or by issuing a secondary select statement.

A lazy relationship is fetched only when being accessed for the first time, so the association is initialized using a secondary select statement.

By default, `@ManyToOne` and `@OneToOne` associations are fetched eagerly, while the `@OneToMany` and `@ManyToMany` relationships are loaded lazily. During entity mapping, it is possible to overrule the implicit fetching strategies through the `fetch` association attribute, and, combining the implicit fetching strategies with the explicitly declared ones, the *default entity graph* is formed.

While executing a direct fetching call or an entity query, Hibernate inspects the default entity graph to know what other entity associations must be fetched additionally.

JPA 2.1 added support for custom entity graphs which, according to the specification, can be used to override the default entity graph on a per-query basis. However, lazy fetching is only a hint, and the underlying persistence provider might choose to simply ignore it.

Entity graphs

These default fetching strategies are a consequence of conforming to the Java Persistence specification. Prior to JPA, Hibernate would fetch every association lazily (`@ManyToOne` and the `@OneToOne` relationships used to be loaded lazily too).

Just because the JPA 1.0 specification says that `@ManyToOne` and the `@OneToOne` must be fetched eagerly, it does not mean that this is the right thing to do, especially in a high-performance data access layer. Even if JPA 2.1 defines the `javax.persistence.fetchgraph` hint which can override a `FetchType.EAGER` strategy at the query level, in reality, Hibernate ignores it and fetches the eager association anyway.

While a lazy association can be fetched eagerly during a query execution, eager associations cannot be overruled on a query basis. For this reason, `FetchType.LAZY` associations are much more flexible to deal with than `FetchType.EAGER` ones.

14.3.3.1 FetchType.EAGER

Assuming that the `PostComment` entity has a `post` attribute which is mapped as follows:

```
@ManyToOne
private Post post;
```

By omitting the `fetch` attribute, the `@ManyToOne` association is going to inherit the default `FetchType.EAGER` strategy so the `post` association is going to be initialized whenever a `PostComment` entity is being loaded in the currently running Persistence Context. This way, when fetching a `PostComment` entity:

```
PostComment comment = entityManager.find(PostComment.class, 1L);
```

Hibernate generates a select statement that joins the `post_comment` and `post` tables so that the `PostComment` entity has its `post` attribute fully initialized.

```
SELECT pc.id AS id1_1_0_, pc.post_id AS post_id3_1_0_,
       pc.review AS review2_1_0_, p.id AS id1_0_1_, p.title AS title2_0_1_
FROM   post_comment pc
LEFT OUTER JOIN post p ON pc.post_id = p.id
WHERE  pc.id = 1
```

When fetching the `PostComment` entity using the following JPQL query:

```
PostComment comment = entityManager.createQuery(
    "select pc " +
    "from PostComment pc " +
    "where pc.id = :id", PostComment.class)
.setParameter("id", commentId)
.getSingleResult();
```

Hibernate generates two queries: one for loading the PostComment entity and another one for initializing the post association.

```
SELECT pc.id AS id1_1_, pc.post_id AS post_id3_1_, pc.review AS review2_1_
FROM    post_comment pc
WHERE   pc.id = 1

SELECT p.id AS id1_0_0_, p.title AS title2_0_0_
FROM    post p
WHERE   p.id = 1
```

While the PostComment entity is fetched explicitly as specified in the select clause, the post attribute is fetched implicitly according to the default entity graph.

 Every time an entity is fetched via an entity query (JPQL or Criteria API) without explicitly fetching all the FetchType.EAGER associations, Hibernate generates additional SQL queries to initialize those relationships as well.

To execute a single SQL query that joins the post_comment and the post table, the JPQL query must use the fetch directive on the post attribute join clause:

```
PostComment comment = entityManager.createQuery(
    "select pc " +
    "from PostComment pc " +
    "left join fetch pc.post p " +
    "where pc.id = :id", PostComment.class)
.setParameter("id", commentId)
.getSingleResult();
```

The SQL query is similar to the one generated by the direct fetching mechanism:

```
SELECT pc.id AS id1_1_0_, p.id AS id1_0_1_, pc.post_id AS post_id3_1_0_,
       pc.review AS review2_1_0_, p.title AS title2_0_1_
FROM    post_comment pc
LEFT OUTER JOIN post p ON pc.post_id = p.id
WHERE   pc.id = 1
```

Although collections can also be fetched eagerly, most often, this is a very bad idea. Because the eager fetching strategy cannot be overridden, every parent entity direct fetching call or entity query is going to load the FetchType.EAGER collection as well.

However, if these collections are not needed by every business case, the eagerly fetched associations will be just a waste of resources and a major cause of performance issues.

To prove it, the following example features a Post entity with two FetchType.EAGER collections:

```
@OneToMany(mappedBy = "post", fetch = FetchType.EAGER)
private Set<PostComment> comments = new HashSet<>();


@ManyToMany(fetch = FetchType.EAGER)
@JoinTable(name = "post_tag",
    joinColumns = @JoinColumn(name = "post_id"),
    inverseJoinColumns = @JoinColumn(name = "tag_id")
)
private Set<Tag> tags = new HashSet<>();
```

When loading multiple Post entities while eager fetching the comments and tags collections:

```
List<Post> posts = entityManager.createQuery(
    "select p " +
    "from Post p " +
    "left join fetch p.comments " +
    "left join fetch p.tags", Post.class)
.getResultList();
```

Hibernate generates a Cartesian Product between the post_comment and the post_tag tables.

```
SELECT p.id AS id1_0_0_, p.title AS title2_0_0_,
       pc.post_id AS post_id3_1_1_, pc.id AS id1_1_1_, pc.id AS id1_1_2_,
       pc.post_id AS post_id3_1_2_, pc.review AS review2_1_2_,
       pt.post_id AS post_id1_2_3_,
       t.id AS tag_id2_2_3_, t.id AS id1_3_4_, t.name AS name2_3_4_
FROM   post p
LEFT OUTER JOIN post_comment pc ON p.id = pc.post_id
LEFT OUTER JOIN post_tag pt ON p.id = pt.post_id
LEFT OUTER JOIN tag t ON pt.tag_id = t.id
```

Even if there is a single Post entity with 20 PostComment(s) and 10 Tag(s), this SQL query will fetch 200 entries. For 100 Post(s), the associated ResultSet will contain 20 000 entries. That's why the Cartesian Product is undesirable from a performance perspective.

The aforementioned example uses Set(s) because fetching multiple List(s) ends up with a MultipleBagFetchException. On the other hand, Set(s) and ordered List(s) are allowed to be fetched concomitantly with other collections.

If the previous entity query omits the JPQL fetch directive, then, instead of a Cartesian Product, two additional queries are going to be executed. so that the tags and comments collections are initialized, as required by the FetchType.EAGER strategy.

```
SELECT p.id AS id1_0_, p.title AS title2_0_
FROM   post p
WHERE  p.id = 1


SELECT pt.post_id AS post_id1_2_0_, pt.tag_id AS tag_id2_2_0_,
       t.id AS id1_3_1_, t.name AS name2_3_1_
FROM   post_tag pt
INNER JOIN tag t ON pt.tag_id = t.id
WHERE  pt.post_id = 1


SELECT pc.post_id AS post_id3_1_0_, pc.id AS id1_1_0_, pc.id AS id1_1_1_,
       pc.post_id AS post_id3_1_1_, pc.review AS review2_1_1_
FROM   post_comment pc
WHERE  pc.post_id = 1
```

 The more associations are fetched eagerly, the slower the entity fetching will get because it either involves many table joins or a large number of secondary queries. If there are 1000 posts, each post with 50 comments and 5 tags, the Cartesian Product query is going to fetch $1000 \times 50 \times \times 5 = 2500000$ rows. On the other hand, if the collections are not fetched during the query execution, there are going to be 2000 additional queries (1000 for fetching comments and another 1000 queries to fetch the tags of every individual Post entity).

For this purpose, it is better to avoid the FetchType.EAGER strategy, especially for @OneToMany and @ManyToMany associations.

14.3.3.2 FetchType.LAZY

By now, it is obvious that marking associations as FetchType.LAZY is a much better alternative for a high-performance application. The fetching strategy is driven by the business use case data access requirements, so the entity graph should be constructed on a per-query basis. Just because a relationship was annotated as FetchType.LAZY, it does not mean it cannot be fetched eagerly as well.

Considering that the PostComment entity has a post attribute that is annotated with the FetchType.LAZY attribute:

```
@ManyToOne(fetch = FetchType.LAZY)
private Post post;
```

When the PostComment entity is fetched either through direct fetching or a JPQL query, Hibernate is going to generate a single post_comment select statement. The post attribute is referencing a Proxy which is only initialized when the attribute is being accessed for the first time.

To visualize the lazy fetching strategy, the following example is going to select a PostComment entity, and then log the title of it its associated Post parent entity:

```
PostComment comment = entityManager.find(PostComment.class, 1L);

LOGGER.info("Loaded comment entity");
LOGGER.info("The post title is '{}'", comment.getPost().getTitle());
```

When the post attribute is being navigated, Hibernate executes a select statement to fetch the uninitialised Post entity Proxy:

```
SELECT pc.id AS id1_1_0_, pc.post_id AS post_id3_1_0_, pc.review AS review2_1_0_
FROM   post_comment pc
WHERE  pc.id = 1

INFO - Loaded comment entity

SELECT p.id AS id1_0_0_, p.title AS title2_0_0_
FROM   post p
WHERE  p.id = 1

INFO - The post title is 'Post nr. 1'
```

For @OneToMany and @ManyToMany associations, Hibernate uses its own collection Proxy implementations (e.g. PersistentBag, PersistentList, PersistentSet, PersistentMap) which can execute the lazy loading SQL statement on demand.

Navigating the lazy association is just one way to initialize the underlying Proxy or collection. The lazy association can also be fetched eagerly using a custom entity graph.

```
EntityGraph<PostComment> postEntityGraph = entityManager.createEntityGraph(
    PostComment.class);
postEntityGraph.addAttributeNodes(PostComment_.post);

PostComment comment = entityManager.find(PostComment.class, 1L,
    Collections.singletonMap("javax.persistence.fetchgraph", postEntityGraph)
);
```

When running the example above, Hibernate generates the following SQL statement:

```
SELECT pc.id AS id1_1_0_, pc.post_id AS post_id3_1_0_,
       pc.review AS review2_1_0_, p.id AS id1_0_1_, p.title AS title2_0_1_
FROM   post_comment pc
LEFT OUTER JOIN post p ON pc.post_id = p.id
WHERE  pc.id = 1
```

In the example above, the EntityGraph specifies that it needs to fetch the post attribute which is identified by the type-safe Metamodel Attribute (e.g. PostComment_.post). This way, the default entity graph is substituted for the duration of the currently executing query.

The same effect can be obtained with an entity query using a fetch directive on the join clause.

```
PostComment comment = entityManager.createQuery(
    "select pc " +
    "from PostComment pc " +
    "join fetch pc.post p " +
    "where pc.id = :id", PostComment.class)
.setParameter("id", 1L)
.getSingleResult();
```

14.3.3.2.1 The N+1 query problem

Unfortunately, the lazy associations are not without problems, and the most common issue is called the N+1 *query problem*. This situation can be observed in the following example:

```java
List<PostComment> comments = entityManager.createQuery(
    "select pc " +
    "from PostComment pc " +
    "where pc.review = :review", PostComment.class)
.setParameter("review", review)
.getResultList();

LOGGER.info("Loaded {} comments", comments.size());

for(PostComment comment : comments) {
    LOGGER.info("The post title is '{}'", comment.getPost().getTitle());
}
```

Which generates the following SQL statements:

```sql
SELECT pc.id AS id1_1_, pc.post_id AS post_id3_1_, pc.review AS review2_1_
FROM    post_comment pc
WHERE   pc.review = 'Excellent!'

INFO - Loaded 3 comments

SELECT pc.id AS id1_0_0_, pc.title AS title2_0_0_
FROM    post pc
WHERE   pc.id = 1

INFO - The post title is 'Post nr. 1'

SELECT pc.id AS id1_0_0_, pc.title AS title2_0_0_
FROM    post pc
WHERE   pc.id = 2

INFO - The post title is 'Post nr. 2'

SELECT pc.id AS id1_0_0_, pc.title AS title2_0_0_
FROM    post pc
WHERE   pc.id = 3

INFO - The post title is 'Post nr. 3'
```

First, Hibernate executes the JPQL query, and a list of PostComment entities is fetched. Then, for each PostComment, the associated post attribute is used to generate a log message containing the Post title. Because the post association is not initialized, Hibernate must fetch the Post entity with a secondary query, and for N PostComment entities, N more queries are going to be executed (hence the N+1 query problem).

 The more queries are executed, the bigger the impact of the N+1 query problem. Although it is commonly associated with the FetchType.LAZY associations, the N+1 query problem can manifest even when using FetchType.EAGER. When executing a JPQL query, if the eager associations are not explicitly fetched as well, Hibernate is going to initialize every eager association with a secondary select query, therefore causing a N+1 query problem.

To fix the N+1 query problem, the Post(s) must be fetched along their PostComment child entities:

```
List<PostComment> comments = entityManager.createQuery(
    "select pc " +
    "from PostComment pc " +
    "join fetch pc.post p " +
    "where pc.review = :review", PostComment.class)
.setParameter("review", review)
.getResultList();
```

This time, Hibernate generates a single SQL statement and the N+1 query problem is gone:

```
SELECT pc.id AS id1_1_0_, p.id AS id1_0_1_, pc.post_id AS post_id3_1_0_,
       pc.review AS review2_1_0_, p.title AS title2_0_1_
FROM   post_comment pc
INNER JOIN post p ON pc.post_id = p.id
WHERE  pc.review = 'Excellent!'

INFO - Loaded 3 comments

INFO - The post title is 'Post nr. 1'
INFO - The post title is 'Post nr. 2'
INFO - The post title is 'Post nr. 3'
```

14.3.3.2.2 How to catch N+1 query problems during testing

When an application feature is implemented, the development team must assert the number of statements generated, therefore making sure that the number of statements is the expected one. However, a change in the entity fetch strategy can ripple in the data access layer causing N+1 query problems. For this reason, it is better to automate the statement count validation, and this responsibility should be carried by integration tests.

The datasource-proxy statement logging framework provides various listeners to customize the statement interception mechanism. Additionally, the framework ships with a built-in DataSourceQueryCountListener, which counts all statements executed by a given DataSource.

```
ChainListener listener = new ChainListener();
listener.addListener(new SLF4JQueryLoggingListener());
listener.addListener(new DataSourceQueryCountListener());

DataSource dataSourceProxy = ProxyDataSourceBuilder.create(dataSource)
    .name(dataSourceProxyName())
    .listener(listener)
.build();
```

First, an SQLStatementCountMismatchException can be defined to capture the expected and the recorded count values. Because the query counters are stored in the QueryCountHolder utility, it is desirable to isolate integration tests from the underlying datasource-proxy specific API, therefore the SQLStatementCountValidator is an adapter for the datasource-proxy utilities.

```
public class SQLStatementCountMismatchException extends RuntimeException {

    private final int expected;
    private final int recorded;

    public SQLStatementCountMismatchException(int expected, int recorded) {
        super(String.format("Expected %d statement(s) but recorded %d instead!",
            expected, recorded)
        );
        this.expected = expected;
        this.recorded = recorded;
    }

    public int getExpected() { return expected; }

    public int getRecorded() { return recorded; }
}
```

```java
public final class SQLStatementCountValidator {

    public static void reset() {
        QueryCountHolder.clear();
    }

    public static void assertSelectCount(int expectedSelectCount) {
        QueryCount queryCount = QueryCountHolder.getGrandTotal();
        int recordedSelectCount = queryCount.getSelect();
        if (expectedSelectCount != recordedSelectCount) {
            throw new SQLStatementCountMismatchException(expectedSelectCount,
                recordedSelectCount);
        }
    }

    public static void assertInsertCount(int expectedInsertCount) {
        QueryCount queryCount = QueryCountHolder.getGrandTotal();
        int recordedInsertCount = queryCount.getInsert();
        if (expectedInsertCount != recordedInsertCount) {
            throw new SQLStatementCountMismatchException(expectedInsertCount,
                recordedSelectCount);
        }
    }

    public static void assertUpdateCount(int expectedUpdateCount) {
        QueryCount queryCount = QueryCountHolder.getGrandTotal();
        int recordedUpdateCount = queryCount.getUpdate();
        if (expectedUpdateCount != recordedUpdateCount) {
            throw new SQLStatementCountMismatchException(expectedUpdateCount,
                recordedUpdateCount);
        }
    }

    public static void assertDeleteCount(int expectedDeleteCount) {
        QueryCount queryCount = QueryCountHolder.getGrandTotal();
        int recordedDeleteCount = queryCount.getDelete();
        if (expectedDeleteCount != recordedDeleteCount) {
            throw new SQLStatementCountMismatchException(expectedDeleteCount,
                recordedDeleteCount);
        }
    }
}
```

The N+1 query detection integration test looks like this:

```
SQLStatementCountValidator.reset();
List<PostComment> comments = entityManager.createQuery(
    "select pc " +
    "from PostComment pc " +
    "where pc.review = :review", PostComment.class)
.setParameter("review", review)
.getResultList();
SQLStatementCountValidator.assertSelectCount(1);
```

If the PostComment entity post attribute is changed to FetchType.EAGER, this test is going to throw a SQLStatementCountMismatchException because Hibernate executes an additional query statement to initialize the post attribute.

In case there were N PostComment entities being selected, Hibernate would generate N+1 queries according to the FetchType.EAGER contract.

```
SELECT pc.id AS id1_1_, pc.post_id AS post_id3_1_, pc.review AS review2_1_
FROM   post_comment pc
WHERE  pc.review = 'Excellent!'

SELECT p.id AS id1_0_0_, p.title AS title2_0_0_
FROM   post p
WHERE  p.id = 1
```

```
com.vladmihalcea.book.hpjp.hibernate.logging.SQLStatementCountMismatchException:
    Expected 1 statement(s) but recorded 2 instead!
```

Whenever statements are generated automatically, it is mandatory to validate their number using an integration test assertion mechanism, and Hibernate makes no exception. Having such tests ensures the number of generated statements does not change, as the tests would fail otherwise.

The datasource-proxy statement count validator supports other DML statements too, and it can be used to validate that insert, update, and delete statements are batched properly.

14.3.3.2.3 LazyInitializationException

Another common issue associated with lazy fetching is the infamous `LazyInitializationException`. As previously explained, `@ManyToOne` and `@OneToOne` associations are replaced with Proxies, while collections are substituted with Hibernate internal Proxy `Collection` implementations. As long as the Persistence Context is open, Hibernate can initialize such Proxies lazily. When the underlying `Session` is closed, attempting to navigate an uninitialized Proxy is going to end with a `LazyInitializationException`.

Assuming that the `PostComment` entity has a `FetchType.LAZY post` attribute, when executing the following example:

```
PostComment comment = null;
EntityManager entityManager = null;
EntityTransaction transaction = null;
try {
    entityManager = entityManagerFactory().createEntityManager();
    transaction = entityManager.getTransaction();
    transaction.begin();
    comment = entityManager.find(PostComment.class, 1L);
    transaction.commit();
} catch (Throwable e) {
    if ( transaction != null && transaction.isActive())
        transaction.rollback();
    throw e;
} finally {
    if (entityManager != null) {
        entityManager.close();
    }
}
LOGGER.info("The post title is '{}'", comment.getPost().getTitle());
```

Hibernate throws a `LazyInitializationException` because the `comment.getPost()` Proxy is disconnected from the original `Session`:

```
org.hibernate.LazyInitializationException: could not initialize proxy -
    no Session
at org.hibernate.proxy.AbstractLazyInitializer.initialize
at org.hibernate.proxy.AbstractLazyInitializer.getImplementation
at org.hibernate.proxy.pojo.javassist.JavassistLazyInitializer.invoke
at com.vladmihalcea.book.hpjp.hibernate.forum.Post_$$_jvst15e_0.getTitle
```

The best way yo deal with the `LazyInitializationException` is to fetch all the required associations as long as the Persistence Context is open. Using the `fetch` JPQL directive, a custom entity graph, or the `initialize` method of the `org.hibernate.Hibernate` utility, the lazy associations that are needed further up the stack (in the service or the view layer) must be loaded before the Hibernate `Session` is closed.

Unfortunately, there are bad ways to deal with the `LazyInitializationException` too. One quick fix would be to change the association in question to `FetchType.EAGER`. While this would work for the current business use case, the `FetchType.EAGER` is going to affect all other queries where the root entity of this association is fetched.

 The fetching strategy is a query time responsibility, and each query should only fetch just as much data that is needed by the current business use case. On the other hand, `FetchType.EAGER` is a mapping time decision that is taken outside the business logic context where the association is meant to be used.

There is also the *Open Session in View* anti-pattern that is sometimes proposed as a solution for the `LazyInitializationException`.

14.3.3.2.4 The Open Session in View Anti-Pattern

Open Session in View is an architectural pattern that proposes to hold the Persistence Context open throughout the whole web request. This way, if the service layer fetched an entity without fully initializing all its associations further needed by the UI, then the view layer could silently trigger a Proxy initialization on demand.

Spring framework comes with a `javax.servlet.Filter`[1] implementation of the Open Session in View pattern. The `OpenSessionInViewFilter` gets a `Session` from the underlying `SessionFactory` and registers it in a `ThreadLocal` storage where the `HibernateTransactionManager` can also locate it. This service layer is still responsible for managing the actual JDBC or JTA transaction, but the `Session` is no longer closed by the `HibernateTransactionManager`[2].

---

[1]https://docs.spring.io/spring/docs/current/javadoc-api/org/springframework/orm/hibernate5/support/OpenSessionInViewFilter.html

[2]https://docs.spring.io/spring/docs/current/javadoc-api/org/springframework/orm/hibernate5/HibernateTransactionManager.html

To visualize the whole process, consider the following sequence diagram:

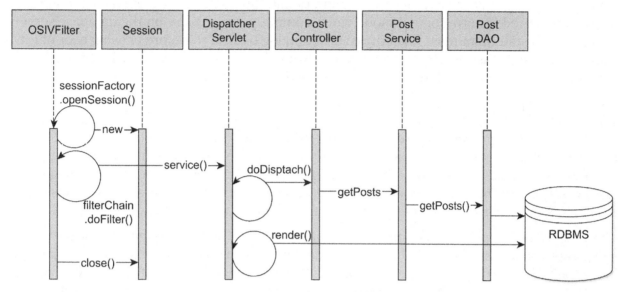

Figure 14.3: Open Session in View lifecycle

- The `OpenSessionInViewFilter` calls the `openSession` method of the underlying `SessionFactory` and obtains a new `Session`.
- The `Session` is bound to the `TransactionSynchronizationManager`[3].
- The `OpenSessionInViewFilter` calls the `doFilter` of the `javax.servlet.FilterChain` object reference and the request is further processed
- The `DispatcherServlet`[4] is called, and it routes the HTTP request to the underlying `PostController`.
- The `PostController` calls the `PostService` to get a list of `Post` entities.
- The `PostService` opens a new transaction, and the `HibernateTransactionManager` reuses the same `Session` that was opened by the `OpenSessionInViewFilter`.
- The `PostDAO` fetches the list of `Post` entities without initializing any lazy association.
- The `PostService` commits the underlying transaction, but the `Session` is not closed because it was opened externally.
- The `DispatcherServlet` starts rendering the UI, which, in turn, navigates the lazy associations and triggers their initialization.
- The `OpenSessionInViewFilter` can close the `Session`, and the underlying database connection is released as well.

At a first glance, this might not look like a terrible thing to do, but, once you view it from a database perspective, a series of flaws start to become more obvious.

---

[3]http://docs.spring.io/spring/docs/current/javadoc-api/org/springframework/transaction/support/TransactionSynchronizationManager.html

[4]http://docs.spring.io/spring/docs/current/javadoc-api/org/springframework/web/servlet/DispatcherServlet.html

The service layer opens and closes a database transaction, but afterward, there is no explicit transaction going on. For this reason, every additional statement issued from the UI rendering phase is executed in auto-commit mode. Auto-commit puts pressure on the database server because each statement must flush the transaction log to disk, therefore causing a lot of I/O traffic on the database side. One optimization would be to mark the Connection as read-only which would allow the database server to avoid writing to the transaction log.

There is no separation of concerns anymore because statements are generated both by the service layer and by the UI rendering process. Writing integration tests that assert the number of statements being generated requires going through all layers (web, service, DAO), while having the application deployed on a web container. Even when using an in-memory database (e.g. HSQLDB) and a lightweight web server (e.g. Jetty), these integration tests are going to be slower to execute than if layers were separated and the back-end integration tests used the database, while the front-end integration tests were mocking the service layer altogether.

The UI layer is limited to navigating associations which can, in turn, trigger N+1 query problems, as previously explained. Although Hibernate offers @BatchSize[5] for fetching associations in batches, and FetchMode.SUBSELECT[6] to cope with this scenario, the annotations are affecting the default fetch plan, so they get applied to every business use case. For this reason, a data access layer query is much more suitable because it can be tailored for the current use case data fetch requirements.

Last but not least, the database connection is held throughout the UI rendering phase which increases connection lease time and limits the overall transaction throughput due to congestion on the database connection pool. The more the connection is held, the more other concurrent requests are going to wait to get a connection from the pool.

The Open Session in View is a solution to a problem that should not exist in the first place, and the most likely root cause is relying exclusively on entity fetching.

If the UI layer only needs a view of the underlying data, then the data access layer is going to perform much better with a DTO projection. A DTO projection forces the application developer to fetch just the required data set and is not susceptible to LazyInitializationException(s).

This way, the separation of concerns is no longer compromised, and performance optimizations can be applied at the data access layer since all statements are confined to the boundaries of the currently executing transaction.

---

[5]https://docs.jboss.org/hibernate/orm/current/javadocs/org/hibernate/annotations/BatchSize.html
[6]https://docs.jboss.org/hibernate/orm/current/javadocs/org/hibernate/annotations/FetchMode.html#SUBSELECT

14.3.3.2.5 Temporary Session Lazy Loading Anti-Pattern

Analogous to the Open Session in View, Hibernate offers the `hibernate.enable_lazy_load_-no_trans` configuration property which allows an uninitialized lazy association to be loaded outside of the context of its original Persistence Context.

```
<property name="hibernate.enable_lazy_load_no_trans" value="true"/>
```

With this configuration property in place, the following code snippets can be executed without throwing any `LazyInitializationException`:

```
List<PostComment> comments = null;

EntityManager entityManager = null;
EntityTransaction transaction = null;
try {
    entityManager = entityManagerFactory().createEntityManager();
    transaction = entityManager.getTransaction();
    transaction.begin();

    comments = entityManager.createQuery(
        "select pc " +
        "from PostComment pc " +
        "where pc.review = :review", PostComment.class)
    .setParameter("review", review)
    .getResultList();

    transaction.commit();
} catch (Throwable e) {
    if ( transaction != null && transaction.isActive())
        transaction.rollback();
    throw e;
} finally {
    if (entityManager != null) {
        entityManager.close();
    }
}
for(PostComment comment : comments) {
    LOGGER.info("The post title is '{}'", comment.getPost().getTitle());
}
```

Behind the scenes, a temporary `Session` is opened just for initializing every `post` association. Every temporary `Session` implies acquiring a new database connection, as well as a new database transaction.

The more associations being loaded lazily, the more additional connections are going to be requested which puts pressure on the underlying connection pool. Each association being loaded in a new transaction, the transaction log is forced to flush after each association initialization.

Just like Open Session in View, the `hibernate.enable_lazy_load_no_trans` configuration property is an anti-pattern as well because it only treats the symptoms and does not solve the actual cause of the `LazyInitializationException`.

By properly initializing all lazy associations prior to closing the initial Persistence Context, and switching to DTO projections where entities are not even necessary, the `LazyInitializationException` is prevented in a much more efficient way.

14.3.3.3 Associations and pagination

As previously explained, paginating result sets has many benefits, from lowering the response time to ensuring that the application works with the ever increasing data sets. Also, fetching a collection with the `join fetch` JPQL directive can prevent N+1 query problems and `LazyInitializationException(s)` as well. Unfortunately, mixing collection fetching and pagination does not work very well together.

Collections must always be fetched fully because otherwise the collection size might not be consistent with the number of child entries associated with a given parent. On the other hand, SQL pagination can truncate the collection before returning all child records, therefore breaking the aforementioned consistency guarantee.

To visualize this process, the following entity query is going to load a list of `Post` entities, filtered by their `title`, and also, fetch all comments associated with a given `Post` record.

When specifying a `maxResults` restriction:

```
List<Post> posts = entityManager.createQuery(
    "select p " +
    "from Post p " +
    "left join fetch p.comments " +
    "where p.title like :title " +
    "order by p.id", Post.class)
.setParameter("title", titlePattern)
.setMaxResults(50)
.getResultList();
```

Hibernate issues a warning message saying that pagination is done in memory, and the SQL query shows no sign of limiting the result set:

```
WARN - firstResult/maxResults specified with collection fetch;
       applying in memory!

SELECT p.id AS id1_0_0_, pc.id AS id1_1_1_, p.title AS title2_0_0_,
       pc.post_id AS post_id3_1_1_, pc.review AS review2_1_1_,
       pc.post_id AS post_id3_1_0__, pc.id AS id1_1_0__
FROM   post p
LEFT OUTER JOIN post_comment pc ON p.id = pc.post_id
WHERE  p.title LIKE 'high-performance%'
ORDER BY p.id
```

So, Hibernate fetches the whole result set, and then it limits the number of root entities according to the `maxResults` query attribute value.

Compared to SQL-level pagination, entity query result set size restriction is not very efficient, causing the database to fetch the whole result set.

Entity queries vs DTO projections

By now, it is obvious that entity queries, although useful in certain scenarios, are not a universal solution to fetching data from a relational database. It can be detrimental to application performance to rely only on entity queries exclusively. As a rule of thumb, entity queries should be used when there is a need to modify the currently selected entities.

For read-only views, DTO projections can be more efficient because there are fewer columns being selected, and the queries can be paginated at the SQL-level. While the entity query language (JPQL and HQL) offers a wide range of filtering criteria, a native SQL query can take advantage of the underlying relational database querying capabilities.

JPQL/HQL and SQL queries are complementary solutions, both having a place in an enterprise system developer's toolkit.

14.3.4 Attribute lazy fetching

When fetching an entity, all attributes are going to be loaded as well. This is because every entity attribute is implicitly marked with the @Basic[7] annotation whose default fetch policy is FetchType.EAGER.

However, the attribute fetch strategy can be set to FetchType.LAZY, in which case the entity attribute is loaded with a secondary select statement upon being accessed for the first time.

```
@Basic(fetch = FetchType.LAZY)
```

This configuration alone is not sufficient because Hibernate requires bytecode instrumentation to intercept the attribute access request and issue the secondary select statement on demand.

When using the Maven bytecode enhancement plugin, the enableLazyInitialization configuration property must be set to true as illustrated in the following example:

```
<plugin>
    <groupId>org.hibernate.orm.tooling</groupId>
    <artifactId>hibernate-enhance-maven-plugin</artifactId>
    <version>${hibernate.version}</version>
    <executions>
        <execution>
            <configuration>
                <failOnError>true</failOnError>
                <enableLazyInitialization>true</enableLazyInitialization>
            </configuration>
            <goals>
                <goal>enhance</goal>
            </goals>
        </execution>
    </executions>
</plugin>
```

With this configuration in place, all JPA entity classes are going to be instrumented with lazy attribute fetching. This process takes place at build time, right after entity classes are compiled from their associated source files.

The attribute lazy fetching mechanism is very useful when dealing with column types that store large amounts of data (e.g. BLOB, CLOB, VARBINARY). This way, the entity can be fetched without automatically loading data from the underlying large column types, therefore improving performance.

To demonstrate how attribute lazy fetching works, the following example is going to use an Attachment entity which can store any media type (e.g. PNG, PDF, MPEG).

---

[7]http://docs.oracle.com/javaee/7/api/javax/persistence/Basic.html#fetch--

```java
@Entity @Table(name = "attachment")
public class Attachment {

    @Id
    @GeneratedValue
    private Long id;

    private String name;

    @Enumerated
    @Column(name = "media_type")
    private MediaType mediaType;

    @Lob
    @Basic(fetch = FetchType.LAZY)
    private byte[] content;

    //Getters and setters omitted for brevity
}
```

Attributes such as the entity identifier, the name or the media type are to be fetched eagerly on every entity load. On the other hand, the media file content should be fetched lazily, only when being accessed by the application code.

After the Attachment entity is instrumented, the class bytecode is changed as follows:

```java
@Transient
private transient PersistentAttributeInterceptor
    $$_hibernate_attributeInterceptor;

public byte[] getContent() {
    return $$_hibernate_read_content();
}

public byte[] $$_hibernate_read_content() {
    if ($$_hibernate_attributeInterceptor != null) {
        this.content = ((byte[]) $$_hibernate_attributeInterceptor
            .readObject(this, "content", this.content));
    }
    return this.content;
}
```

The content attribute fetching is done by the PersistentAttributeInterceptor object reference, therefore providing a way to load the underlying BLOB column only when the getter is called for the first time.

Figure 14.4: The attachment database table

When executing the following test case:

```
Attachment book = entityManager.find(Attachment.class, bookId);

LOGGER.debug("Fetched book: {}", book.getName());

assertArrayEquals(Files.readAllBytes(bookFilePath), book.getContent());
```

Hibernate generates the following SQL queries:

```
SELECT a.id AS id1_0_0_,
       a.media_type AS media_ty3_0_0_,
       a.name AS name4_0_0_
FROM   attachment a
WHERE  a.id = 1

-- Fetched book: High-Performance Java Persistence

SELECT a.content AS content2_0_
FROM   attachment a
WHERE  a.id = 1
```

Because it is marked with the FetchType.LAZY annotation and lazy fetching bytecode enhancement is enabled, the content column is not fetched along with all the other columns that initialize the Attachment entity. Only when the data access layer tries to access the content attribute, Hibernate issues a secondary select to load this attribute as well.

Just like FetchType.LAZY associations, this technique is prone to N+1 query problems, so caution is advised. One slight disadvantage of the bytecode enhancement mechanism is that all entity attributes, not just the ones marked with the FetchType.LAZY annotation, are going to be transformed, as previously illustrated.

14.3.5 Fetching subentities

Another approach to avoid loading table columns that are rather large is to map multiple subentities to the same database table.

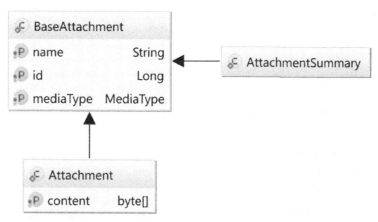

Figure 14.5: Attachment and AttachmentSummary entities

Both the `Attachment` entity and the `AttachmentSummary` subentity inherit all common attributes from a `BaseAttachment` superclass.

```
@MappedSuperclass
public class BaseAttachment {

    @Id
    @GeneratedValue
    private Long id;

    private String name;

    @Enumerated
    @Column(name = "media_type")
    private MediaType mediaType;

    //Getters and setters omitted for brevity
}
```

While `AttachmentSummary` extends `BaseAttachment` without declaring any new attribute:

```
@Entity @Table(name = "attachment")
public class AttachmentSummary extends BaseAttachment {}
```

The `Attachment` entity inherits all the base attributes from the `BaseAttachment` superclass and maps the `content` column as well.

```
@Entity @Table(name = "attachment")
public class Attachment extends BaseAttachment {

    @Lob
    private byte[] content;

    //Getters and setters omitted for brevity
}
```

When fetching the `AttachmentSummary` subentity:

```
AttachmentSummary bookSummary = entityManager.find(
    AttachmentSummary.class, bookId);
```

The generated SQL statement is not going to fetch the content column:

```
SELECT a.id as id1_0_0_, a.media_type as media_ty2_0_0_, a.name as name3_0_0_
FROM attachment a
WHERE   a.id = 1
```

However, when fetching the `Attachment` entity:

```
Attachment book = entityManager.find(Attachment.class, bookId);
```

Hibernate is going to fetch all columns from the underlying database table:

```
SELECT a.id as id1_0_0_, a.media_type as media_ty2_0_0_,
        a.name as name3_0_0_, a.content as content4_0_0_
FROM attachment a
WHERE   a.id = 1
```

 When it comes to reading data, subentities are very similar to DTO projections. However, unlike DTO projections, subentities can track state changes and propagate them to the database.

14.4 Entity reference deduplication

Considering that the Post comment has a bidirectional @OneToMany association with a PostComment entity, and the database contains the following entities:

```
Post post = new Post();
post.setId(1L);
post.setTitle("High-Performance Java Persistence");
post.addComment(new PostComment("Excellent!"));
post.addComment(new PostComment("Great!"));

entityManager.persist(post);
```

When fetching a Post entity along with all its PostComment child entries:

```
List<Post> posts = entityManager.createQuery(
    "select p " +
    "from Post p " +
    "left join fetch p.comments " +
    "where p.title = :title", Post.class)
.setParameter("title", "High-Performance Java Persistence")
.getResultList();

LOGGER.info("Fetched {} post entities: {}", posts.size(), posts);
```

Hibernate generates the following output:

```
SELECT p.id AS id1_0_0_ , pc.id AS id1_1_1_ , p.title AS title2_0_0_ ,
       pc.post_id AS post_id3_1_1_, pc.review AS review2_1_1_
FROM   post p
LEFT OUTER JOIN post_comment pc ON p.id = pc.post_id
WHERE  p.title = 'High-Performance Java Persistence'

-- Fetched 2 post entities: [
    Post{id=1, title='High-Performance Java Persistence'},
    Post{id=1, title='High-Performance Java Persistence'}]
```

Because the underlying SQL query result set size is given by the number of post_comment rows, and the post data is duplicated for each associated post_comment entry, Hibernate is going to return 2 Post entity references.

Because the Persistence Context guarantees application-level repeatable reads, the posts list contains two references to the same Post entity object. To enable entity reference deduplication, JPA and Hibernate provide the distinct keyword.

Therefore, when adding distinct to the previous entity query:

```
List<Post> posts = entityManager.createQuery(
    "select distinct p " +
    "from Post p " +
    "left join fetch p.comments " +
    "where p.title = :title", Post.class)
.setParameter("title", "High-Performance Java Persistence")
.getResultList();
```

Hibernate generates the following output:

```
SELECT DISTINCT
        p.id AS id1_0_0_ , pc.id AS id1_1_1_ , p.title AS title2_0_0_ ,
        pc.post_id AS post_id3_1_1_, pc.review AS review2_1_1_
FROM    post p
LEFT OUTER JOIN post_comment pc ON p.id = pc.post_id
WHERE   p.title = 'High-Performance Java Persistence'

-- Fetched 1 post entities: [
    Post{id=1, title='High-Performance Java Persistence'}]
```

So, the duplicated entries have been removed from the result set, but the DISTINCT keyword was passed to the underlying SQL query. While this would be beneficial for scalar queries, for entity queries, this can affect the query execution plan.

When executing the query above that with the DISTINCT keyword on PostgreSQL, the following execution plan is obtained:

```
HashAggregate
  Group Key: p.id, pc.id, p.title, pc.post_id, pc.review
  -> Hash Right Join
    Hash Cond: (pc.post_id = p.id)
    -> Seq Scan on post_comment pc
    -> Hash
        -> Seq Scan on post p
            Filter: (title = 'High-Performance Java Persistence')
```

The HashAggregate is going to execute a sort the result set so that duplicate entries can be removed much faster. In this particular use case, this extra sorting phase is completely redundant because there are no duplicate entries to be removed. Therefore, the overall response time is going to be increased unnecessarily.

For this reason, Hibernate 5.2.2 adds an optimization via the DISTINCT_PASS_THROUGH query hint. When providing this query hint, and rerunning the previous entity query:

```
List<Post> posts = entityManager.createQuery(
    "select distinct p " +
    "from Post p " +
    "left join fetch p.comments " +
    "where p.title = :title", Post.class)
.setParameter("title", "High-Performance Java Persistence")
.setHint(QueryHints.HINT_PASS_DISTINCT_THROUGH, false)
.getResultList();
```

Hibernate is going to generate the following output:

```
SELECT p.id AS id1_0_0_ , pc.id AS id1_1_1_ , p.title AS title2_0_0_ ,
       pc.post_id AS post_id3_1_1_, pc.review AS review2_1_1_
FROM   post p
LEFT OUTER JOIN post_comment pc ON p.id = pc.post_id
WHERE  p.title = 'High-Performance Java Persistence'

-- Fetched 1 post entities: [
   Post{id=1, title='High-Performance Java Persistence'}]
```

So, the entity references have been deduplicated while the distinct JPA keyword was not passed through the underlying SQL statement. This time, the PostgreSQL execution plan looks as follows:

```
Hash Right Join
  Hash Cond: (pc.post_id = p.id)
  -> Seq Scan on post_comment pc
  -> Hash
        -> Seq Scan on post p
              Filter: (title = 'High-Performance Java Persistence')
```

As illustrated by the execution plan above, there is no HashAggregate step this time. Therefore, the unnecessary sorting phase is skipped, and the query execution is going to be faster.

14.5 Query plan cache

There are two types of entity queries: dynamic and named queries. For dynamic queries, the EntityManager offers the createQuery method, while for named queries, there is a createNamedQuery alternative. There is no obvious performance gain for using named queries over dynamic ones because, behind the scenes, a named query caches only its definition (e.g. NamedQueryDefinition), and the actual query plan cache is available for both dynamic and named queries.

Every query must be compiled prior to being executed, and, because this process might be resource intensive, Hibernate provides a QueryPlanCache for this purpose. For entity queries, the query String representation is parsed into an Abstract Syntax Tree. For native queries, the parsing extracts information about named parameters and query return type.

The query plan cache is shared by entity and native queries, and its size is controlled by the following configuration property:

```
<property name="hibernate.query.plan_cache_max_size" value="2048"/>
```

By default, the QueryPlanCache stores 2048 plans which is sufficient for many small and medium-sized enterprise applications.

For native queries, the QueryPlanCache stores also the ParameterMetadata which holds info about parameter name, position, and associated Hibernate type. The ParameterMetadata cache is controlled via the following configuration property:

```
<property name="hibernate.query.plan_parameter_metadata_max_size" value="128"/>
```

If the application executes much more queries than the QueryPlanCache can hold, there is going to be an impact due to query compilation phase.

The following test executes only two queries while varying the QueryPlanCache and the ParameterMetadata cache size from 1 to 100. When the plan cache size is 1, the queries are always compiled, and the average duration can be visualized in the following table:

Table 14.1: Query plan cache performance

Query type	Cache miss time (ms)	Cache hit time (ms)
Entity	0.68425	0.00092
Native	0.00313	0.00136

Only for entity queries, the plan cache can really make a difference in terms of performance. For native queries, the gain is less significant. The plan cache storing both entity and native queries, it is important to adjust its size so that it can accommodate all queries being executed. Otherwise, some entity queries might have to be recompiled, therefore increasing the current transaction response time.

15. Caching

15.1 Caching flavors

Caching is everywhere. For instance, the CPU has several caching layers to decrease the latency associated with accessing data from the main memory. Being close to the processing unit, the CPU cache is very fast. However, compared to the main memory, the CPU cache is very small and can only store frequently-accessed data.

To speed up reading and writing to the underlying disk drive, the operating system uses caching as well. Data is read in pages that are cached into main memory, so frequently-accessed data is served from OS buffers rather than the disk drive. Disk cache improves the write operations as well because modifications can be buffered and flushed at once, therefore improving write throughput.

Since indexes and data blocks are better off served from memory, most relational database systems employ an internal caching layer.

So even without explicitly setting up a caching solution, an enterprise application already uses several caching layers. Nevertheless, enterprise caching is most often a necessity, and there are several solutions that can be used for this purpose.

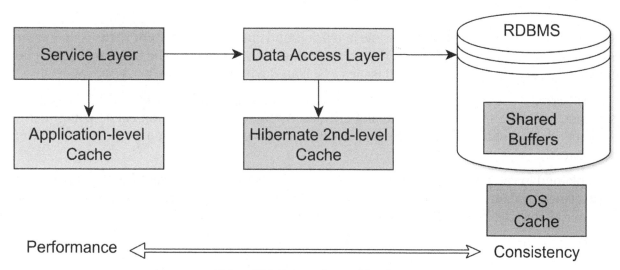

Figure 15.1: Enterprise caching layers

As illustrated in the diagram above, caching entails a trade-off. On one hand, bypassing the underlying data access layer can speed up reads and writes. However, the farther the caching solution is situated, the more difficult it is for it to maintain consistency with the underlying database system.

For it guarantees ACID transactions, the database cache is highly consistent, so, from a data integrity perspective, it entails no risk of reading stale data. However, the database engine can only spare disk access, and so it cannot alleviate the networking overhead. More, if the data access layer needs to fetch an aggregate that spans over multiple database tables, the result set would either contain many joins, or it will require multiple secondary queries. The more complex the data access pattern, the more work a database server has to do, and, for this reason, it is common to use an application-level cache as well.

Most often, application-level caches are key-value stores. Once an aggregate is fetched from the database, it can be stored in the application cache so that any successive request can bypass the database entirely. The application-level cache can outperform the database engine because it can bypass the networking overhead associated with fetching result sets.

 Another very important reason for using an application-level caching solution is that it can provide a safety hook for when the database has to be taken down for maintenance.

If the front-end cache stores a sufficient amount of data, it can serve as a temporary replacement for the database system, allowing read-only operations to be served from the cache. Even if write operations are prevented while the database system is unavailable, the read-only mode increases the overall system availability.

However, application-level caches come at a price, and ensuring consistent reads is no longer a trivial thing to do. Because of its tight integration with Hibernate, the second-level cache can avoid many consistency-related issues associated with application-level caches.

The Hibernate second-level cache is a data access caching solution that aims to reduce database load when it comes to fetching entities. Along with it collection cache component, the second-level cache allows retrieving an entire entity graph without a single access to the database.

As explained in the previous chapter, fetching entities is usually associated with propagating entity state transitions. Therefore, the second-level cache can improve response time for read-write transactions without compromising data consistency.

 Application-level caches are useful for read scenarios, while the second-level cache consistency guarantee is better suited for offloading write traffic.

15.2 Cache synchronization strategies

In database nomenclature, the system of record represents the source of truth when information is scattered among various data providers. Duplicating data, so that it resides closer to application layers, can improve response time at the price of making it more difficult to synchronize the two data copies. To avoid inconsistent reads and data integrity issues, whenever a change occurs in the system, it is very important to synchronize both the database and the cache.

There are various ways to keep the cache and the underlying database in sync, and this section is going to present some of the most common cache synchronization strategies.

15.2.1 Cache-aside

The application code manually manages both the database system and the caching layer.

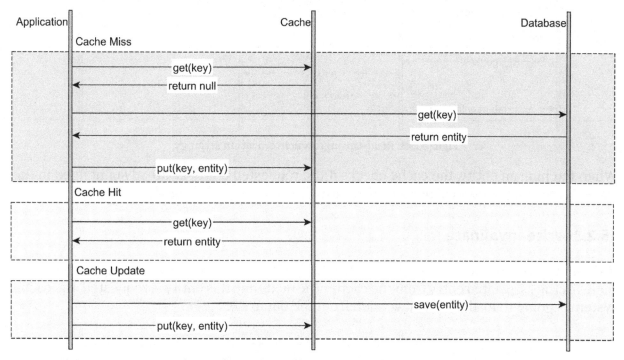

Figure 15.2: Cache-aside synchronization strategy

Before hitting the database, the application logic inspects the cache to see if the requested entity was previously loaded. Whenever an entity changes, the application must update both the database and the cache store.

Mixing application logic with caching management semantics breaks the Single Responsibility Principle. For this reason, it is good practice to move the caching logic into an AOP (aspect-oriented programming) interceptor, therefore decoupling the cache management logic from the business logic code.

15.2.2 Read-through

Instead of managing both the database and the cache, the application layer interacts only with the cache system; the database management logic being hidden behind the caching API. Compared to the cache-aside use case, the data access logic is simplified since there is only one data source to communicate with.

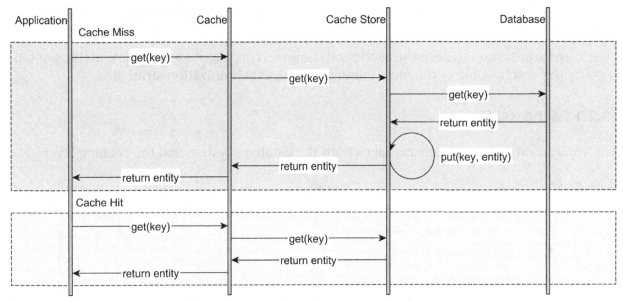

Figure 15.3: Read-through synchronization strategy

When fetching an entity, the cache checks if the requested entity is already contained in the cache store, and, upon a cache miss, the entity is loaded from the database.

15.2.3 Write-invalidate

If the entity is modified, the cache propagates the change to the underlying database and removes the associated entry from the cache. The next time this entity is requested, the cache system is going to load the latest version from the database.

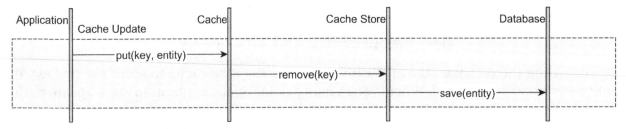

Figure 15.4: Write-invalidate synchronization strategy

15.2.4 Write-through

If the entity is modified, the changed is propagated to the underlying database and the cache as well.

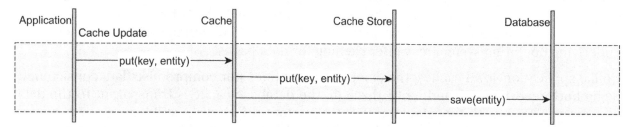

Figure 15.5: Write-through synchronization strategy

If the caching layer supports JTA transactions, the cache and the database can be committed at once. Although XA transactions can simplify development, the two-phase commit protocol incurs a significant performance overhead.

An alternative is to use soft locks on the cache side to hide the cache entry modification until the database transaction is committed, so that, until the lock is released, other concurrent transactions must load the entity from the database.

15.2.5 Write-behind

If strong consistency is not mandated, the change requests can be enqueued and flushed at once to the database.

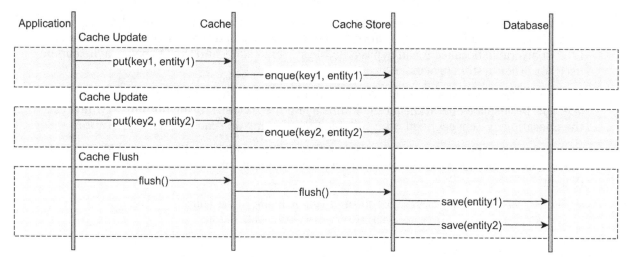

Figure 15.6: Write-behind synchronization strategy

This strategy is employed by the JPA Persistence Context, all entity state transitions being flushed towards the end of the currently running transaction or prior to executing a query.

15.3 Database caching

As explained at the beginning of this chapter, most database engines make use of internal caching mechanisms to speed up read and write operations. The most common database cache component is the in-memory buffers, but there might be other components as well such as the execution plan cache or query result buffer. Even without a database cache, the underlying operating system may offer caching for data pages.

Unlike application-level caches, the database cache does not compromise data consistency. Being both read-through and write-through, the database cache is transparent to the data access layer. Even with the advent of SSD (solid-state drive), disks still have a much higher latency than RAM. For this purpose, it makes much sense to load frequently-accessed data from memory, rather than going to disk.

Oracle

Oracle has multiple mechanisms for caching, such as:

- Buffer pool - storing blocks of data that are loaded from the underlying disk drive.
- Shared pool - storing parsed SQL statements, schema object metadata, sequence numbers.
- Large pool - stores results for parallel queries, large I/O buffers that are used for recovery management and backup or restore procedures.
- Result cache - stores results for SQL queries (when using the RESULT_CACHE query hint) and PL/SQL functions (when using the RESULT_CACHE directive).

On Unix systems, all I/O goes through the OS page cache. However, the same data is going to be cached in the Buffer pool, therefore data blocks are cached twice. For this reason, direct I/O[a] is desirable because it can bypass the file system cache, and the OS page cache can be used for other system processes.

There are also use cases when Oracle does not use the Buffer pool for caching data blocks (e.g. TEMP tablespace operations, LOB columns using the NOCACHE storing option), in which case the operating system cache may be suitable for speeding up read and write operations.

Although each caching structure can be configured manually, it is often a good idea to leave this responsibility to the automatic memory management[b] mechanism, which is enabled by default.

---

[a]http://docs.oracle.com/database/121/TGDBA/pfgrf_os.htm#TGDBA94410
[b]https://docs.oracle.com/database/121/TGDBA/memory.htm#TGDBA505

SQL Server

To provide very low transaction response times, SQL Server strives for reducing I/O operations (which are a source of performance-related issues in many database systems). For this reason, the database engine tries to use as much system memory as possible so that frequently-accessed data and index disk pages are served from RAM rather than the disk drive.

Upon startup, SQL Server allocates a portion of the system memory and uses it as a buffer pool. The buffer pool is divided into multiple pages of 8KB. Both data and index pages are read from disk into buffer pages, and, when the in-memory pages are modified, they are written back to disk.

SQL Server 2014 supports buffer pool extensions[a], which allow it to use SSD drives to increase the buffer cache size beyond the capabilities of the current system available memory.

[a]https://msdn.microsoft.com/en-us/library/dn133176.aspx

PostgreSQL

For improving read and write operation performance, PostgreSQL relies heavily on the underlying operating system caching capabilities. However, most operating systems use a LRU (least recently used) page replacement policy which is unaware of the data access patterns or other database-related considerations.

For this reason, PostgreSQL defines a shared buffers structure which stores disk pages into 8KB in-memory page cache entries. The shared buffer size is controlled via the `shared_buffers` configuration property. Unlike the OS cache, the shared buffers use a LFU (least frequently used) algorithm called clock sweep which counts the number of times a disk page is used. The more often a disk page is being used, the longer it is going to linger in the shared buffer database internal cache.

That being said, the shared buffer structure is more useful for storing frequently-accessed data blocks, while the operating system cache can be used for everything else. The shared buffer cache should not be set too high because the database engine requires memory for other operations as well (sorting, hashing, building indexes, vacuuming).

Although the shared buffers structure is very important for speeding up reads and writes, it is good practice to limit the shared buffer size[a] to the size of the current working set, therefore leaving enough memory for other database-related tasks.

[a]http://www.postgresql.org/docs/current/static/runtime-config-resource.html

MySQL

MySQL uses its internal buffer pool to cache data and indexes. The buffer pool is implemented as a linked list of memory pages. If the buffer pool size is smaller than the overall InnoDB tablespace size, a LRU-based algorithm is going to be used to deallocate older page entries.

The pool size is given by the `innodb_buffer_pool_size` configuration property which, ideally, should be adjusted so that it can hold all data and indexes in memory. Care must be taken to allow enough memory for the OS, as well for other MySQL structures and processes (e.g. threads allocated for each individual connection, sort buffers, query cache).

On Linux, to avoid double buffering caused by the operating system caching mechanism, the `innodb_flush_method`[a] configuration property should be set to `O_DIRECT`.

Nevertheless, the OS cache is useful for storing the InnoDB transaction log (used for ensuring ACID transactions), the binary log (used for database replication), and other MySQL structures that are not covered by the InnoDB buffer pool.

---

[a]http://dev.mysql.com/doc/refman/5.7/en/innodb-parameters.html#sysvar_innodb_flush_method

Essential, but not sufficient

Database caching is very important for a high-performance enterprise application. However, database caching only applies to a single node, and, if the database size is bigger than the capacity of a single node, then this solution alone is no longer sufficient. One workaround is to use database sharding, but that is not without challenges.

Even if database caching improves performance considerably, the networking overhead still plays a significant role in the overall transaction response time. If the application operates on graphs of entities, fetching an entire graph might require lots of joins or many secondary select statements. For this reason, it makes sense to cache the whole entity aggregate and have it closer to the application layer.

If the enterprise system relies only on the database system alone to serve read requests, the database becomes a single point of failure. This availability can be increased by using database replication. However, if all database nodes are collocated (to reduce the synchronization overhead caused by networking latency), the database system can still become unavailable if the data center is facing a sudden power outage.

For all these reasons, it is good practice to use an application-layer caching solution to address database caching limitations.

15.4 Application-level caching

Application caches are a necessity for high-performance enterprise applications, and this section is going to explore this topic in greater detail. No matter how well tuned a database engine is, the statement response time is highly dependent on the incoming database load. A traffic spike incurs a high contention of database system resources, which can lead to higher response times.

For instance, most internet applications expose a sitemap which is used by Search Engine bots to index the content of the site in question and make it available for searches. From a business perspective, having a high page rank is highly desirable because it can translate to more revenue. However, the Search Engine bot can generate a sudden traffic spike, which, in turn, can lead to a spike in transaction response time. Unfortunately, high response times can affect the site page rank. That being said, the translation response time must be relatively low even during high traffic loads.

The application-level cache can, therefore, level up traffic spikes because the cache fetching complexity is O(1). More, if the application-level cache holds a significant portion of the entire data set, the application can still work (even if in a read-only mode) when the database is shut down for maintenance or due to a catastrophic event.

15.4.1 Entity aggregates

In a relation database, data is normalized, and, for a complex enterprise application, it is usually spread across multiple tables. On the other hand, the business logic might operate on entity graphs which assemble information from various database tables.

To better visualize the entity aggregate, consider the following diagram depicting all entities associated with a single Post in a particular forum.

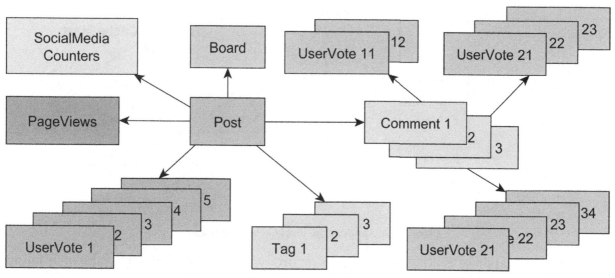

Figure 15.7: Entity aggregates

The Post entity is the root since all other entities relate to it, either directly or indirectly. A Post belongs to a Board entity, and it can have several Tag(s). The PageViews entity summarizes statistics about how popular a given Post might be. There is also a SocialMediaCounters entity to hold the number of shares for social media platforms. Users can add Comment(s) to a Post, and they can also cast a vote on both the Post or the Comment entity.

The sitemap contains the list of all Post(s) so that Search Engines can index all questions and answers. When a Post is requested, the whole entity aggregate is required to render the display. Without application-level caching, the data access layer would have to either join all the associated entities or use secondary select statements.

To avoid a Cartesian Product, the Post entity should be joined to its Tag(s), as well as with other many-to-one relationships (e.g. Board, PageViews, SocialMediaCounters). A secondary query is used to fetch the UserVote(s) associated with the current Post. The Comment(s) can be fetched with a secondary select, and this is desirable since there might be many Comment(s), and the secondary query can better use pagination. The Comment query could also join the UserVote(s) so that these two entities are fetched with a single query as well.

15.4.2 Distributed key-value stores

While the underlying data resides in the relational database, the entity aggregate can also be saved in a distributed cache, such as Redis or Memcached. Key-value stores are optimized for storing data structures in memory, and the lookup complexity is O(1). This is ideal for high-performance enterprise applications since response time can stay low even during unforeseen traffic spikes.

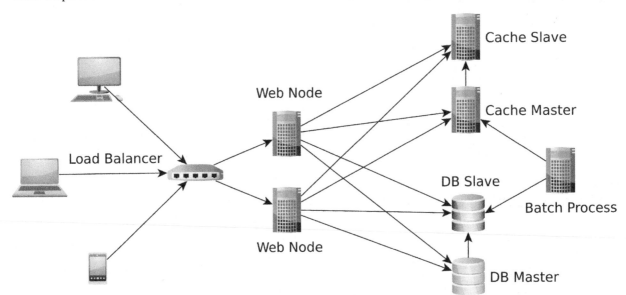

Figure 15.8: Application-level cache integration

The relational database is still the system of record, while the key-value caching solution is used as an alternate data provider.

15.4.3 Cache synchronization patterns

Unfortunately, duplicating data among two data sources is not without issues. Ideally, both the relational database and the application-level cache should be in sync, every update being applied synchronously to both data stores. In reality, not all business use cases have strict consistency requirements.

For instance, the PageViews and the SocialMediaCounters can be updated periodically by a batch processor which can aggregate the database counters and update the cache entry with the latest aggregated values. On the other hand, some actions need a more strict consistency guarantees. For Comment entries, read-your-writes consistency is needed because otherwise users might miss their own changes.

 Caching is always about trade-offs, and not all business use cases are equal in terms of consistency guarantees. For strict consistency, some transactions might need to bypass the cache entirely and read from the database.

Once a user or a batch process makes a change to the underlying database records, the cache needs to be updated as well. As explained in the cache concurrency strategies section, there are several ways to implement the synchronization logic.

15.4.4 Synchronous updates

If cache-aside is being used, the business logic must update both the database and all associated cache entries in the same transaction. Because most key-value stores do not use XA transactions, the cache entries can be either invalidated (in which case there is no risk of reading stale data), or they can be updated after the database transaction has been committed (in which case there is a slight time interval when a concurrent transaction can read a stale entry from the cache).

For the previous Domain Model, Comment entities should be processed synchronously. Adding or modifying a UserVote entry can also be done synchronously, or at least for the comments that are associated with the currently logged user.

15.4.5 Asynchronous updates

If eventual consistency is tolerated, then asynchronous updates are also a viable solution, and the application logic can be simplified since the caching logic is decoupled from business logic. This is also necessary when there are multiple data stores that need to be updated according to the latest changes that happened in the database. For instance, the enterprise application might need to propagate changes to a cache, an in-memory data processing framework (e.g.

Spark) which might monitor the forum for spam messages, or to a data warehouse. In this case, the changes must be captured from the database and propagated to all other subsystems that are interested in being notified about these updates.

15.4.5.1 Change data capture

In database terminology, change data capture (CDC) is an assembly of patterns that are responsible for recording database changes.

One solution is to record the timestamp version of every row that is either inserted, updated, or deleted. This pattern only works if records are not actually physically removed, but instead, they are simply marked as deleted (soft deleting), and hidden away from any database query.

Another implementation would be to capture changes using database triggers so that an event is recorded whenever a row is inserted, updated, or deleted. Unfortunately, triggers might slow down write operations which is undesirable especially if there is only one database Master node because the longer the write transactions take, the less throughput the Master node will accommodate.

A more efficient approach is to use a framework that can parse the database transaction log. Unlike database triggers, this approach does not incur any additional performance penalty for write operations since the transaction log is being parsed asynchronously. The only drawback is that not all database support this natively, and the transaction log entries can change from one database version to the other.

Oracle

Oracle GoldenGate[a] is a change data capture tool that can be used either for database replication or as an ETL (extract, transform, and load) process in order to feed a data warehouse. Another approach is to use Databus[b], which is an open-source framework developed by Linkedin for log mining.

[a]http://www.oracle.com/us/products/middleware/data-integration/goldengate/overview/index.html
[b]https://github.com/linkedin/databus

SQL Server

Since version 2008, SQL Server offers a Change Data Capture[a] solution that can be configured at the database, table, or even column level.

[a]https://msdn.microsoft.com/en-us/library/cc627369.aspx

PostgreSQL

Even if there is no native CDC solution, PostgreSQL 9.4 has introduced logical decoding[a] which can be used for extracting row-level modifications.

---

[a]http://www.postgresql.org/docs/9.5/static/logicaldecoding.html

MySQL

There are multiple solutions that are able to parse the MySQL binary log, and the most notable is Databus which supports both Oracle and MySQL.

Denormalization ripple effect

In the previous Domain Model, storing the Board and the list of Tag(s) associated with every particular Post entity graph is appropriate only if the Board and the Tag are practically immutable. Otherwise, changing the Board entity could ripple throughout the cache, causing a large number of entries to be updated as well. This problem is even more acute if cache entry invalidation is being used. For Tag(s), the Post aggregate should store only a list of Tag identifiers, the actual Tag names being resolved upon fetching the Post entity aggregate from the cache.

On the other hand, Comment(s) and UserVote(s) are more related to a single Post entry, so they are more suitable for being stored in the Post entity aggregate. To avoid the ripple effect, the UserVote entity should only contain virtually immutable user-related columns (e.g. user identifier).

 The higher the data denormalization degree associated with entity aggregates, the bigger the data change ripple. Therefore, it is good practice to avoid storing associations that might be shared among many entity graphs cache entries.

15.5 Second-level caching

While the Persistence Context has long been referred to as the first-level cache, in reality, it is meant to provide application-level repeatable reads rather than lowering fetch execution time. The first-level cache is not thread-safe, and, once the Hibernate Session is closed, the cached entities are no longer accessible.

On the other hand, the second-level cache is bound to a SessionFactory, it is thread-safe, and it provides a solution for optimizing entity aggregate loading time. Hibernate only defines the contract for the second-level cache API and does not provide a reference implementation for this specification. The second-level cache API is implemented by third-party caching providers, such as Infinispan[1], Ehcache[2], or Hazelcast[3].

Being tightly integrated with Hibernate, the second-level cache does not require any data access layer code change. While application-level caches operate in a cache-aside synchronization mode, the second-level cache offers read-through and write-through cache update strategies.

Unlike an application-level caching solution, the second-level does not store entity aggregates. Instead, entities are saved in a row-level data format which is closer to the associated database row values. Although it features a collection-level cache component, behind the scenes, it only saves the entity identifiers contained in a particular collection instance. The same is true for the entity query caching, whose cache entries contain only the entity identifiers that satisfy a given query filtering criteria.

For all the aforementioned reasons, the second-level cache is not a replacement or a substitute for application-level caches. The biggest gain for using the Hibernate second-level cache is that, in a Master-Slave database replication scheme, it can optimize read-write transactions. While read-only queries can be executed on many Slave nodes, read-write transactions can only be executed by the Master node.

 Being capable of working in read-through and write-through mode, the second-level cache can help reduce read-write transactions response time by reducing the amount of work the Master node is required to do.

---

[1]http://infinispan.org/
[2]http://www.ehcache.org/
[3]http://hazelcast.org/

15.5.1 Enabling the second-level cache

By default, the `hibernate.cache.use_second_level_cache` configuration is set to `true`. However, this is not sufficient because Hibernate requires a `CachingRegionFactory` implementation as well, and, without specifying any third-party implementation, Hibernate defaults to using the `NoCachingRegionFactory` implementation, meaning that nothing is actually being cached.

For this reason, it is mandatory to supply the `hibernate.cache.region.factory_class` configuration property, which takes the fully-qualified class name of the `CacheRegionFactory` third-party implementation.

```
<property name="hibernate.cache.region.factory_class"
          value="org.hibernate.cache.ehcache.EhCacheRegionFactory"/>
```

After enabling the second-level cache, the application developer must instruct Hibernate which entities should be cached. Although JPA 2.0 defined the `@Cacheable` annotation, Hibernate also requires a cache concurrency strategy.

For this reason, the `org.hibernate.annotations.Cache` annotation should be provided as well.

```
@Entity
@Cache(usage = CacheConcurrencyStrategy.READ_WRITE)
public class Post {

    //Fields, getters, and setters omitted for brevity
}
```

Hibernate defines the `hibernate.cache.default_cache_concurrency_strategy` configuration property which applies the same synchronization strategy to all cacheable entities.

When this configuration property is set, the `@Cache` annotation is no longer mandatory, and the `@Cacheable` annotation can be used instead. By supplying a `@Cache` annotation, the default cache concurrency strategy can be overridden on a per-entity basis.

15.5.2 Entity cache loading flow

Once the second-level cache is activated for a particular entity, it participates automatically in the entity loading mechanism.

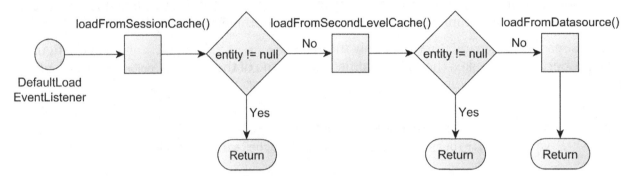

Figure 15.9: Entity loading control flow

When loading an entity, Hibernate always checks the Persistence Context first. This behavior guarantees application-level repeatable reads. Once an entity becomes managed, Hibernate will use the same entity instance when loading it directly or including it in an entity query.

If the entity is not found in the currently running Persistence Context and the second-level cache is configured properly, Hibernate checks the second-level cache. Only if the second-level cache does not contain the entity in question, Hibernate will fetch the entity from the underlying database.

15.5.3 Entity cache entry

Internally, every entity is stored as a `CacheEntry`. As previously explained, Hibernate does not store aggregates, and the second-level cache entry is close to the underlying table row representation.

> ### Hydrated and disassembled state
>
> In Hibernate nomenclature, *hydration* represents the process of transforming a JDBC `ResultSet` into an array of raw values.
>
> The *hydrated state* is saved in the currently running Persistence Context as an `EntityEntry` object which encapsulated the loading time entity snapshot. The hydrated state is then used by the default dirty checking mechanism which compares the current entity data against the loading time snapshot.
>
> The second-level cache entry values contain the hydrated state of a particular entity. However, for the second-level cache the hydrated state is called *disassembled state*.

To visualize the disassembled entity state, consider the following entity model:

```java
@Entity @Cache(usage = CacheConcurrencyStrategy.READ_WRITE)
public class Post {
    @Id
    private Long id;

    private String title;

    @Version
    private int version;

    //Getters and setters omitted for brevity
}

@Entity @Cache(usage = CacheConcurrencyStrategy.READ_WRITE)
public class PostDetails {
    @Id
    private Long id;

    private Date createdOn;

    private String createdBy;

    @OneToOne
    @MapsId
    private Post post;

    //Getters and setters omitted for brevity
}

@Entity @Cache(usage = CacheConcurrencyStrategy.READ_WRITE)
public class PostComment {
    @Id
    private Long id;

    @ManyToOne
    private Post post;

    private String review;

    //Getters and setters omitted for brevity
}
```

Upon saving and fetching the following Post entity:

```
Post post = new Post();
post.setId(1L);
post.setTitle("High-Performance Java Persistence");
entityManager.persist(post);
```

Hibernate stores the following second-level cache entry:

```
item = {org.hibernate.cache.ehcache.internal.strategy.AbstractReadWriteEhcacheAc\
cessStrategy$Item}
  value = {org.hibernate.cache.spi.entry.StandardCacheEntryImpl}
    disassembledState = {java.io.Serializable[1]}
      0 = "High-Performance Java Persistence"
    subclass = "com.vladmihalcea.book.hpjp.hibernate.cache.Post"
  version = 0
  timestamp = 5990528746983424
```

The disassembledState is an Object[] array which, in this case, contains a single entry that represents the Post title. The version attribute is stored separately, outside of the disassembledState array. The entity identifier is stored in the cache entry key which looks as follows:

```
key = {org.hibernate.cache.internal.OldCacheKeyImplementation}
  id = {java.lang.Long} "1"
  type = {org.hibernate.type.LongType}
  entityOrRoleName = "com.vladmihalcea.book.hpjp.hibernate.cache.Post"
  tenantId = null
  hashCode = 31
```

The cache entry key contains the entity type (e.g. entityOrRoleName), the identifier (e.g. id), and the identifier type (e.g. type). When multitenancy is being used, the tenant identifier (e.g. tenantId) is stored as well.

When storing a PostDetails entity:

```
PostDetails details = new PostDetails();
details.setCreatedBy("Vlad Mihalcea");
details.setCreatedOn(new Date());
details.setPost(post);
entityManager.persist(details);
```

The second-level cache entry looks like this:

```
item = {org.hibernate.cache.ehcache.internal.strategy.AbstractReadWriteEhcacheAc\
cessStrategy$Item}
  value = {org.hibernate.cache.spi.entry.StandardCacheEntryImpl}
    disassembledState = {java.io.Serializable[3]}
      0 = "Vlad Mihalcea"
      1 = {java.util.Date} "Fri May 06 15:45:10 EEST 2016"
    subclass = "com.vladmihalcea.book.hpjp.hibernate.cache.PostDetails"
  version = null
  timestamp = 5990558557458432
```

The `version` attribute is null because the `PostDetails` entity does not feature a `@Version` attribute. The `disassembledState` array has a length of 3, although just the `createdBy` and the `createdOn` attributes are visible. The `@OneToOne` association information is stored as null in the `disassembledState` array because Hibernate knows that the entity identifier is sufficient to locate the associated parent relationship.

When persisting a `PostComment` entity:

```
PostComment comment1 = new PostComment();
comment1.setId(1L);
comment1.setReview("JDBC part review");
comment1.setPost(post);
entityManager.persist(comment1);
```

The disassembled state will contain the `review` attribute and the foreign key value that is used for identifying the `@ManyToOne` association:

```
item = {org.hibernate.cache.ehcache.internal.strategy.AbstractReadWriteEhcacheAc\
cessStrategy$Item}
  value = {org.hibernate.cache.spi.entry.StandardCacheEntryImpl}
    disassembledState = {java.io.Serializable[2]}
      0 = {java.lang.Long} "1"
      1 = "JDBC part review"
    subclass = "com.vladmihalcea.book.hpjp.hibernate.cache.PostComment"
  version = null
  timestamp = 5990563491569665
```

15.5.3.1 Entity reference cache store

Hibernate can also store entity references directly in the second-level cache, therefore avoiding the performance penalty of reconstructing an entity from its disassembled state. However, not all entity types are allowed to benefit from this optimization.

For an entity to be cached as a reference, it must obey the following rules:

- The entity must be immutable, meaning that it must be marked with the `@org.hibernate.annotations.Immutable` annotation.
- It might not feature any entity association (`@ManyToOne`, `@OneToOne`, `@OneToMany`, `@ManyToMany`, or `@ElementCollection`).
- The `hibernate.cache.use_reference_entries` configuration property must be enabled.

Among the previously Domain Model entities, only the `Post` entity could be stored as an entity reference because `PostDetails` has a `@OneToOne` `Post` association, while `PostComment` has a `@ManyToOne` `Post` relationship. Therefore, the `Post` entity only needs to be marked with the `@Immutable` annotation:

```
@Entity @Immutable
@Cache(usage = CacheConcurrencyStrategy.READ_ONLY)
public class Post implements Serializable {

    @Id
    private Long id;

    private String title;

    @Version
    private int version;

    //Getters and setters omitted for brevity
}
```

 It is good practice to make the entity `Serializable` because the cache provider might need to persist the entity reference on disk. Because entities are immutable, the `READ_ONLY` is the most obvious `CacheConcurrencyStrategy` to use in this case.

When storing the same Post entity instance that was used for the disassembled state use case, the cache entry value is going to look as follows:

```
value = {org.hibernate.cache.spi.entry.ReferenceCacheEntryImpl}
  reference = {com.vladmihalcea.book.hpjp.hibernate.cache.Post}
    id = {java.lang.Long} "0"
    title = "High-Performance Java Persistence"
    version = 0
  subclassPersister = {org.hibernate.persister.entity.SingleTableEntityPersister}
```

To understand the performance gain for storing and retrieving entity references, the following test case is going to measure how much time it takes to fetch 100, 500, 1000, 5000, and 10 000 entities from the second-level cache when using the default entity disassembled state mechanism or the entity reference cache store.

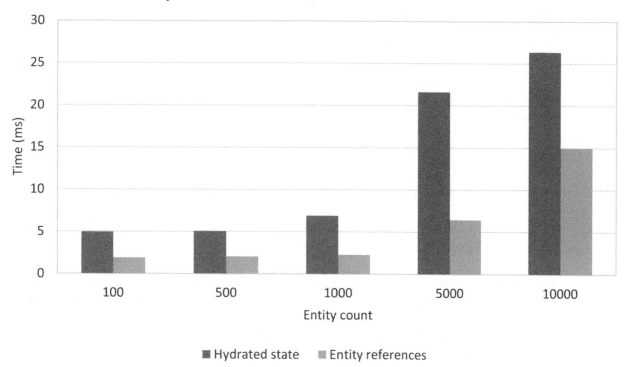

Figure 15.10: Disassembled state vs Entity references

Fetching entity references is much more efficient since new objects are not required to be instantiated and populated with the entity disassembled state. The more entities are fetched from the cache, the more apparent the time gap between the default entity cache store and its entity reference alternative.

Although the `hibernate.cache.use_reference_entries` configuration allows reducing the cache fetching time, it's not a general purpose second-level cache optimization technique because it's only applicable to entities that do not have any association mapping.

15.5.4 Collection cache entry

The collection cache allows storing the entity identifiers that are contained within a given collection instance. Because it only stores identifiers, it is mandatory that the contained entities are cached as well.

The collection cache is activated by the `hibernate.cache.use_second_level_cache` configuration property, just like the regular entity caching mechanism.

The `Post` entity has a bidirectional one-to-many `PostComment` association that is mapped as follows:

```
@OneToMany(cascade = CascadeType.ALL, mappedBy = "post", orphanRemoval = true)
@Cache(usage = CacheConcurrencyStrategy.READ_WRITE)
private List<PostComment> comments = new ArrayList<>();
```

For the next example, two `PostComment` child entities are going to be associated with a managed `Post` entity:

```
Post post = entityManager.find(Post.class, 1L);

PostComment comment1 = new PostComment();
comment1.setId(1L);
comment1.setReview("JDBC part review");
post.addComment(comment1);

PostComment comment2 = new PostComment();
comment2.setId(2L);
comment2.setReview("Hibernate part review");
post.addComment(comment2);
```

Because the collection is marked with the `@Cache` annotation, upon accessing the collection for the first time, Hibernate is going to cache its content using the following cache entry key:

```
key = {org.hibernate.cache.internal.OldCacheKeyImplementation}
  id = {java.lang.Long} "1"
  type = {org.hibernate.type.LongType}
  entityOrRoleName = "com.vladmihalcea.book.hpjp.hibernate.cache.Post.comments"
  tenantId = null
  hashCode = 31
```

The collection cache entry key is almost identical with the entity cache one, the only difference being the cache region name, which is constructed by appending the collection attribute name to the fully-qualified entity class name.

As previously explained, the associated cache entry value contains `PostComment` entity identifiers that are contained within the currently used `Post` entity `comment` collection:

```
item = {org.hibernate.cache.spi.entry.CollectionCacheEntry}
  state = {java.io.Serializable[2]}
    0 = {java.lang.Long} "1"
    1 = {java.lang.Long} "2"
```

 Along with the entity cache, the collection cache allows retrieving an entity aggregate without having to hit the database even once. Although fetching an entire entity graph requires multiple cache calls, the major advantage of storing entities and collections separately is that invalidation or updates affect a single cache entry.

15.5.5 Query cache entry

Just like the collection cache, the query cache is strictly related to entities, and it draws an association between a search criteria and the entities satisfying the given filtering condition. The query cache is disabled by default, and, to activate it, the following configuration property needs to be supplied:

```
<property name="hibernate.cache.use_query_cache" value="true"/>
```

Even if the query cache is enabled, queries must be explicitly marked as cacheable. When using the Hibernate native API, the setCacheable method must be used:

```
List<Post> posts = (List<Post>) session.createQuery(
        "select p from Post p " +
        "where p.title like :token")
.setParameter("token", "High-Performance%")
.setCacheable(true)
.list();
```

For the Java Persistence API, the `org.hibernate.cacheable` query hint must be provided, so when executing the following query:

```java
List<Post> posts = entityManager.createQuery(
    "select p from Post p " +
    "where p.title like :token", Post.class)
.setParameter("token", "High-Performance%")
.setHint("org.hibernate.cacheable", true)
.getResultList();
```

Hibernate stores it using the following cache entry key:

```
key = {QueryKey}
  sqlQueryString = "select p0_.id as id1_0_, p0_.title as title2_0_, p0_.version\
 as version3_0_ from Post p0_ where p0_.title like ?"
  positionalParameterTypes = {org.hibernate.type.Type[0]}
  positionalParameterValues = {java.lang.Object[0]}
  namedParameters = {java.util.HashMap}  size = 1
    0 = {java.util.HashMap$Node} "token" -> "High-Performance%"
  firstRow = null
  maxRows = null
  tenantIdentifier = null
  filterKeys = null
  customTransformer = {org.hibernate.transform.CacheableResultTransformer}
  hashCode = -221304300
```

The cache entry value associated with the query above looks like this:

```
element = {net.sf.ehcache.Element}
  key = {org.hibernate.cache.spi.QueryKey}
  value = {java.util.ArrayList}  size = 2
    0 = {java.lang.Long} "5990928755007489"
    1 = {java.lang.Long} "1"
    2 = {java.lang.Long} "2"
  version = 1
  hitCount = 1
  timeToLive = 120
  timeToIdle = 120
  creationTime = 1462629167305
  lastAccessTime = 1462629171227
  lastUpdateTime = 1462629167305
  cacheDefaultLifespan = true
  id = 0
```

The first entry represents the timestamp of the Session that stored the given query cache result. When the query cache entry is read, Hibernate checks if the query timestamp is greater than the associated tablespace update timestamps, and it only returns the cached element if there was no update since the cached result was stored.

The second and the third value entries represent the entity identifiers that satisfied these query filtering criteria.

 Just like the collection cache, because the query cache only stores entity identifiers, it is mandatory that the associated entities are cached as well.

15.5.6 Cache concurrency strategies

The usage property of the @Cache annotation specifies the CacheConcurrencyStrategy in use for a particular entity or collection. There are four distinct strategies to choose from (READ_ONLY, NONSTRICT_READ_WRITE, READ_WRITE, TRANSACTIONAL), each one defining a distinct behavior when it comes to inserting, updating, or deleting entities:

Before starting explaining each particular cache concurrency strategy, it is better to provide some guidelines related to visualizing the cache content. Hibernate can gather statistics about the second-level cache usage, and, as explained in the Hibernate statistics section, the hibernate.generate_statistics configuration property must be set to true.

Once statistics are enabled, it is very easy to inspect the second-level cache regions using the following utility method:

```
protected void printCacheRegionStatistics(String region) {
    SecondLevelCacheStatistics statistics =
        sessionFactory().getStatistics().getSecondLevelCacheStatistics(region);
    LOGGER.debug("\nRegion: {},\nStatistics: {},\nEntries: {}",
        region, statistics, statistics.getEntries());
}
```

As previously explained, enterprise caching requires diligence because data is duplicated between the database, which is also the system of record, and the caching layer. To make sure that the two separate sources of data do not drift apart, Hibernate must synchronize the second-level cache entry whenever the associated entity state is changed. Because it has a great impact on data integrity, as well as on application performance, the following sections will discuss in greater detail each of those cache concurrency strategies.

15.5.6.1 READ_ONLY

If the cached data is immutable, there is no risk of data inconsistencies, so read-only data is always a good candidate for caching.

15.5.6.1.1 Inserting READ_ONLY cache entries

Considering that the previous Post entity is using the READ_ONLY cache concurrency strategy, when persisting a new entity instance:

```
doInJPA(entityManager -> {
    Post post = new Post();
    post.setId(1L);
    post.setTitle("High-Performance Java Persistence");
    entityManager.persist(post);
});
printCacheRegionStatistics(Post.class.getName());
```

Hibernate generates the following output:

```
INSERT INTO post (title, version, id)
VALUES ('High-Performance Java Persistence', 0, 1)

Region: com.vladmihalcea.book.hpjp.hibernate.cache.Post,
Statistics: SecondLevelCacheStatistics[hitCount=0,missCount=0,putCount=1],
Entries: {1=CacheEntry(Post)[1,High-Performance Java Persistence,0]}
```

The putCount value is 1, so the entity is cached on insert, meaning that READ_ONLY is a write-through strategy. Afterward, when issuing a direct load operation, Hibernate generates the following cache statistics:

```
doInJPA(entityManager -> {
    Post post = entityManager.find(Post.class, 1L);
    printCacheRegionStatistics(post.getClass().getName());
});
```

```
Region: com.vladmihalcea.book.hpjp.hibernate.cache.Post,
Statistics: SecondLevelCacheStatistics[hitCount=1,missCount=0,putCount=1],
Entries: {1=CacheEntry(Post)[1,High-Performance Java Persistence,0]}
```

The hitCount value is 1 because the entity was loaded from the cache, therefore bypassing the database.

For generated identifiers, the write-though entity caching works only for sequences and table generator, so when inserting a Post entity that uses the GenerationType.SEQUENCE strategy:

```
doInJPA(entityManager -> {
    Post post = new Post();
    post.setTitle("High-Performance Java Persistence");
    entityManager.persist(post);
});
printCacheRegionStatistics(Post.class.getName());
```

Hibernate is going to generate the following output:

```
INSERT INTO post (title, version, id)
VALUES ('High-Performance Java Persistence', 0, 1)

Region: com.vladmihalcea.book.hpjp.hibernate.cache.Post,
Statistics: SecondLevelCacheStatistics[hitCount=0,missCount=0,putCount=1],
Entries: {1=CacheEntry(Post)[1,High-Performance Java Persistence,0]}
```

Unfortunately, for identity columns, READ_ONLY uses a read-through cache strategy instead. If the Post entity uses the GenerationType.IDENTITY strategy, upon inserting the same Post entity instance, the second-level cache is not going to store the newly persisted entity:

```
Region: com.vladmihalcea.book.hpjp.hibernate.cache.Post,
Statistics: SecondLevelCacheStatistics[hitCount=0,missCount=0,putCount=0],
Entries: {}
```

On the other hand, when the entity is fetched for the first time:

```
doInJPA(entityManager -> {
    Post post = entityManager.find(Post.class, 1L);
    printCacheRegionStatistics(post.getClass().getName());
});
```

Hibernate is going to store the entity into the second-level cache:

```
SELECT p.id AS id1_0_0_, p.title AS title2_0_0_, p.version AS version3_0_0_
FROM   post p
WHERE  p.id = 1
```

```
Region: com.vladmihalcea.book.hpjp.hibernate.cache.readonly.Post,
Statistics: SecondLevelCacheStatistics[hitCount=0,missCount=1,putCount=1],
Entries: {1=CacheEntry(Post)[High-Performance Java Persistence,0]}
```

Considering that the Post entity has a bidirectional @OneToMany PostComment association, and the collection is cached using the READ_ONLY strategy, when adding two comments:

```
doInJPA(entityManager -> {
    Post post = entityManager.find(Post.class, 1L);

    PostComment comment1 = new PostComment();
    comment1.setId(1L);
    comment1.setReview("JDBC part review");
    post.addComment(comment1);

    PostComment comment2 = new PostComment();
    comment2.setId(2L);
    comment2.setReview("Hibernate part review");
    post.addComment(comment2);
});
printCacheRegionStatistics(Post.class.getName() + ".comments");
```

Hibernate inserts the two comments in the database, while the collection cache region is not updated:

```
INSERT INTO post_comment (post_id, review, id)
VALUES (1, 'JDBC part review', 1)
INSERT INTO post_comment (post_id, review, id)
VALUES (1, 'Hibernate part review', 2)

Region: com.vladmihalcea.book.hpjp.hibernate.cache.Post.comments,
Statistics: SecondLevelCacheStatistics[hitCount=0,missCount=0,putCount=0],
Entries: {}
```

However, upon requesting the collection for the first time:

```
Post post = entityManager.find(Post.class, 1L);
assertEquals(2, post.getComments().size());
printCacheRegionStatistics(Post.class.getName() + ".comments");
```

Hibernate executes the SQL query and updates the cache as well:

```
SELECT pc.post_id AS post_id3_1_0_, pc.id AS id1_1_0_, pc.review AS review2_1_1_
FROM   post_comment pc
WHERE  pc.post_id = 1
```

```
Region: com.vladmihalcea.book.hpjp.hibernate.cache.Post.comments,
Statistics: SecondLevelCacheStatistics[hitCount=0,missCount=1,putCount=1],
Entries: {1=CollectionCacheEntry[1,2]}
```

Once the collection is cached, any further collection fetch request is going to be served from the cache, therefore bypassing the database.

As opposed to the READ_ONLY entity cache, the READ_ONLY collection cache is not write-through. Instead, it uses a read-through caching strategy.

15.5.6.1.2 Updating READ_ONLY cache entries

The READ_ONLY strategy disallows updates, so when trying to modify a Post entity, Hibernate throws the following exception:

```
java.lang.UnsupportedOperationException: Can't write to a readonly object
```

As of writing (Hibernate 5.1.0), Hibernate allows removing elements from a READ_ONLY cached collection. However, it does not invalidate the collection cache entry.

This way, when removing a PostComment from the Post entity comments collection:

```
doInJPA(entityManager -> {
    Post post = entityManager.find(Post.class, 1L);
    PostComment comment = post.getComments().remove(0);
    comment.setPost(null);
});

printCacheRegionStatistics(Post.class.getName());
printCacheRegionStatistics(PostComment.class.getName());

doInJPA(entityManager -> {
    Post post = entityManager.find(Post.class, 1L);
});
```

Hibernate generates the following output:

```
DELETE FROM post_comment WHERE id = 1

Region: com.vladmihalcea.book.hpjp.hibernate.cache.Post.comments,
Statistics: SecondLevelCacheStatistics[hitCount=0,missCount=1,putCount=1],
Entries: {1=CollectionCacheEntry[1,2]}

Region: com.vladmihalcea.book.hpjp.hibernate.cache.PostComment,
Statistics: SecondLevelCacheStatistics[hitCount=0,missCount=0,putCount=2],
Entries: {2=CacheEntry(PostComment)[1,Hibernate part review]}

javax.persistence.EntityNotFoundException: Unable to find
com.vladmihalcea.book.hpjp.hibernate.cache.PostComment with id 1
```

In reality, every READ_ONLY entity and collection should be marked with the @Immutable annotation:

```
@Entity @Immutable @Cache(usage = CacheConcurrencyStrategy.READ_ONLY)
public class Post {

    @OneToMany(cascade = CascadeType.PERSIST, mappedBy = "post")
    @Immutable @Cache(usage = CacheConcurrencyStrategy.READ_ONLY)
    private List<PostComment> comments = new ArrayList<>();

    //Code omitted for brevity
}
```

This way, when trying to update a PostComment collection, Hibernate is going to throw the following exception:

```
org.hibernate.HibernateException: changed an immutable collection instance:
[com.vladmihalcea.book.hpjp.hibernate.cache.Post.comments#1]
```

15.5.6.1.3 Deleting READ_ONLY cache entries

While updates should never occur for READ_ONLY entities (which signals a data access logic issue), deletes are permitted.

When deleting a Post entity that happens to be stored in the second-level cache:

```
printCacheRegionStatistics(Post.class.getName());
printCacheRegionStatistics(PostComment.class.getName());

doInJPA(entityManager -> {
    Post post = entityManager.find(Post.class, 1L);
    entityManager.remove(post);
});

printCacheRegionStatistics(Post.class.getName());
printCacheRegionStatistics(PostComment.class.getName());
```

Hibernate generates the following output:

```
Region: com.vladmihalcea.book.hpjp.hibernate.cache.Post,
Statistics: SecondLevelCacheStatistics[hitCount=2,missCount=0,putCount=1],
Entries: {1=CacheEntry(Post)[1,High-Performance Java Persistence,0]}

Region: com.vladmihalcea.book.hpjp.hibernate.cache.PostComment,
Statistics: SecondLevelCacheStatistics[hitCount=0,missCount=0,putCount=2],
Entries: {1=CacheEntry(PostComment)[1,JDBC part review],
          2=CacheEntry(PostComment)[1,Hibernate part review]}

DELETE FROM post_comment WHERE id = 1
DELETE FROM post_comment WHERE id = 2
DELETE FROM post WHERE id = 1 AND version = 0

Region: com.vladmihalcea.book.hpjp.hibernate.cache.Post,
Statistics: SecondLevelCacheStatistics[hitCount=3,missCount=0,putCount=1],
Entries: {}

Region: com.vladmihalcea.book.hpjp.hibernate.cache.PostComment,
Statistics: SecondLevelCacheStatistics[hitCount=2,missCount=0,putCount=2],
Entries: {}
```

The Post and PostComment entities are successfully removed form the database and the second-level cache as well.

15.5.6.2 NONSTRICT_READ_WRITE

The NONSTRICT_READ_WRITE concurrency strategy is designed for entities that are updated infrequently, and when strict consistency is not a mandatory requirement. The following examples are going to reuse the same entities that were previously employed, the only thing being different is that the Post and PostComment entities, as well as the comments collections, are using the @Cache(usage = CacheConcurrencyStrategy.NONSTRICT_READ_WRITE) annotation.

15.5.6.2.1 Inserting NONSTRICT_READ_WRITE cache entries

First of all, unlike other strategies, NONSTRICT_READ_WRITE is not write-through. Therefore, when persisting a Post entity, the second-level cache is not going to store the newly inserted object. Instead, NONSTRICT_READ_WRITE is a read-through cache concurrency strategy.

```
doInJPA(entityManager -> {
    Post post = new Post();
    post.setId(1L);
    post.setTitle("High-Performance Java Persistence");

    PostComment comment1 = new PostComment();
    comment1.setId(1L);
    comment1.setReview("JDBC part review");
    post.addComment(comment1);

    PostComment comment2 = new PostComment();
    comment2.setId(2L);
    comment2.setReview("Hibernate part review");
    post.addComment(comment2);

    entityManager.persist(post);
});
printCacheRegionStatistics(Post.class.getName());
printCacheRegionStatistics(Post.class.getName() + ".comments");

LOGGER.info("Load Post entity and comments collection");
doInJPA(entityManager -> {
    Post post = entityManager.find(Post.class, 1L);
    assertEquals(2, post.getComments().size());
    printCacheRegionStatistics(post.getClass().getName());
    printCacheRegionStatistics(Post.class.getName() + ".comments");
});
```

When executing the test case above, the Post entity and PostComment collections are going to be cached upon being fetched for the first time.

```
INSERT INTO post (title, version, id)
VALUES ('High-Performance Java Persistence', 0, 1)

INSERT INTO post_comment (post_id, review, id) VALUES (1, 'JDBC part review', 1)
INSERT INTO post_comment (post_id, review, id)
VALUES (1, 'Hibernate part review', 2)

Region: com.vladmihalcea.book.hpjp.hibernate.cache.Post,
Statistics: SecondLevelCacheStatistics[hitCount=0,missCount=0,putCount=0],
Entries: {}

Region: com.vladmihalcea.book.hpjp.hibernate.cache.Post.comments,
Statistics: SecondLevelCacheStatistics[hitCount=0,missCount=0,putCount=0],
Entries: {}

--Load Post entity and comments collection
SELECT p.id AS id1_0_0_, p.title AS title2_0_0_, p.version AS version3_0_0_
FROM    post p
WHERE   p.id = 1

SELECT pc.post_id AS post_id3_1_0_, pc.id AS id1_1_0_, pc.review AS review2_1_1_
FROM    post_comment pc
WHERE   pc.post_id = 1

Region: com.vladmihalcea.book.hpjp.hibernate.cache.Post,
Statistics: SecondLevelCacheStatistics[hitCount=0,missCount=1,putCount=1],
Entries: {1=CacheEntry(Post)[1,High-Performance Java Persistence,0]}

Region: com.vladmihalcea.book.hpjp.hibernate.cache.Post.comments,
Statistics: SecondLevelCacheStatistics[hitCount=0,missCount=1,putCount=1],
Entries: {1=CollectionCacheEntry[1,2]}
```

 For it removes cache entries, NONSTRICT_READ_WRITE is only appropriate when entities are rarely changed. Otherwise, if the cache miss rate is too high, the cache renders inefficient.

15.5.6.2.2 Updating NONSTRICT_READ_WRITE cache entries

Unlike the READ_ONLY cache concurrency strategy, NONSTRICT_READ_WRITE supports entity and collection modifications.

```
doInJPA(entityManager -> {
    Post post = entityManager.find(Post.class, 1L);
    post.setTitle("High-Performance Hibernate");
    PostComment comment = post.getComments().remove(0);
    comment.setPost(null);
});
printCacheRegionStatistics(Post.class.getName());
printCacheRegionStatistics(Post.class.getName() + ".comments");
printCacheRegionStatistics(PostComment.class.getName());
```

When executing the test case above, Hibernate generates the following output:

```
UPDATE post
SET title = 'High-Performance Hibernate', version = 1
WHERE id = 1 AND version = 0

DELETE FROM post_comment WHERE id = 1

Region: com.vladmihalcea.book.hpjp.hibernate.cache.Post,
Statistics: SecondLevelCacheStatistics[hitCount=1,missCount=1,putCount=1],
Entries: {}

Region: com.vladmihalcea.book.hpjp.hibernate.cache.Post.comments,
Statistics: SecondLevelCacheStatistics[hitCount=1,missCount=1,putCount=1],
Entries: {}

Region: com.vladmihalcea.book.hpjp.hibernate.cache.PostComment,
Statistics: SecondLevelCacheStatistics[hitCount=2,missCount=0,putCount=2],
Entries: {2=CacheEntry(PostComment)[1,Hibernate part review]}
```

15.5.6.2.3 Risk of inconsistencies

NONSTRICT_READ_WRITE does not offer strict consistency because it takes no locks on the cache entries that get modified. For this reason, on very tiny time interval, it is possible that the database and the cache might render different results.

During an entity update, the flow of operations goes like this:

1. The current Hibernate transaction (e.g. `JdbcTransaction` or `JtaTransaction`) is flushed.
2. The `DefaultFlushEventListener` executes all pending actions contained in the current `ActionQueue`.
3. The `EntityUpdateAction` calls the `update` method of the `EntityRegionAccessStrategy`.
4. The `NonStrictReadWriteEhcacheCollectionRegionAccessStrategy` removes the cache entry from the underlying 'EhcacheEntityRegion.

After the database transaction is committed, the cache entry is removed once again:

1. The after transaction completion callback is called.
2. The current `Session` propagates this event to its internal `ActionQueue`.
3. The `EntityUpdateAction` calls the `afterUpdate` method on the `EntityRegionAccessStrategy`.
4. The `NonStrictReadWriteEhcacheCollectionRegionAccessStrategy` calls the `remove` method on the underlying `EhcacheEntityRegion`.

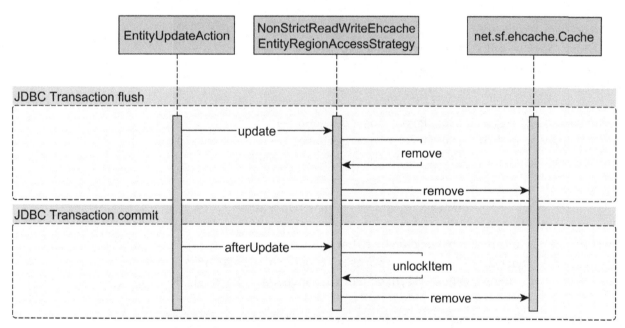

Figure 15.11: NONSTRICT_READ_WRITE update flow

The cache invalidation is not synchronized with the current database transaction. Even if the associated cache region entry gets invalidated twice (before and after transaction completion), there is still a tiny time window when the cache and the database might drift apart.

15.5.6.2.4 Deleting NONSTRICT_READ_WRITE cache entries

When deleting a Post entity that cascades the remove event to the PostComment collection:

```
printCacheRegionStatistics(Post.class.getName());
printCacheRegionStatistics(Post.class.getName() + ".comments");
printCacheRegionStatistics(PostComment.class.getName());

doInJPA(entityManager -> {
    Post post = entityManager.find(Post.class, 1L);
    entityManager.remove(post);
});

printCacheRegionStatistics(Post.class.getName());
printCacheRegionStatistics(Post.class.getName() + ".comments");
printCacheRegionStatistics(PostComment.class.getName());
```

Hibernate is going to remove all associated cache regions:

```
Region: com.vladmihalcea.book.hpjp.hibernate.cache.Post,
Statistics: SecondLevelCacheStatistics[hitCount=0,missCount=1,putCount=1],
Entries: {1=CacheEntry(Post)[1,High-Performance Java Persistence,0]}

Region: com.vladmihalcea.book.hpjp.hibernate.cache.Post.comments,
Statistics: SecondLevelCacheStatistics[hitCount=0,missCount=1,putCount=1],
Entries: {1=CollectionCacheEntry[1,2]}

Region: com.vladmihalcea.book.hpjp.hibernate.cache.PostComment,
Statistics: SecondLevelCacheStatistics[hitCount=0,missCount=0,putCount=2],
Entries: {1=CacheEntry(PostComment)[1,JDBC part review],
          2=CacheEntry(PostComment)[1,Hibernate part review]}
```

```
DELETE FROM post_comment WHERE id = 1
DELETE FROM post_comment WHERE id = 2
DELETE FROM post WHERE id = 1 AND version = 0
```

```
Region: com.vladmihalcea.book.hpjp.hibernate.cache.Post,
Statistics: SecondLevelCacheStatistics[hitCount=1,missCount=1,putCount=1],
Entries: {}
```

```
Region: com.vladmihalcea.book.hpjp.hibernate.cache.Post.comments,
Statistics: SecondLevelCacheStatistics[hitCount=1,missCount=1,putCount=1],
Entries: {}
```

```
Region: com.vladmihalcea.book.hpjp.hibernate.cache.PostComment,
Statistics: SecondLevelCacheStatistics[hitCount=2,missCount=0,putCount=2],
Entries: {}
```

Just like with update, the cache entry removal is called twice (the first time during flush and the second time after the transaction is committed).

15.5.6.3 READ_WRITE

To avoid any inconsistency risk while still using a write-through second-level cache, Hibernate offers the READ_WRITE cache concurrency strategy. A write-through cache strategy is a much better choice for write-intensive applications since cache entries can be updated rather than being simply removed.

Because the database is the system of record and database operations are wrapped inside one single physical transaction, the cache can either be updated synchronously which requires JTA transactions or asynchronously, right after the database transaction gets committed.

READ_WRITE is an asynchronous cache concurrency strategy, and, to prevent data integrity issues like stale cache entries, it employs a soft locking mechanism that provides the guarantees of a logical transaction isolation.

The following examples are going to reuse the same entities that were previously employed, and the only thing that differs is that the Post and PostComment entities, as well as the comments collections, are using the @Cache(usage = CacheConcurrencyStrategy.READ_WRITE) annotation.

15.5.6.3.1 Inserting READ_WRITE cache entries

Only the entity cache region can work in write-through mode, and, just like with any other cache concurrency strategy, the collection cache is read-through.

When running the same example used for inserting NONSTRICT_READ_WRITE cache entries, Hibernate generates the following output:

```
INSERT INTO post (title, version, id)
VALUES ('High-Performance Java Persistence', 0, 1)

INSERT INTO post_comment (post_id, review, id)
VALUES (1, 'JDBC part review', 1)
INSERT INTO post_comment (post_id, review, id)
VALUES (1, 'Hibernate part review', 2)

Region: com.vladmihalcea.book.hpjp.hibernate.cache.Post,
Statistics: SecondLevelCacheStatistics[hitCount=0,missCount=0,putCount=1],
Entries: {1=[ value = CacheEntry(Post)[1,High-Performance Java Persistence,0],
            version=0, timestamp=5991931785445376 ]}

Region: com.vladmihalcea.book.hpjp.hibernate.cache.Post.comments,
Statistics: SecondLevelCacheStatistics[hitCount=0,missCount=0,putCount=0],
Entries: {1=Lock Source-UUID:7d059ff0-0ec8-490f-b316-e77efad0b15f Lock-ID:0}

--Load Post entity and comments collection

SELECT pc.post_id AS post_id3_1_0_, pc.id AS id1_1_0_, pc.review AS review2_1_1_
FROM   post_comment pc
WHERE  pc.post_id = 1

Region: com.vladmihalcea.book.hpjp.hibernate.cache.Post,
Statistics: SecondLevelCacheStatistics[hitCount=1,missCount=0,putCount=1],
Entries: {1=[ value = CacheEntry(Post)[1,High-Performance Java Persistence,0],
            version=0, timestamp=5991931785445376 ]}

Region: com.vladmihalcea.book.hpjp.hibernate.cache.Post.comments,
Statistics: SecondLevelCacheStatistics[hitCount=0,missCount=1,putCount=1],
Entries: {1=[ value = CollectionCacheEntry[1,2],
            version=null, timestamp=5991931785895936 ]}
```

Unfortunately, this write-though caching does not work for the identity columns, and if the Post entity is using the IDENTITY generator:

```
@Id @GeneratedValue(strategy = GenerationType.IDENTITY)
private Long id;
```

When inserting a `Post` entity:

```
doInJPA(entityManager -> {
    Post post = new Post();
    post.setTitle("High-Performance Java Persistence");
    entityManager.persist(post);
});
printCacheRegionStatistics(Post.class.getName());
```

Hibernate is going to generate the following output:

```
Region: com.vladmihalcea.book.hpjp.hibernate.cache.Post,
Statistics: SecondLevelCacheStatistics[hitCount=0,missCount=0,putCount=0],
Entries: {}
```

> Because it supports write-through `READ_WRITE` entity caching, the sequence generator is preferred over identity columns. The behavior might change in future, so it is better to check the HHH-7964[a] JIRA issue status.
>
> ---
> [a]https://hibernate.atlassian.net/browse/HHH-7964

15.5.6.3.2 Updating READ_WRITE cache entries

As already mentioned, the `READ_WRITE` cache concurrency strategy employs a soft locking mechanism to ensure data integrity.

1. The Hibernate transaction commit procedure triggers a `Session` flush.
2. The `EntityUpdateAction` replaces the current cache entry with a `Lock` object.
3. The `update` method is used for synchronous strategies. Therefore, it is a no-op in this case.
4. The after transaction callbacks are called, and the `EntityUpdateAction` executes the `afterUpdate` method of the `EntityRegionAccessStrategy`.
5. The `ReadWriteEhcacheEntityRegionAccessStrategy` replaces the `Lock` entry with an actual `Item`, encapsulating the entity disassembled state.

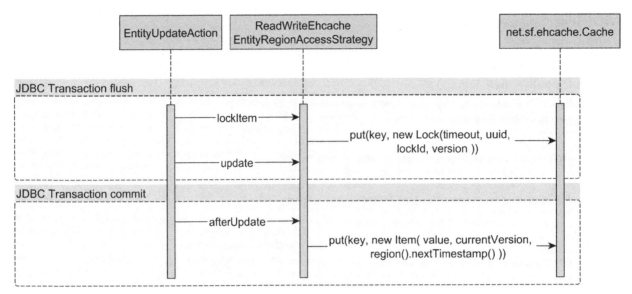

Figure 15.12: READ_WRITE update flow

 Just like with database transactions, changes are applied directly, and locks are used to prevent other concurrent transactions from reading uncommitted data. When reading a Lock object from the cache, Hibernate knows that the associated entry is being modified by an uncommitted transaction. Therefore, it reads the entity from the database.

To visualize the whole process, when running the following test case:

```
doInJPA(entityManager -> {
    Post post = entityManager.find(Post.class, 1L);
    post.setTitle("High-Performance Hibernate");
    PostComment comment = post.getComments().remove(0);
    comment.setPost(null);
    entityManager.flush();

    printCacheRegionStatistics(Post.class.getName());
    printCacheRegionStatistics(Post.class.getName() + ".comments");
    printCacheRegionStatistics(PostComment.class.getName());
    LOGGER.debug("Commit after flush");
});
printCacheRegionStatistics(Post.class.getName());
printCacheRegionStatistics(Post.class.getName() + ".comments");
printCacheRegionStatistics(PostComment.class.getName());
```

Hibernate generates the following output:

```
UPDATE post
SET title = 'High-Performance Hibernate', version = 1
WHERE id = 1 AND version = 0


DELETE FROM post_comment WHERE id = 1


Region: com.vladmihalcea.book.hpjp.hibernate.cache.Post,
Statistics: SecondLevelCacheStatistics[hitCount=1,missCount=0,putCount=1],
Entries: {1=Lock Source-UUID:69c2fd51-11a3-43c1-9db2-91f30624ac74 Lock-ID:0}


Region: com.vladmihalcea.book.hpjp.hibernate.cache.Post.comments,
Statistics: SecondLevelCacheStatistics[hitCount=0,missCount=1,putCount=1],
Entries: {1=Lock Source-UUID:e75094c1-6bc2-43f3-87e3-1dcdf6bee083 Lock-ID:1}


Region: com.vladmihalcea.book.hpjp.hibernate.cache.PostComment,
Statistics: SecondLevelCacheStatistics[hitCount=0,missCount=0,putCount=2],
Entries: {1=Lock Source-UUID:99aafdef-7816-43ee-909d-5f10ab759c60 Lock-ID:0,
        2=[ value = CacheEntry(PostComment)[1,Hibernate part review],
            version=null, timestamp=5992022222598145 ]}


--Commit after flush


Region: com.vladmihalcea.book.hpjp.hibernate.cache.Post,
Statistics: SecondLevelCacheStatistics[hitCount=1,missCount=0,putCount=2],
Entries: {1=[ value = CacheEntry(Post)[1,High-Performance Hibernate,1],
            version=1, timestamp=5992019884548096 ]}


Region: com.vladmihalcea.book.hpjp.hibernate.cache.Post.comments,
Statistics: SecondLevelCacheStatistics[hitCount=0,missCount=1,putCount=1],
Entries: {1=Lock Source-UUID:db769a0a-d65a-4911-952e-1d0bb851ed8d Lock-ID:1}


Region: com.vladmihalcea.book.hpjp.hibernate.cache.PostComment,
Statistics: SecondLevelCacheStatistics[hitCount=0,missCount=0,putCount=2],
Entries: {1=Lock Source-UUID:f357da6a-665e-40d1-84c0-760e450df421 Lock-ID:0,
        2=[ value = CacheEntry(PostComment)[1,Hibernate part review],
            version=null, timestamp=5992019884109825 ]}
```

Right after the Persistence Context is flushed, Hibernate executes the associated SQL statements and adds Lock objects into the cache entries associated with the currently modifying Post entity and comments collection, as well as for the deleting PostComment entity.

After the transaction is committed, the `Post` entity cache entry is replaced with an `Item` object containing the updated disassembled state. Since `READ_WRITE` collections are not write-through, the `comments` collection cache entry is still a `Lock` object even after commit. Since the `PostComment` entity has been deleted, its cache entry is represented by a `Lock` entry.

15.5.6.3.3 Deleting READ_WRITE cache entries

Deleting entities is similar to the update process, as we can see from the following sequence diagram:

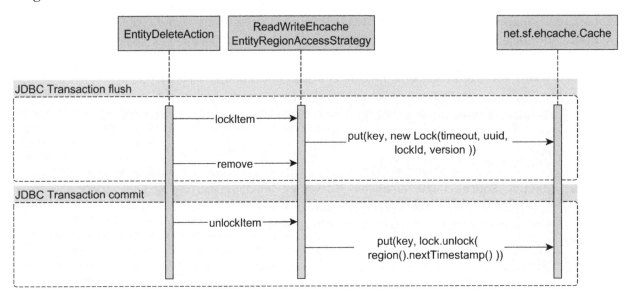

Figure 15.13: READ_WRITE delete flow

1. The Hibernate transaction commit procedure triggers a `Session` flush.
2. The `EntityDeleteAction` replaces the current cache entry with a `Lock` object
3. The `remove` method call doesn't do anything since `READ_WRITE` is an asynchronous cache concurrency strategy.
4. The after transaction callbacks are called, and the `EntityDeleteAction` executes the `unlockItem` method of the `EntityRegionAccessStrategy`.
5. The `ReadWriteEhcacheEntityRegionAccessStrategy` replaces the `Lock` entry with another `Lock` object whose timeout period is further increased.

After an entity is deleted, its associated second-level cache entry will be replaced by a `Lock` object, so that any subsequent request is redirected to reading from the database instead of using the second-level cache entry.

When running the same example used for deleting `NONSTRICT_READ_WRITE` cache entries, Hibernate generates the following output:

```
Region: com.vladmihalcea.book.hpjp.hibernate.cache.Post,
Statistics: SecondLevelCacheStatistics[hitCount=1,missCount=0,putCount=1],
Entries: {1=[ value = CacheEntry(Post)[1,High-Performance Java Persistence,0],
            version=0, timestamp=5992355751620608 ]}

Region: com.vladmihalcea.book.hpjp.hibernate.cache.Post.comments,
Statistics: SecondLevelCacheStatistics[hitCount=0,missCount=1,putCount=1],
Entries: {1=[ value = CollectionCacheEntry[1,2],
            version=null, timestamp=5992355752042496 ]}

Region: com.vladmihalcea.book.hpjp.hibernate.cache.PostComment,
Statistics: SecondLevelCacheStatistics[hitCount=0,missCount=0,putCount=2],
Entries: {1=[ value = CacheEntry(PostComment)[1,JDBC part review],
            version=null, timestamp=5992355751624704 ],
         2=[ value = CacheEntry(PostComment)[1,Hibernate part review],
            version=null, timestamp=5992355751624705 ]}

DELETE FROM post_comment WHERE id = 1
DELETE FROM post_comment WHERE id = 2
DELETE FROM post WHERE id = 1 AND version = 0

Region: com.vladmihalcea.book.hpjp.hibernate.cache.Post,
Statistics: SecondLevelCacheStatistics[hitCount=2,missCount=0,putCount=1],
Entries: {1=Lock Source-UUID:b042192a-9ac6-4877-8663-018f898f1cdb Lock-ID:0}

Region: com.vladmihalcea.book.hpjp.hibernate.cache.Post.comments,
Statistics: SecondLevelCacheStatistics[hitCount=1,missCount=1,putCount=1],
Entries: {1=Lock Source-UUID:e75f034a-0346-4696-88fd-1b5100658a6f Lock-ID:1}

Region: com.vladmihalcea.book.hpjp.hibernate.cache.PostComment,
Statistics: SecondLevelCacheStatistics[hitCount=2,missCount=0,putCount=2],
Entries: {1=Lock Source-UUID:1d13b830-e96d-40f5-aa2b-6a402fa6135d Lock-ID:0,
         2=Lock Source-UUID:1d13b830-e96d-40f5-aa2b-6a402fa6135d Lock-ID:1}
```

The delete operation does not remove entries from the second-level cache, but instead it replaces the previous Item entries with Lock objects. The next time a deleted cache entry is being read, Hibernate is going to redirect the request to the database, therefore guaranteeing strong consistency.

15.5.6.3.4 Soft locking concurrency control

Because the database is the system of record, strong consistency implies that uncommitted cache changes should not be read by other concurrent transactions. The READ_WRITE can store either an Item or a Lock.

The Item holds the entity disassembled state, as well as the entity version and a timestamp. The version and the timestamp are used for concurrency control as follows:

- An Item is readable only from a Session that has been started after the cache entry creation timestamp.
- An Item entry can be written only if the incoming version is greater than the current one held in the cache entry.

When an entity or a collection is either updated or deleted, Hibernate replaces the cached Item entry with a Lock, whose concurrency control mechanism works as follows:

- Since it overwrites an Item cache entry, the Lock object instructs a concurrent Session to read the entity or the collection from the database.
- If at least one Session has managed to lock this entry, any write operation is forbidden.
- A Lock entry is writable only if the incoming entity state has a version which is newer than the one contained in the Lock object, or if the current Session creation timestamp is greater than the Lock timeout threshold.

If the database transaction is rolled back, the current cache entry holds a Lock instance which cannot be undone to the previous Item state. For this reason, the Lock must time out to allow the cache entry to be replaced by an actual Item cache entry.

 For Ehcache, the default Lock timeout is 120 seconds, and it can be customized via the net.sf.ehcache.hibernate.cache_lock_timeout configuration property.

The READ_WRITE concurrency strategy offers a write-through caching mechanism without requiring JTA transactions.

However, for heavy write contention scenarios, when there is a chance of rolling back transactions, the soft locking concurrency control can lead to having other concurrent transactions hitting the database for the whole duration of the lock timeout period. For this kind of situations, the TRANSACTIONAL concurrency strategy might be more suitable.

15.5.6.4 TRANSACTIONAL

While READ_WRITE is an asynchronous write-though cache concurrency strategy, TRANSACTIONAL uses a synchronous caching mechanism.

To enlist two data sources (the database and the second-level cache) in the same global transaction, a JTA transaction manager is needed. When using Java EE, the application server provides JTA transactions by default. For stand-alone enterprise applications, there are multiple transaction managers to choose from (e.g. Bitronix, Atomikos, Narayana).

For JTA transactions, Ehcache offers two failure recovery options: xa_strict and xa.

15.5.6.4.1 XA_Strict mode

In this mode, the second-level cache exposes a XAResource interface so that it can participate in the two-phase commit (2PC) protocol.

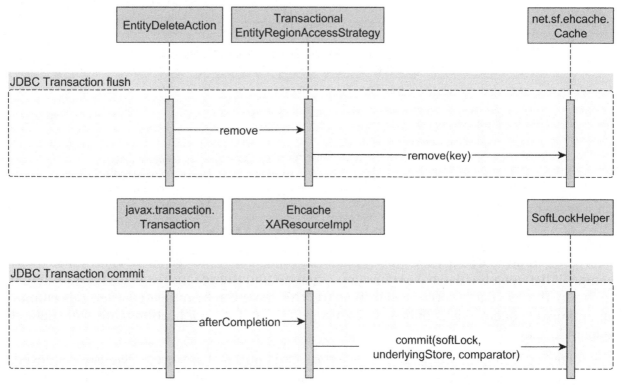

Figure 15.14: TRANSACTIONAL XA_Strict flow

The entity state is modified both in the database and in the cache, but these changes are isolated from other concurrent transactions, and they become visible once the current XA transaction gets committed.

The database and the cache remain consistent even in the case of an application crash.

15.5.6.4.2 XA mode

If only one DataSource participates in a global transaction, the transaction manager can apply the one-phase commit optimization. The second-level cache is managed through a javax.transaction.Synchronization transaction callback. The Synchronization does not actively participate in deciding the transaction outcome, therefore following the current database transaction outcome:

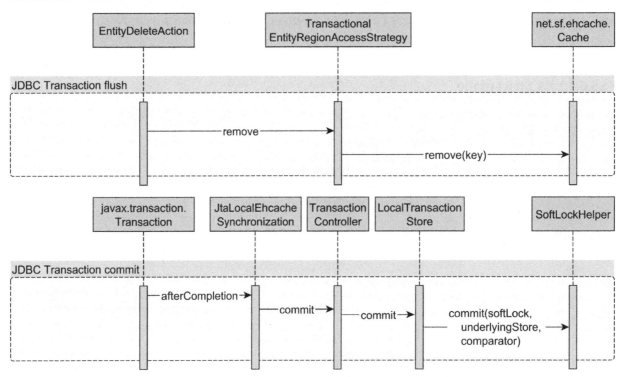

Figure 15.15: TRANSACTIONAL XA flow

This mode trades durability for a lower response time, and in the case of a server crash (happening in between the database transaction commit and the second-level cache transaction callback), the two data sources will drift apart. This issue can be mitigated if entities employ an optimistic concurrency control mechanism, so, even if the application reads stale data, it will not lose updates upon writing it back.

The following examples are going to reuse the same entities that were previously employed, and the only thing that differs is that the Post and PostComment entities, as well as the comments collections, are using the @Cache(usage = CacheConcurrencyStrategy.TRANSACTIONAL) annotation. The transaction boundaries are managed by Spring framework, and the actual JTA transaction logic is coordinated by Bitronix Transaction Manager.

15.5.6.4.3 Inserting TRANSACTIONAL cache entries

When running the same example used for inserting NONSTRICT_READ_WRITE cache entries, Hibernate generates the following output:

```
INSERT INTO post (title, version, id)
VALUES ('High-Performance Java Persistence', 0, 1)

INSERT INTO post_comment (post_id, review, id)
VALUES (1, 'JDBC part review', 1)
INSERT INTO post_comment (post_id, review, id)
VALUES (1, 'Hibernate part review', 2)

Region: com.vladmihalcea.book.hpjp.hibernate.cache.Post,
Statistics: SecondLevelCacheStatistics[hitCount=0,missCount=0,putCount=1],
Entries: {1=CacheEntry(Post)[1,High-Performance Java Persistence,0]}

Region: com.vladmihalcea.book.hpjp.hibernate.cache.Post.comments,
Statistics: SecondLevelCacheStatistics[hitCount=0,missCount=0,putCount=00],
Entries: {}

--Load Post entity and comments collection

SELECT pc.post_id AS post_id3_1_0_, pc.id AS id1_1_0_, pc.review AS review2_1_1_
FROM   post_comment pc
WHERE  pc.post_id = 1

Region: com.vladmihalcea.book.hpjp.hibernate.cache.Post,
Statistics: SecondLevelCacheStatistics[hitCount=1,missCount=0,putCount=1],
Entries: {1=CacheEntry(Post)[1,High-Performance Java Persistence,0]}

Region: com.vladmihalcea.book.hpjp.hibernate.cache.Post.comments,
Statistics: SecondLevelCacheStatistics[hitCount=0,missCount=1,putCount=1],
Entries: {1=CollectionCacheEntry[1,2]}
```

Just like READ_WRITE, the TRANSACTIONAL cache concurrency strategy is write-through for entities (unless using the identity generator in which case it is read-through), and read-though for collections.

15.5.6.4.4 Updating TRANSACTIONAL cache entries

Because the TRANSACTIONAL cache is synchronous, all changes are applied directly to cache, as illustrated by the following example:

```
doInJPA(entityManager -> {
    printCacheRegionStatistics(Post.class.getName());
    printCacheRegionStatistics(Post.class.getName() + ".comments");
    printCacheRegionStatistics(PostComment.class.getName());

    Post post = entityManager.find(Post.class, 1L);
    post.setTitle("High-Performance Hibernate");
    PostComment comment = post.getComments().remove(0);
    comment.setPost(null);

    entityManager.flush();

    printCacheRegionStatistics(Post.class.getName());
    printCacheRegionStatistics(Post.class.getName() + ".comments");
    printCacheRegionStatistics(PostComment.class.getName());

    LOGGER.debug("Commit after flush");
});
printCacheRegionStatistics(Post.class.getName());
printCacheRegionStatistics(Post.class.getName() + ".comments");
printCacheRegionStatistics(PostComment.class.getName());
```

For which Hibernate generates the following output:

```
Region: com.vladmihalcea.book.hpjp.hibernate.cache.Post,
Statistics: SecondLevelCacheStatistics[hitCount=1,missCount=0,putCount=1],
Entries: {1=CacheEntry(Post)[1,High-Performance Java Persistence,0]}

Region: com.vladmihalcea.book.hpjp.hibernate.cache.Post.comments,
Statistics: SecondLevelCacheStatistics[hitCount=0,missCount=1,putCount=1],
Entries: {1=CollectionCacheEntry[1,2]}

Region: com.vladmihalcea.book.hpjp.hibernate.cache.PostComment,
Statistics: SecondLevelCacheStatistics[hitCount=0,missCount=0,putCount=2],
Entries: {1=CacheEntry(PostComment)[1,JDBC part review],
          2=CacheEntry(PostComment)[1,Hibernate part review]}
```

```
UPDATE post
SET title = 'High-Performance Hibernate', version = 1
WHERE id = 1 AND version = 0

DELETE FROM post_comment WHERE id = 1

Region: com.vladmihalcea.book.hpjp.hibernate.cache.Post,
Statistics: SecondLevelCacheStatistics[hitCount=2,missCount=0,putCount=2],
Entries: {1=CacheEntry(Post)[1,High-Performance Hibernate,1]}

Region: com.vladmihalcea.book.hpjp.hibernate.cache.Post.comments,
Statistics: SecondLevelCacheStatistics[hitCount=1,missCount=1,putCount=1],
Entries: {}

Region: com.vladmihalcea.book.hpjp.hibernate.cache.PostComment,
Statistics: SecondLevelCacheStatistics[hitCount=2,missCount=0,putCount=2],
Entries: {2=CacheEntry(PostComment)[1,Hibernate part review]}

--Commit after flush

Region: com.vladmihalcea.book.hpjp.hibernate.cache.Post,
Statistics: SecondLevelCacheStatistics[hitCount=2,missCount=0,putCount=2],
Entries: {1=CacheEntry(Post)[1,High-Performance Hibernate,1]}

Region: com.vladmihalcea.book.hpjp.hibernate.cache.Post.comments,
Statistics: SecondLevelCacheStatistics[hitCount=1,missCount=1,putCount=1],
Entries: {}

Region: com.vladmihalcea.book.hpjp.hibernate.cache.PostComment,
Statistics: SecondLevelCacheStatistics[hitCount=2,missCount=0,putCount=2],
Entries: {2=CacheEntry(PostComment)[1,Hibernate part review]}
```

Unlike the READ_WRITE cache concurrency strategy, TRANSACTIONAL does not use Lock cache entries, but instead it offers transaction isolation through the second-level cache provider internal locking mechanisms. After the Post entity and the comments collections are modified, Hibernate applies all the changes synchronously.

The Post entity modification is immediately visible in the cache, but only for the currently running transaction. Other transactions will not see any pending modifications until the current transaction is committed.

The PostComment entity that was deleted from the database is going to be removed from the entity cache region as well.

The Post.comments collection cache region is invalidated, and all its content is being removed.

From the current running transaction perspective, the TRANSACTIONAL cache concurrency strategy offers read-your-own-writes consistency guarantees. Once the transaction is committed, all pending database and cache changes are becoming visible to other concurrent transactions as well.

15.5.6.4.5 Deleting TRANSACTIONAL cache entries

When running the same example used for deleting NONSTRICT_READ_WRITE cache entries, Hibernate generates the following output:

```
Region: com.vladmihalcea.book.hpjp.hibernate.cache.Post,
Statistics: SecondLevelCacheStatistics[hitCount=1,missCount=0,putCount=1],
Entries: {1=CacheEntry(Post)[1,High-Performance Java Persistence,0]}

Region: com.vladmihalcea.book.hpjp.hibernate.cache.Post.comments,
Statistics: SecondLevelCacheStatistics[hitCount=0,missCount=1,putCount=1],
Entries: {1=CollectionCacheEntry[1,2]}

Region: com.vladmihalcea.book.hpjp.hibernate.cache.PostComment,
Statistics: SecondLevelCacheStatistics[hitCount=0,missCount=0,putCount=2],
Entries: {1=CacheEntry(PostComment)[1,JDBC part review],
          2=CacheEntry(PostComment)[1,Hibernate part review]}

DELETE FROM post_comment WHERE id = 1
DELETE FROM post_comment WHERE id = 2
DELETE FROM post WHERE id = 1 AND version = 0

Region: com.vladmihalcea.book.hpjp.hibernate.cache.Post,
Statistics: SecondLevelCacheStatistics[hitCount=2,missCount=0,putCount=1],
Entries: {}

Region: com.vladmihalcea.book.hpjp.hibernate.cache.Post.comments,
Statistics: SecondLevelCacheStatistics[hitCount=1,missCount=1,putCount=1],
Entries: {}

Region: com.vladmihalcea.book.hpjp.hibernate.cache.PostComment,
Statistics: SecondLevelCacheStatistics[hitCount=2,missCount=0,putCount=2],
Entries: {}
```

Unlike the READ_WRITE cache concurrency strategy which replaces the deleted Item cache entry with a Lock object, TRANSACTIONAL removes all the previously stored cache entries.

Choosing the right cache concurrency strategy

The concurrency strategy choice is based on the underlying data access patterns, as well as on the current application consistency requirements. By analyzing the second-level cache statistics, the application developer can tell how effective a cache concurrency strategy renders. A high `hitCount` number indicates that the data access layer benefits from using the current cache concurrency strategy, while a high `missCount` value tells the opposite.

Although analyzing statistics is the best way to make sure that a strategy is a right choice, there are still some general guidelines that can be used to narrow the choice list.

For immutable data, the `READ_ONLY` strategy makes much sense because it even disallows updating cache entries.

If entities are changed infrequently and reading a stale entry is not really an issue, then the `NONSTRICT_READ_WRITE` concurrency might be a good candidate.

For strong consistency, the data access layer can either use `READ_WRITE` or `TRANSACTIONAL`. `READ_WRITE` is a good choice when the volume of write operations, as well as the chance of rolling back transaction, are rather low.

If the read and write ratio is balanced, `TRANSACTIONAL` might be a good alternative because updates are applied synchronously. If the roll back ratio is high (e.g. due to optimistic locking exceptions), the `TRANSACTIONAL` strategy is a much better choice because it allows rolling back cache entries, unlike `READ_WRITE` cache mode which maintains a `Lock` entry until it times out. Depending on the caching provider, even the `TRANSACTIONAL` cache concurrency strategy might offer different consistency modes (e.g. `xa`, `xa_strict`) so that the application developer can balance strong consistency with throughput. To overcome the overhead of the two-phase commit protocol, the Ehcache XA mode can leverage the one-phase commit optimization.

The concurrency strategy choice might be affected by the second-level cache topology as well. If the volume of data is high, a single node might not be sufficient, so data needs to be distributed across multiple nodes. A distributed cache increases cache availability because, if one node crashes, the cached data still lives on other machines. However, most distributed second-level cache providers do not support the `TRANSACTIONAL` cache concurrency strategy, leaving the application developer to choose either `NONSTRICT_READ_WRITE` or `READ_WRITE`.

15.5.7 Query cache strategy

The query cache does not take into consideration the cache concurrency strategy of the associated cached entities, so it has its own rules when it comes to ensuring data consistency. Just like the collection cache, the query cache uses a read-through approach, so queries are cached upon being executed for the first time.

`org.hibernate.cache.internal.StandardQueryCache` is the second-level cache region where query results are being stored.

To visualize how the read-through query cache works, consider the following query:

```
public List<PostComment> getLatestPostComments(EntityManager entityManager) {
    return entityManager.createQuery(
        "select pc " +
        "from PostComment pc " +
        "order by pc.post.id desc", PostComment.class)
    .setMaxResults(10)
    .setHint(QueryHints.HINT_CACHEABLE, true)
    .getResultList();
}
```

 The QueryHints.HINT_CACHEABLE constant can be used to supply the JPA query hint that enables the second-level query cache.

If the current database contains the following entities:

```
Post post = new Post();
post.setId(1L);
post.setTitle("High-Performance Java Persistence");

PostComment comment = new PostComment();
comment.setId(1L);
comment.setReview("JDBC part review");
post.addComment(comment);

entityManager.persist(post);
```

When running the aforementioned query and printing the associated query cache region statistics:

```
doInJPA(entityManager -> {
    printCacheRegionStatistics(StandardQueryCache.class.getName());
    assertEquals(1, getLatestPostComments(entityManager).size());
    printCacheRegionStatistics(StandardQueryCache.class.getName());
});
```

Hibernate generates the following output:

```
Region: org.hibernate.cache.internal.StandardQueryCache,
Statistics: SecondLevelCacheStatistics[hitCount=0,missCount=0,putCount=0],
Entries: {}

SELECT pc.id AS id1_1_, pc.post_id AS post_id3_1_, pc.review AS review2_1_
FROM   post_comment pc ORDER BY pc.post_id DESC LIMIT 10

Region: org.hibernate.cache.internal.StandardQueryCache,
Statistics: SecondLevelCacheStatistics[hitCount=0,missCount=1,putCount=1],
Entries: {sql: ; named parameters: {}; max rows: 10; = [5992563495481345, 1]}
```

For brevity, the query cache entry was shortened. As expected, once the query is being executed, the matching entity identifiers are stored in the query cache entry.

15.5.7.1 Tablespace query cache invalidation

To understand query cache invalidation, considering the following exercise:

```
doInJPA(entityManager -> {
    assertEquals(1, getLatestPostComments(entityManager).size());
    printCacheRegionStatistics(StandardQueryCache.class.getName());

    LOGGER.info("Insert a new PostComment");
    PostComment newComment = new PostComment();
    newComment.setId(2L);
    newComment.setReview("JDBC part review");
    Post post = entityManager.find(Post.class, 1L);
    post.addComment(newComment);
    entityManager.flush();

    assertEquals(2, getLatestPostComments(entityManager).size());
    printCacheRegionStatistics(StandardQueryCache.class.getName());
});
LOGGER.info("After transaction commit");
printCacheRegionStatistics(StandardQueryCache.class.getName());

doInJPA(entityManager -> {
    LOGGER.info("Check query cache");
    assertEquals(2, getLatestPostComments(entityManager).size());
});
printCacheRegionStatistics(StandardQueryCache.class.getName());
```

Hibernate generates the following output:

```
Region: org.hibernate.cache.internal.StandardQueryCache,
Statistics: SecondLevelCacheStatistics[hitCount=0,missCount=1,putCount=1],
Entries: {sql: ; named parameters: {}; max rows: 10;=[5992617470844929, 1]]}
```

```
-- Insert a new PostComment
```

```
INSERT INTO post_comment (post_id, review, id)
VALUES (1, 'JDBC part review', 2)
```

```
UpdateTimestampsCache - Pre-invalidating space [post_comment],
timestamp: 5992617717362689
UpdateTimestampsCache - [post_comment] last update timestamp: 5992617717362689,
result set timestamp: 5992617470844929
StandardQueryCache - Cached query results were not up-to-date
```

```
SELECT pc.id AS id1_1_, pc.post_id AS post_id3_1_, pc.review AS review2_1_
FROM   post_comment pc ORDER BY pc.post_id DESC LIMIT 10
```

```
Region: org.hibernate.cache.internal.StandardQueryCache,
Statistics: SecondLevelCacheStatistics[hitCount=0,missCount=2,putCount=2],
Entries: {sql: ; named parameters: {}; max rows: 10; =[5992617470844929, 2, 1]]}
```

```
UpdateTimestampsCache - Invalidating space [post_comment],
timestamp: 5992617471619075
```

```
--After transaction commit
```

```
Region: org.hibernate.cache.internal.StandardQueryCache,
Statistics: SecondLevelCacheStatistics[hitCount=0,missCount=2,putCount=2],
Entries: {sql: ; named parameters: {}; max rows: 10; =[5992617470844929, 2, 1]]}
```

```
--Check query cache
```

```
StandardQueryCache - Checking query spaces are up-to-date: [post_comment]
UpdateTimestampsCache - [post_comment] last update timestamp: 5992617471619075,
result set timestamp: 5992617470844929
StandardQueryCache - Cached query results were not up-to-date
```

```
Region: org.hibernate.cache.internal.StandardQueryCache,
Statistics: SecondLevelCacheStatistics[hitCount=0,missCount=3,putCount=3],
Entries: {sql: ; named parameters: {}; max rows: 10;=[5992617471627265, 2, 1]]}
```

Hibernate second-level cache favors strong-consistency and the query cache is no different. Whenever tablespaces are changing, the query cache invalidates all entries that are using the aforementioned tablespaces. The flow goes like this:

- Once the PostComment persist event is flushed, Hibernate pre-invalidates the post_comment tablespace timestamp (5992617717362689).
- When a tablespace is pre-invalidated, its timestamp is set to the cache region timeout timestamp value, which, by default, is set to 60 seconds.
- The query cache compares the cache entry timestamp with the tablespace pre-invalidation timeout timestamp value.
- Because the post_comment tablespace timestamp (5992617717362689) is greater than query result fetch timestamp (5992617470844929), the query cache ignores the cached entry value, and Hibernate executes the database query.
- The result set that is now fetched from the database goes to the cache without updating the result set timestamp (5992617470844929).
- When the current database transaction is committed, the post_comment tablespace is invalidated. Therefore, the tablespace timestamp is set to the transaction commit timestamp (5992617471619075).
- Even after the current database transaction is committed, the query cache timestamp is still seeing the old query result (5992617470844929).
- A new Session wants to execute the query, and because the query cache timestamp (5992617471619075) is still older than the post_comment tablespace timestamp, Hibernate executes the database query.
- Because this Session has not modified any tablespace, Hibernate updates the query cache with the current result set and the cache entry timestamp is set to the current Session timestamp (5992617471627265).

This flow guarantees strict consistency, and the query cache timestamp acts like a soft locking mechanism, preventing other concurrent transactions from reading stale entries.

15.5.7.2 Native SQL statement query cache invalidation

Hibernate can only parse JPQL and HQL statements, so it knows what tablespaces are required by a particular entity statement. For native statements, Hibernate cannot know if a tablespace is going to be affected directly or indirectly, and, by default, every native update statement is going to invalidate all query cache entries.

When executing the following example:

```
assertEquals(1, getLatestPostComments(entityManager).size());
printCacheRegionStatistics(StandardQueryCache.class.getName());

entityManager.createNativeQuery(
    "UPDATE post SET title = '\"'||title||'\"' ")
.executeUpdate();

assertEquals(1, getLatestPostComments(entityManager).size());
printCacheRegionStatistics(StandardQueryCache.class.getName());
```

Hibernate generates the following output:

```
Region: org.hibernate.cache.internal.StandardQueryCache,
Statistics: SecondLevelCacheStatistics[hitCount=0,missCount=1,putCount=1],
Entries: {sql: ; named parameters: {}; max rows: 10;=[5992657080082432, 1]}

UpdateTimestampsCache - Pre-invalidating space [post_comment],
timestamp: 5992657328578560
UpdateTimestampsCache - Pre-invalidating space [post],
timestamp: 5992657328578560

UPDATE post SET title = '"'||title||'"'

StandardQueryCache - Checking query spaces are up-to-date: [post_comment]
UpdateTimestampsCache - [post_comment] last update timestamp: 5992657328578560,
result set timestamp: 5992657080082432
StandardQueryCache - Cached query results were not up-to-date

SELECT pc.id AS id1_1_, pc.post_id AS post_id3_1_, pc.review AS review2_1_
FROM    post_comment pc
ORDER BY pc.post_id DESC
LIMIT 10

Region: org.hibernate.cache.internal.StandardQueryCache,
Statistics: SecondLevelCacheStatistics[hitCount=0,missCount=2,putCount=2],
Entries: {sql: ; named parameters: {}; max rows: 10;=[5992657080082432, 1]}

UpdateTimestampsCache - Invalidating space [post], timestamp: 5992668528799744
UpdateTimestampsCache - Invalidating space [post_comment],
timestamp: 5992668528799744
```

The flow goes like this:

- Initially, the query result is stored in the cache.
- Upon executing the native DML statement, Hibernate pre-invalidates all tablespaces (e.g. post and post_comment).
- When the data access layer executes the previously cached PostComment query, Hibernate checks the cache entry timestamp validity.
- Because the post_comment timestamp was set to the timeout value, Hibernate is prevented from using the cached result, so it executes the database query.
- When the transaction is committed, all tablespaces are invalidated, their associated timestamps being set to the current transaction commit timestamp.

To prevent Hibernate from invalidating all entries in the StandardQueryCache region, the native query must explicitly specify the tablespaces that are going to be affected:

```
entityManager.createNativeQuery(
    "UPDATE post SET title = '\"'||title||'\"' ")
.unwrap(SQLQuery.class).addSynchronizedEntityClass(Post.class)
.executeUpdate();
```

This time, Hibernate generates the following output:

```
Region: org.hibernate.cache.internal.StandardQueryCache,
Statistics: SecondLevelCacheStatistics[hitCount=0,missCount=1,putCount=1],
Entries: {sql: ; named parameters: {}; max rows: 10;=[5992666396459009, 1]}


UpdateTimestampsCache - Pre-invalidating space [post],
timestamp: 5992666644185088


UPDATE post SET title = '"'||title||'"'


StandardQueryCache - Checking query spaces are up-to-date: [post_comment]
UpdateTimestampsCache - [post_comment] last update timestamp: 5992666396422146,
result set timestamp: 5992666396459009
StandardQueryCache - Returning cached query results


Region: org.hibernate.cache.internal.StandardQueryCache,
Statistics: SecondLevelCacheStatistics[hitCount=1,missCount=1,putCount=1],
Entries: {sql:; named parameters: {}; max rows: 10;f2=[5992666396459009, 1]}


UpdateTimestampsCache - Invalidating space [post], timestamp: 5992666398470144
```

Because this time only the post tablespace is invalidated, and since the entity query uses the post_comment table, the previously cached query result can be reused to satisfy the current entity query fetching requirements.

Query cache applicability

As explained in the Fetching chapter, DTO projections are suitable for executing read-only queries. For this purpose, the query cache is not a general purpose solution since it can only select entities.

However, fetching entities is appropriate for read-write transactions, and any entity modification can trigger a ripple effect in the `StandardQueryCache` second-level cache region. For this purpose, the query cache works better for immutable entities, or for entities that rarely change.

16. Concurrency Control

As explained in the JDBC Transactions chapter, every SQL statement executes within the scope of a database transaction. To prevent conflicts, database engines employ row-level locks. Database physical locks can either be acquired implicitly or explicitly. Whenever a row is changed, the relational database acquires an implicit exclusive lock on the aforementioned record to prevent write-write conflicts.

Locks can also be acquired explicitly, in which case the concurrency control mechanism is called pessimistic locking. Exclusive locks can be acquired explicitly on most database systems, whereas shared locks are not universally supported.

Pessimistic locking deals with concurrency conflicts through prevention, which can impact application performance and scalability. For this reason, to increase transaction throughput while still ensuring strong consistency, many data access frameworks provide optimistic locking support as well.

16.1 Hibernate optimistic locking

Even if pessimistic locking has only been added in JPA 2.0, optimistic locking has been supported since version 1.0. Just like pessimistic locking, the optimistic concurrency control mechanism can be used implicitly or explicitly.

16.1.1 The implicit optimistic locking mechanism

To enable the implicit optimistic locking mechanism, the entity must provide a @Version attribute:

```
@Entity @Table(name = "post")
public class Post {

    @Id
    private Long id;

    private String title;

    @Version
    private int version;

    //Getters and setters omitted for brevity
}
```

Logical vs. Physical clocks

Using timestamps to order events is rarely a good idea. System time is not always monotonically incremented, and it can even go backward due to network time synchronization (NTP protocol).

More, time accuracy across different database systems varies from nanoseconds (Oracle[a]) to 100 nanoseconds (SQL Server[b]), to microseconds (PostgreSQL[c] and MySQL 5.6.4[d] and even seconds (previous versions of MySQL). In distributed systems, logical clocks (e.g. vector clocks or Lamport timestamps) are always preferred to physical timestamps (wall clocks) when it comes to ordering events.

 For this reason, employing a numerical version is more appropriate than using a timestamp.

[a]http://docs.oracle.com/database/121/LNPCB/pco04dat.htm#LNPCB269
[b]https://msdn.microsoft.com/en-us/library/bb677335.aspx
[c]http://www.postgresql.org/docs/9.5/static/datatype-datetime.html
[d]http://dev.mysql.com/doc/refman/5.6/en/fractional-seconds.html

To visualize the optimistic concurrency control, when executing the following test case:

```
doInJPA(entityManager -> {
    Post post = new Post();
    post.setId(1L);
    post.setTitle("High-Performance Java Persistence");
    entityManager.persist(post);

    entityManager.flush();
    post.setTitle("High-Performance Hibernate");
});
```

Hibernate generates the following output:

```
INSERT INTO post (title, version, id)
VALUES ('High-Performance Java Persistence', 0, 1)

UPDATE post SET title = 'High-Performance Hibernate', version = 1
WHERE id = 1 AND version = 0
```

Whenever an update occurs, Hibernate is going to filter the database record according to the expected entity version. If the version has changed, the update count is going to be 0, and a OptimisticLockException is going to be thrown.

To visualize the conflict detection mechanism, consider the following exercise:

```
doInJPA(entityManager -> {
    Post post = entityManager.find(Post.class, 1L);
    executeSync(() -> {
        doInJPA(_entityManager -> {
            Post _post = _entityManager.find(Post.class, 1L);
            _post.setTitle("High-Performance JDBC");
        });
    });
    post.setTitle("High-Performance Hibernate");
});
```

When executing the aforementioned test case, Hibernate generates the following output:

```
-- Alice selects the Post entity
SELECT p.id AS id1_0_0_, p.title AS title2_0_0_, p.version AS version3_0_0_
FROM    post p
WHERE   p.id = 1


-- Bob also selects the same Post entity
SELECT p.id AS id1_0_0_, p.title AS title2_0_0_, p.version AS version3_0_0_
FROM    post p
WHERE   p.id = 1


-- Bob updates the Post entity
UPDATE post SET title = 'High-Performance JDBC', version = 1
WHERE id = 1 AND version = 0


-- Alice also wants to update the Post entity
UPDATE post SET title = 'High-Performance Hibernate', version = 1
WHERE id = 1 AND version = 0


--Exception thrown
javax.persistence.RollbackException: Error while committing the transaction
Caused by: javax.persistence.OptimisticLockException:
Caused by: org.hibernate.StaleStateException:
Batch update returned unexpected row count from update [0];
actual row count: 0; expected: 1
```

Because this example uses the Java Persistence API, the Hibernate internal StaleStateException is wrapped in the OptimisticLockException defined by the JPA specification.

The flow of operations can be summarized as follows:

- Alice fetches a `Post` entity and then her thread is suspended.
- Bob thread is resumed, he fetches the same `Post` entity and changes the `title` to `High-Performance JDBC`. The entity `version` is set to 1.
- When Alice's thread is resumed, she tries to update the `Post` entity `title` to `High-Performance Hibernate`.
- An `OptimisticLockException` is thrown because the second update statement is expecting to filter the entity version with a value of 0, while the `version` column value is now 1.

16.1.1.1 Resolving optimistic locking conflicts

While pessimistic locking prevents conflict occurrences, optimistic locking mechanisms, just like MVCC, use conflict detection instead. So anomalies are detected and prevented from being materialized by aborting the currently running transactions, and Hibernate optimistic locking can prevent the *lost update* anomaly.

As explained in the application-level transactions section, when using a multi-request workflow, the database isolation level can no longer prevent lost updates. On the other hand, the optimistic locking mechanism can prevent losing updates as long as the entity state is preserved from one request to the other.

Optimistic locking discards all incoming changes that are relative to a stale entity version. However, everything has its price and optimistic locking is no different.

If two concurrent transactions are updating distinct entity attribute subsets, then there should be no risk of losing any update. However, the optimistic concurrency control mechanism takes an all-or-nothing approach even for non-overlapping changes. For this reason, two concurrent updates, both starting from the same entity version, are always going to collide. It is only the first update that is going to succeed, the second one failing with an optimistic locking exception.

This strict policy acts as if all changes are going to overlap, and, for highly concurrent write scenarios, the single version strategy can lead to a large number of transactions being rolled back.

To visualize the non-overlapping conflict, consider the following `Post` entity class:

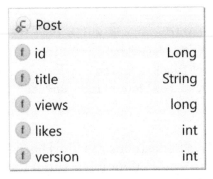

Figure 16.1: Post entity with a single global version

In the following example, Alice modifies the `Post` entity `title` attribute, Bob increments the `likes` counter, and Carol sets the `views` attribute to a value that was aggregated from an external batch processor.

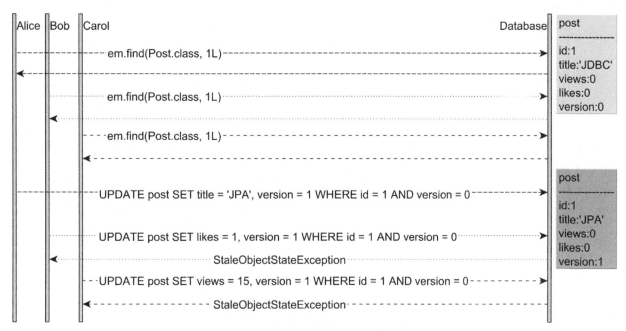

Figure 16.2: Optimistic locking non-overlapping conflict

The flow of operations can be explained as follows:

- All three users are loading the same `Post` entity version.
- Alice modifies the `title`. Therefore, the `Post` entity `version` is incremented.
- Bob tries to increment the `likes` counter but rolls back because it expects the `version` to be 0, but now it has a value of 1.
- Carol's transaction is also aborted because of the entity version mismatch.

The optimistic locking mechanism allows only monotonically increasing version updates. If changes were dependent one to another, then getting an `OptimisticLockException` is less of an issue than losing an update. However, if from a business logic perspective, the changing attributes are not overlapping, having a single global version is no longer sufficient.

For this reason, the single global version must be split into multiple subversions, and this can be done in two ways:

- Instead of having a single optimistic locking counter, there can be a distinct version for each individual attribute set.
- Each changing attribute can be compared against its previously known value, so lost updates are relative only to the attribute in question.

16.1.1.2 Splitting entities

The Post entity can be split into several sub-entities according to the three distinct set of attributes:

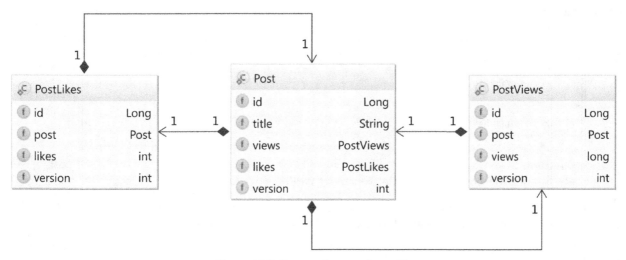

Figure 16.3: Post entity version split

While the title attribute remains in the Post parent entity, the likes, and the views attributes are moved to distinct entities. The PostLikes and PostViews entities are associated with the Post parent entity in a bidirectional one-to-one relationship. The PostLikes and PostViews entity identifiers are also foreign keys to the post table primary key.

Each entity has its own version attribute. Whenever the Post title is changed, it is only the Post entity version that is checked and incremented. When the views attribute is updated, only the PostViews entity is going to be affected. The same is true for incrementing likes which are stored in the PostLikes entity.

While breaking a larger entity into several sub-entities can help address optimistic locking conflicts, this strategy has its price. This rather extreme data normalization strategy can have an impact on read operation performance because data is scattered across several tables. If the whole aggregate is needed to be fetched, the data access layer will require to join several tables or execute additional secondary select statements.

The second-level cache can mitigate the read operation performance penalty. Actually, the root entity split can improve the second-level cache performance, especially for read-through strategies (e.g. NONSTRICT_READ_WRITE). If the views attribute is modified, only the PostViews cache entry needs to be invalidated, whereas the Post and the PostLikes remain unaffected.

When running the previous exercise, there is no longer any conflict being generated:

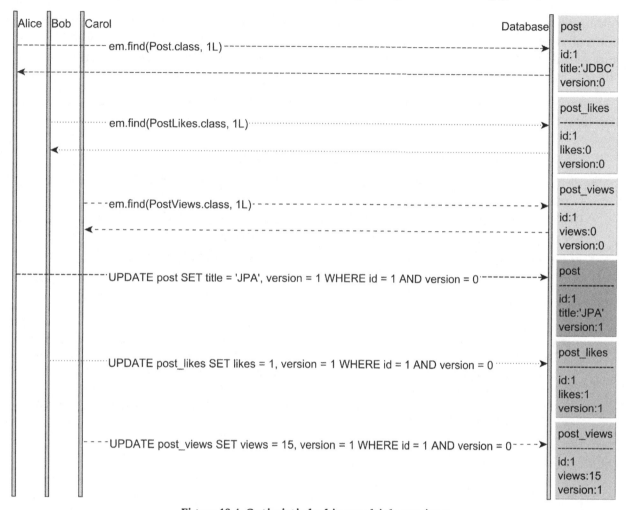

Figure 16.4: Optimistic locking multiple versions

Lost updates are prevented at the entity-level only so the three distinct attributes can be updated concurrently without generating any conflict. However, conflicts can still occur if the same attribute is getting updated by two concurrent transactions.

 Designing a Domain Model must take into consideration both read and write data access patterns. Splitting entities by write responsibility can reduce optimistic locking false positives when the write ratio is relatively high.

16.1.1.3 Versionless optimistic locking

Although having a numerical version attribute is the most common optimistic concurrency control strategy, Hibernate offers a versionless optimistic locking mechanism which is not supported by JPA 2.1 specification. To switch to the versionless optimistic locking mechanism, the `@OptimisticLocking` annotation must be configured at the entity level.

The `org.hibernate.annotations.OptimisticLocking` annotation comes with a `type` attribute that can take the following values:

- NONE - The implicit optimistic locking mechanism is disabled.
- VERSION - The implicit optimistic locking mechanism uses a numerical or a timestamp version attribute.
- DIRTY - The implicit optimistic locking mechanism uses only the attributes that have been modified in the currently running Persistence Context.
- ALL - The implicit optimistic locking mechanism uses all entity attributes.

`OptimisticLockType.ALL` and `OptimisticLockType.DIRTY` also require the `@DynamicUpdate` annotation because update statements must be rewritten so that either all attributes or the ones that were modified are included in the where clause criteria. For these two optimistic lock types, the entity versioning mechanism is based on the hydrated state snapshot that was stored when the entity was first loaded in the currently running Persistence Context.

To see how the `OptimisticLockType.ALL` option works, consider the following `Post` entity mapping:

```
@Entity @Table(name = "post") @DynamicUpdate
@OptimisticLocking(type = OptimisticLockType.ALL)
public class Post {

    @Id
    private Long id;

    private String title;

    //Getters and setters omitted for brevity
}
```

When using the aforementioned Post entity to rerun the example defined at the beginning of the Hibernate implicit optimistic locking section, Hibernate generates the following output:

```
INSERT INTO post (title, version, id)
VALUES ('High-Performance Java Persistence', 0, 1)

UPDATE post SET title = 'High-Performance JDBC'
WHERE id = 1 AND title = 'High-Performance Java Persistence'
```

If the Post entity had more attributes, all of them would be included in the SQL where clause.

 The OptimisticLockType.ALL is useful when the underlying database table cannot be altered in order to add a numerical version column. Because it takes into consideration all entity attributes, the OptimisticLockType.ALL option behaves just like a single global version attribute, and write conflicts can occur even if two concurrent transactions are modifying non-overlapping attribute sets.

Even if the entity splitting method can address the non-overlapping attribute sets conflict, too much data normalization can affect read operation performance. The OptimisticLockType.DIRTY option can deal with this issue, and so lost updates are prevented for the currently modified attributes.

To demonstrate it, the following Post entity mapping is going to be used while running the same test case employed in the resolve optimistic locking conflicts section:

```
@Entity @Table(name = "post") @DynamicUpdate
@OptimisticLocking(type = OptimisticLockType.DIRTY)
public class Post {

    @Id
    private Long id;

    private String title;

    private long views;

    private int likes;

    //Getters and setters omitted for brevity
}
```

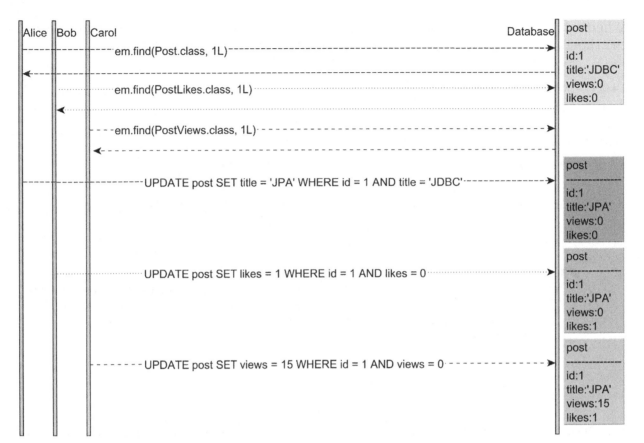

Figure 16.5: Optimistic locking dirty attributes

The `OptimisticLockType.DIRTY` option allows concurrent users to update distinct attributes without causing any conflict. However, conflicts can still occur when two concurrent transactions are updating the same attribute. Therefore, lost updates are prevented on a per-attribute basis.

 For heavy-write data access layers, it is not uncommon to split an entity into multiple parts, each individual subentity containing attributes that need to be updated atomically. If, from a writing perspective, attributes are independent, then the `OptimisticLockType.DIRTY` mechanism is also a viable alternative.

Preventing lost updates is essential for data integrity, but the prospect of having transactions aborted due to non-overlapping attribute changes is undesirable. To cope with this issue, entities need to be carefully modeled based on both read and write data access patterns.

16.1.1.3.1 OptimisticLockType.DIRTY update caveat

In spite of being very useful for preventing optimistic locking conflicts, the `OptimisticLock-Type.DIRTY` mechanism has one limitation: it does not work with the `Session.update()` method.

```
Post detachedPost = doInJPA(entityManager -> {
    LOGGER.info("Alice loads the Post entity");
    return entityManager.find(Post.class, 1L);
});

executeSync(() -> {
    doInJPA(entityManager -> {
        LOGGER.info("Bob loads the Post entity and modifies it");
        Post post = entityManager.find(Post.class, 1L);
        post.setTitle("Hibernate");
    });
});

doInJPA(entityManager -> {
    LOGGER.info("Alice updates the Post entity");
    detachedPost.setTitle("JPA");
    entityManager.unwrap(Session.class).update(detachedPost);
});
```

When running the test case above, Hibernate generates the following statements:

```
-- Alice loads the Post entity
SELECT p.id AS id1_0_0_, p.likes AS likes2_0_0_, p.title AS title3_0_0_,
       p.views AS views4_0_0_
FROM   post p
WHERE  p.id = 1

-- Bob loads the Post entity and modifies it
SELECT p.id AS id1_0_0_, p.likes AS likes2_0_0_, p.title AS title3_0_0_,
       p.views AS views4_0_0_
FROM   post p
WHERE  p.id = 1

UPDATE post SET title = 'Hibernate' WHERE id = 1 AND title = 'JDBC'

-- Alice updates the Post entity
UPDATE post SET likes=0, title='JPA', views=0 WHERE id=1
```

Bob's update benefits from dirty attribute optimistic locking, just as expected. On the other hand, Alice's update is not using any optimistic locking at all.

That is because the reattached Post entity misses the loaded state information, so the dirty checking mechanism cannot be executed in this case. For this reason, Hibernate schedules an update statement that simply copies the current entity state to the underlying database record. Unfortunately, this can lead to lost updates since Alice is not aware of Bob's latest modification. If optimistic locking were working, Alice's update would be prevented.

The @SelectBeforeUpdate annotation allows Hibernate to fetch the entity snapshot prior to executing the update query. This way, Hibernate can run the dirty checking mechanism and make sure that the update is really necessary.

```
@Entity(name = "Post") @Table(name = "post")
@OptimisticLocking(type = OptimisticLockType.DIRTY)
@DynamicUpdate
@SelectBeforeUpdate
public static class Post {

    @Id
    private Long id;

    private String title;

    private long views;

    private int likes;

    //Getters and setters omitted for brevity
}
```

Unfortunately, even when using @SelectBeforeUpdate, the optimistic locking mechanism is still circumvented, and Alice update transaction executes the following statements:

```
SELECT p.id AS id1_0_0_, p.likes AS likes2_0_0_, p.title AS title3_0_0_,
       p.views AS views4_0_0_
FROM   post p
WHERE  p.id = 1

UPDATE post SET title='JPA' WHERE id = 1
```

The dynamic update works since the update statement contains only the modified attribute, but there is no optimistic locking filtering criteria.

If Alice uses the `EntityManager.merge()` operation:

```
doInJPA(entityManager -> {
    detachedPost.setTitle("JPA");
    entityManager.merge(detachedPost);
});
```

Hibernate executes the following SQL statements:

```
SELECT p.id AS id1_0_0_, p.likes AS likes2_0_0_, p.title AS title3_0_0_,
       p.views AS views4_0_0_
FROM   post p
WHERE  p.id = 1


UPDATE post SET title='JPA' WHERE id = 1 AND title = 'Hibernate'
```

The optimistic locking mechanism is used, but it is relative to the newly loaded entity state. This time, lost updates can only be detected if, while merging the detached entity, Carol would update the same `Post` entity `title`.

Statefulness to the rescue

Unfortunately, Bob's update is still undetected by the versionless optimistic locking mechanism. The current entity state alone is no longer sufficient when merging a detached entity version because the Persistence Context cannot determine which attributes have been changed and which reference values are to be used in the where clause filtering criteria.

To fix it, the entity must store the loading-time attribute state so that the Persistence Context can use it later for the optimistic locking where clause criteria, therefore, preventing any lost update occurrence. However, this is impractical, and so the entity state must be stored either in a stateful Persistence Context, or its loading-time version value be saved separately.

Using a numerical version is practical, but it can lead to optimistic locking conflicts because all attributes are treating as a global all-or-nothing update attribute set. On the other hand, the Persistence Context does not need to be closed. Only the database connection needs to be released to allow other concurrent transactions to execute in the user think time. The Persistence Context can be kept open so that entities never become detached. This way, the entity loading-time state is never lost, and the versionless optimistic locking mechanism will work even across multiple transactions. When using Java EE, a `PersistenceContextType.EXTENDED` can be used inside a `@Stateful` EJB. Spring Webflow allows registering a Persistence Context in the `HttpSession` so that the `EntityManager` remains open throughout the whole lifecycle of the current flow.

16.2 The explicit locking mechanism

While the implicit locking mechanism is suitable for many application concurrency control requirements, there might be times when a finer-grained locking strategy is needed. JPA offers a concurrency control API, on top of which the application developer can implement really complex data integrity rules. The explicit locking mechanism works for both pessimistic and optimistic locking.

For pessimistic concurrency control, JPA abstracts the database-specific locking semantics, and, depending on the underlying database capabilities, the application developer can acquire exclusive or shared locks.

If the implicit optimistic locking mechanism controls the entity version automatically, and the application developer is not allowed to make changes to the underlying version attribute, the explicit optimistic lock modes allow incrementing an entity version even if the entity was not changed by the currently running transaction. This is useful when two distinct entities need to be correlated so that a child entity modification can trigger a parent entity version incrementation.

JPA offers various `LockModeType(s)` that can be acquired for the direct loading mechanism (e.g. `entityManager.find`, `entityManager.lock`, `entityManager.refresh`) as well as for any JPQL or Criteria API query (e.g. `Query.setLockMode()`).

The following table lists all `LockModeType(s)` that can be acquired by a particular entity:

Table 16.1: `LockModeType(s)`

Lock Mode Type	Description
NONE	In the absence of explicit locking, the application uses the default implicit locking mechanism.
OPTIMISTIC or READ	Issues a version check upon transaction commit.
OPTIMISTIC_FORCE_INCREMENT or WRITE	Increases the entity version prior to committing the current running transaction.
PESSIMISTIC_FORCE_INCREMENT	An exclusive database lock is acquired, and the entity version is incremented right away.
PESSIMISTIC_READ	A shared database lock is acquired to prevent any other transaction from acquiring an exclusive lock.
PESSIMISTIC_WRITE	An exclusive lock is acquired to prevent any other transaction from acquiring a shared/exclusive lock.

The following sections will analyze each individual `LockModeType` in greater detail.

16.2.1 PESSIMISTIC_READ and PESSIMISTIC_WRITE

To acquire row-level locks, JPA defines two `LockModeType`: PESSIMISTIC_READ, for shared locks, and PESSIMISTIC_WRITE, for exclusive locks. Unfortunately, there is no standard definition for acquiring shared and exclusive locks, and each database system defines its own syntax.

Oracle

Only exclusive locks are supported for which Oracle defines the FOR UPDATE[a] clause. Rows that were selected with the FOR UPDATE clause cannot be locked or modified until the current transaction either commits or rolls back.

[a]https://docs.oracle.com/database/121/SQLRF/statements_10002.htm#SQLRF01702

SQL Server

SQL Server does not define a FOR UPDATE select statement clause, but instead it defines several table hints[a]. The WITH (HOLDLOCK, ROWLOCK) is equivalent to acquiring a shared lock until the current running transaction is ended, whereas the WITH (UPDLOCK, ROWLOCK) hint can be used to acquire an exclusive lock.

[a]https://msdn.microsoft.com/en-us/library/ms187373.aspx

PostgreSQL

The select clause can take multiple locking clauses[a] among which FOR SHARE is used to acquire a shared lock, whereas FOR UPDATE takes an exclusive lock on each selected row.

[a]https://www.postgresql.org/docs/9.5/static/sql-select.html#SQL-FOR-UPDATE-SHARE

MySQL

Just like PostgreSQL, the FOR UPDATE clause can be used to acquire an exclusive lock, while LOCK IN SHARE MODE[a] is used for shared locks.

[a]http://dev.mysql.com/doc/refman/5.7/en/innodb-locking-reads.html

When using Hibernate, the application developer needs not to worry about the locking syntax employed by the underlying database system. To acquire an exclusive lock, the PESSIMISTIC_-WRITE lock type must be used, and Hibernate will pick the underlying Dialect lock clause.

For instance, when running the following entity lock acquisition request on PostgreSQL:

```
Post post = entityManager.find(Post.class, 1L, LockModeType.PESSIMISTIC_WRITE);
```

Hibernate is going to generate the following query:

```
SELECT p.id AS id1_0_0_, p.body AS body2_0_0_, p.title AS title3_0_0_,
       p.version AS version4_0_0_
FROM   post p
WHERE  p.id = 1
FOR UPDATE
```

If the relational database offers support for acquiring shared locks explicitly, the PESSIMISTIC_-READ lock type must be used instead. When fetching an entity directly using the PESSIMISTIC_-READ lock type on PostgreSQL:

```
Post post = entityManager.find(Post.class, 1L, LockModeType.PESSIMISTIC_READ);
```

Hibernate is going to use the FOR SHARE select clause:

```
SELECT p.id AS id1_0_0_, p.body AS body2_0_0_, p.title AS title3_0_0_,
       p.version AS version4_0_0_
FROM   post p
WHERE  p.id = 1
FOR SHARE
```

 If the underlying database does not support shared locks, when using the PESSIMISTIC_READ lock type, an exclusive lock is acquired instead. When running the previous PESSIMISTIC_READ direct fetching example on Oracle, Hibernate will use a FOR UPDATE select clause.

Although it is much more convenient to lock entities at the moment they are fetched from the database, entities can also be locked even after they are loaded in the currently running Persistence context.

For this purpose, the `EntityManager` interface defines the `lock` method which takes a managed entity and a `LockModeType`:

```
Post post = entityManager.find(Post.class, 1L);
entityManager.lock(post, LockModeType.PESSIMISTIC_WRITE);
```

When running the aforementioned example, Hibernate is going to execute the following statements:

```
SELECT p.id AS id1_0_0_, p.body AS body2_0_0_, p.title AS title3_0_0_,
       p.version AS version4_0_0_
FROM   post p
WHERE  p.id = 1


SELECT id
FROM   post
WHERE  id = 1 AND version = 0
FOR UPDATE
```

Only a managed entity can be passed to the `lock` method when using the Java Persistence API. Otherwise, an `IllegalArgumentException` is being thrown indicating that the entity is not contained within the currently running Persistence Context.

On the other hand, the Hibernate native API offers entity reattachment upon locking as demonstrated by the following example:

```
Post post = doInJPA(entityManager -> {
    return entityManager.find(Post.class, 1L);
});


doInJPA(entityManager -> {
    LOGGER.info("Lock and reattach");
    Session session = entityManager.unwrap(Session.class);
    session.buildLockRequest(
        new LockOptions(LockMode.PESSIMISTIC_WRITE))
    .lock(post);
    post.setTitle("High-Performance Hibernate");
});
```

When running the test case above, Hibernate manages to acquire an exclusive lock on the associated database record while also propagating the entity state change to the database:

```
SELECT p.id AS id1_0_0_, p.body AS body2_0_0_, p.title AS title3_0_0_,
       p.version AS version4_0_0_
FROM   post p
WHERE  p.id = 1


-- Lock and reattach
SELECT id
FROM   post
WHERE  id = 1 AND version = 0
FOR UPDATE


UPDATE post
SET body = 'Chapter 17 summary', title = High-Performance Hibernate'
WHERE id = 1 AND version = 0
```

Because the detached entity becomes managed, the entity modification triggers an update statement at flush time.

16.2.1.1 Lock scope

By default, the lock scope is bound to the entity that is being locked explicitly. However, just like other entity state transitions, the lock acquisition request can be cascaded to child associations like the `PostDetails` and `PostComment(s)` entities in the next diagram.

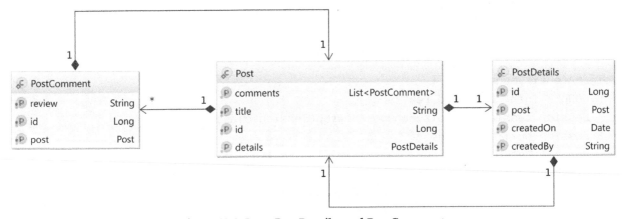

Figure 16.6: Post, PostDetails, and PostComment

The easiest way to lock a whole entity graph is to apply the `LockModeType` at the entity query level.

When executing the following entity query:

```
Post post = entityManager.createQuery(
    "select p " +
    "from Post p " +
    "join fetch p.details " +
    "join fetch p.comments " +
    "where p.id = :id", Post.class)
.setParameter("id", 1L)
.setLockMode(LockModeType.PESSIMISTIC_WRITE)
.getSingleResult();
```

Hibernate generates the following SQL query:

```
SELECT p.id AS id1_0_0_, p.body AS body2_0_0_, p.title AS title3_0_0_,
       p.version AS version4_0_0_, pd.id AS id1_2_1_,
       pd.created_by AS created_2_2_1_, pd.created_on AS created_3_2_1_,
       pd.version AS version4_2_1_, pc.id AS id1_1_2_,
       pc.post_id AS post_id4_1_2_, pc.review AS review2_1_2_,
       pc.version AS version3_1_2_, pc.post_id AS post_id4_1_0__,
       pc.id AS id1_1_0__
FROM   post p
INNER JOIN post_details pd ON p.id = pd.id
INNER JOIN post_comment pc ON p.id = pc.post_id
WHERE  p.id = 1
FOR UPDATE
```

The FOR UPDATE clause is applied to all records that are being selected, therefore, the whole result set is being locked. In this particular case, the lock scope depends on the query filtering criteria.

Aside from entity queries, Hibernate can also propagate a lock acquisition request from a parent entity to its children when using direct fetching. For this purpose, the child associations must be annotated with the Hibernate specific CascadeType.Lock[1] attribute.

 CascadeType.Lock can also be inherited implicitly when the child association is annotated with the CascadeType.ALL attribute.

---

[1]https://docs.jboss.org/hibernate/orm/current/javadocs/org/hibernate/annotations/CascadeType.html#LOCK

To demonstrate how the lock can be cascaded, the Post entity is changed so that the CascadeType.ALL attribute is set on both comments and details child associations:

```
@OneToMany(cascade = CascadeType.ALL, mappedBy = "post", orphanRemoval = true)
private List<PostComment> comments = new ArrayList<>();

@OneToOne(cascade = CascadeType.ALL, mappedBy = "post", orphanRemoval = true,
          fetch = FetchType.LAZY, optional = false)
private PostDetails details;
```

The implicit or explicit CascadeType.Lock is not sufficient because the LockRequest[2] declares a scope attribute which is disabled by default. For the lock to be cascaded, the scope attribute must be set to true as in the following example:

```
Post post = entityManager.find(Post.class, 1L);
entityManager.unwrap(Session.class)
.buildLockRequest(
    new LockOptions(LockMode.PESSIMISTIC_WRITE))
.setScope(true)
.lock(post);
```

However, when executing the test case above, Hibernate is going to lock only the Post entity:

```
SELECT p.id AS id1_0_0_, p.body AS body2_0_0_, p.title AS title3_0_0_,
       p.version AS version4_0_0_
FROM   post p
WHERE  p.id = 1

SELECT id
FROM   post
WHERE  id = 1 AND version = 0
FOR UPDATE
```

For managed entities, Hibernate does not cascade the lock acquisition request even if the scope attribute is provided, therefore, the entity query alternative is preferred.

When locking a detached entity graph, Hibernate is going to reattach every entity that enabled cascade propagation while also propagating the lock request.

---

[2]https://docs.jboss.org/hibernate/orm/current/javadocs/org/hibernate/Session.LockRequest.html

```
Post post = doInJPA(entityManager -> {
    return entityManager.createQuery(
        "select p " +
        "from Post p " +
        "join fetch p.details " +
        "join fetch p.comments " +
        "where p.id = :id", Post.class)
    .setParameter("id", 1L)
    .getSingleResult();
});

doInJPA(entityManager -> {
    entityManager.unwrap(Session.class)
    .buildLockRequest(
        new LockOptions(LockMode.PESSIMISTIC_WRITE))
    .setScope(true)
    .lock(post);
});
```

When executing the test case above, Hibernate generates the following queries:

```
SELECT p.id AS id1_0_0_, pd.id AS id1_2_1_, pc.id AS id1_1_2_,
       p.body AS body2_0_0_, p.title AS title3_0_0_, p.version AS version4_0_0_,
       pd.created_by AS created_2_2_1_, pd.created_on AS created_3_2_1_,
       pd.version AS version4_2_1_, pc.post_id AS post_id4_1_2_,
       pc.review AS review2_1_2_, pc.version AS version3_1_2_,
       pc.post_id AS post_id4_1_0__, pc.id AS id1_1_0__
FROM   post p
INNER JOIN post_details pd ON p.id = pd.id
INNER JOIN post_comment pc ON p.id = pc.post_id
WHERE  p.id = 1

SELECT id FROM post_comment WHERE id = 2 AND version = 0 FOR UPDATE
SELECT id FROM post_comment WHERE id = 3 AND version = 0 FOR UPDATE

SELECT id FROM post_details WHERE id = 1 AND version = 0 FOR UPDATE

SELECT id FROM post WHERE id =1 AND version =0 FOR UPDATE
```

Not only the Post entity is being locked but also the PostDetails and every PostComment child entity.

However, if the `Post` entity is loaded without initializing any child association:

```
Post post = doInJPA(entityManager -> (Post) entityManager.find(Post.class, 1L));
```

When running the previous test case, Hibernate is going to execute the following statements:

```
SELECT p.id AS id1_2_0_, p.created_by AS created_2_2_0_,
       p.created_on AS created_3_2_0_, p.version AS version4_2_0_
FROM   post_details p
WHERE  p.id = 1

SELECT id from post_details WHERE id =1 AND version = 0 FOR UPDATE

SELECT id from post WHERE id =1 AND version = 0 FOR UPDATE
```

Only the `Post` and `PostDetails` entities are locked this time. Because the `PostDetails` entity had not been fetched previously, the detached `Post` entity was using a proxy which only held the child association identifier and the child entity type. The one-to-one `PostDetails` association propagates all entity state transitions. Hence, the lock acquisition request is going to be applied to the `PostDetails` proxy as well. When being reassociated, the `@OneToOne` and `@ManyToOne` associations are fetched right away, and the lock is, therefore, propagated.

On the other hand, the `PostComment` child entries are not locked because Hibernate needs not to fetch `@OneToMany` and `@ManyToMany` associations upon reattaching the parent `Post` entity. The lock acquisition request is cascaded to child collections only if the collection is already initialized.

Locking too much data can hurt scalability because, once a row-level lock is acquired, other concurrent transactions that need to modify this record are going to be blocked until the first transaction either commits or rolls back. The lock cascading works only with detached entities and only if the `@OneToMany` and `@ManyToMany` associations have been previously fetched.

Being applicable to both managed and detached entities and giving better control over what entities are getting locked, the entity query locking mechanism is a much better alternative than entity lock event cascading.

16.2.1.2 Lock timeout

When acquiring a row-level lock, it is good practice to set a timeout value for which the current request is willing to wait before giving up. Depending on the current database `Dialect`, if the timeout value is greater than zero, Hibernate can use it to limit the lock acquisition request interval.

For the Hibernate native API, the timeout value can be supplied like this:

```
entityManager.unwrap(Session.class)
.buildLockRequest(
    new LockOptions(LockMode.PESSIMISTIC_WRITE)
        .setTimeOut((int) TimeUnit.SECONDS.toMillis(3))
    )
.lock(post);
```

With JPA, the timeout value is given through the following hint:

```
entityManager.lock(post, LockModeType.PESSIMISTIC_WRITE,
    Collections.singletonMap(
        "javax.persistence.lock.timeout",
        TimeUnit.SECONDS.toMillis(3)
    )
);
```

When running the aforementioned lock acquisition request on Oracle, Hibernate generates the following SQL query:

```
SELECT id
FROM   post
WHERE  id = 1 AND version = 0
FOR UPDATE WAIT 3
```

 Even if the timeout value is given in milliseconds, the Hibernate `Dialect` converts it to the underlying database supported format (e.g. seconds for Oracle).

To avoid any waiting, Hibernate comes with a NO_WAIT lock option which simply sets the
timeout value to 0.

```
entityManager.unwrap(Session.class)
.buildLockRequest(
    new LockOptions(LockMode.PESSIMISTIC_WRITE)
    .setTimeOut(LockOptions.NO_WAIT))
.lock(post);
```

The JPA alternative looks as follows:

```
entityManager.lock(post, LockModeType.PESSIMISTIC_WRITE,
    Collections.singletonMap("javax.persistence.lock.timeout", 0)
);
```

When running the lock acquisition request above on PostgreSQL, Hibernate is going to use
the NO WAIT PostgreSQL clause:

```
SELECT id
FROM   post
WHERE  id = 1 AND version = 0
FOR UPDATE NOWAIT
```

 The LockOptions.NO_WAIT option can only be used only if the underlying database
supports such a construct (e.g. Oracle and PostgreSQL). For other database systems,
this option is ignored and a regular pessimistic write lock clause is going to be used
instead.

When using NO WAIT or some other timeout value greater than 0, if the row is already locked,
the lock acquisition request is going to be aborted with the following exception:

```
ORA-00054: resource busy and acquire with NOWAIT specified or timeout expired
```

The exception is meant to notify the database client that the lock could not be acquired.
However, getting an exception is not always desirable, especially when implementing a job
queue mechanism.

For the following example, consider that Post entries need to be moderated to avoid spam
messages or inappropriate content.

The Post entity is going to use a status attribute which indicates if the Post can be safely displayed or it requires manual intervention from a site administrator.

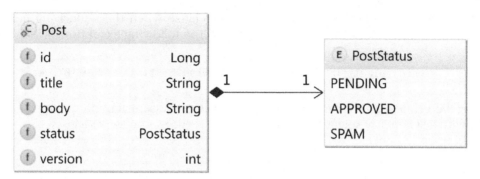

Figure 16.7: Post with PostStatus

The Post entities can be moderated by multiple administrators, so, in order to prevent them from approving the same entries, each administrator acquires a lock on the currently selected Post entities.

```
List<Post> pendingPosts = entityManager.createQuery(
    "select p " +
    "from Post p " +
    "where p.status = :status", Post.class)
.setParameter("status", PostStatus.PENDING)
.setFirstResult(5).setMaxResults(7)
.setLockMode(LockModeType.PESSIMISTIC_WRITE)
.setHint("javax.persistence.lock.timeout", 0)
.getResultList();
```

When Alice runs the aforementioned query on Oracle, Hibernate will generate the following statements:

```
SELECT * FROM (
    SELECT  row_.*, rownum rownum_ FROM (
        SELECT p.id AS id1_0_, p.body AS body2_0_, p.status AS status3_0_,
               p.title AS title4_0_, p.version AS version5_0_
        FROM   post p
        WHERE  p.status = 0
    ) row_
    WHERE   rownum <= 7
)
WHERE rownum_ > 5

SELECT id FROM post WHERE id = 5 AND version = 0 FOR UPDATE
SELECT id FROM post WHERE id = 6 AND version = 0 FOR UPDATE
```

Follow-on locking

The Oracle `Dialect` cannot employ the FOR UPDATE clause when the underlying query uses pagination because otherwise the database throws the following exception:

```
ORA-02014: cannot select FOR UPDATE from view with DISTINCT, GROUP BY, etc.
```

Because the original query cannot use the FOR UPDATE clause, each matching row must be locked with a secondary select statement.

After Alice has locked some Post records and started to moderate them, Bob decides to do the same thing, but, when he tries to run the same query as Alice, he will get an exception because the same rows are already locked. To address this usability issue, some database systems (e.g. Oracle 10g, PostgreSQL 9.5) define a SKIP LOCKED clause so a query can filter out row entries that are already locked. The following example is going to demonstrate how SKIP LOCKED works:

```java
private List<Post> pendingPosts(EntityManager entityManager, int lockCount,
                                int maxResults, Integer maxCount) {
    LOGGER.debug("Attempting to lock {} Post(s) entities", maxResults);
    List<Post> posts= entityManager.createQuery(
        "select p from Post p where p.status = :status", Post.class)
    .setParameter("status", PostStatus.PENDING)
    .setMaxResults(maxResults)
    .unwrap(org.hibernate.Query.class)
    .setLockOptions(new LockOptions(LockMode.UPGRADE_SKIPLOCKED))
    .list();

    if(posts.isEmpty()) {
        if(maxCount == null) {
            maxCount = pendingPostCount(entityManager);
        }
        if(maxResults < maxCount || maxResults == lockCount) {
            maxResults += lockCount;
            return pendingPosts(entityManager, lockCount, maxResults, maxCount);
        }
    }
    LOGGER.debug("{} Post(s) entities have been locked", posts.size());
    return posts;
}
```

The pendingPostCount method calculates the maximum number of Post entities that are eligible for moderation.

```
private int pendingPostCount(EntityManager entityManager) {
    int postCount = ((Number) entityManager.createQuery(
        "select count(*) from Post where status = :status")
    .setParameter("status", PostStatus.PENDING)
    .getSingleResult()).intValue();

    LOGGER.debug("There are {} PENDING Post(s)", postCount);
    return postCount;
}
```

Because the aforementioned pendingPost is private, the following simplified overloaded method is going to be used by the service layer:

```
public List<Post> pendingPosts(EntityManager entityManager, int lockCount) {
    return pendingPosts(entityManager, lockCount, lockCount, null);
}
```

With this new method in place, Alice and Bob can moderate distinct Post entries without risking any pessimistic locking conflict.

```
doInJPA(entityManager -> {
    final int lockCount = 2;
    LOGGER.debug("Alice wants to moderate {} Post(s)", lockCount);
    List<Post> pendingPosts = pendingPosts(entityManager, lockCount);
    List<Long> ids = pendingPosts
        .stream().map(Post::getId).collect(toList());
    assertTrue(ids.size() == 2 && ids.contains(0L) &&
        ids.contains(1L));

    executeSync(() -> {
        doInJPA(_entityManager -> {
            LOGGER.debug("Bob wants to moderate {} Post(s)", lockCount);
            List<Post> _pendingPosts = pendingPosts(_entityManager, lockCount);
            List<Long> _ids = _pendingPosts
                .stream().map(Post::getId).collect(toList());
            assertTrue(_ids.size() == 2 &&
                _ids.contains(2L) && _ids.contains(3L));
        });
    });
});
```

When running the aforementioned test case, Hibernate generates the following output:

```
-- Alice wants to moderate 2 Post(s)
-- Attempting to lock 2 Post(s) entities
SELECT * FROM (
    SELECT p.id AS id1_0_, p.body AS body2_0_, p.status AS status3_0_,
           p.title AS title4_0_, p.version AS version5_0_
    FROM   post p
    WHERE  p.status = 0
)
WHERE  rownum <= 2
FOR UPDATE SKIP LOCKED
-- 2 Post(s) entities have been locked

-- Bob wants to moderate 2 Post(s)
-- Attempting to lock 2 Post(s) entities
SELECT * FROM (
    SELECT p.id AS id1_0_, p.body AS body2_0_, p.status AS status3_0_,
           p.title AS title4_0_, p.version AS version5_0_
    FROM   post p
    WHERE  p.status = 0
)
WHERE  rownum <= 2
FOR UPDATE SKIP LOCKED

SELECT COUNT(*) AS col_0_0_
FROM   post p
WHERE  p.status = 0
-- There are 10 PENDING Post(s)

-- Attempting to lock 4 Post(s) entities
SELECT * FROM (
    SELECT p.id AS id1_0_, p.body AS body2_0_, p.status AS status3_0_,
           p.title AS title4_0_, p.version AS version5_0_
    FROM   post p
    WHERE  p.status = 0
)
WHERE  rownum <= 4
FOR UPDATE SKIP LOCKED
-- 2 Post(s) entities have been locked
```

The flow can be explained as follows:

- The `lockCount` variable dictates how many Post entities a user should be locking at once.
- Alice tries to lock 2 Post entities with a status of PENDING, and since no other user has locked any such entity, she manages to lock the first 2 Post records.
- Bob also attempts to lock 2 Post entities.
- At first, Bob's tries to lock 2 PENDING Post(s), but the query returns no record. This happens because the SKIP LOCKED clause ignores the matching records that are already locked (by Alice).
- Bob counts the number of Post entities to know many records are eligible for moderation. Even if Alice locked two rows, because Oracle uses MVCC, the `pendingPostCount` query is able to count both locked and unlocked database table records.
- Knowing that there are still some records that might not be locked, he increments the `maxResults` variable with the `lockCount` value.
- The `maxResults` tells the maximum number of entities that can be scanned by the current iteration.
- Because the `maxResults` has a value of 4, there are 4 Post records being scanned. However, since Alice has locked the first two entries (identifiers 0 and 1), Bob can only lock the next 2 records (identifiers 2 and 3).
- Because Bob has managed to lock at least one Post entity, he can continue with the moderation process.

LockMode.UPGRADE_SKIPLOCKED

Long before JPA 1.0, Hibernate defined its own LockMode(s), which have been later used as the base of the Java Persistence LockModeType(s). Although JPA 2.1 does not offer support for skipping locks, when using Hibernate, by setting the timeout value to LockOptions.SKIP_LOCKED (e.g. value of -2) the SKIP LOCKED clause is applied to the pessimistic locking clause. However, because of the follow-on locking behavior on Oracle, the SKIP LOCKED cannot by applied to the original query, so, not only the expected goal is not achieved, but this query will fail due to a stale state false positive. If a given row is already locked, the secondary follow-on locking query will not find any row, and Hibernate is going to assume that the row version has changed, or the row was deleted in the meanwhile, causing an OptimisticLockingException.

Fortunately, with Hibernate 5.1, the LockMode.UPGRADE_SKIPLOCKED bypasses the follow-on locking mechanism, as demonstrated by the previous example. Nevertheless, the locking query cannot use any ORDER BY, GROUP BY, or offset pagination. Otherwise, Oracle is going to throw an exception[a].

[a]https://docs.oracle.com/database/121/SQLRF/statements_10002.htm#SQLRF55371

Hibernate 5.2.1 follow-on locking improvements

Since Hibernate 5.2.1, the Oracle Dialect does not resort to *follow-on locking* on every situation. Therefore, the follow-on locking mechanism is activated if the underlying query contains one of the subsequent directives:

- DISTINCT
- GROUP BY
- UNION or UNION ALL
- Pagination with ORDER BY or with OFFSET (e.g. setFirstResult)

For this reason, on Hibernate 5.2.1, the previous example which was using UPGRADE_SKIPLOCKED LockMode to bypass the follow-on locking mechanism can be rewritten as follows:

```
List<Post> posts= entityManager.createQuery(
    "select p from Post p where p.status = :status", Post.class)
.setParameter("status", PostStatus.PENDING)
.setMaxResults(maxResults)
.unwrap(org.hibernate.Query.class)
.setLockOptions(new LockOptions(LockMode.PESSIMISTIC_WRITE)
    .setTimeOut(LockOptions.SKIP_LOCKED))
.list();
```

The aforementioned query works since it does not use any directive that would otherwise require the follow-on locking mechanism.

More, if there is any situation where the follow-on locking mechanism is being chosen although the underlying SQL query can successfully apply the row-level lock acquisition request, the LockOptions now offers the possibility of manually setting the follow-on locking strategy:

```
List<Post> posts= entityManager.createQuery(
    "select p from Post p where p.status = :status", Post.class)
.setParameter("status", PostStatus.PENDING)
.setMaxResults(maxResults)
.unwrap(org.hibernate.Query.class)
.setLockOptions(new LockOptions(LockMode.PESSIMISTIC_WRITE)
    .setTimeOut(LockOptions.SKIP_LOCKED)
    .setFollowOnLocking(false))
.list();
```

16.2.2 LockModeType.OPTIMISTIC

To understand how `LockModeType.OPTIMISTIC` works, the following entities are going to be used in the upcoming test cases:

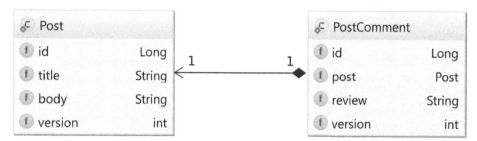

Figure 16.8: Post and PostComment entities

Once a `Post` is published, users can add `PostComment(s)` to review and share their opinions about the content of the aforementioned `Post`. Even if both entities have a `version` attribute, lost updates can be prevented at the entity level only. However, the `PostComment` entity is strictly related to the state of the `Post` entity that was used for reviewing. If a concurrent user modified the `Post` entity content, the `PostComment` might no longer be relevant.

In the following example, Alice is going to select a `Post` entity, and, while she is reviewing the `Post` entity, Bob is changing its content so that it now references the 17th chapter of the book. Alice, being unaware of the latest `Post` change, she adds a `PostComment` for the 16th chapter of the book.

```
doInJPA(entityManager -> {
    LOGGER.info("Alice loads the Post entity");
    Post post = entityManager.find(Post.class, 1L);

    executeSync(() -> {
        doInJPA(_entityManager -> {
            LOGGER.info("Bob loads the Post entity and modifies it");
            Post _post = _entityManager.find(Post.class, 1L);
            _post.setBody("Chapter 17 summary");
        });
    });

    LOGGER.info("Alice adds a PostComment to the previous Post entity version");
    PostComment comment = new PostComment();
    comment.setId(1L);
    comment.setReview("Chapter 16 is about Caching.");
    comment.setPost(post);
    entityManager.persist(comment);
});
```

When executing the test case above, Hibernate generates the following output:

```
-- Alice loads the Post entity
SELECT p.id AS id1_0_0_, p.body AS body2_0_0_, p.title AS title3_0_0_,
       p.version AS version4_0_0_
FROM   post p
WHERE  p.id = 1

-- Bob loads the Post entity and modifies it
SELECT p.id AS id1_0_0_, p.body AS body2_0_0_, p.title AS title3_0_0_,
       p.version AS version4_0_0_
FROM   post p
WHERE  p.id = 1

UPDATE post
SET    body = 'Chapter 17 summary' ,
       title = 'High-Performance Java Persistence' ,
       version = 1
WHERE  id = 1 AND version = 0

-- Alice adds a PostComment review to the previous Post entity version
INSERT INTO post_comment (post_id, review, version, id)
VALUES (1, 'Chapter 16 is about Caching.', 0, 1)
```

This is still a lost update that would never happen if Alice were taking a shared lock on the Post entity. Unfortunately, a shared lock would compromise application scalability because Alice reviews the Post in the user-think time. For this reason, an optimistic lock should be acquired on the Post entity to ensure that the entity state hasn't change since it was first loaded.

```
entityManager.lock(post, LockModeType.OPTIMISTIC);

LOGGER.info("Alice adds a PostComment to the previous Post entity version");
PostComment comment = new PostComment();
comment.setId(1L);
comment.setReview("Chapter 16 is about Caching.");
comment.setPost(post);
entityManager.persist(comment);
```

LockModeType.OPTIMISTIC does not acquire an actual lock right way, but instead it schedules a version check towards the end of the currently running transaction.

When executing the test case above while also acquiring the `LockModeType.OPTIMISTIC` on the `Post` entity, Hibernate generates the following output:

```
-- Alice adds a PostComment review to the previous Post entity version
INSERT INTO post_comment (post_id, review, version, id)
VALUES (1, 'Chapter 16 is about Caching.', 0, 1)

SELECT version FROM post WHERE id = 1

javax.persistence.OptimisticLockException: Newer version [1] of entity
[[Post#1]] found in database
```

`LockModeType.OPTIMISTIC` instructs Hibernate to check the `Post` entity version towards the end of the transaction. If the version has changed, an `OptimisticLockException` is thrown.

16.2.2.1 Inconsistency risk

Unfortunately, this kind of application-level check is always prone to inconsistencies due to bad timing. For example, after Hibernate executes the version check select statement, a concurrent transaction can simply update the `Post` entity without the first transaction noticing anything.

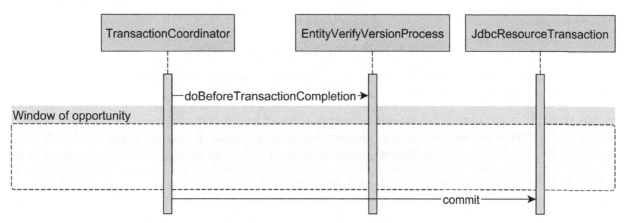

Figure 16.9: LockModeType.OPTIMISTIC window of opportunity

During that *window of opportunity*, another concurrent transaction might change the `Post` entity record before the first transaction commits its changes. To prevent such an incident, the
`LockModeType.OPTIMISTIC` should be accompanied by a shared lock acquisition:

```
entityManager.lock(post, LockModeType.OPTIMISTIC);
entityManager.lock(post, LockModeType.PESSIMISTIC_READ);
```

This way, no other concurrent transaction can change the `Post` entity until the current transaction is ended.

16.2.3 LockModeType.OPTIMISTIC_FORCE_INCREMENT

`LockModeType.OPTIMISTIC_FORCE_INCREMENT` allows incrementing the locked entity version even if the entity hasn't changed at all in the currently running Persistence Context.

> The `@Version` attribute should never have a setter method because this attribute is managed automatically by Hibernate. To increment the version of a given entity, one of the two `FORCE_INCREMENT` lock strategies must be used instead.

To understand how the `LockModeType.OPTIMISTIC_FORCE_INCREMENT` strategy works, consider the following Version Control system:

Figure 16.10: Repository, Commit, and Change

The `Repository` is the root entity, and each change is represented by a `Commit` entry which, in turn, may contain one or more `Change` embeddable types.

In this particular example, the `Repository` version must be incremented with each new `Commit` being added. The `Repository` entity version is used to ensure that commits are applied sequentially, and a user is notified if a newer commit was added since she has updated her working copy.

The following example depicts the user flow for this particular Version Control system:

```
Repository repository = entityManager.find(Repository.class, 1L,
        LockModeType.OPTIMISTIC_FORCE_INCREMENT);


Commit commit = new Commit(repository);
commit.getChanges().add(new Change("FrontMatter.md", "0a1,5..."));
commit.getChanges().add(new Change("HibernateIntro.md", "17c17..."));


entityManager.persist(commit);
```

When Alice executes the commit command, every file that she changes is going to be represented by a `Change` embeddable which also holds the diff between the original and the current file content. The `Repository` entity is loaded using the `LockModeType.OPTIMISTIC_FORCE_-INCREMENT` lock strategy so that its version is going to be incremented at the end of the current transaction.

Upon running the aforementioned test case, Hibernate generates the following statements:

```
SELECT r.id AS id1_2_0_, r.name AS name2_2_0_, r.version AS version3_2_0_
FROM   repository r WHERE  r.id = 1

INSERT INTO commit (repository_id, id) VALUES (1, 2)

INSERT INTO commit_change (commit_id, diff, path)
VALUES (2, '0a1,5...', 'FrontMatter.md')
INSERT INTO commit_change (commit_id, diff, path)
VALUES (2, '17c17...', 'HibernateIntro.md')

UPDATE repository SET version = 1 WHERE id = 1 AND version = 0
```

The `Repository` version is incremented before transaction completion, and, unlike `LockMode-Type.OPTIMISTIC`, data integrity is guaranteed by the current transaction isolation level. If the `Repository` version changed in between, the update will fail and an `OptimisticLockingException` is going to trigger a transaction rollback.

In the following example, both Alice and Bob are going to issue two commits concurrently:

```
doInJPA(entityManager -> {
    Repository repository = entityManager.find(Repository.class, 1L,
        LockModeType.OPTIMISTIC_FORCE_INCREMENT);

    executeSync(() -> {
        doInJPA(_entityManager -> {
            Repository _repository = _entityManager.find(Repository.class, 1L,
                LockModeType.OPTIMISTIC_FORCE_INCREMENT);

            Commit _commit = new Commit(_repository);
            _commit.getChanges().add(new Change("Intro.md", "0a1,2..."));
            _entityManager.persist(_commit);
        });
    });

    Commit commit = new Commit(repository);
    commit.getChanges().add(new Change("FrontMatter.md", "0a1,5..."));
    commit.getChanges().add(new Change("HibernateIntro.md", "17c17..."));
    entityManager.persist(commit);
});
```

When running the aforementioned test case, Hibernate generates the following output:

```
-- Alice selects the Repository entity
SELECT r.id AS id1_2_0_, r.name AS name2_2_0_, r.version AS version3_2_0_
FROM   repository r
WHERE  r.id = 1

-- Bob selects the Repository entity
SELECT r.id AS id1_2_0_, r.name AS name2_2_0_, r.version AS version3_2_0_
FROM   repository r
WHERE  r.id = 1

-- Bob adds a new Commit entity
INSERT INTO commit (repository_id, id) VALUES (1, 2)

INSERT INTO commit_change (commit_id, diff, path)
VALUES (2, '0a1,2...', 'Intro.md')

-- Bob increments the Repository version
UPDATE repository SET version = 1 WHERE id = 1 AND version = 0

-- Alice adds a new Commit entity
INSERT INTO commit (repository_id, id) VALUES (1, 3)

INSERT INTO commit_change (commit_id, diff, path)
VALUES (3, '0a1,5...', 'FrontMatter.md')

INSERT INTO commit_change (commit_id, diff, path)
VALUES (3, '17c17...', 'HibernateIntro.md')

-- Alice increments the Repository version
UPDATE repository SET version = 1 WHERE id = 1 AND version = 0

--Exception thrown
javax.persistence.RollbackException: Error while committing the transaction
Caused by: javax.persistence.OptimisticLockException:
Caused by: org.hibernate.StaleObjectStateException:
Row was updated or deleted by another transaction
(or unsaved-value mapping was incorrect)
```

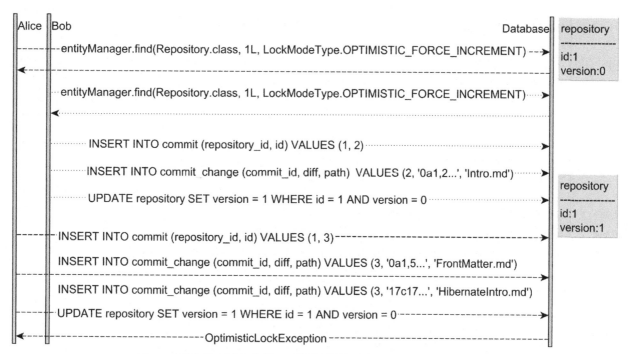

Figure 16.11: LockModeType.OPTIMISTIC_FORCE_INCREMENT

The flow can be explained as follows:

- Alice fetches the Repository entity and instructs Hibernate to acquire an OPTIMISTIC_- FORCE_INCREMENT application-level lock.
- Alice's thread is suspended by the JVM thread scheduler, so Bob gets the chance to fetch the Repository entity using the OPTIMISTIC_FORCE_INCREMENT lock strategy.
- Bob manages to add a new Commit entity, and his transaction is committed. Therefore, the Repository entity version is also incremented.
- Alice thread is resumed, and she adds one Commit entity and initiates a transaction commit.
- The optimistic locking update fails because the Repository version has changed.

OPTIMISTIC_FORCE_INCREMENT is useful for propagating a child entity state change to the parent entity optimistic locking version. By applying an optimistic lock on a common parent entity, it is, therefore, possible to coordinate multiple child entities whose changes need to be applied sequentially so that no update is being lost.

16.2.4 LockModeType.PESSIMISTIC_FORCE_INCREMENT

Just like OPTIMISTIC_FORCE_INCREMENT, PESSIMISTIC_FORCE_INCREMENT can be used to increment the version of any given entity. However, if for OPTIMISTIC_FORCE_INCREMENT the entity version is incremented towards the end of the currently running transaction, the PESSIMISTIC_FORCE_IN-CREMENT forces the version incrementation right away, as demonstrated by the test case below.

```
Repository repository = entityManager.find(Repository.class, 1L,
        LockModeType.PESSIMISTIC_FORCE_INCREMENT);

Commit commit = new Commit(repository);
commit.getChanges().add(new Change("FrontMatter.md", "0a1,5..."));
commit.getChanges().add(new Change("HibernateIntro.md", "17c17..."));

entityManager.persist(commit);
```

Hibernate generates the following statements:

```
SELECT r.id AS id1_2_0_, r.name AS name2_2_0_, r.version AS version3_2_0_
FROM   repository r
WHERE  r.id = 1
FOR UPDATE

UPDATE repository SET version = 1 WHERE id = 1 AND version = 0

INSERT INTO commit (repository_id, id) VALUES (1, 2)

INSERT INTO commit_change (commit_id, diff, path)
VALUES (2, '0a1,5...', 'FrontMatter.md')

INSERT INTO commit_change (commit_id, diff, path)
VALUES (2, '17c17...', 'HibernateIntro.md')
```

The Repository is locked using a FOR UPDATE SQL clause in the select statement that fetches the aforementioned entity. The Repository entity is also incremented before the entity is returned to the data access layer.

In the following example, Alice is going to lock the Repository only after she previously fetched the very same entity. However, in the meanwhile, Bob is going to increment the Repository entity version using a PESSIMISTIC_FORCE_INCREMENT lock.

```
Repository repository = entityManager.find(Repository.class, 1L);

executeSync(() -> {
    doInJPA(_entityManager -> {
        Repository _repository = _entityManager.find(Repository.class, 1L,
            LockModeType.PESSIMISTIC_FORCE_INCREMENT);

        Commit _commit = new Commit(_repository);
        _commit.getChanges().add(new Change("Intro.md", "0a1,2..."));
        _entityManager.persist(_commit);
    });
});

entityManager.lock(repository, LockModeType.PESSIMISTIC_FORCE_INCREMENT);
```

When running the test case above, Hibernate generates the following output:

```
-- Alice selects the Repository entity
SELECT r.id AS id1_2_0_, r.name AS name2_2_0_, r.version AS version3_2_0_
FROM   repository r
WHERE  r.id = 1

-- Bob selects the Repository entity
SELECT r.id AS id1_2_0_, r.name AS name2_2_0_, r.version AS version3_2_0_
FROM   repository r
WHERE  r.id = 1
FOR UPDATE

-- Bob increments the Repository version upon fetching the Repository entity
UPDATE repository SET version = 1 WHERE id = 1 AND version = 0

-- Bob adds a new Commit entity
INSERT INTO commit (repository_id, id) VALUES (1, 2)

INSERT INTO commit_change (commit_id, diff, path)
VALUES (2, '0a1,2...', 'Intro.md')

-- Alice tries to increment the Repository entity version
UPDATE repository SET version = 1 WHERE id = 1 AND version = 0

-- Exception thrown
javax.persistence.OptimisticLockException:
Caused by: org.hibernate.StaleObjectStateException:
```

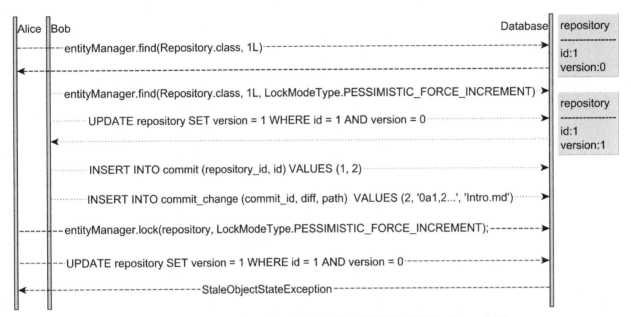

Figure 16.12: Fail fast PESSIMISTIC_FORCE_INCREMENT lock acquisition

The flow can be explained as follows:

- Alice fetches the `Repository` entity without acquiring any physical or logical lock.
- Alice's thread is suspended by the JVM thread scheduler, so Bob gets the chance to fetch the `Repository` entity using the `PESSIMISTIC_FORCE_INCREMENT` lock strategy.
- The `Repository` entity version is incremented right away.
- Bob manages to add a new `Commit` entity, and his transaction is committed.
- Alice thread is resumed, and she attempts to acquire a `PESSIMISTIC_FORCE_INCREMENT` on the already fetched `Repository` entity.
- The optimistic locking update fails because the `Repository` version was changed by Bob.

 The instantaneous version incrementation has the following benefits:

- Because the entity is locked at the database row level, the entity version incrementation is guaranteed to succeed.
- If the entity was previously loaded without being locked and the `PESSIMISTIC_FORCE_INCREMENT` version update fails, the currently running transaction can be rolled back right away.

Once a transaction acquires the PESSIMISTIC_FORCE_INCREMENT lock and increments the entity version, no other transaction can acquire a PESSIMISTIC_FORCE_INCREMENT lock because the second select statement is blocked until the first transaction releases the row-level physical lock.

The following example aims to demonstrate how two concurrent transactions can be coordinated through a common entity PESSIMISTIC_FORCE_INCREMENT lock acquisition.

```
doInJPA(entityManager -> {
    Repository repository = entityManager.find(Repository.class, 1L,
        LockModeType.PESSIMISTIC_FORCE_INCREMENT);

    executeAsync(() -> doInJPA(_entityManager -> {
        startLatch.countDown();
        Repository _repository = _entityManager.find(Repository.class, 1L,
            LockModeType.PESSIMISTIC_FORCE_INCREMENT);

        Commit _commit = new Commit(_repository);
        _commit.getChanges().add(new Change("Intro.md", "0a1,2..."));
        _entityManager.persist(_commit);
        _entityManager.flush();
        endLatch.countDown();
    }));
    awaitOnLatch(startLatch);
    LOGGER.info("Sleep for 500ms to delay the other transaction");
    sleep(500);

    Commit commit = new Commit(repository);
    commit.getChanges().add(new Change("FrontMatter.md", "0a1,5..."));
    commit.getChanges().add(new Change("HibernateIntro.md", "17c17..."));

    entityManager.persist(commit);
});
endLatch.await();
```

 The awaitOnLatch and sleep method utilities have the role of converting the InterruptedException into a RuntimeException which, unlike checked exceptions, can be propagated throughout a lambda expression without having to add unnecessary try/catch clauses.

When executing the test case above, Hibernate generates the following statements:

```
-- Alice selects the Repository entity
SELECT r.id AS id1_2_0_, r.name AS name2_2_0_, r.version AS version3_2_0_
FROM   repository r
WHERE  r.id = 1
FOR UPDATE

-- Alice increments the Repository version upon fetching the Repository entity
UPDATE repository SET version = 1 WHERE id = 1 AND version = 0

-- Bob tries to select the Repository entity, but his select is blocked
SELECT r.id AS id1_2_0_, r.name AS name2_2_0_, r.version AS version3_2_0_
FROM   repository r
WHERE  r.id = 1
FOR UPDATE

-- Alice waits 500 ms to delay Bob's lock acquisition request

-- Alice adds a new Commit entity
INSERT INTO commit (repository_id, id) VALUES (1, 2)

INSERT INTO commit_change (commit_id, diff, path)
VALUES (2, '0a1,5...', 'FrontMatter.md')

INSERT INTO commit_change (commit_id, diff, path)
VALUES (2, '17c17...', 'HibernateIntro.md')

-- Bob's increments the Repository version upon fetching the Repository entity
UPDATE repository SET version = 2 WHERE id = 1 AND version = 1

-- Bob adds a new Commit entity
INSERT INTO commit (repository_id, id) VALUES (1, 3)

INSERT INTO commit_change (commit_id, diff, path)
VALUES (3, '0a1,2...', 'Intro.md')
```

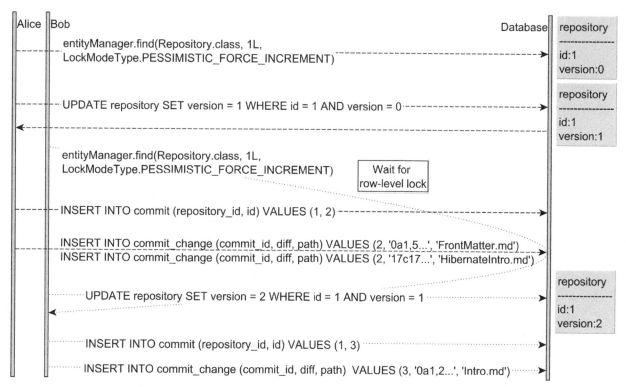

Figure 16.13: LockModeType.PESSIMISTIC_FORCE_INCREMENT

The flow can be explained as follows:

- Alice fetches the Repository entity while also acquiring a row-level lock and incrementing the entity version.
- Alice's thread is suspended by the JVM thread scheduler, so Bob gets the chance to fetch the Repository entity using the PESSIMISTIC_FORCE_INCREMENT lock strategy.
- Because it uses a FOR UPDATE clause, Bob Repository entity select statement is blocked by Alice's row-level lock.
- Alice thread is resumed, and she waits for 500 ms to delay Bob's lock acquisition request.
- Alice adds a new Commit entity, and her transaction is committed. Therefore, the Repository entity row-level lock is released.
- Bob can resume his select statement, and he acquires a row-level lock on the Repository entity.
- The Repository entity version is incremented by the PESSIMISTIC_FORCE_INCREMENT lock strategy.
- Bob manages to add his Commit entity and commits his transaction.

Once the row-level lock is acquired, the entity version update is guaranteed to succeed, therefore, reducing the likelihood of getting an OptimisticLockingException.

III JOOQ

17. Why jOOQ matters

When working with a relational database, it all boils down to SQL statements.

As previously explained, Hibernate entity queries are suitable for read-write logical transactions. For reporting, analytics or ETL (Extract, Transform, Load) native SQL queries are the best choice since they can take advantage of database-specific features like window functions or Common Table Expressions. Even for CRUD operations, there might be times when a database-specific syntax is more suitable like it's the case for the upsert SQL operation[1].

While Hibernate does a very good job to automate the vast majority of statements, it is unlikely that you can rely on Hibernate alone for every business use case. Therefore, native queries are a necessity for most enterprise applications.

As demonstrated in the Native query DTO projection section, both JPA and Hibernate provide a way to execute native SQL statements. Being able to execute any SQL statement is great, but, unfortunately, the JPA approach is limited to static statements only. To build native SQL statement dynamically, JPA and Hibernate are no longer enough.

17.1 How jOOQ works

JOOQ is a query builder framework that allows you generate a great variety of database-specific statements using a Java API. The DSLContext is the starting point to building any SQL statement, and it requires two things:

- a reference to a JDBC Connection
- a database dialect so that it can translate the Java API query representation into a database-specific SQL query

For instance, when using PostgreSQL 9.5, the DSLContext can be constructed as follows:

```
DSLContext sql = DSL.using(connection, SQLDialect.POSTGRES_9_5);
```

17.2 DML statements

With the DSLContext in place, it's time to show some simple DML statements like insert, update, delete, as well as a trivial select query. What's worth noticing is that the Java API syntax is almost identical to its SQL counterpart, so most jOOQ queries are self-describing.

---

[1]https://en.wikipedia.org/wiki/Merge_(SQL)

To delete all records for the post table, the following jOOQ statement must be used:

```
sql
.deleteFrom(table("post"))
.execute();
```

Which translates to the following SQL statement:

```
DELETE FROM post
```

To insert a new post table row, the following jOOQ statement can be used:

```
assertEquals(1, sql
    .insertInto(table("post")).columns(field("id"), field("title"))
    .values(1L, "High-Performance Java Persistence")
    .execute()
);
```

Just like in JDBC, the execute method return the affected row count for the current insert, update, or delete SQL statement.

When running the previous jOOQ query, the following SQL statement is being executed:

```
INSERT INTO post (id, title)
VALUES (1, 'High-Performance Java Persistence')
```

When updating the previously inserted record:

```
sql
.update(table("post"))
.set(field("title"), "High-Performance Java Persistence Book")
.where(field("id").eq(1))
.execute();
```

JOOQ generates the following SQL statement:

```
UPDATE post
SET title = 'High-Performance Java Persistence Book'
WHERE id = 1
```

Selecting the previously updated record is just as easy:

```
assertEquals("High-Performance Java Persistence Book", sql
    .select(field("title"))
    .from(table("post"))
    .where(field("id").eq(1))
    .fetch().getValue(0, "title")
);
```

To execute the statement and return the SQL query result set, the fetch method must be used. As expected, the previous jOOQ query generates the following SQL statement:

```
SELECT title FROM post WHERE id = 1
```

17.3 Java-based schema

All the previous queries were referencing the database schema explicitly, like the table name or the table columns. However, just like JPA defines a Metamodel API for Criteria queries, jOOQ allows generating a Java-based schema that mirrors the one in the database.

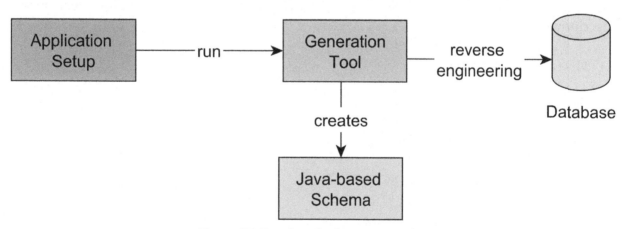

Figure 17.1: Java-based schema generation

There are many advantages to having access to the underlying database schema right from the Java data access layer. For instance, when executing a database stored procedure, the argument types can be bound at compile-time. The same argument holds for query parameters or the result set obtained from running a particular query.

When a column name needs to be modified, there is no risk of forgetting to update a given jOOQ statement because a Java-based schema violation will prevent the application from compiling properly. From a development perspective, the Java-based schema enables the IDE to autocomplete jOOQ queries, therefore increasing productivity and reducing the likelihood of typos.

After generating the Java-based schema, the application developer can use it to build any type-safe jOOQ query.

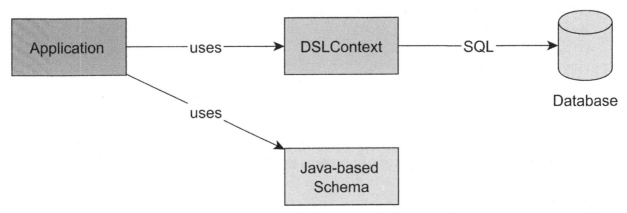

Figure 17.2: Typesafe schema usage

To rewrite the previous DML statements to use the Java-based schema, the generated schema classes need to be imported first:

```
import static com.vladmihalcea.book.hpjp.jooq.pgsql.schema.Tables.POST;
```

With the Java-based schema in place, the previous DML statements become even more descriptive:

```
sql.deleteFrom(POST).execute();

assertEquals(1, sql
    .insertInto(POST).columns(POST.ID, POST.TITLE)
    .values(1L, "High-Performance Java Persistence")
    .execute()
);

sql
.update(POST)
.set(POST.TITLE, "High-Performance Java Persistence Book")
.where(POST.ID.eq(1L))
.execute();

assertEquals("High-Performance Java Persistence Book", sql
    .select(POST.TITLE)
    .from(POST)
    .where(POST.ID.eq(1L))
    .fetch().getValue(0, POST.TITLE)
);
```

Although jOOQ can work just fine without a Java-based schema, it is much more practical to use typesafe queries whenever possible.

17.4 Upsert

In database terminology, an upsert statement is a mix between an insert and an update statement. First, the insert statement is executed and if it succeeds, the operation return successfully. If the insert fails, it means that there is already a database row matching the same unique constraints with the insert statement. In this case, an update is issued against the database row that matches the given filtering criteria.

The SQL:2003 and SQL:2008 standards define the MERGE statement, which among other scenarios, it can be used to emulate the upsert operation. However, MERGE acts more like an if-then-else statement, therefore being possible to combine insert, update, and delete statements. While upsert implies the same database table, MERGE can also be used to synchronize the content of two different tables.

Oracle and SQL Server implement the MERGE operation according to the standard specification, whereas MySQL and PostgreSQL provide only an implementation for the upsert operation.

JOOQ implements the upsert operation, therefore, managing to translate the Java-based query to the underlying database-specific SQL syntax.

To visualize how upsert works, consider the following method which aims to insert a post_-details record if there is none, or to update the existing record if there is already a row with the same primary key:

```
public void upsertPostDetails(
    DSLContext sql, BigInteger id, String owner, Timestamp timestamp) {
    sql
    .insertInto(POST_DETAILS)
    .columns(POST_DETAILS.ID, POST_DETAILS.CREATED_BY, POST_DETAILS.CREATED_ON)
    .values(id, owner, timestamp)
    .onDuplicateKeyUpdate()
    .set(POST_DETAILS.UPDATED_BY, owner)
    .set(POST_DETAILS.UPDATED_ON, timestamp)
    .execute();
}
```

Two users, *Alice* and *Bob*, are going to execute the `upsertPostDetails` method concomitantly, and, because of the upsert logic, the first user is going to insert the record while the second one is going to update it, without throwing any exception:

```
executeAsync(() -> {
    upsertPostDetails(sql, BigInteger.valueOf(1), "Alice",
            Timestamp.from(LocalDateTime.now().toInstant(ZoneOffset.UTC)));
});
executeAsync(() -> {
    upsertPostDetails(sql, BigInteger.valueOf(1), "Bob",
            Timestamp.from(LocalDateTime.now().toInstant(ZoneOffset.UTC)));
});
```

JOOQ is going to translate the upsert Java-based operation to the specific syntax employed by the underlying relational database.

17.4.1 Oracle

On Oracle, jOOQ uses the `MERGE` statement to implement the upsert logic:

```
MERGE INTO "POST_DETAILS" USING
    (SELECT 1 "one" FROM dual) ON ("POST_DETAILS"."ID" = 1)
WHEN MATCHED THEN
    UPDATE SET
        "POST_DETAILS"."UPDATED_BY" = 'Alice',
        "POST_DETAILS"."UPDATED_ON" = '2016-08-11 12:19:48.22'
WHEN NOT MATCHED THEN
    INSERT ("ID", "CREATED_BY", "CREATED_ON")
    VALUES (1, 'Alice', '2016-08-11 12:19:48.22')



MERGE INTO "POST_DETAILS" USING
    (SELECT 1 "one" FROM dual) ON ("POST_DETAILS"."ID" = 1)
WHEN MATCHED THEN
    UPDATE SET
        "POST_DETAILS"."UPDATED_BY" = 'Bob',
        "POST_DETAILS"."UPDATED_ON" = '2016-08-11 12:19:48.442'
WHEN NOT MATCHED THEN
    INSERT ("ID", "CREATED_BY", "CREATED_ON")
    VALUES (1, 'Bob', '2016-08-11 12:19:48.442')
```

17.4.2 SQL Server

Just like with Oracle, jOOQ uses MERGE to implement the upsert operation on SQL Server:

```
MERGE INTO [post_details] USING
    (SELECT 1 [one]) AS dummy_82901439([one]) ON [post_details].[id] = 1
WHEN MATCHED THEN
    UPDATE SET
        [post_details].[updated_by] = 'Alice',
        [post_details].[updated_on] = '2016-08-11 12:36:33.458'
WHEN NOT MATCHED THEN
    INSERT ([id], [created_by], [created_on])
    VALUES (1, 'Alice', '2016-08-11 12:36:33.458')


MERGE INTO [post_details] USING
    (SELECT 1 [one]) AS dummy_82901439([one]) ON [post_details].[id] = 1
WHEN MATCHED THEN
    UPDATE SET
        [post_details].[updated_by] = 'Bob',
        [post_details].[updated_on] = '2016-08-11 12:36:33.786'
WHEN NOT MATCHED THEN
    INSERT ([id], [created_by], [created_on])
    VALUES (1, 'Bob', '2016-08-11 12:36:33.786')
```

17.4.3 PostgreSQL

As opposed to Oracle and SQL Server, PostgreSQL offers the ON CONFLICT clause, which jOOQ uses for implementing upsert:

```
INSERT INTO "post_details" ("id", "created_by", "created_on")
VALUES (1, 'Alice',  CAST('2016-08-11 12:56:01.831' AS timestamp))
ON CONFLICT ("id") DO
UPDATE SET
    "updated_by" = 'Alice',
    "updated_on" = CAST('2016-08-11 12:56:01.831' AS timestamp)


INSERT INTO "post_details" ("id", "created_by", "created_on")
VALUES (1, 'Bob', CAST('2016-08-11 12:56:01.865' AS timestamp))
ON CONFLICT ("id") DO
UPDATE SET
    "updated_by" = 'Bob',
    "updated_on" = CAST('2016-08-11 12:56:01.865' AS timestamp)
```

17.4.4 MySQL

Almost identical to PostgreSQL, MySQL uses the ON DUPLICATE KEY for upsert:

```
INSERT INTO `post_details` (`id`, `created_by`, `created_on`)
VALUES (1, 'Alice', '2016-08-11 13:27:53.898')
ON DUPLICATE KEY
UPDATE
    `post_details`.`updated_by` = 'Alice',
    `post_details`.`updated_on` = '2016-08-11 13:27:53.898'

INSERT INTO `post_details` (`id`, `created_by`, `created_on`)
VALUES (1, 'Bob', '2016-08-11 13:27:53.905')
ON DUPLICATE KEY
UPDATE
    `post_details`.`updated_by` = 'Bob',
    `post_details`.`updated_on` = '2016-08-11 13:27:53.905'
```

17.5 Batch updates

As previously explained, JDBC batching plays a very important role in tuning the data access layer write operation performance. While Hibernate offers automated JDBC batching, for entities using identity columns, insert statements do not benefit from this feature. This is because Hibernate requires the entity identifier upon persisting the entity, and the only way to know the identity column value is to execute the insert statement.

Instead of implementing an automatic entity state management mechanism like Hibernate, jOOQ takes a WYSIWYG (what you see is what you get) approach to persistence. Even if nowadays many relational database systems offer sequences (Oracle, SQL Server 2012, PostgreSQL, MariaDB), the identity generator is still the only viable option for MySQL (e.g. AUTO_INCREMENT). However, since MySQL has a very significant market share, it is important to know that, with jOOQ, JDBC batching works just fine with insert statements.

To batch the insert statements associated to three Post entries, jOOQ offers the following API:

```
BatchBindStep batch = sql.batch(sql.insertInto(POST, POST.TITLE).values("?"));

for (int i = 0; i < 3; i++) {
    batch.bind(String.format("Post no. %d", i));
}
int[] insertCounts = batch.execute();
```

Running this test case on MySQL, jOOQ generates the following output:

```
INSERT INTO `post` (`title`) VALUES (Post no. 0), (Post no. 1), (Post no. 2)
```

As illustrated, jOOQ manages to batch all inserts in a single database roundtrip.

 When using Hibernate with MySQL and need to perform lots of inserts, it is a good idea to execute the batch inserts with jOOQ.

17.6 Inlining bind parameters

By default, just like Hibernate, jOOQ uses PreparedStatement(s) and bind parameter values. This is a very good default strategy since prepared statements can benefit from statement caching, as previously explained.

However, every rule has an exception. Because the bind parameter values might influence the execution plan, reusing a cached plan might be suboptimal in certain scenarios. Some database systems use statistics to monitor the efficiency of a cached execution plan, but the automatic adjustment process might take time.

For this reason, it is not uncommon to want to bypass the execution plan cache for certain queries that take skewed bind parameter values. Because the query string forms the cache key, by inlining the bind parameter values into the SQL statement, it is for sure that the database will either generate a new plan or pick the cached execution plan that was generated for the very same SQL statement.

This workaround can address the issue when bind parameter values are skewed, but it requires building the SQL statement dynamically. The worst thing to do would be to start concatenating string fragments and risk SQL injection attacks. Fortunately, jOOQ offers a way to inline the bind parameters right into the SQL statements without exposing the data access layer to SQL injection vulnerabilities. The jOOQ API ensures the bind parameter values match the expected bind parameter types.

Because by default jOOQ relies on PreparedStatement(s), to switch to using an inlined Statement, it is required to provide the following setting upon creating the DSLContext:

```
DSLContext sql = DSL.using(connection, sqlDialect(),
    new Settings().withStatementType(StatementType.STATIC_STATEMENT));
```

Afterward, when executing a parameterized query:

```
List<String> titles = sql
.select(POST.TITLE)
.from(POST)
.where(POST.ID.eq(1L))
.fetch(POST.TITLE);
```

JOOQ is going to inline all bind parameter values into the SQL statement String:

```
SELECT `post`.`title`
FROM   `post`
WHERE  `post`.`id` = 1
```

Without supplying the StatementType.STATIC_STATEMENT setting, when using *datasource-proxy* to intercept the executed SQL statement, the actual executed statement looks as follows:

```
Query:["select `post`.`title` from `post` where `post`.`id` = ?"],
Params:[(1)]
```

Previous Hibernate and jOOQ SQL snippet format

Although most SQL snippets generated by Hibernate or jOOQ in this book give the impression that bind parameters are inlined, that was just for readability sake since the bind parameter values were manually inlined after extracting the SQL statement from the actual logs.

In reality, all Hibernate statements as well as all jOOQ statements using the default StatementType.PREPARED_STATEMENT type are using bind parameter placeholders as illustrated in the aforementioned *datasource-proxy* output.

17.7 Complex queries

In the Native query DTO projection section, there was an SQL query using Window Functions, Derived Tables, and Recursive CTE (Common Table Expressions). Not only that it's possible to rewrite the whole query in Java, but that can be done programmatically.

The postCommentScores method shows how Derived Tables and Window Functions work with jOOQ. In fact, the jOOQ API resembles almost identically the actual SQL statement.

```java
public List<PostCommentScore> postCommentScores(Long postId, int rank) {
    return doInJOOQ(sql -> {
        return sql
        .select(field(name(TSG, "id"), Long.class),
            field(name(TSG, "parent_id"), Long.class),
            field(name(TSG, "review"), String.class),
            field(name(TSG, "created_on"), Timestamp.class),
            field(name(TSG, "score"), Integer.class)
        )
        .from(sql
            .select(field(name(ST, "id")), field(name(ST, "parent_id")),
                field(name(ST, "review")), field(name(ST, "created_on")),
                field(name(ST, "score")),
                denseRank().over(orderBy(field(name(ST, "total_score")).desc()))
                .as("rank"))
            .from(sql
                .select(field(name(SBC, "id")),
                    field(name(SBC, "parent_id")), field(name(SBC, "review")),
                    field(name(SBC, "created_on")), field(name(SBC, "score")),
                    sum(field(name(SBC, "score"), Integer.class))
                        .over(partitionBy(field(name(SBC, "root_id"))))
                        .as("total_score")
                )
                .from(sql
                    .withRecursive(withRecursiveExpression(sql, postId))
                    .select(field(name(PCS, "id")),
                        field(name(PCS, "parent_id")),
                        field(name(PCS, "root_id")), field(name(PCS, "review")),
                        field(name(PCS, "created_on")),
                        field(name(PCS, "score")))
                    .from(table(PCS)).asTable(SBC)
                ).asTable(ST)
            )
            .orderBy(
                field(name(ST, "total_score")).desc(),
                field(name(ST, "id")).asc()
            ).asTable(TSG)
        )
        .where(field(name(TSG, "rank"), Integer.class).le(rank))
        .fetchInto(PostCommentScore.class);
    });
}
```

Because following a very large query is sometimes difficult, with jOOQ, it's fairly easy to break a query into multiple building blocks. In this particular example, the WITH RECURSIVE query is encapsulated in its own method. Aside from readability, it is possible to reuse the withRecursiveExpression query method for other use cases, therefore reducing the likelihood of code duplication.

```
private CommonTableExpression<Record7<Long, Long, Long, Long, String, Timestamp,
    Integer>> withRecursiveExpression(DSLContext sql, Long postId) {
    return name(POST_COMMENT_SCORE).fields("id", "root_id", "post_id",
        "parent_id", "review", "created_on", "score")
        .as(sql.select(
            POST_COMMENT.ID, POST_COMMENT.ID, POST_COMMENT.POST_ID,
            POST_COMMENT.PARENT_ID, POST_COMMENT.REVIEW,
            POST_COMMENT.CREATED_ON, POST_COMMENT.SCORE)
        .from(POST_COMMENT)
        .where(POST_COMMENT.POST_ID.eq(postId)
            .and(POST_COMMENT.PARENT_ID.isNull()))
        .unionAll(
            sql.select(
                POST_COMMENT.ID,
                field(name("post_comment_score", "root_id"), Long.class),
                POST_COMMENT.POST_ID, POST_COMMENT.PARENT_ID,
                POST_COMMENT.REVIEW, POST_COMMENT.CREATED_ON,
                POST_COMMENT.SCORE)
            .from(POST_COMMENT)
            .innerJoin(table(name(POST_COMMENT_SCORE)))
            .on(POST_COMMENT.PARENT_ID.eq(
                field(name(POST_COMMENT_SCORE, "id"), Long.class)))
            .where(POST_COMMENT.PARENT_ID.eq(
                field(name(POST_COMMENT_SCORE, "id"), Long.class)))
        )
    );
}
```

To fetch the list of PostCommentScore entries, the application developer just has to call the postCommentScores method. However, the application requires the PostCommentScore entries to be arranged in a tree-like structure based on the parentId attribute. This was also the case with Hibernate, and that was the reason for providing a custom ResultTransformer. Therefore, a PostCommentScoreRootTransformer is added for the jOOQ query as well.

```
List<PostCommentScore> postCommentScores = PostCommentScoreRootTransformer.
    INSTANCE.transform(postCommentScores(postId, rank));
```

The `PostCommentScoreRootTransformer` class is almost identical to the `PostCommentScoreResult-` `Transformer` used in the Hibernate Fetching chapter.

```java
public class PostCommentScoreRootTransformer {

    public static final PostCommentScoreRootTransformer INSTANCE =
        new PostCommentScoreRootTransformer();

    public List<PostCommentScore> transform(
        List<PostCommentScore> postCommentScores) {
        Map<Long, PostCommentScore> postCommentScoreMap = new HashMap<>();
        List<PostCommentScore> roots = new ArrayList<>();

        for (PostCommentScore postCommentScore : postCommentScores) {
            Long parentId = postCommentScore.getParentId();
            if (parentId == null) {
                roots.add(postCommentScore);
            } else {
                PostCommentScore parent = postCommentScoreMap.get(parentId);
                if (parent != null) {
                    parent.addChild(postCommentScore);
                }
            }
            postCommentScoreMap.putIfAbsent(
                postCommentScore.getId(), postCommentScore);
        }
        return roots;
    }
}
```

17.8 Stored procedures and functions

When it comes to calling stored procedures or user-defined database functions, jOOQ is probably the best tool for this job. Just like it scans the database metadata and builds a Java-based schema, jOOQ is capable of generating Java-based stored procedures as well.

For example, the previous query can be encapsulated in a stored procedure which takes the `postId` and the `rankId` and returns a `REFCURSOR` which can be used to fetch the list of `PostCommentScore` entries.

```
CREATE OR REPLACE FUNCTION post_comment_scores(postId BIGINT, rankId INT)
    RETURNS REFCURSOR AS
$BODY$
    DECLARE
        postComments REFCURSOR;
    BEGIN
        OPEN postComments FOR
            SELECT id, parent_id, review, created_on, score
            FROM (
                SELECT
                    id, parent_id, review, created_on, score,
                    dense_rank() OVER (ORDER BY total_score DESC) rank
                FROM (
                    SELECT
                        id, parent_id, review, created_on, score,
                        SUM(score) OVER (PARTITION BY root_id) total_score
                    FROM (
                        WITH RECURSIVE post_comment_score(id, root_id, post_id,
                            parent_id, review, created_on, score) AS (
                            SELECT
                                id, id, post_id, parent_id, review, created_on,
                                score
                            FROM post_comment
                            WHERE post_id = postId AND parent_id IS NULL
                            UNION ALL
                            SELECT pc.id, pcs.root_id, pc.post_id, pc.parent_id,
                                pc.review, pc.created_on, pc.score
                            FROM post_comment pc
                            INNER JOIN post_comment_score pcs
                            ON pc.parent_id = pcs.id
                            WHERE pc.parent_id = pcs.id
                        )
                        SELECT id, parent_id, root_id, review, created_on, score
                        FROM post_comment_score
                    ) score_by_comment
                ) score_total
                ORDER BY total_score DESC, id ASC
            ) total_score_group
            WHERE rank <= rankId;
        RETURN postComments;
    END;
$BODY$ LANGUAGE plpgsql
```

When the Java-based schema was generated, jOOQ has created a `PostCommentScore` class for the `post_comment_scores` PostgreSQL function. The `PostCommentScore` jOOQ utility offers a very trivial API, so calling the `post_comment_scores` function is done like this:

```
public List<PostCommentScore> postCommentScores(Long postId, int rank) {
    return doInJOOQ(sql -> {
        PostCommentScores postCommentScores = new PostCommentScores();
        postCommentScores.setPostid(postId);
        postCommentScores.setRankid(rank);
        postCommentScores.execute(sql.configuration());
        return postCommentScores.getReturnValue().into(PostCommentScore.class);
    });
}
```

 With jOOQ, calling database stored procedures and user-defined functions is as easy as calling a Java method.

17.9 Streaming

When processing large result sets, it's a good idea to split the whole data set into multiple subsets that can be processed in batches. This way, the memory is better allocated among multiple running threads of execution.

One way to accomplish this task is to split the data set at the SQL level, as explained in the DTO projection pagination section. Streaming is another way of controlling the fetched result set size, and jOOQ makes it very easy to operate on database cursors.

To demonstrate how streaming works, let's consider a forum application which allows only one account for every given user. A fraud detection mechanism must be implemented to uncover users operating on multiple accounts.

To identify a user logins, the IP address must be stored in the database. However, the IP alone is not sufficient since multiple users belonging to the same private network might share the same public IP. For this reason, the application requires additional information to identify each particular user. Luckily, the browser sends all sorts of HTTP headers which can be combined and hashed into a user fingerprint. To make the fingerprint as effective as possible, the application must use the following HTTP headers: User Agent, Content Encoding, Platform, Timezone, Screen Resolution, Language, List of Fonts, etc.

The user_id, the ip and the fingerprint are going to be stored in a post_comment_details table. Every time a post_comment is being added, a new post_comment_details is going to be inserted as well. Because of the one-to-one relationship, the post_comment and the "post_comment_details' tables can share the same Primary Key.

Figure 17.3: The post_comment_details table

The fraud detection batch process runs periodically and validates the latest added post_comment_details. Because there can be many records to be scanned, a database cursor is used.

JOOQ offers a Java 8 stream API for navigating the underlying database cursor, therefore, the batch process job can be implemented as follows:

```
try (Stream<PostCommentDetailsRecord> stream = sql
    .selectFrom(POST_COMMENT_DETAILS)
    .where(POST_COMMENT_DETAILS.ID.gt(lastProcessedId))
    .stream()) {
    processStream(stream);
}
```

 The try-with-resources statement is used to ensure that the underlying database stream always gets closed after being processed.

Because there can be thousands of posts added in a day, when processing the stream, a fixed-size HashMap is used to prevent the application from running out of memory.

To solve this issue, a custom-made MaxSizeHashMap can be used so that it provides a FIFO (first-in, first-out) data structure to hold the current processing data window. Implementing a MaxSizeHashMap is pretty straight forward since java.util.LinkedHashMap offers a removeEldestEntry extension callback which gets called whenever a new element is being added to the Map.

```
public class MaxSizeHashMap<K, V> extends LinkedHashMap<K, V> {
    private final int maxSize;

    public MaxSizeHashMap(int maxSize) {
        this.maxSize = maxSize;
    }

    @Override
    protected boolean removeEldestEntry(Map.Entry<K, V> eldest) {
        return size() > maxSize;
    }
}
```

The `IpFingerprint` class is used for associating multiple user ids to a specific IP and fingerprint. Because the `IpFingerprint` object is used as a `Map` key, the `equals` and `hashCode` methods must be implemented so that they use the associated IP and fingerprint.

```
public class IpFingerprint {
    private final String ip;
    private final String fingerprint;

    public IpFingerprint(String ip, String fingerprint) {
        this.ip = ip;
        this.fingerprint = fingerprint;
    }

    @Override
    public boolean equals(Object o) {
        if (this == o) return true;
        if (o == null || getClass() != o.getClass()) return false;
        IpFingerprint that = (IpFingerprint) o;
        return Objects.equals(ip, that.ip) &&
                Objects.equals(fingerprint, that.fingerprint);
    }

    @Override
    public int hashCode() {
        return Objects.hash(ip, fingerprint);
    }
}
```

With these utilities in place, the `processStream` must create a tree structure that can be navigated as follows: `post_id` -> `IpFingerprint` -> list of `user_id`.

The `processStream` method iterates the underlying database cursor and builds a `Map` where the key is the `post_id` and the value is a `Map` of fingerprints and user ids.

```
private void processStream(Stream<PostCommentDetailsRecord> stream) {
    Map<Long, Map<IpFingerprint, List<Long>>> registryMap =
        new MaxSizeHashMap<>(25);

    stream.forEach(postCommentDetails -> {
        Long postId = postCommentDetails
            .get(POST_COMMENT_DETAILS.POST_ID);
        String ip = postCommentDetails
            .get(POST_COMMENT_DETAILS.IP);
        String fingerprint = postCommentDetails
            .get(POST_COMMENT_DETAILS.FINGERPRINT);
        Long userId = postCommentDetails
            .get(POST_COMMENT_DETAILS.USER_ID);

        Map<IpFingerprint, List<Long>> fingerprintsToPostMap =
            registryMap.get(postId);
        if(fingerprintsToPostMap == null) {
            fingerprintsToPostMap = new HashMap<>();
            registryMap.put(postId, fingerprintsToPostMap);
        }

        IpFingerprint ipFingerprint = new IpFingerprint(ip, fingerprint);

        List<Long> userIds = fingerprintsToPostMap.get(ipFingerprint);
        if(userIds == null) {
            userIds = new ArrayList<>();
            fingerprintsToPostMap.put(ipFingerprint, userIds);
        }

        if(!userIds.contains(userId)) {
            userIds.add(userId);
            if(userIds.size() > 1) {
                notifyMultipleAccountFraud(postId, userIds);
            }
        }
    });
}
```

If the `user_id` list contains more than one entry, it means there have been multiple users identified by the same fingerprint, therefore, a notification must be sent to the system administrator.

Even if streaming is a very good fit for processing very large results sets, most often, it is much more appropriate to operate on smaller batches to avoid long-running transactions.

17.10 Keyset pagination

As explained in the DTO projection pagination section, pagination can improve performance since the application only fetches as much data as it's required to be rendered by the current view. The default pagination technique supported by JPA and Hibernate is called the *offset* method, and it is efficient only for small result sets or when navigating the first pages of a large result set. The further the page, the more work is going to be done by the database to fetch the current subset of data. To overcome the offset pagination limitation, the application developer has two alternatives.

The first choice is to narrow down the result set as much as possible using multiple filtering criteria. From a user experience perspective, this is probably the best option as well since the user can select the exact subset of data that she is interested in operating. If the filtered subset is rather small, the offset pagination limitation is not going to be a big issue.

However, if the filtered subset is still large and there is no more filtered that can be further applied, then keyset pagination becomes a better alternative to using the SQL-level offset support. Keyset pagination uses the database table primary key to mark the position of the current fetching data subset.

If JPA 2.1 and Hibernate 5.2 do not offer support for keyset pagination, jOOQ provides a `seek()` method which translate to a database-specific keyset pagination query syntax.

Considering the front page of a forum application which displays all the posts in the descending order of their creation, the application requires a paginated view over the following `PostSummary` records:

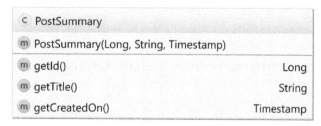

Figure 17.4: The PostSummary class

The keyset pagination query is rather trivial as illustrated by the following code snippet:

```java
public List<PostSummary> nextPage(String user, int pageSize,
    PostSummary offsetPostSummary) {
    return doInJOOQ(sql -> {
        SelectSeekStep2<Record3<Long, String, Timestamp>, Timestamp, Long>
        selectStep = sql
        .select(POST.ID, POST.TITLE, POST_DETAILS.CREATED_ON)
        .from(POST)
        .join(POST_DETAILS).on(POST.ID.eq(POST_DETAILS.ID))
        .where(POST_DETAILS.CREATED_BY.eq(user))
        .orderBy(POST_DETAILS.CREATED_ON.desc(), POST.ID.desc());
        return (offsetPostSummary != null)
            ? selectStep
            .seek(offsetPostSummary.getCreatedOn(), offsetPostSummary.getId())
            .limit(pageSize)
            .fetchInto(PostSummary.class)
            : selectStep
            .limit(pageSize)
            .fetchInto(PostSummary.class);
    });
}
```

To fetch the first page, the offset PostSummary is null:

```java
List<PostSummary> results = nextPage(pageSize, null);
```

When fetching the first page on PostgreSQL, jOOQ executes the following SQL query:

```sql
SELECT "post"."id", "post"."title", "post_details"."created_on"
FROM "post"
JOIN "post_details" on "post"."id" = "post_details"."id"
ORDER BY "post_details"."created_on" DESC, "post"."id" DESC
LIMIT 5
```

After fetching a page of results, the last entry becomes the offset PostSummary for the next page:

```java
PostSummary offsetPostSummary = results.get(results.size() - 1);
results = nextPage(pageSize, offsetPostSummary);
```

When fetching the second page on PostgreSQL, jOOQ executes the following query:

```
SELECT "post"."id", "post"."title", "post_details"."created_on"
FROM "post"
JOIN "post_details" on "post"."id" = "post_details"."id"
WHERE (
    1 = 1 AND
    ("post_details"."created_on", "post"."id") <
    (CAST('2016-08-24 18:29:49.112' AS timestamp), 95)
)
ORDER BY "post_details"."created_on" desc, "post"."id" desc
LIMIT 5
```

On Oracle 11g, jOOQ uses the following SQL query:

```
SELECT "v0" "ID", "v1" "TITLE", "v2" "CREATED_ON"
FROM (
    SELECT "x"."v0", "x"."v1", "x"."v2", rownum "rn"
    FROM (
        SELECT
            "POST"."ID" "v0", "POST"."TITLE" "v1",
            "POST_DETAILS"."CREATED_ON" "v2"
        FROM "POST"
        JOIN "POST_DETAILS" on "POST"."ID" = "POST_DETAILS"."ID"
        WHERE (
            1 = 1 and (
                "POST_DETAILS"."CREATED_ON" <= '2016-08-25 03:04:57.72' and (
                    "POST_DETAILS"."CREATED_ON" < '2016-08-25 03:04:57.72' or (
                        "POST_DETAILS"."CREATED_ON" =
                        '2016-08-25 03:04:57.72' and
                        "POST"."ID" < 95
                    )
                )
            )
        )
        ORDER BY "v2" desc, "v0" desc
    ) "x"
    WHERE rownum <= (0 + 5)
)
WHERE "rn" > 0
ORDER BY "rn"
```

Because Oracle 11g does not support comparison with row value expressions as well a dedicated SQL operator for limiting the result set, jOOQ must emulate the same behavior, hence the SQL query is more complex than the one executed on PostgreSQL.

> Keyset pagination is a very handy feature when the size of the result set is rather large. To get a visualization of the performance gain obtain when switching to keyset pagination, Markus Winand has a No-Offset article[a] explaining in great detail why offset is less efficient than keyset pagination.
>
> ――――――――――
> [a]http://use-the-index-luke.com/no-offset

Index

Made in the USA
Las Vegas, NV
31 October 2023

79998795R00267